Contents

The Emergence of a New Turkcy

Democracy and the AK Parti

M. Hakan Yavuz, editor

*Utah Series in Turkish
and Islamic Studies*

The University of Utah Press
Salt Lake City

Utah Series in Turkish and Islamic Studies
M. Hakan Yavuz, editor

 The Defiance House Man colophon is a registered trademark of the University of Utah Press. It is based upon a four-foot-tall, Ancient Puebloan pictograph (late PIII) near Glen Canyon, Utah.

10 09 08 07 06   5 4 3 2 1

LIBRARY OF CONGRESS CATALOGING-IN-PUBLICATION DATA

The emergence of a new Turkey : democracy and the AK Parti /
  M. Hakan Yavuz, editor.
    p. cm. —(Utah series in Turkish and Islamic studies)
  Includes index.
  ISBN-13: 978-0-87480-863-6 (pbk. : alk. paper)
  ISBN-10: 0-87480-863-4 (pbk. : alk. paper)
    1. Turkey—Politics and government—1980–   . I. Yavuz, M.
  Hakan. II. Series.
  DR603.E46 2006
  324.2561'082—dc22   2006001355

The Emergence of a New Turkey

Acronyms and Abbreviations

ADD	Atatürkçü Düşünce Derneği (Association for Kemalist Thought)
BRSA	Bank Regulation and Supervision Authority
CDMEC	Central Decision Making and Executive Committee
CDU-CSU	Christian Democratic Union
CSU	Christian Social Union
DEHAP	Demokratik Halkın Partisi (Democratic People's Party, DPP)
DC	Democrazia Cristiana (Christian Democracy Party)
DEP	Democracy Party (Demokrasi Partisi)
DLP	Democratic Left Party (Demokratik Sol Party; DSP)
DP	Democrat Party (Demokrat Parti; DP)
DRA	Directorate of Religious Affairs (Diyanet İşleri Başkanlığı)
ECHR	European Court of Human Rights
ESK	Economic and Social Council
EU	European Union
FIS	Islamic Salvation Front
FP	Felicity Party (Saadet Partisi; SP)
GUP	Greater Unity Party (Büyük Birlik Partisi; BBP)
HDS	Guardians of the Salafi Call
ICFTU	International Confederation of Free Trade Unions
İHL	İmam Hatip Liseleri
IMF	International Monetary Fund
JDP	Justice and Development Party (Adalet ve Kalkınma Partisi; AKP)
JP	Justice Party (Adalet Partisi; AP)
MLSS	Ministry of Labor and Social Security (Çalışma ve Sosyal Güvenlik Bakanlığı; ÇSGB)
MP	Motherland Party (Anavatan Partisi; ANAP)
MRP	Mouvement républicain populaire

MÜSİAD	Independent Industrialists and Businessmen's Association
NAP	Nationalist Action Party (Milliyetçi Hareket Partisi; MHP)
NOM	National Outlook Movement (Milli Görüş Hareketi)
NOP	National Order Party (Milli Nizam Partisi; MNP)
NSC	National Security Council
NSP	National Salvation Party (Milli Selamet Partisi; MSP)
NTP	New Turkey Party (Yeni Türkiye Partisi; NTP)
NTSB	National Turkish Students Union (Milli Türk Talebe Birliği; MTTB)
NWP	Nationalist Work Party (Milliyetçi Calışma Partisi; MCP)
OIC	Organization of the Islamic Conference
PKK	Partiya Karkeren Kurdistan (Kurdistan Workers' Party)
PWP	People's Work Party (Halkın Emek Partisi; HEP)
RPF	Rassemblement du peuple français (Rally of the French People)
RPP	Republican People's Party (Cumhuriyet Halk Partisi; CHP)
SMC	Supreme Military Council (Yüksek Askeri Şura)
SPD	Social Democrat Party of Germany
TCK	Turkish Penal Code (Türk Ceza Kanunu)
TGS	Turkish General Staff (Genel Kurmay Başkanlığı)
TESEV	Türkiye Ekonomik ve Sosyal Etüdler Vakfı (Turkish Economic and Social Studies Foundation)
TİSK	Confederation of Turkish Employers' Associations
TOBB	Turkish Union of Chambers and Commodity Exchanges (Türkiye Odalar ve Borsalor Birliği)
TPP	True Path Party (Doğru Yol Partisi; DYP)
TRT	Turkish Radio and Television
TÜSİAD	Turkish Industrialists and Businessmen's Association
VP	Virtue Party (Fazilet Partisi; FP)
WP	Welfare Party (Refah Partisi; RP)
YÖK	Council of Higher Education (Yüksek Öğretim Kurulu)
YP	Young Party (Genç Parti; GP)

Acknowledgments

This book owes many debts to friends and colleagues. Some of my preliminary ideas about the Justice and Development Party (JDP) were sketched out in my earlier book, *Islamic Political Identity in Turkey* (2003). When I decided to organize a workshop on the JDP, Ibrahim Karawan, the director of the Middle East Center of the University of Utah, supported the idea eagerly. The workshop was generously funded by a Department of Education grant via the Middle East Center. I owe a large debt of gratitude to Ibrahim. Particular thanks go to Steve Ott and Steven Reynolds of the College of Social and Behavioral Sciences, and Ron Hrebenar, the chair of the Political Science Department, for their valuable financial help and collegial support in the preparation of this book.

I would also thank the workshop discussants and colleagues, Chadra Kukathas, Korkut Ertürk, Fred Quinn, Yasin Aktay, and Eric Hooglund, who commented as draft papers were presented at four panels. Lastly, this book would have not been possible without encouragement and stimulation provided by colleagues, including Payam Faroughi, Erol Olçok, Yalçın Akdoğan, Edibe Sözen, Erol Kaya, Fahrettin Altun, Tolga Köker, Hasan Kösebalaban, Peter von Sivers, and Etga Uğur. Special gratitude goes to June Marvel of the University of Utah for her untiring editorial help and Jeff Grathwohl of the University of Utah Press for his patience and the unfailing support that made this volume possible.

The Role of the New Bourgeoisie in the Transformation of the Turkish Islamic Movement

■ *M. Hakan Yavuz*

Adalet ve Kalkınma Partisi (the Justice and Development Party; JDP) is also called AK Parti, meaning the "uncontaminated" or "pure" party to differentiate itself from the other political parties that were involved in widespread corruption before the November 2002 Turkish national elections. The JDP was victorious in the 2002 national elections because it moved to the center of the political spectrum, and voters regarded this shift as credible and positive. What explains the transformation of the JDP? Given its Islamic roots, and the past activities and statements of its leaders, the party's programs, growth, and conquest of power in Turkish politics merit attention. One needs to explain how and why the party adopted a more liberal line. The transformation of the Islamic movement in the form of shifting from oppositional to propositional is an outcome of underlying changes in Turkish society, especially changes in the new business class and new intellectuals. Although the pressures put on the JDP to undertake changes to satisfy the Copenhagen criteria for European Union (EU) membership are important, they are insufficient to fully explain the JDP's path of change. It is a sociological error to reduce the compass of political change solely to the Copenhagen criteria. In this sense, the JDP is not the cause of the silent revolution occurring in Turkey, but rather the outcome. The prime agent of this transformation is the new emerging bourgeoisie rooted in Anatolia. This new Anatolian business class evolved as a result of Prime Minister Turgut Özal's neoliberal economic revolution. The second key agent is the new intellectual class outside the control of the state.

Some scholars tend to read the current experiment in Turkey as the successful political integration of an Islamic movement within a democracy.[1]

Several facts support such an interpretation. Although the JDP leadership denies its Islamic background and claims to be a conservative democratic party, nonetheless the party did emerge out of the ashes of the Welfare and Virtue parties that were closed down by the Constitutional Court on charges of being a forum and proponent of antisecular activities.[2] Moreover, the majority of the JDP's deputies are observant Muslims in their daily lives. For instance, their spouses continue to wear headscarves, which have been banned at public offices, ceremonies, and universities because they are regarded as a challenge to the secular nature of Turkey. Nonetheless Turkey's experience with the JDP raises several complicated questions: Is the JDP an Islamic party? Is it possible for an ex-Islamic movement to become a-Islamic or un-Islamic? Is the commitment of the members of the JDP to religious values in their personal life enough to label the party Islamic? When does a movement or a party become or cease to be Islamic? Even if the administration of the party denies any connection with political Islam, can we still consider the party Islamic?

On the other hand, one may read JDP's denial of its Islamic connections as simply a compromise between the state and the JDP. The JDP, as the argument goes, is free to govern the country as long as it stays within Turkey's strictly proscribed constitutional framework and ignores many religious claims of its conservative constituency. This alternative interpretation further complicates the issue and raises the following question: Is the case of the JDP, rather than being a success story of *an Islamic movement* that has adapted to a host of new conditions, a story of *the ability of the Turkish system* to transform and domesticate political Islam to the extent that it denies its Islamism, even its explicit Islamic roots?

Despite popular arguments to the contrary, it is problematic to propose Turkey as a model for Islamic democracy, and the Turkish experiment cannot be recreated in other Muslim countries.[3] For instance, Turkey itself has not persuasively solved significant problems regarding the integration of political Islam into its system by accommodating it, but rather it has used extrajudicial means to transform political Islam to the point that the movement seeks refuge in the denial of its past and reacts negatively when it is called Islamic or Muslim. As such, the JDP refuses to define itself as an Islamic or Muslim party.

I would argue that if an Islamic political movement actively hinders the articulation of arguments on the basis of Islamic values, it is no longer Islamic. A movement is Islamic to the extent that it is making political claims on religious—Islamic—grounds. In the case of Turkey, we see such a process, the process of post-Islamism or the shift from the politics of identity to the politics of services—*hizmet partisi*. One sees the realization/materialization of liberal politics in Turkey in the sense that a political movement is not engaged in the politics of identity, which tend to be conflict-ridden and confrontational, but rather in the politics of services, based on compromise and cooperation. A new social and political contract, as a result, is evolving in the case of Turkey on the basis of neoliberal economic and political values. This can be seen as the normalization of Turkish politics since it hints at the positive integration of the country into many of the macro trends taking place on a global scale. The JDP, being the product of these transformations, is not a party of identity but rather a party that strives to provide better services. It does not develop or articulate any claims on the basis of Islam or other forms of identity, but acts as an agent of the country's integration into neoliberal economic and political spaces.

Going back to our main question, that is, when and under what conditions a movement ceases to be Islamic, I contend that it ceases to be Islamic if it fails to articulate policies based on Islamic identity but makes claims on the basis of public reasoning.

Based on the activities of the JDP, it is possible to conclude that the Islamic political movement has helped to consolidate democracy in Turkey by offering the country's marginalized groups an alternative avenue for political participation. Yet this positive role is very much an outcome of expanding opportunity spaces and the contracting of military-legal institutions, made possible in large part through the actions and the trendsetter role played by a new and rising Anatolian bourgeoisie who have refused to support confrontational policies. The democratic bargaining between the state establishment and the JDP forced the latter group to give up any search for governmental "hegemony" and to accept EU-oriented democratic norms. Turkey's Islamic groups, more than the secularists, reluctantly support this new democratic bargain because they intrinsically understand that this was the only way for them to come to power.

Turkey's accession process to the EU helped to domesticate and force not only the state but also the antisystemic actors to change their perceptions and strategies and to adopt EU norms as the point of reference to create a new social contract in Turkey. When a possible accession date is given by the EU, what the JDP is going to do is not clear. Although some members of the JDP are in the process of formulating some sort of post-EU platform/program, other broad-based programs, which would appeal to the sectors of the population that have supported the JDP in the past, have yet to be articulated. There is still a high likelihood that Turkish voters will return to the identity-based parties they have voted for in the past, having used the JDP "like a streetcar" to get to their desired destination, namely EU membership, and to cleanse the political landscape of corrupt politicians. I believe this is the biggest question facing Turkish politics in the near future, the question of whether politics in Turkey has really shifted from the politics of identity to the politics of issues/services, or whether the case of the JDP is simply a temporary development, if not an anomaly.

THE SOURCE OF SILENT REVOLUTION: THE NEW BOURGEOISIE

The Turkish case challenges two dominant Orientalist theses: that is, that Islam and democracy, on the one hand, and capitalism and Islam, on the other, are incompatible. In the case of Turkey, one sees the evolution of Islam that is entrepreneurial and capitalist-oriented. The rise of an Islamic bourgeoisie is a challenge to the Weberian reading of the relationship between Islam and capitalism as incompatible and antagonist. By Islamic entrepreneurs, I mean those pious individuals who identify Islam as their identity and formulate their everyday cognitive map by using Islamic ideas and history to vernacularize (Islamicize) modern economic relations that promote the market forces and cherish neoliberal projects.

Political Islam is most often depicted as the enemy of the West and the Western values of capitalism, democracy, human rights, and modernity. Throughout the 1990s the image of *Mecca* vs. *Mechanization* of Daniel Lerner has been replaced with Benjamin Barber's *Jihad* vs. *McWorld*. The case of Turkey is useful to challenge and question this dichotomous mode of thinking. It not only indicates the prospects for the compatibility of Islam with democracy and Islam with capitalism but also demonstrates how the new wave of globalization has opened new spaces for the evolution and consolidation of Islamic economic actors. The Islamic movement in Turkey, which is led by counter-elite with a counter project, is progressive in several aspects. While it challenges state ideology (Kemalism) and a secular bloc (military-bureaucracy-capitalist), it also critiques "traditional/folk" Islamic ways of doing and thinking. This is a case whereby the neoliberal project produced new Islamic actors, and these actors, in turn, shaped Islamic discourse and practices. The expansions of the market, the increasing role of the middle class, and the strengthening of civil society have had profound impact on Islamic actors and their identities.

In order to understand the origins and policies of the JDP, one has to explore not only the social and political context of the new Muslim actors, that is, the Islamic bourgeoisie, but also the JDP's identity, its politics, and its relationship with Islamic political groups. It is important to study the role of the Islamic bourgeoisie and its relationship to Islamic groups because the bourgeoisie provides the financial means to develop the new political movement through its charities, TV stations, radios, and newspapers, and, as such, has boosted its social status.

Who are these actors? What are their identity and politics? How do they shape the orientation of the JDP? What is the role of the Islamic bourgeoisie in the fragmentation, and even in the end, of Islamism? The Islamic movement is not shaped by the shantytowns surrounding large cities in Turkey but rather by rising social groups in terms of wealth and education. Thus, it is these rising social groups, especially the Islamic bourgeoisie, that fuel the locomotive of Islamization regarding consumer patterns and are the vanguard of Turkey's recent democratization.

The Islamic bourgeoisie evolved out of the state's neoliberal economic policies that created conducive economic conditions and the emerging transnational financial networks as a result of deregulation and the opening of the Turkish economy. The Islamic bourgeoisie has also benefited from the local governments of the Welfare Party, especially after 1994. This new actor is both a cause and an outcome of the neoliberal economic policies of Özal, the former reformist Turkish prime minister and president who died in 1993. The symbiotic relationship between the state and the large Istanbul-based capitalists had been based on agreement over secularism and the Kemalist ideology. The emergence of an Anatolian-based Islamic bourgeoisie ran counter to the existing economic and cultural alliance between the state and the Istanbul-based capitalists.

Islamic entrepreneurs consist mostly of a first generation of college graduates who are the children of an Anatolian-based petty bourgeoisie who benefited from Özal's neoliberal economic policies that increased their social mobility, which allowed them to establish their own medium-sized and small-sized firms. They are the first generation of urbanizing economic elite who continue to maintain strong ties with the provincial towns and villages of Anatolia. Most of them were born and raised in provincial towns and villages and only settled in the big cities of Turkey after their college education.

They were first introduced to Islamic values in their provincial towns and villages and later spent several years in university dormitories, mostly run by Nurcu or Nakşibendi Sufi orders, and objectified Islam as an alternative project, becoming conscious Muslims who had a clear and concise notion of what constituted an Islamic identity. Thus, a closer study indicates that most of the members of MÜSİAD (Independent Industrialists and Businessmen's Association), a consciously Muslim businessmen's association, appear to have come from a conservative Muslim social environment with a history of antiestablishment discontent. They were and are critical of state subsidies for the Istanbul-based business class and have always been disgruntled with Turkey's history of state–big business connections. The Anatolian-based petty bourgeoisie were mostly excluded and marginalized by the import-substitution policies of the state, and the state, from the foundation of the Turkish Republic onwards, always favored a secular-oriented big city–based bourgeoisie as the carrier of its modernization projects and purveyor of its prescribed lifestyles as well. Most of this new urbanizing economic elite became involved in the growing textile and construction trade. Eventually services, transportation, and tourism became important fields of activity. Most of these small and medium firms are family owned and they maintain family structures with conservative religious values. In other words, even though they all come from a traditional petty bourgeoisie background and culturally marginalized milieu, they used education and the new economic and political conditions of the post-1980s to develop entrepreneurial and organizational skills to reposition themselves as the new economic actors of Anatolia with the goal of modernizing their cities and lifestyles through Islamization. They identified the state's interventionist policies and its ties to big business as being responsible for Turkey's uneven economic development and socioeconomic problems that excluded large sectors of the petty bourgeoisie. Islamic identity, which was marginalized and identified as the cause of Turkey's backwardness by the Kemalist elite, was mobilized by these new actors to challenge state policies and to form a new organization to articulate their policies. In other words, Islamic identity was not a cause but rather was used as the lubricant to prime the workings of market forces and as an instrument of carving their share of the market. The transformative history of MÜSİAD is the history of this new urbanizing economic elite who were steeped in Islamic ethics and networks. This entrepreneurial Islam is the outcome of this new elite, who critique the Istanbul-based secularist elite and traditional Islamic conception of *esnaf* (small merchants).

The expansion of the economic opportunity spaces not only facilitated the evolution of more moderate political forces but also enhanced the civil society and private education. The autonomous economic groups supported a number of cultural projects, along with new TV stations, radio channels, and magazines.

This transformation of Turkey's Islamic movement could be called a conservative revolution because it wants to maintain Turkey's generally conservative traditions and bring local norms and identities to the national level; it is a normative revolution in that it seeks to moralize the political institutions and networks. By conservative revolution I mean not advocating wholesale change or a sharp transformation but rather creating new cognitive spaces for different imaginations of the past and the reconstruction of the present. This conservative revolution is very much based on the Ottoman imperial dream of becoming "bigger" and "better" by overcoming the rigid nation-state ideology. This imagination is not carried out by the intelligentsia. It is a bottom-up imagination of those who felt excluded and dissatisfied with the prevailing sociopolitical conditions of Turkey. For a new Turkey, the JDP leadership has looked toward reconfiguring alliances and redistributing political power, has sought ways to create new institutions and new values, and more importantly has attempted to overthrow the ingrained Kemalist mode or patterns of "progressive" and elitist thinking. The main goal is to level the society so that top and bottom are not widely separated. In short, the JDP's dream is to shape politics along the identity and needs of civil society. But the party's dream of putting power in the hands of the people has not been fully materialized because of the authoritarian temptations of the leaders of the JDP and the political culture of modern Turkey.

RELIGIOUS AND CIVIL SOCIETIES

Contemporary Turkish society is often pragmatic rather than ideological, inclusive rather than exclusive, and essentially nonviolent. Turks—as in Turkish citizens of all ethnicities including Kurds—seek to build civic institutions by utilizing religious idioms and practices in order to gain better lives. Individuals, whether in rural or urban areas, are not able, however, to act together for their common good that somehow transcends the immediate material interests of the family or their neighborhood. Most provincial foundations and associations are formed around a religious idea or institution. Many Turks live with their families, and single households remain the exception rather than the rule. Turkish businesses are mostly family owned, with fewer than twenty employees. Here family loyalty is paramount, under patriarchal control, exhibiting very little trust in the government. These small shop owners and merchants are the principal supporters of the JDP and its leader Erdoğan, giving him a much larger percentage of votes compared to the rest of the parties. Since many Turks live in a condition of habitual illegality (either their home or shop has been built on state property; or they do not pay proper taxes) and because they live in conflict with the establishment over its own moral code and lifestyle, they easily identify with Erdoğan as a symbol of their own condition. His understanding of liberty is very much defined in negative terms, however—that is, in terms of removing all impediments and interferences.

Many scholars of Turkish politics and society tend to view Turkey's Islamic movement in opposition to the state rather than focusing on the symbiotic relationship between the two. This dominant framework of reading the inevitable clash of Kemalist and Islamist ideologies ignores the more nuanced evolution and mutual transformation of state and society. One of the logical outcomes of this framework is to read the rise of political Islam as the failure of Kemalism or the demise of Islamism as the rise of Kemalism. This mutually exclusive mode of reading has become the dominant mode in Turkish studies. The long-term impact of reformist policies of the Kemalist elite and economic liberalization facilitated the formation of opportunity spaces, and these spaces, in turn, became the site of the reconstitution of Islam. Because of this imagined Kemalist secularism as an antireligious ideology, almost all scholars see the 1980 military coup's initiative of reconciliation with Islam and Islamic activism as the cause of post-1980 Islamism in Turkey. This mode of reading ignores the complex and multifaceted relationship between Islam and the state. The main source of the legitimacy for the Turkish state has always been Islam and its close ties with Islamic groups. Islamic and Republican secularism are not separate worlds in conflict, but are symbiotic parts of the same historic whole. The Islamic movement evolved and was defined very much as a result of its oppositional interaction with the state. Yet the interactions between the state and Islamic movements are not about the bipolar clash of identities and ideologies but rather occasional cooptation, confrontation, and overall symbiotic interaction. The Turkish religious landscape consists of four actors: political Islam, social Islam of widespread (neo)Sufi groups, the state Islam of the Directorate of Religious Affairs (DRA),[4] and radical Islam.

The presence of an Islamic party and its role in local and national politics are important in terms of domesticating the excesses of Islamic claims and "learning" to articulate religious interests and claims in the secular idiom of politics. With the multiparty system in the 1950s, it was the center-right Democrat Party that first brought Islamic claims to the political sphere in terms of human rights and respect for culture.

For a variety of reasons the voters of Turkey overwhelmingly voted for the JDP in 2002 and swept away a generation of established politicians to give what was essentially Erdoğan's party enough seats in Parliament to form a single-party government. These election results provided one of the most interesting experiences in the Muslim world and begged the question: Was a modern democratic party with deep roots in political Islam capable of expanding civil liberties and maintaining a democratic system?

Against this background, this book will examine the social and political roots of the JDP. It will attempt to answer whether the JDP is a product of temporal conditions and if so, how will these changes shape the future of Turkey and the party itself? What are the major constitutive principles of the ideology and identity of the JDP, and how is the party different from earlier Islamic parties in Turkey? How does the JDP resemble or differ from other Islamic parties and Islamic movements in the wider Middle East? How does it view the separation of church (mosque) and state? Does it actually favor a secular or a Muslim Turkey and what are the building principles of the JDP's self-declared "conservative democracy"?

Furthermore, in regard to Turkey's overall political landscape, what is the JDP's relationship with the Kemalist secular military and how does the military view the party? Also, what kind of radical solutions, if any, does the party propose for alleviating Turkey's enduring problems on the issue of the Kurds, individual freedoms, the Armenian question, and human rights? How do these views influence and affect possible EU candidacy for Turkey? Furthermore, how and why has Turkey's diverse and powerful Islamic movement reconstructed a positive view of integration with Europe? As a corollary question, what is the link between domestic politics and foreign policy; that is, is the EU essential for the JDP's survival and how have domestic politics affected Turkey's strategic relationship with the United States in the aftermath of the occupation of Iraq? How does the United States view the party and vice versa, and how will this view affect the significant United States–Turkey partnership of the last fifty years? In regard to democracy and social issues, how democratic is the JDP structurally as a party? How does the party view the role of women in society? This book seeks to answer these pertinent questions and also to highlight the deeply rooted contradictions of the JDP.

The analyses in this book suggest that the JDP is wrapped in a number of contradictions: It seeks to "reform" the political system and state-society relations while at the same time declaring its identity as a "conservative" democracy; it champions for political participation and pluralism while at the same time the party does not allow much room for its own internal democracy; the party identifies decentralization and local-based governance as a solution to Turkey's overburdened bureaucracy while it seeks to centralize JDP's own party structure and decision making. The party eliminated almost all bottom-up channels, and Erdoğan rules it with his all-male advisors.

For one, there are a number of reasons for the JDP's centralized politics: Since the JDP is a coalition of diverse people who came together under the pre-2002 political conditions, it is not homogenous and it needs a strong leader to rule over it. Moreover, Turkish politics has always been dominated by personalities, and "personal networks" count more than principles. On the other hand, the party's proposed identity of conservative democracy is very much like a "space" where people with diverse identities and interests meet to express their desire for change of the status quo. For instance, Erol Kaya, the mayor of Pendik, argues that the JDP is a "supermarket" where people come to meet their need and as such, by itself, "it has not formed an identity." Its claimed identity of conservative democracy does not necessarily reflect in all its policies, but rather it is an identity tool for external legitimacy. Ahmet Yıldız argues that the JDP's conservative democracy does not seek to lead or guide its party policies but rather to overcome the suspicions of outside countries, especially the United States and the EU states.[5] The party's image of a conservative democracy, according to Yıldız, also carves a space in the center-right spectrum of Turkish politics to overcome the secularist suspicion, and seeks to connect with Islamist-oriented masses. In short, Yıldız is right to conclude that the JDP's conservative democracy tries to define the party for others rather than serving as a guiding ideology for the party itself.

ORGANIZATION OF THE BOOK

This introduction and the first chapter of part 1 (Identity, Ideology, and Leadership) form the historical and theoretical background of the rest of the chapters. The introduction examines the historic context of the evolution of the Islamic movement into a more a-Islamic or non-Islamic movement in the case of the JDP, and focuses on the determinant role of the political economy in the evolution of a more liberal Islamic movement in Turkey. In chapter 1, Massimo Introvigne provides a theoretical framework to examine the pluralization and evolution of Turkish Islamic movements. By utilizing religious economy theories developed by R. Stark,

L. Iannaccone, and others, he argues that religious competition taking place in a "religious market" where "religious firms" compete for the allegiance of "religious consumers" is at the core of the pluralization of Islamic movements. Introvigne also examines the sociopolitical consequences of the state intervention into the religious market before and after the 2002 elections.

The chapters by Yalçın Akdoğan and William Hale analyze the meaning of "conservative democracy." Akdoğan provides the official version of the concept and responds to some of the critics of the definition and the use of the concept by the JDP. He defines it in opposition to the Islamic identity of the previous pro-Islamic parties of the National Outlook Movement. Hale's chapter brings in the comparative dimension by comparing the Christian democracy in Europe with the "conservative democracy" of the JDP. However, Hale treats the JDP as a pro-Islamic party attempting to redefine the role of Islam in a democratic context. Both chapters indicate that "conservative democracy" is a concept in the making in Turkey, and it is made in practice rather than imposed on Turkish political realities. İhsan Dağı examines the connection between the insecurity of the JDP (felt exclusion) and the degree to which the party has internalized the human rights discourse in its policies. This paradox of a deep sense of insecurity despite huge electoral support of the JDP makes it very sensitive to the politics of human rights. Dağı displays how the JDP has instrumentalized both human rights and EU membership in its search for systemic legitimacy and security. He argues that under such circumstances the JDP has developed a three-layered strategy: It has adopted a language of human rights and democracy as a "discursive shield"; it has mobilized popular support as a form of "democratic legitimacy"; and it has built a liberal-democratic coalition with modern secular sectors within Turkey's political spectrum that have recognized the JDP as a legitimate actor. Sultan Tepe directly deals with some of the issues raised in Dağı's chapter about the party's role in the consolidation of democracy. Tepe concludes that an overall analysis shows that the JDP is a party shaped by the centrifugal forces of Turkey's highly volatile electoral politics and fragmented party system. The party's ideology, its conservative democratic demeanor, and its organization are still in the making. Rather than being a novel political project rooted in Islam, the party's ideology marginalizes the role of Islam in the public sphere or reduces it to a set of traditional values.

Ahmet Kuru starts where Tepe leaves the reader, with a number of questions about the role of Islam in the public sphere. Kuru seeks to cope with this issue by focusing on the JDP's conceptualization of secularism. He starts with the following question: "Is secularism a universally monolithic phenomenon with a standard meaning or a contextually changing concept based on varying interpretations?" This question has been at the core of debates on state-religion relations in several predominantly secular states. Turkey provides an intriguing example to examine fundamental and changing aspects of secularism regarding distinct normative backgrounds of political actors and their conflicting policy decisions. In contemporary Turkish politics, powerful institutions, for example the military and the Constitutional Court, have had conventional attitudes toward secularism. Following the November 2002 national elections, the JDP joined the political balance of power with an unpredictable view of secularism. Today, both the followers and the discontents of the mainstream understanding of secularism in Turkey are trying to understand the JDP, which also tries to recreate itself on the issue of secularism.

Kuru thus analyzes the debates on secularism in Turkey through the lens of the JDP case. He provides the appropriate theoretical and historical backgrounds on this important issue. He covers the general theoretical framework of his argument through a conceptual survey of secularism with a comparative perspective. He then briefly looks at the historical origin of and contemporary disagreements on secularism in two prominent Western countries—the United States and France. Kuru's aim is to specify the commonalities and differences between secularism and laicism, essential to understanding secularism in Turkey. Following these two background sections, the main body of Kuru's chapter examines three issues: first, the external challenges that the JDP has faced on secularism from state institutions, its constituency, and the EU. Second, he examines the JDP's policies for the last two years to understand the party's general attitude toward secularism. Finally, the chapter contributes to our understanding of the JDP's new self-professed ideology—"conservative democracy"—since a balancing view of secularism has a crucial place in the party's self-identification as a conservative party.

Ali Çarkoğlu argues that the rise in support for the JDP marks the progression of electoral collapse of centrist politics in Turkey. His chapter focuses on the main characteristics of the electoral support for the party in two elections. The first one is the general elections in November 2002. The second is the municipality elections in March 2004. Çarkoğlu's main questions are: From where is the JDP's support coming? How different are these support bases compared to earlier Turkish pro-Islamists?

Part 2 of the book (The JDP Policies) deals with the JDP's economic policies (Ziya Öniş), JDP-Turkish military ties (Gareth Jenkins); the party's gender policies (Edibe Sözen); its labor relations (Engin Yıldırım); and the party's foreign policy stances as seen through the "Islamic civilizational" lens (Burhanettin Duran) and the Iraqi war crisis of 2003 (Saban Kardaş). Since the JDP's program is largely shaped by its commitment to fulfilling the political criteria for EU membership, the main policy framework is the EU accession rules and norms. Thus the relations between the JDP government and the Turkish military have taken place against the backdrop of—and been largely shaped by—Turkey's progress toward fulfilling the political criteria for EU accession. Civilian control of the military is a sine qua non for EU membership. For the party, EU accession is thus not only attractive in itself but provides the opportunity to contain arguably its most implacable domestic opponent: the Kemalist secularist-oriented military establishment. Jenkins argues that although it's still doubtful that the EU will ever grant Turkey full membership, the Turkish General Staff (TGS) nevertheless supports accession because it sees it as the culmination of Atatürk's policy of Westernization and because it believes that accession will result in higher levels of welfare and education, which in turn will erode electoral support for Islamism via parties such as the JDP. Equally important, the TGS is aware that the vast majority of the Turkish public supports EU membership, and being seen as opposed to membership would undermine the military's still considerable public prestige.

Yıldırım's chapter examines the JDP's approach to labor in the context of the party's socioeconomic and Islamic backgrounds, membership requirements of the EU, and International Monetary Fund–led economic policies. He argues that the party's relations with labor are influenced by two contradictory processes: On the one hand, the JDP seems to have followed the anti-labor pattern set in the early 1980s when Turkey's labor market was deregulated to achieve competitiveness through increased market flexibility and its trade unions suffered from political assaults and economic setbacks. On the other hand, having received significant support from the lower classes whose interests often, if not always, clash with those of business owners, the party has been aware that it must also please the economically disadvantaged with its policies. Indeed, reconciling interests of the laboring classes and (conservative) business owners has been a real challenge for the JDP government. The party has thus oscillated between respecting labor rights and favoring policies that defend the interests of employers. The party's understanding of social justice probably revolves around maintaining and strengthening traditional relations of charity, solidarity, and cooperation rather than strengthening individual and social rights.

The last two chapters deal with the foreign policy of Turkey: Burhanettin Duran examines the role of Islamic civilizational identity in the foreign policy making of the JDP. Duran argues that the party has been transforming both the parameters of Turkish politics and Islamist politics through "Europeanization" and "internationalization" of internal issues. The task of transforming both itself and Turkey, argues Duran, is based on a careful balance between Islamist and secularist expectations in domestic politics and between the United States and Europe in international context. The transformation has not been limited to Turkish domestic and foreign policies. A more critical process of change can be observed in respect to Islamic political identity and discourses in Turkey. Duran claims that the party's foreign policy represents a departure from the Islamism of the National Outlook Movement, which embraced an anti-Western/European stance from the 1970s to the 1990s. The JDP expects that EU membership will allow Turkey to further a process of promoting its relations with the Middle East and the Muslim world. But this expectation seems to be ignoring the possible difficulties of pursuing a multidimensional foreign policy within the Union. Duran concludes that apart from the EU harmonization process, it is difficult to say that the JDP has successfully triggered political debates over the sensitive issues of identity politics. The party's political identity of "conservative democracy" is not theorized properly, according to Duran, in order to resolve the tensions of identity politics in Turkey. In the context of the EU accession process and globalization, the primary challenge of the JDP's foreign policy is thus to redefine the Turkish national identity.

Saban Kardaş focuses on the more specific issue of the Iraqi crisis to examine the role of identity and national interests in the formulation of the foreign policy of Turkey under the JDP. By comparing the party leadership's strategic language with that of Turkey's security and foreign policy elite, Kardaş seeks to better account for the dynamic interaction between the continuities and changes, and identity and interests, in Turkish foreign policy. He argues that throughout the Iraqi crisis involving critical decisions by Turkey, the JDP leadership employed a rhetoric that dismissed an ideological-ideational approach to foreign policy and prioritized the country's national interests, paying due attention to material and practical considerations—a foreign policy based on *realpolitik*, if you will. He concludes that the differences between the JDP's leadership and the establishment, to the extent that they existed at the commencement of the Iraqi crisis, have been more in the details than in the substance of foreign policy.

The title of this book (*The Emergence of a New Turkey*) illustrates the main thesis of these chapters that a new Turkish elite in terms of its regional, social, and religious cultural background has emerged on the scene. The book's focus is on the JDP. The architects of this new Turkey are the Anatolian bourgeoisie, new intellectuals, and the JDP. These new agents of political change created an alliance in response to the February 28 military coup and the 2001 economic crisis. As the new Turkey is in the making, two major defining characteristics need to be revealed. One of them is the evolution of a new political discourse. This discourse consists of democracy, civil society, human rights, and freedom of speech. This new discourse empowers the marginalized sectors of Turkish society and opens new ways of imagining state-society relations. This language opened a national debate over key issues of political and national identity centering on the state, security, Turkishness, Islam, Alevism, and Kurdishness. Almost all key concepts of the old Kemalist contract are contested and redefined in accordance with the new wave of globalization and, most importantly, the demands of the Copenhagen criteria. This is an outcome of the dynamic public sphere in Turkey, which has resurfaced as a result of the burgeoning financial and economic sectors outside the control of the state. In the evolution of this new political language, the Anatolian bourgeoisie played an important role by financing private education, newspapers, journals, and radio stations. The new bourgeoisie has provided the necessary material support to put demands for greater democracy and a more open civil society into practice. The transformation of political Islam is also the story of the support of this new class and its ability to carry its ideas into the political domain. This class first supported the Welfare Party, engineered a transformation within the party, and eventually came out in support of the Gül-Erdoğan ticket.

As part of the evolution of a new political language, a major revolution has taken place at the cognitive level. With EU institutional support, new interest groups want to guarantee their intrinsic freedoms and transform state-society relations. Another major change is taking place in regards to the definitions of the state, politics, and nation. Politics in Turkey has always been treated as an instrument for proclaiming bureaucratic decision demands to the public, and not as an instrument for articulating societal claims and demands through political contestation. Thus, political debates in Turkey have always focused on the protection and consolidation of state power, and nation is defined as an extension of the state.

A popular saying in Turkey goes: "May God protect the state and the nation" (*Allah devlete ve millete zeval vermesin*). For instance, opposition parties are not monitoring state activities on the basis of societal interests but rather from the perspective of state interests. Although politics was presented as a conflict between the forces of modernity and religious fanaticism, it was an elite-centered instrument managing the process of exclusion and inclusion into and out of the system. In Turkish political culture, the state used to have a semisacred meaning and the Turkish nation and faith existed in order to serve the state. This situation has changed, and the state is now regarded as a set of institutions to serve the people and protect the value structure of society. The supporters of the JDP do not want the party to define itself in terms of the concerns and the politics of the center. They have redefined the perceived core values of the social center and have demanded that the party restructure the existing political center (the state) in terms of societal values in Turkey.

The second defining characteristic of this new Turkey is the end of dual sovereignty or "parallel governments" in Turkey as a result of the curtailing of the power of the military. Sovereignty in Turkey has always been divided between those who are elected and those who are appointed, such as the military and civilian bureaucracy. The latter group had the preponderance of power to set the framework of Parliament and the functioning rules of democracy and has also determined whose voices are deemed legitimate or illegitimate. In previous decades, those who were appointed were never held accountable by the populace and derived their legitimacy simply by "preserving the Kemalist ideology." As guardians of the state ideology, they protected their own power and position and, among other things, sought to keep the elected government within the boundaries of the state ideology by manipulating and using the media, the military, and the judiciary. Their goal was to protect the state and its ideology from the populace and democratically elected politicians who might have challenged their authority and ideology from an independent power base. This appointed group determined and formulated its own "defensive and protective task" of Kemalism. They, like the Council of the Guardians in neighboring Iran, designated the boundaries of elected government. This dual government came to an end with the constitutional changes of 2004. This change came with the support of domestic forces, especially the coalition that developed between Istanbul and the new Anatolian-based bourgeoisie. The end of the military's power came about because of two interrelated events.[6]

With the 1997 soft coup, by implementing harsh policies against Muslim groups and the presence of Islamic symbols and discourse in the public sphere, the military lost a great deal of its popular base of support amongst pious Anatolian Sunni-Turks who had traditionally been willing to grant a great deal of deference to the Pashas because of the war of liberation of 1919–21. Furthermore, the Copenhagen criteria called for the separation of military decision making from the civilian political system. Turkey's Euro-skeptic conservative Muslims became Europhiles almost overnight after the 1997 coup. Many realized that domestic forces did not have the necessary resources and ability to end the military's power and antireligious authoritarianism and recognized the Copenhagen criteria as the only way of rolling back those in the military and bureaucratic establishment who interpreted Kemalism in a militant and anti-Islamic fashion. Today, because of this process, one sees the emergence of a democratic Turkey and the corollary expansion of political freedoms. Since 1999, the Turkish Parliament enacted seven major reform packages and a number of harmonization laws to fulfill the Copenhagen political criteria for EU membership.[7]

One of the major cognitive impacts of these changes is the redefinition of security and the role of the security forces (military and police). The previous paradigm of protecting the state from society has shifted to a paradigm espousing the protection of society from state interventions. The new agent of change in Turkey is no longer the military but the evolving bourgeoisie. The new class of intellectuals, who are funded by the bourgeoisie and work outside the state institutions, play an important role in the process of redefining the political language of Turkey in accordance with the global discourses of human rights, democracy, and market economy. In short, now the people are not a subject but an object of their own destiny. They do not want to be defined by the state but seek to define the state instead. Turkey is searching for a new social contract outside of the rigid Kemalist public philosophy. It is important in this process to redefine state-society relations and the role of state institutions. The EU process, along with the decisions of the European Court of Human Rights, has offered a framework for this new social contract in Turkish society by stressing the secular and democratic nature of the Republic in which individual rights are protected with legal mechanisms. In the constitution of this new social contract, the role and meaning of politics is crucial. By reducing politics into "rendering social services," the JDP has not developed a necessary framework for public debate.

Recep Tayyip Erdoğan's new conception of politics and globalized discourse, along with his charismatic personality, is behind his electoral success in November 2002. As an activist of Islamic politics within the National Outlook Movement of Necmettin Erbakan and then as the mayor of Istanbul, Erdoğan understood that political success and consolidation occurs at the local level, as İhsan Dağı aptly explains in his chapter. At the local level, politics is not about big ideas or liberation ideologies but rather about rendering social services and proving to the population that issues of corruption and accountability are addressed in a fashion markedly superior to previous administrations. Politics, for Erdoğan, is about serving and improving one's everyday life and a pragmatic instrument to articulate the claims of people. On the basis of his experience in Istanbul, Erdoğan became aware that the main source of the JDP's legitimacy is based on meeting the needs of people and providing social services to all. This awareness makes him the most pragmatic leader in Turkish history, and at the same time the least ideologically committed. It is locally based politics on a national scale.

Although the leadership of the JDP lacks a developed ideological map of action, they have a good understanding of Ottoman history. This history provides them a rich laboratory of insights and lessons that are useful for guiding current politics. In the case of the JDP leadership, history, especially the classical period of the Ottoman Empire, becomes an "ideology." The makers of new Turkey, the Anatolian bourgeoisie, the new intellectuals, and the JDP leadership, especially Erdoğan, Abdullah Gül, and Bülent Arınç, the speaker of the Parliament, are informed by the grandeur and self-confidence of the Ottoman Classical age, which represented one of the high-water marks in Islamic and indeed world civilization more than the Republican fears of "partition of the country and the collapse of the state."

As this brief sketch shows, a great many problems are addressed, or at least touched upon, by the authors of this collection of essays. This is the first comprehensive study on the governing Justice and Development Party. Many other issues of the party and Turkey also need to be explored, as the JDP struggles to define the concept of conservative democracy in practice. This edited volume, therefore, is but a first step in what, it is hoped, will eventually become a well-developed area of political party studies in comparative politics.

NOTES

1. Graham E. Fuller, "Turkey's Strategic Model: Myths and Realities," *Washington Quarterly* 27, no. 3 (Summer 2004): 51–64. Daniel Pipes also argued that "The Justice and Development Party in Turkey is very different from the Taliban in its means, but not so different in its ends. If the party gained full control over Turkey, it could be as dangerous as the Taliban were in Afghanistan." Washington Institute, *Policy Watch* 746 (April 10, 2003), http://www.washingtoninstitute.org/watch/policywatch/policy watch2003/746.htm.

2. M. Hakan Yavuz, *Islamic Political Identity in Turkey* (New York: Oxford University Press, 2003).

3. Etga Uğur, "Intellectual Roots of 'Turkish Islam' and Approaches to the 'Turkish Model,'" *Journal of Muslim Minority Affairs* 24, no. 2 (October 2004): 327–46.

4. DRA is one of the largest state institutions, with its own branches and budget both inside and outside Turkey. It has the second largest representation outside of Turkey after the Ministry of Foreign Affairs. It owns over 120 mosques and has several hundred employees in various European states. The DRA licenses mosques, appoints all prayer leaders (Imams), pays their salaries, and controls all their activities and speeches. The education of the personnel of religious institutions is carried out by the Ministry of Education and the autonomous Council of Higher Education, known as YÖK. Education and religious services and the meaning of Islam are tightly controlled in Turkey. This state Islam regularly contains and contests diverse interpretations of Islam.

5. Ahmet Yıldız, "Muhafazakarlığın Yerlileştirilmesi ya da AKP'nin 'Yeni Muhafazakar Demokratlığı,'" *Karizma* 7 (January–March 2004): 54; Fahrettin Altun, "İslamcılık ve Muhafazakar Demokrasi," *Anlayış*, December 2005, 41–43; Altun, "Ak Parti'nin Topuğu," *Anlayış*, January 2006, 26–28; Yasin Aktay, "İkrar ile İnkar Arasında Ak Parti'nin kimliği," *Anlayış*, December 2005, 51–54; Necdet Subaşı, *Ara Dönem Din Politikaları* (Istanbul: Küre, 2005), 155–73.

6. For a very different reading of the role of the military in the EU process, see Ersel Aydinli, Nihat Ali Özcan, and Dogan Akyaz, "The Turkish Military's March toward Europe," *Foreign Affairs* 85, no. 1 (January–February 2006): 77–90.

7. Bertil Emrah Oder, "Enhancing the Human Face of Constitutional Reality in Turkey through Accession Partnership with the EU," in *Turkey: The Road Ahead?* ed. Bertil Duner (Stockholm: Swedish Institute of International Affairs, 2002), 72–104.

I.
IDENTITY, IDEOLOGY, AND LEADERSHIP

CHAPTER I

Turkish Religious Market(s)

A View Based on the Religious Economy Theory

■ *Massimo Introvigne*

SECULARIZATION VS. RELIGIOUS ECONOMY

This chapter discusses the relevance of the sociological theory of religious economy for analyzing the competition in the semimonopolistic religious market of a country with a large Islamic majority such as Turkey. The theory of religious economy applied here was summarized by Rodney Stark and Roger Finke in their seminal book *Acts of Faith*.[1] The antithesis of the Marxist reduction of religion to economy, it uses tools taken from modern economic science and the metaphor of the market to study religion as a largely independent field whose very specific social dynamics are not simply consequences of nonreligious psychological or economic factors. In this section, I briefly mention general methodological issues, building on a previous study of Italy (a semimonopolistic market because of its large Roman Catholic majority), before applying the theory to Islam and focusing in particular on Turkey. How the religious market in Turkey compares with non-Muslim religious markets in Europe is particularly relevant in light of the controversies, in which religion played a central role, before and after the December 17, 2004, decision by European governments to start talks on October 3, 2005, aimed at granting full membership in the European Union to Turkey.[2]

One of the main tenets of the religious economy theory is that to the degree that religious economies are unregulated and competitive, overall levels of religious commitment will be high. (Conversely, lacking competition, the dominant firm[s] will be too inefficient to sustain vigorous marketing efforts, and the result will be a low overall level of religious commitment, with the average person minimizing and delaying payment of religious costs.[3])

The theory predicts that, contrary to the secularization thesis, religiousness levels will be higher and religious organizations will be stronger where pluralism is greater.

Italy offers an interesting test case. As Stark and I have discussed elsewhere, religious attendance consistently declined in Italy after World War II as long as religious pluralism was minimal and the state tried to protect a Roman Catholic monopoly.[4] When the religious economy became somewhat deregulated, with massive immigration of non-Catholics and legislation that effectively protected religious minorities, religious attendance in general began to grow rather than decline, an exceptional phenomenon in Western Europe. This analysis met with several objections from Italian sociologists. They conceded that Italian data are an effective weapon against any theory that regards secularization as a necessary correlate of modernization and democratization. In fact, modernization and the expansion of religious liberty and pluralism in Italy caused church attendance to experience moderate growth rather than decline. But, these sociologists argued, these Italian data do not really corroborate the religious economy theory either. In fact, Italian religious pluralism is mostly theoretical. According to data I published in 2001, all religions other than the Roman Catholic Church account for only 1.9 percent of Italian citizens and 3.5 percent of those living in Italy, including noncitizen immigrants and guest workers.[5] We thus have in Italy, or so the objection goes, a growth of religious attendance in a situation of de facto religious monopoly, where the religious economy theory would in fact associate monopoly and decline.

This has been called, by a sociologist sympathetic to religious economy, "the Italian puzzle."[6] The puzzle, however, is not without solutions. First of all, Stark and I argued that perceived pluralism is at least as important as real pluralism. In Italy, political events leading to the end of the Christian Democrat hegemony in 1994, new legislation on religion, and, above all, a spectacular increase in immigration during the 1980s and 1990s, mostly from Muslim countries, made religious pluralism a hotly debated cultural and political issue. While the average Italian living outside the largest cities before the 1970s might never have seen a non-Christian, with the exception of a very small Jewish minority (and, of course, atheists), in the 1990s and 2000s even the most remote village was host to Muslim, Hindu, and other non-Christian immigrants.[7] The terrorist attacks of September 11, 2001, of course, greatly increased the perception of a "Muslim invasion," popularized by the controversial best-sellers of Italian journalist Oriana Fallaci,[8] although the number of

Muslims remains much smaller than in other Western European countries. This increased perception of pluralism might perhaps have the same effects as real pluralism.

On the other hand, religious competition, like competition in other fields, may be either interbrand or intrabrand. For example, competition shows its healthy effects in the car market not only when several car manufacturers compete in the same market, but also when a semimonopolistic car company is able to differentiate between very different product lines and models, thus creating intrabrand alternatives where little interbrand competition exists. This might also be true for religion. Outside the religious economy field, sociologist Niklas Luhmann analyzed large churches as conglomerates of several different microchurches (congregations, movements, religious orders), each with a very large degree of internal autonomy and at times pursuing competing agendas.[9] Italian sociologists have long perceived differentiation as both a key feature of Italian Roman Catholicism and a source of its strength, compared to the situation in neighboring countries such as France or Switzerland, where the Catholic organization is much more centralized and is still mostly focusing on the parish system.[10] In Italy, largely autonomous movements, brotherhoods, and similar institutions account for the large majority of churchgoers. In short, Roman Catholicism is so large that what appears at first sight to be a Catholic monopoly in fact hides a vibrant intrabrand religious market in which semi-independent Catholic firms compete for the allegiance of the largely Roman Catholic population. This intrabrand competition is, of course, not identical to interbrand competition. It might, however, cause similar effects, particularly when one considers that in the market on which religious economy theory was originally based, that of the United States, the most visible competition is intra-Protestant, with the different Protestant "firms" largely recognizing the other firms as legitimate participants in a common Christian enterprise. Competing Roman Catholic firms in Italy would claim just the same.

RELIGIOUS MARKETS AND NICHES

Religious economy focuses on supply. It postulates that demand remains comparatively stable, even in the long term. This happens, the theory argues, because consumers, including consumers of religion, tend to distribute themselves in market niches according to their demographics, financial capabilities, and preferences, the latter being perhaps, as Gary S. Becker argued,[11] the most important factor in markets of symbolic goods. Niches tend, in turn, to remain stable.

Stark and Finke have created several models of religious demand that distinguish between niches according to the concept of strictness and according to costs.[12] Religion is stricter when its symbolic costs are higher and when its members are expected to believe and behave in a more traditional and conservative way than society at large. Religious consumers distribute themselves in niches of different strictness. By simplifying more complex models, we can distinguish among five niches: ultrastrict, strict, moderate-conservative, liberal, and ultraliberal. The liberal niche includes those consumers who are prepared to accept the liberal values that prevail in modern society; the ultraliberal niche includes "modernists" (intended here to mean those who regard modernity as positive and "good for religion"; the term *modernism*, of course, has many different meanings) who enthusiastically embrace these liberal values and are willing to give them a religious sanction. By contrast, consumers in the strict niche see the prevailing liberal values as negative and dangerous, and those in the ultrastrict niche require absolute separation from these values, which are perceived as truly perverse and even demonic. Consumers in the moderate-conservative niche do not utterly reject modern values but feel free to reinterpret them on the basis of religious tradition while in turn reinterpreting religion to make it relevant to the modern world.

Religious consumers may also occupy different niches according to their ideas and aspirations about the relationship between religion, culture, and politics (although this may vary from country to country). Ultrastrict religious consumers identify religion and culture (and religion and politics) and would not admit any distinction. Those in the strict niche regard the identification as desirable but realize that it is not always possible and leave room for some pragmatic compromise. Liberals accept, and ultraliberals promote, modern separation between religion and culture (above all, between religion and politics). Moderate-conservatives appreciate that there is, and should be, a distinction between religion, culture, and politics but would like religion to remain a relevant factor in the public arena. They accept distinction but reject separation. It is because of this attitude that those in the strict niche may be called "fundamentalist" and those in the ultrastrict niche may be called "ultrafundamentalist." I am, of course, aware of the epistemological ambiguity of the category of "fundamentalism," a subject of great controversy. I use the term here without reference to specific historical movements but rather to refer to *an attitude regarding as desirable a nondistinction between religion and culture* (including, again, between religion and politics).

TABLE I.I. Niches in the Religious Market

NICHES	TRENDS	RELATIONSHIP BETWEEN RELIGION AND CULTURE
Ultrastrict	Ultrafundamentalism	Total identification
Strict	Fundamentalism or traditionalism	Identification (some compromise accepted)
Moderate-conservative	Conservatism, reformism	Distinction (but not separation)
Liberal	Religious liberalism	Separation (accepted)
Ultraliberal	Modernism	Separation (promoted)

Table 1.1 shows a very much simplified model of the niche theory as applied in this paper.

One of the conclusions of the religious economy theory most supported by empirical data is that niches are not equal in dimensions. There are, indeed, more consumers in the central moderate-conservative niche than in the others, and the strict niche alone is larger than its liberal and ultraliberal counterparts combined. Religious economy has confirmed what Dean M. Kelley argued in 1972 in his *Why Conservative Churches Are Growing*,[13] and has answered Kelley's many critics. American data have confirmed in a quite spectacular way the growth of conservative and moderately conservative churches and the decline of liberal denominations. The religious economy theory, particularly through the works of Laurence R. Iannaccone, has contributed an explanation based on the free rider theory. A religious group plagued by a high number of free riders would offer to its members boring and unsatisfying religious experiences, and many would simply walk away. Conservative and (moderately) strict groups, with their high costs, include a smaller number of free riders, thus enjoying more success than their liberal counterparts.[14] It is also the case that the liberal and ultraliberal religious niches are smaller because consumers who are interested in the symbolic goods offered in these niches have a great number of secular alternatives, which is not true for the other niches. A consumer who wishes to express support for modern liberal values may do so in dozens of nonreligious organizations without having to pay the specific costs associated with even the most liberal forms of religion.

Religious consumers thus are willing to pay reasonably high costs for obtaining the benefits associated with intense and satisfying religious experiences offered by groups in which the number of free riders is limited. These costs, however, should remain reasonable. If costs are too high, only a handful of radicals will be prepared to pay them. This explains why the ultrastrict, or ultrafundamentalist, niche remains smaller than the strict one and much smaller than the moderate-conservative niche.[15] It should also be noted that while niches normally remain stable, religious organizations move from niche to niche. Many organizations start in the ultrastrict niche but, as their foundational charisma becomes routinized,[16] gradually move toward the mainstream, first to the strict and then to the moderate-conservative niche. They may also go on to move farther left to the liberal and ultraliberal niches, but in this case, their membership will normally decline. Very few extremist groups remain forever in the ultrastrict or ultrafundamentalist niche, where they end up declining or turning to violence. Most move on. This is, of course, a religious economic way of revisiting the classic "sect to church" model elaborated by H. Richard Niebuhr,[17] with the difference that there is nothing unavoidable in the process,[18] and that confronted with the decline experienced when they reach the liberal niche, some organizations may experience conservative revivals and in fact go back "from church to sect."[19]

At least this is what happens in normal conditions. I have argued elsewhere that several possible circumstances can distort the religious demand and the normal functioning of the niches.[20] Perhaps we can use the term *war religious economy* to describe a situation in which a widespread domestic or transnational conflict is perceived by participants as a religious struggle or crusade (whatever its "real" causes as assessed by outside observers). In this case, the ultrastrict and strict niches may experience an abnormal growth, as consumers are more interested in a religion that is literally prepared for war. On the other hand, an *economy of war against religion* is one in which the government persecutes or strictly controls most religious groups, claiming that extremist religion threatens to destroy the existing social order. The unintended result of this policy is, more often than not, a growth of the very ultrastrict or ultrafundamentalist niche the government hoped to control. In fact, if every religious group with the exception of those that support a nonreligious government is persecuted, the normal bridges where religious demand and religious supply meet would be cut. Moderate groups would not be accustomed to operating underground or illegally. Extremist groups would, and they could end up being the only organizations available for supplying religious goods to a wider public that, in other circumstances, might have preferred merely strict or moderately conservative organizations. The latter, however, cannot function in an economy of war against religion, since they have no experience or skills for operating underground.

INTRABRAND RELIGIOUS MARKETS IN THE MUSLIM WORLD

As Anthony J. Gill noted in 2002, there is no reason that the religious economy theory should not apply to the Islamic world.[21] Roman Catholicism and Islam are the largest religions in the world in number of members. They have developed various forms of interbrand competition, which continue today in Africa and elsewhere. For the purposes of this chapter, however, it is crucial to note that intrabrand competition is as prominent in Islam as it is in Roman Catholicism. It was mentioned earlier that a supposed "Catholic monopoly" in Italy is in fact an umbrella category encompassing a vigorous intra-Catholic competition between various very different organizations. The same is true for many allegedly monopolistic religious economies in the Islamic world.

What country would appear to be more religiously monopolistic than Saudi Arabia? Surely there should be no religious competition there, and "Wahhabi" Islam should be in full control of a monopoly. *Wahhabism* is a word coined by Western scholars in the early nineteenth century to designate the puritanical brand of Sunni Islam adopted by the Saud dynasty (that is, the present Saudi royal family) that is based on the teachings of traditionalist preacher Muhammad ibn 'Abd al-Wahhab (1703–1792). Saudis normally reject the word *Wahhabism* as a Western construction and prefer to refer to their brand of Islam as *Salafism* (a reference to *Salaf,* a word indicating the first companions of the Prophet, although this term is also controversial and is used today by some as a synonym for "Islamic extremism"). Terminology aside, it is not the case that there is in Saudi Arabia today a monolithic Wahhabi monopoly, according to scholarly surveys such as the one published by Pascal Ménoret in 2003.[22] Instead, we find a rich religious market in which state ulamas (that is, professional Islamic scholars) compete with a vast unregulated private sector, offering all shades of Islam from ultrafundamentalist to moderately liberal, different interpretations of Wahhabism, and even frank opposition to it, not to mention the presence of both non-Wahhabi Sunni minorities and Shiite minorities. Not surprisingly, the growth of intra-Islamic competition has resulted in Saudi Arabia in what many call simply "the Revival."

Religious supply within the Islamic world covers, in fact, all niches.

Although Islamic religious supply is obviously very different from its Christian counterparts, the theory of religious economy would suggest that religious *demand* may be conceptualized by using similar categories. As a consequence, the theory of religious niches should also be applicable to Islamic religious markets. As predictably as in the Christian world, the ultraliberal Islamic niche that enthusiastically embraces Western values and is occasionally advertised as "the Islamic Enlightenment" (*l'Islam des Lumières* in France) remains small, more popular among elite circles of intellectuals than among the population at large. A description of the other niches should take into account the holistic character of Islam, the fact that Islamic trends and movements offer solutions to all domains of human life, and the fact that many religious groups have immediate political expressions as well.

An intra-Islamic and, particularly, intra-Sunni religious market seems to have originated in the nineteenth century, with the growing awareness that the Islamic world was experiencing serious problems and solutions were needed. Itzchak Weismann has described nineteenth-century Damascus as a main center of this revival,[23] but there were others as well. Calling themselves Salafis (as was mentioned earlier, a term implying a reference to the glorious Muslim ancestors), reformers such as Jamal al-Din Afghani (1839–1897) and Muhammad 'Abduh (1849–1905) tried both to modernize Islam and to Islamize modernity. Their teachings, however, were read in quite different ways by the following generation of reformers. Through Rashid Rida (1865–1935), the nineteenth-century Salafiya developed toward what would become, with the foundation of the Muslim Brotherhood in Egypt, modern Islamic fundamentalism. (The term *Salafi* today designates fundamentalist and even terrorist movements in several countries, but this was by no means the original meaning.) At the opposite extreme, authors such as 'Ali 'Abdel Raziq (1888–1966) developed an Islamic modernism (*Raziqism*) that closely parallels movements in the Western ultraliberal niche and remains both controversial and confined to comparatively small intellectual circles.[24] In the center, a moderately conservative reformism tried to avoid both fundamentalism and secularism, more often than not by allying itself with Sufi brotherhoods (that is, movements that focus on the mystical path to Islam, although, unlike their Christian counterparts, such mystical movements may have millions of members).

This schema refers to the Arab Middle East, but the same situation seems to have developed elsewhere. Islamic revivals in the nineteenth and early twentieth centuries called for a return to past glory and eventually developed in the opposite directions of fundamentalism and modern-ism. This was the case in Indonesia and Malaysia with several groups; in Yemen with the reformism of Muhammad al-Shawkānī (1760–1834), who led the country from Zaydite Shiism to traditionalist Sunnism;[25] and in sub-Saharan Africa with Shaykh al-Amin ibn ʿAli al-Mazruʾi (1890–1947) and several others.[26] Almost everywhere, those who develop the insights of the earlier reformers toward fundamentalism are anti-Sufi and ask for an interpretation of Islamic law, Shariʿa, based on *taqlid* (tradi-tion) only, while the moderate-conservatives often have Sufi connections and call for interpreting Shariʿa through *ijtihad* (interpretation based on principles of analogy).

The strict niche does not include only fundamentalists in the lineage of the Muslim Brotherhood (or parallel organizations outside the Arab Middle East). In competition, and occasional cooperation, with funda-mentalists, we find in the strict niche also "traditionalists." They are the heirs of a previous wave of reformism that proposed to free Islam from allegedly superstitious elements derived from Sufism and popular reli-gion. These included Wahhabis in Saudi Arabia and Ahl-i Hadith in India, while the Indian Deobandis, although sharing a severe puritan-ism with Wahhabis, are in fact much more tolerant of Sufi practices. Traditionalist movements such as the Wahhabis or the Deobandis do not belong to the historical lineage of fundamentalism. Unlike funda-mentalists, they have a tradition of quietist respect for the powers that be and a much more radical aversion to modernity. Although political alliances have confused the issues, differences between fundamentalists and traditionalists remain significant, as they compete for the allegiance of consumers in the same strict niche. From both fundamentalist and traditionalist lineages, finally, derive groups in the ultrastrict niche that either separate themselves radically from mainstream society or resort to violence and terrorism. Terrorist forms of ultrafundamentalism should not be confused with the more mainstream tradition of fundamental-ism, whose main organizations do not promote terrorism (although they often condone it in particular war situations such as those in Palestine or Chechnya). In this sense, the term *fundamentalism*, referring to the tra-dition of the Muslim Brotherhood and similar organizations, has a quite precise historical meaning in Islam and should not be used as a synonym for terrorism or illegal activities.

As for the liberal niche, it is occupied both by liberal, "modernized" forms of Sufism (such as the Turkish Melamiya, of which more later) and by those secular nationalist movements (such as the less secular wing

TABLE 1.2. A Model of the Islamic Religious Market

NICHES	TRENDS	MOVEMENTS (EXAMPLES)
Ultrastrict	Ultrafundamentalism	Al-Qa'ida, GIA
Strict	(a) Fundamentalism (b) Traditionalism	(a) Muslim Brotherhood (b) "Wahhabism," Deobandism
Moderate-conservative	(a) Conservative political Islam (b) Mainline Sufism (c) Centrist Reformism	(a) JDP, Wasat* (b) Nakşibendiya (c) Nahdlatul Ulama, Nur
Liberal	(a) Islamo-Nationalism (b) Liberal Sufism	Ba'ath, Algerian nationalism, Melamiya
Ultraliberal	Modernism	Islamo-Marxism, Raziqism

*Wasat in Egypt remains somewhat ambiguous and maintains ties with forms of fundamentalism.

of the Ba'ath Party, which was once in power in Iraq and still controls Syria) that maintain a role for religion (unlike other nationalist movements that reject religion altogether). Algerian nationalism is a case in point, although the fact that both the government and its fundamentalist opponents now claim for themselves the heritage of the reformism of Malek Bennabi (1905–1973) confirms that even in the Maghreb countries, it is not impossible to go back from present-day modernism and fundamentalism to common earlier reformist roots. From the same roots may develop a moderate-conservative center. "Centrist" is indeed an expression that is part of Egyptian political lexicon, indicating as it does the members of a political party that was originally established in 1996 as Hizb al-Wasat (the Centre Party) and reformed in 1998 as Hizb al-Wasat al-Mizri (the Egyptian Centre Party). The new name did not prevent a consistent refusal by Egypt's Political Parties Committee (PPC) to legalize the Centrists. Although the Centrists claimed to regard Islam for political purposes as a "civilizational" rather than "religious" element (a formula also used by Bennabi in Algeria) and the party included Christians as well as Muslims, the fact that several prominent members were ex-Muslim Brothers made the government highly suspicious of the Wasat.[27] However, although perhaps incomplete and occasionally ambiguous, the Egyptian "centrism" may be an interesting attempt of a part of the Muslim Brotherhood to move from the fundamentalist niche to the moderately conservative niche, where a significant constituency is obviously believed to exist.

Table 1.2 shows a model of the niche theory as applied to Islamic religious markets in general.

Islamic Exceptionalism?

Religious economy should consider Islamic reformism in its various shapes from a supply-side perspective. Reformism and revival, be they in nineteenth-century Plymouth, Boston, or Damascus, do not arise because of an alleged inherent newness of the religious demand. Reformers and revivalists understand that the demand is already there and create a supply adequate to meet it—hence their success. The theory would postulate that in the long term, ultrafundamentalist (and ultraliberal) movements will meet with only a limited degree of success, fundamentalist movements will be more successful than their liberal counterparts, and movements capable of occupying the centrist moderate-conservative niche will enjoy the greatest success of all. Many would object that this is not true in the Islamic world. Either the theory of religious economy is not universally applicable, they would say, or there is an "Islamic exceptionalism." But is there really?

First of all, in our post-9/11 situation, ultrafundamentalism is over-reported. Almost nobody in the general public in the West has heard the names of organizations such as the Indonesian Nahdlatul Ulama, a centrist conservative group, or Mohammadiyya, a group that can be classified among the less extremist expressions of fundamentalism. They have an estimated forty million and thirty million members, respectively, and appear to be much larger than the Muslim Brotherhood, not to mention al-Qa'ida. The same is true for the Turkish Fethullah Gülen movement, which is both large and international yet hardly a household name in the West.

On the other hand, there are, as was mentioned earlier, abnormal situations conducive to a distortion of the niches, with an alarming but temporary expansion of the ultrastrict segment. In the *war religious economy* that prevails in Palestine, the largest local branch of the Muslim Brotherhood, Hamas, is an expression of the Brotherhood's move from the strict niche it occupies in other countries to the ultrastrict one, owing to exceptional local circumstances. War religious economy polarizes the alternatives between an ultrafundamentalist group, Hamas, and secular nationalism, making as difficult as all observers claim the emergence of a centrist leadership that would be a more reliable partner in international negotiations. Similar comments may apply to Chechnya, Kashmir, and other war situations.

In other countries, governments have banned a large number of religious organizations. As was mentioned earlier, the most extreme groups in the ultrafundamentalist niche are the ones that are able to resist such persecution and operate underground, where moderate-conservative groups and even the less extremist organizations of the fundamentalist niche may simply disappear. Extremist ultrafundamentalists are thus able to meet a large segment of the religious demand, with virtually no competition, and are paradoxically reinforced by the same legal measures that are aimed at eliminating them. Saddam Hussein's Iraq was a case in point. Particularly before 1991, the regime sought to eliminate all independent religious organizations, Sunnis as well as Shiites. Those who managed to survive underground were, predictably, the most extreme, including some branches of the Muslim Brotherhood and semiterrorist groups that had international connections. The situation that prevailed during Saddam's religious repression (an economy of war against religion, or at least against *independent* religion) is somewhat repeated in the present religious war economy, in which extremist groups may gain a larger audience than in "normal" times. Polls and the 2005 elections, however, seem to show that most religious consumers in Iraq, whose ideas are perhaps underreported in the media, do look for alternatives in the centrist, moderately conservative niche represented by Najaf's traditional Shiite authorities and those Sunni political parties that have joined the new government.

Islamic ultrafundamentalist terrorism is obviously a complex phenomenon whose causes are not only cultural or religious. However, the Algerian case seems to confirm the dangers of repression. The army coup of January 11, 1992, banned a whole spectrum of Islamic organizations. Some went into exile, but among those who were able to continue an illegal existence in Algeria were, predictably, the most extreme wings of the ultrafundamentalist movement. These, soon divided into a plethora of conflicting organizations (some of them infiltrated by the Algerian intelligence, others by al-Qa'ida), were responsible for a bloody civil war that probably claimed some 100,000 victims. The situation has now evolved. Only small pockets of terrorist and guerrilla activities by the GIA (Armed Islamic Group), the GSPC (Salafi Group for Preaching and Combat), and the HDS (Guardians of the Salafi Call) remain operative. It is certainly true that the main terrorist organizations were defeated through military action, although with a high cost in human lives. It is also the case, however, that actions taken by President Bouteflika (who was reelected in 2004) in granting amnesty to several insurgents, freeing from jail the leaders of the banned FIS (Islamic Salvation Front), legalizing parties with connections to the Muslim Brotherhood (although not the FIS itself), and reclaiming the common heritage of Bennabi's reformism and the contribution of political Islam to Algeria's national anticolonial struggle have opened the religious market and have created a number of alternative options to ultrafundamentalism. Conservative and fundamentalist religious demand may now be legally met by a number of legitimate groups, which offer serious competition for those ultrafundamentalist organizations that remain committed to violence, although Algeria's problems are far from being solved.

Religious Market(s) in Turkey

Although Turkey does have its share of religious minorities, the analysis will focus here on its intrabrand Muslim market. Turkey offers an ideal test case for a number of reasons. Thierry Zarcone claims that Islam in Turkey has always been highly pluralistic and still maintains the heritage of tensions between large cities and the rural countryside, between Istanbul and Anatolia, between Turkish identity and the Arabic Koran. This French scholar sees what we would call the Turkish religious market as resulting historically from the competition of five trends during the Ottoman period:

1. Islam as the official religion of the Ottoman Empire, whose orthodoxy was guaranteed by the state ulamas. In imperial Turkey, they controlled the administration of justice through the kadis (religious judges) and through religious instruction as a whole, from elementary to secondary, interpreting the Shari'a through the lens of the Hanafi legal school.

2. Sufi Islam of the large brotherhoods, which perpetuated a substantially orthodox Sunni Islam outside the circle of the religiously educated through their large networks of *tekkes* (halls of shrines used for Sufi meetings). Since many shaykhs (local leaders) of the most important brotherhoods were themselves ulamas, there were no substantial conflicts with the first group. Zarcone, however, suggests a distinction between three groups of Sufi brotherhoods: one claiming to fully respect the Shari'a as defined by the Hanafi ulamas (Nakşibendiya, Chaziliya); one divided between a respect for orthodoxy and sympathy for the mysticism of Ibn Arabi (1165–1240), which is despised by most state ulamas (Halvetiya,

Mevleviya); and one engaged in a difficult attempt to harmonize pre-Islamic and non-Sunni influences with Sunnism (Bektaşiya, Melamiya, Hamzeviya).

3. Heterodox Islam of the countryside, grounded in the syncretistic Turcoman heritage with Shiite influences. In fact, the most relevant groups were not technically Shiite (though a Shiite minority did exist in Turkey) but part of what many scholars now call the "hyper-Shiite tradition."[28] *Hyper-Shiism* is a style of religious thought that both regards as a divine incarnation Ali (600–661, the son-in-law and fourth successor of the Prophet Muhammad whose claim to the caliphate, when challenged by Muawiyah I [602–680], led his followers to establish Shiism as a branch separate from the "Sunni" Islam originally led by Muawiyah and his successors, the Umayyad caliphs) and considers its subsequent leaders to be Ali's reincarnations. Neither claim is made, or accepted, by mainstream Shiism. An exact typology of different groups within the hyper-Shiite tradition is the subject matter of complicated discussions. Zarcone does not believe that the Bektaşis are part of this tradition, while he includes here the Kızılbaş, which in part still exist under this name in villages of Thrace and Anatolia and in part merged with, or were influenced by, the Alevis, whose complicated recent evolution, however, calls into question their inclusion in the "hyper-Shiite" fold.

4. What Zarcone calls the heterodox Islam of the "doctor-philosophers," in the tradition of Bedreddin Simavli (1359–1416) and of a series of independent mystics verging on pantheism.

5. The popular Sunni Islam of "country ulamas," which took great pride in distinguishing itself from the crypto-Shiite or hyper-Shiite heterodoxy yet incorporated a number of beliefs of non-Sunni origin, focused on the rural shrines of the saints, and were often regarded by both the state ulamas and the larger brotherhoods as superstitious. In fact, the Ottoman establishment regarded the three latter competitors as somewhat illegitimate. However, they managed to survive.[29]

Although the personal ideas about religion of the father of the modern Turkish Republic, Kemal Atatürk (1881–1938), are the subject of some debate,[30] there is little doubt that he was inspired by the sociological theories of Auguste Comte (1798–1857) and regarded traditional religion as an obstacle to progress. Kemalism involved a complex de-Islamization process whereby the official Islam was separated from the judiciary (which was secularized) and brought under the strict control of the secular state, Sufi brotherhoods were formally dissolved in 1925, and the rural shrines of the saints were closed. Admirer as he was of the French *laïcité*, Atatürk realized that the French model could not simply be imported into a Muslim country. The *laïcité* in France was aimed at reducing religion to an affair of the individual, entirely separated from the state. Unlike French Roman Catholicism, Turkish Islam was not easily amenable to a process of deinstitutionalization. It was just too intrinsically institutional and operated within a framework in which the distinction between public and private and between religious and cultural was much less evident. The Turkish *laiklik* therefore did not ignore religion, as the French *laïcité* proclaimed to do (at least theoretically), but rather put it under the direct control of the prime minister's office via its Directorate of Religious Affairs, instituted in 1924.

The de-Islamization process in fact greatly reduced the number of available options in the Turkish religious market. Although circumscribed by the secular state, official Islam maintained its prominence. The large brotherhoods did not disappear, but the official dissolution forced them to perform what M. Hakan Yavuz calls an "inward migration" away from the public domain into the sphere of family and household.[31] Rural Islam experienced difficulties and problems due to the official prohibition against the cult of the saints and the general de-Islamization policy but managed to survive. Heterodoxy in general celebrated Kemalism as its ally in revenge against previous discrimination. Kızılbaş, Alevis, and even Bektaşis presented themselves as staunch supporters of Kemalism, although this support, as David Shankland has demonstrated,[32] converted some of their organizations into secular-cultural associations with feeble religious references, while, on the other hand, the laws against the brotherhoods did create problems for these groups also.

As the religious economy theory would predict, the official regulation of the religious market caused several extremist reactions: an insurrection in the southeast in 1925 combining Kurdish ethnonationalism and religious reaction, the so-called conspiracy of the Tarikat-i Salahiya (Brotherhood of the Virtue) between 1920 and 1925, and religiously oriented popular uprisings such as the "Menemen incident" of 1925, in which a Kemalist officer was lynched by the populace. The government reacted with a stricter control on religion, which experienced its worst period between 1925 and 1945. Between 1932 and 1954, the People's Houses and the Village Institutes tried to replace the mosque and the *tekke* as the (secular) centers of village life.[33] Kemalism, whose secularizing experiment took place in Sunni Turkey, has often been compared to similar efforts by the Pahlavi dynasty in Iran, a Shiite country. As Touraj Atabaki and Erik J. Zürcher have noted, both efforts did achieve some results but were never entirely or permanently successful.[34]

On the other hand, as Yavuz noted, "the secularization policies of the state did not succeed fully, because they focused on the public sphere and were not able to touch the grassroots level of informal societal networks."[35] According to Yavuz, it was Sufism that in the face of state coercion was most able to resist, thanks to its ability to withdraw into the inner domestic and familial sphere. However, the Sufi orders that relied on conspicuous external rituals, clothing, buildings, and ceremonies such as the Mevleviya experienced more difficulties. The Nakşibendis, on the other hand, whose system does not necessarily require a *tekke*, whose clothing is not peculiar, and who are able to privilege the silent (and inconspicuous) *zikr* (a Sufi ritual for remembering God through meditation and prayer, also, however, occasionally including songs and dances) were able to survive both the legal ban of 1925 and the persecution of the 1930s. Together with the Nakşibendis, a "movement of resistance to the ongoing Kemalist modernization" that was capable, according to Yavuz,[36] of being at the same time "forward-looking and proactive" emerged in the shape of the Nurcu, or Nur, movement of Said Nursi (1876–1960). Nursi's followers, known as Nurcus, who proclaimed the harmonization of Islam and modern science and, as Ian Markham and Ibrahim Özdemir emphasize, truly opened Islam to modern interreligious dialogue,[37] in fact occupied a space outside the public sphere that Kemalism had denied to religion: the sphere of culture, of successful books, and of their readers. Although Nursi had been a member of the Nakşibendis and defended the brotherhoods against the Kemalist ban, he founded a peculiar centrist-conservative (but not fundamentalist) tradition that is not, strictly speaking, part of Sufism and is not affiliated with any Sufi brotherhood (including the Nakşibendis).[38] Nakşibendis and Nurcus thus were at the forefront of a new relevance of Islam that emerged when, in the 1950s, the Turkish religious market started to be deregulated. Faced with the new threat of communism, the Kemalist establishment and the military granted more latitude to religion, which was regarded as both a necessary component of the nation's moral fabric and an element capable of unifying all Turkish citizens, transcending their ethnic diversities, particularly the contrast between Turks and Kurds. Turkish secularism, or *laiklik*, as

Andrew Davison has noted, became something still more different from the French *laïcité*.[39] The differences with France were perhaps there, Davison argues, from the very beginning.[40] The government of Turgut Özal (1927–1993) in the 1980s epitomized this new approach. Özal was himself part of the circle of the popular shaykh Mehmed Zahid Kotku (1897–1980), head of the Nakşibendi branch known as Gümüşhanevi headquartered at the İskenderpaşa Camii mosque in Istanbul.[41] The teachings of Kotku, whose circle also included future prime ministers Necmettin Erbakan and Recep Tayyip Erdoğan, emphasized the perfect compatibility between Islam and modernity, including economic development.

While the political consequences, developments, and reactions to the deregulation of the Turkish religious market deserve a larger discussion and are treated elsewhere in this book, a general map of this market according to the theory of religious niches may be proposed. The map can, of course, include only some of the many trends and groups active in Turkey and leaves largely aside the Kurdish and Shiite minorities. I will also try to apply to Turkey the general model of the Islamic religious market outlined in the section above on Islamic exceptionalism.

Ultrafundamentalism, defined as the total rejection of the modern political order and the attempt to subvert it through violent means, appears to be very rare in contemporary Turkey, even though Turkey has had its sad share of terrorist attacks claimed by ultrafundamentalist Islamic groups (and a considerably higher number of incidents attributed to Kurdish separatists or Marxist-Leninists). However, a simple statistical table would reveal that ultrafundamentalist terrorism declined with the opening and deregulation of the Turkish religious market.[42] This is in accordance with the religious economy theory, which predicts that extremist groups find more followers when conservative but nonviolent alternatives are not easily available to religious consumers or are harassed in their public activity by the state. On the other hand, when religious consumers are comparatively free to choose fundamentalist (but nonviolent) and conservative (but not fundamentalist) competing groups, ultrafundamentalism declines. Recent incidents have been attributed to foreign influences (perhaps with al-Qa'ida connections). Even a terrorist organization with such a quintessentially Turkish name as the Knights of the Great Orient, which has claimed some recent attacks, remains somewhat ambiguous. *Büyük Doğu*, meaning "Great Orient," was both the title of a journal founded in 1943 by influential Islamic intellectual Necip Fazıl (1904–1983) and its term for Islam as "a holistic and totalistic ideology."[43] There are, however, no clear links between the contemporary terrorist Knights of the Great Orient and Fazıl's ideas. Certain scholars of terrorism even think that the Knights might originally have been a creation of factions of the Turkish intelligence establishment that were eager to blame terrorism on Islamic fundamentalism,[44] although of course this opinion remains controversial.

The word *fundamentalism* is as ambiguous in the Turkish context as it is elsewhere. Considering the difference between Turkish and Arab political Islam, one might prefer to use some expression other than *fundamentalism*. Its use here, however, refers strictly to the niche theory outlined above and is not a value judgment. In this sense, Turkish political Islam as represented by Necmettin Erbakan occupies the fundamentalist niche of the religious market. It is perhaps not coincidental that Erbakan's first meeting as newly installed prime minister in 1996 was "with the leader of Egypt's Muslim Brotherhood,"[45] the movement that largely defines international Islamic fundamentalism (which, again, should not be confused with ultrafundamentalism or terrorism). The fact that Erbakan had Sufi connections and enjoyed the support of Sufi brotherhoods is not incompatible with a collocation of its supporters in the fundamentalist niche. Fundamentalists are not everywhere anti-Sufi, and the founder of the Muslim Brotherhood, Hasan al-Banna (1906–1949), was himself a Sufi.[46]

Fundamentalism, as was mentioned earlier, competes with traditionalism—a different religious style—for the allegiance of consumers in the strict niche. The largest (four million members) traditionalist organization in Turkey is the *cemaat* (community) of the Süleymancıs, established by Süleyman Hilmi Tunahan (1888–1959). A cemaat is not technically a brotherhood, and the Turkish system of the cemaat created what Zarcone defines as "Sufism without 'brotherhoodism.'"[47] Tunahan in fact denounced the decadence of the brotherhoods system, although he remained attached to its tradition, rooted in the Indian branch of the Nakşibendis, to which, not coincidentally, the founders of the largest international traditionalist movement, Deobandism, also swore allegiance.

It is worth noting that the term *traditionalism* is used here with reference, once again, to the niche model described above rather than technically in order to identify the school of thought mostly defined by, if not exclusively originating from, René Guénon (1886–1951) and often referred to as "Traditionalism" with a capital *T.* Guénon's ideas are popular among a handful of Turkish intellectuals and academics, including Mustafa Tahralı, a professor of theology at Marmara University, and

Mahmud Kılıç, the heir of a prominent Sufi family who helped to pop-
ularize the works of Iranian Traditionalist Seyyed Hossein Nasr in Turkey. A limited number of Turks have also been initiated in Traditionalist
orders, including female movie director Ayşe Şasa, who joined a Traditionalist branch of the Sufi brotherhood known as Khalwatiya. On the
other hand, "there are no Traditionalist organizations in Turkey," nor do
Traditionalists have any political influence,[48] although they are occasionally attacked as dangerous, for opposite reasons, by both Kemalists and
fundamentalists.

What appears unique to the Turkish religious market is the strength
of a conservative-moderate center, which has offerings that are both rich
and diverse and which has met with a notable degree of success. In this
central niche of the religious market, at least three different expressions of
Turkish Sunni Islam compete. We have mentioned that although niches
are stable, movements often move from one niche to another, and it is
not uncommon for a fundamentalist group to evolve toward the central conservative-moderate niche. Several Islamic fundamentalist movements have moved toward the center by rethinking their tradition and
their relationship with the original nineteenth-century Salafiya. We have
described the itinerary of a part of the Egyptian Muslim Brotherhood
toward the formation of centrist political organizations. Similar evolu-
tions have been described in Tunisia among Islamist intellectuals of the
circle of Rachid Gannouchi.[49] In Turkey, this process, although with
characteristics peculiar to that country, emerged with the separation of
Erdoğan's JDP from Erbakan's Felicity Party (Saadet Partisi). The JDP is
regarded by many as a typical "conservative" organization.[50] The results
of the 2002 elections, in which the JDP obtained 34.2 percent of the
votes compared to 2.46 percent for the FP (further reinforced by data
on the 2004 administrative elections), confirmed in their own way that
the conservative-moderate niche is larger than its fundamentalist coun-
terpart even when both are considered in their political projections. It is
by no means arbitrary to discuss political parties within the framework
of an analysis of the religious market. According to Zarcone, the parties
of political Islam up to and including the FP were based on "the dominant model of the [Sufi] brotherhoods."[51] The JDP, while still an expression of political Islam, should be regarded in this perspective as the first
religiously inspired party capable of rejecting the brotherhood model and
adopting "the model of Western Christian Democrat parties." Through
this change of model, "political Islam in Turkey has not failed; quite to
the contrary, it has successfully moved to a new ideological phase."[52]

On the other hand, politics, even in the shape of political Islam, does not exhaust the field of the conservative-moderate niche of the religious market in Turkey, which appears to be as large in Turkey as in the non-Islamic countries typically studied by the religious economy theory. The same religious demand is met by the main branches of the Nakşibendiya, both in the great Istanbul organizations such as the already mentioned Gümüşhanevi, the Erenköy Cemaati,[53] or the group of the Ismail Aga mosque and in the Anatolian brotherhoods such as the Menzil Cemaati of Raşhid Erol (1929–1996). To different degrees, all these branches have succeeded in modernizing Sufi Islam while remaining faithful to the ancient Nakşibendi roots, thus catering to a large moderate-conservative constituency, which in present-day Turkey appears to be larger than the traditionalist audience served by the Süleymancıs.

Finally, the center of the religious market in Turkey is occupied by a very original phenomenon, "the greatest novelty in Turkish religious history": a dozen Nurcu communities claiming the heritage of Said Nursi's reformism.[54] The most important neo-Nur movement is the Fethullah Gülen movement, also the subject of a growing number of scholarly studies in the West.[55] "Neither 'fundamentalist' nor 'secularist,'"[56] the movement combines Turkish nationalism, the Sufi heritage of Anatolia, and Nursi's proposals for a dialogue between Islam and modern science to create a typical centrist and post-Sufi organization. Without recapitulating here the existing scholarship on the Gülen movement, an important point is that it typically addresses the needs of the moderate-conservative niche in the intra-Islamic religious market, perhaps as a result of movement from an original position in the strict niche toward the center, somewhat similar to the evolution of Catholic groups such as Opus Dei.[57] Other neo-Nur groups appeal to diverse audiences. It is also important to note that groups in the moderate-conservative niche do not automatically support the JDP. Yavuz concludes as much with respect to the Gülen movement.[58] Nakşibendi brotherhoods seem to be similarly divided.

There are, of course, also offerings that address the liberal niche of the religious market in Turkey. Several movements have offered a religious interpretation of Kemalism. This appears in the post-brotherhood phase of the branch of the Melamiya, in which Maksud Hulusi (1851–1929) was succeeded by his son Mahmut Sadettin Bilginer (1909–1983) and by his close disciple Hasan Lufti Chuchut (1903–1988). A Sufi brotherhood was transformed into a liberal movement critical of both traditional Sufism and the prevailing conservative-moderate groups. Much more complicated is the situation of the Bektaşiya as reorganized by Bedri Noyan

(1912–1997) and Turgut Koca (1921–1997). According to Zarcone, Noy-an's designated successor, Teoman Güre, was excluded from the direction of the Bektaşiya in 2000 "because of its membership in Freemasonry."[59] This might appear to be a confirmation that the fundamentalist propaganda against all forms of Freemasonry exerts an influence wider than expected within Turkish Islam. But in fact the relationship between the Bektaşiya and the esoteric wing of Turkish Freemasonry (as opposed to its secularist-Kemalist wing) has a long history,[60] and Freemasonry has often been used as a vehicle for integrating Sufism and liberalism, with quite mixed results.

Problems within the Bektaşiya have resulted in what Zarcone calls "quite serious confusions,"[61] with Alevis taking over several Bektaşi tekkes and converting them into Alevi meetinghouses. Some use the expression *Alevi-Bektaşis*, which has a questionable historical status. In fact, one is in principle initiated into a Bektaşi brotherhood, while one is born an Alevi and the initiation simply confirms a status acquired by birth. The Bektaşiya originated as a Sufi and Sunni brotherhood (although with non-Sunni influences and verging on heterodoxy), while Alevism, whatever it may be considered, is not part of Sunnism. Alevism has reinvented itself during the course of the twentieth century, however, trying to occupy the ultraliberal niche and claiming for itself the role of an ultra-Kemalist and occasionally openly Marxist community with a vaguely religious origin. In this sense, it has claimed that one may become an Alevi (rather than being born in the tradition), has initiated even Westerners, and has experienced its share of problems with the international crisis of Marxism. What exactly Alevism is today, or will be in the future, is a matter of considerable debate.[62]

It is, at any rate, difficult for the Bektaşis and the Alevis to reach an audience with no traditional or family attachment to their respective traditions. Those in the liberal and ultraliberal niches might prefer the works of individual Islamo-Kemalist thinkers such as Hasan Ali Yücel (1897–1961) who never created organized movements. In fact, as the religious economy theory would predict, *religious* liberal and ultraliberal organizations remain small because they have to compete with *nonreligious* secular groups that espouse similar values. Jenny B. White has confirmed that, particularly in the large world of Turkish women's organizations, the real competition for the organizations of political Islam comes from secular Kemalist groups, which are not religious.[63] Table 1.3 applies the proposed model of the Islamic religious market to Turkey, obviously in a somewhat schematic form.

TABLE 1.3. A Model of the Turkish Religious Market

NICHES	TRENDS	MOVEMENTS (EXAMPLES)
Ultrastrict	Ultrafundamentalism	Knights of the Great Orient
Strict	(a) Fundamentalism (b) Traditionalism	(a) Saadet Party (b) Süleymancıs
Moderate- conservative	(a) Conservative political Islam (b) Mainline Sufism (c) Centrist Reformism	(a) JDP (b) Mainline Nakşibendiya (c) Nur and neo-Nur groups
Liberal	(a) Islamo-Nationalism (b) Liberal Sufism	(a) Islamo-Kemalism (b) Melamiya, Bektaşiya*
Ultraliberal	Modernism	Islamo-Marxism, Alevism

* The Sufi status of the Bektaşiya is disputed.

What makes Turkey highly unusual among Islamic religious markets are its rich, persuasive, and varied offerings in the central moderate-
conservative niche. Movements in this niche are both religiously and
politically successful, and religion in general appears to be in very good
health in a country that before World War II experienced one of the most
sustained secularist policies of de-Islamization. In a survey conducted in
1999, 92 percent of the respondents reported that they kept the fast during the month of Ramadan, 46 percent that they performed the five daily
canonical prayers, and 62 percent that they attended Friday prayers regularly.[64] In the 1999–2002 wave of the *World Value Survey*, where questions were phrased somewhat differently, 71 percent of the Turk males
reported religious service attendance "once a month or more" (it is traditional for women to visit mosques much less frequently), while 92 percent of all Turks, males and females, said that they "get comfort and
strength from religion" and 82 percent reported that they "pray every
day or more than once a week."[65] Turkey confirms that where offerings
in the moderate-conservative niche abound and the state limits its interference, fundamentalism is contained and ultrafundamentalism is marginalized. This should be good news for those who are preoccupied with
an allegedly unavoidable explosion of fundamentalism—if not ultrafundamentalism—in deregulated religious and political markets within the
Islamic world. The situations in Indonesia and Malaysia, large non-Arab
Islamic countries where the religious economy appears to be in the process of being similarly deregulated, would tend to confirm these conclusions. Whether the same effects would follow deregulation in the Arab

Muslim world is a prediction that the religious economy theory should dare to propose, although it could be tested only when truly deregulated Arab religious markets begin to appear.

NOTES

1. Rodney Stark and Roger Finke, *Acts of Faith: Explaining the Human Side of Religion* (Berkeley: University of California Press, 2000).

2. For an overview, see Netherlands Scientific Council for Government Policy, *The European Union, Turkey and Islam* (Amsterdam: Amsterdam University Press, 2004).

3. Stark and Finke, *Acts of Faith*, 201.

4. Rodney Stark and Massimo Introvigne, *Dio è tornato: Indagine sulla rivincita delle religioni in Occidente* (Casale Monferrato, Italy: Piemme, 2003).

5. Massimo Introvigne, PierLuigi Zoccatelli, Nelly Ippolito Macrina, and Verónica Roldán, *Enciclopedia delle religioni in Italia* (Leumann, Italy: Elledici, 2001).

6. Luca Diotallevi, *Il rompicapo della secolarizzazione italiana: Caso italiano, teorie americane e revisione del paradigma della secolarizzazione* (Soveria Mannelli, Italy: Rubbettino, 2001). See also Diotallevi, "Internal Competition in a National Religious Monopoly: The Catholic Effect and the Italian Case," *Sociology of Religion* 63 (2002): 137–55.

7. See Massimo Introvigne and Rodney Stark, "Religious Competition and Revival in Italy: Exploring European Exceptionalism," *Interdisciplinary Journal of Research on Religion* 1, no. 1 (2005), online at http://www.bepress.com/cgi/viewcontent.cgi?article=1001&context=ijrr.

8. See Oriana Fallaci, *La rabbia e l'orgoglio* (Milan: Rizzoli, 2001; translated as *The Rage and the Pride* [New York: Rizzoli International, 2002]); and *La forza della ragione* (Milan: Rizzoli, 2004; translated as *The Force of Reason* [New York: Rizzoli International, 2005]).

9. See Niklas Luhmann, *Die Religion der Gesellschaft* (Frankfurt am Main: Suhrkamp, 2000).

10. For more on differentiation in Italian Roman Catholicism, see Luigi Berzano, *Differenziazione e religione negli anni Ottanta* (Turin: Giappichelli, 1990); Roberto Cipriani, *La religione dei valori: Indagine nella Sicilia Centrale* (Caltanissetta, Italy: Sciascia, 1992); Franco Garelli, *Forza della religione e debolezza della fede* (Bologna: Il Mulino, 1996).

11. See Gary S. Becker, *The Economic Approach to Human Behavior* (Chicago: University of Chicago Press, 1976).

12. Stark and Finke, *Acts of Faith*, 197; see also Stark and Finke, "Beyond Church and Sect: Dynamics and Stability in Religious Economics," in *Sacred Markets, Sacred Canopies: Essays on Religious Markets and Religious Pluralism*, ed. Ted Jelen (Lanham, MD: Rowman and Littlefield, 2002), 31–82.

13. Dean M. Kelley, *Why Conservative Churches Are Growing: A Study in Sociology of Religion* (New York: Harper and Row, 1972).

14. See Laurence R. Iannaccone, "Sacrifice and Stigma: Reducing Free-Riding in Cults, Communes, and Other Collectives," *Journal of Political Economy* 100 (1992): 271–92; Iannaccone, "Why Strict Churches Are Strong," *American Journal of Sociology* 99 (1994): 1180–211.

15. See Laurence R. Iannaccone, "Toward an Economic Theory of 'Fundamental-ism,'" *Journal of Institutional and Theoretical Economics* 153 (1997): 100–116; Iannaccone, "Religious Extremism: Origins and Consequences," *Contemporary Jewry* 21 (2000): 8–29.

16. The concept of routinization of charisma is obviously derived from Max Weber. The idea of the evolution of religious "firms," however, is reconstructed here according to Stark and Iannaccone's (2003) theory of religious economy and differs from Weber's.

17. See H. Richard Niebuhr, *The Social Sources of Denominationalism* (New York: Henry Holt, 1929).

18. See Roger Finke and Rodney Stark, *The Churching of America, 1776–1990: Winners and Losers in Our Religious Economy* (New Brunswick, NJ: Rutgers University Press, 1992).

19. Stark and Finke, "Beyond Church and Sect," 53.

20. Massimo Introvigne, *Fondamentalismi: I diversi volti dell'intransigenza religiosa* (Casale Monferrato, Italy: Piemme, 2004).

21. Anthony J. Gill, "A Political Economy of Religion," in Jelen, *Sacred Markets, Sacred Canopies*, 115–32. See also Stark and Finke, *Acts of Faith*.

22. Pascal Ménoret, *L'Énigme saoudienne: les Saoudiens et le monde, 1744–2003* (Paris: La Découverte, 2003).

23. See Itzchak Weismann, *Taste of Modernity: Sufism, Salafiyya, and Arabism in Late Ottoman Damascus* (Leiden, The Netherlands: Brill, 2001).

24. See Azzam S. Tamimi, "The Origins of Arab Secularism," in *Islam and Secularism in the Middle East*, ed. John L. Esposito and Azzam S. Tamimi (New York: New York University Press, 2000), 13–28.

25. See Bernard Haykel, *Revival and Reform in Islam: The Legacy of Muhammad al-Shawkānī* (Cambridge, UK: Cambridge University Press, 2003).

26. See Roman Loimeier, "Patterns and Peculiarities of Islamic Reform in Africa," *Journal of Religion in Africa* 33 (2003): 237–62.

27. See Raymond William Baker, *Islam without Fear: Egypt and the New Islamists* (Cambridge, MA: Harvard University Press, 2003).

28. See Tord Olsson, Elisabeth Özdalga, and Catharina Raudvere, eds., *Alevi Identity: Cultural, Religious and Social Perspectives. Papers Read at a Conference Held at the Swedish Research Institute in Istanbul, November 25–27, 1996* (Richmond, UK: Curzon, 1998).

29. Thierry Zarcone, *La Turquie moderne et l'islam* (Paris: Flammarion, 2004). See also Feroz Ahmad, *Turkey: The Quest for Identity* (Oxford, UK: OneWorld, 2003).

30. See Andrew Mango, *Atatürk* (New York: Overlook Press, 2000). For the connection of this question with the symbolic significance of Atatürk's Mausoleum in Ankara, see Alev Çinar, *Modernity, Islam, and Secularism in Turkey: Bodies, Places, and Time* (Minneapolis: University of Minnesota Press, 2005).

31. See M. Hakan Yavuz, *Islamic Political Identity in Turkey* (New York: Oxford University Press, 2003).

32. See David Shankland, *The Alevis in Turkey: The Emergence of a Secular Islamic Tradition* (London: Routledge, 2003).

33. Yavuz, *Islamic Political Identity*, 285–86.

34. See Touraj Atabaki and Erik J. Zürcher, *Men of Order: Authoritarian Modernization under Atatürk and Reza Shah* (London: I. B. Tauris, 2003).

35. Yavuz, *Islamic Political Identity*, 57.

36. Ibid., 151.

37. See Ian Markham and Ibrahim Ozdemir, *Globalization, Ethics and Islam: The Case of Bediüzzaman Said Nursi* (Aldershot, UK: Ashgate, 2005).

38. For different assessments of Nursi, see Ibrahim M. Abu-Rabi', ed., *Islam at the Crossroads: On the Life and Thought of Bediüzzaman Said Nursi* (Albany: State University of New York Press, 2003).

39. See Andrew Davison, *Secularism and Revivalism in Turkey: A Hermeneutic Reconsideration* (New Haven: Yale University Press, 1998).

40. Andrew Davison, "Turkey, A 'Secular' State? The Challenge of Description," *South Atlantic Quarterly* 102 (2003): 333–50.

41. Yavuz, *Islamic Political Identity*, 141.

42. See Richard J. Chasdi, *Tapestry of Terror: A Portrait of Middle East Terrorism, 1994–1999* (Lanham, MD: Lexington Books, 2003). This is also true in the Turkish diaspora in Europe, which is particularly strong in Germany: see Beticül Ergan Argun, *Turkey in Germany: The Transnational Sphere of Deutschkei* (New York: Routledge, 2003); Katherine Pratt Ewing, "Living Islam in the Diaspora: Between Turkey and Germany," *South Atlantic Quarterly* 102 (2003): 405–31.

43. Yavuz, *Islamic Political Identity*, 116.

44. See Michael M. Gunter, *The Kurds and the Future of Turkey* (New York: St. Martin's Press, 1997).

45. Yavuz, *Islamic Political Identity*, 243.

46. In addition to Turkish fundamentalism, Iranian Shiite fundamentalist texts circulate in Turkish translations among the Shiite minority, although the most prominent Turkish Shiite leaders have distanced themselves from the Iranian model. The influence of Saudi Arabian Wahhabi traditionalism (often simply referred to as *fundamentalism*) on certain independent (and often illegal) religious schools is also occasionally mentioned by both Turkish and foreign media but should not be overestimated.

47. Zarcone, *La Turquie moderne*, 281. Mark Sedgwick ("Establishments and Sects in the Islamic World," in *New Religious Movements in the 21st Century: Legal, Political, and Social Challenges in Global Perspective*, ed. Phillip Charles Lucas and Thomas Robbins [New York: Routledge, 2004], 283–312) has developed a model to distinguish between "denominations," "sects," and "cults" within Islam, but the model is based on the Arab world, and it is unclear whether it can be easily applied to non-Arab religious markets such as that of Turkey.

48. Mark Sedgwick, *Against the Modern World: Traditionalism and the Secret Intellectual History of the Twentieth Century* (New York: Oxford University Press, 2004), 256.

49. See Azzam S. Tamimi, *Rachid Gannouchi: A Democrat within Islamism* (New York: Oxford University Press, 2001).

50. See Ahmet İnsel, "The AKP and Normalizing Democracy in Turkey," *South Atlantic Quarterly* 102, nos. 2–3 (Spring/Summer 2003): 293–308.

51. Zarcone, *La Turquie moderne*, 207.

52. Ibid., 208.

53. See Yavuz, *Islamic Political Identity*, 144–45.

54. Ibid., 284.

55. See M. Hakan Yavuz and John L. Esposito, eds., *Turkish Islam and the Secular State: The Gülen Movement* (Syracuse, NY: Syracuse University Press, 2003).

56. John O. Voll, "Fethullah Gülen: Transcending Modernity in the New Islamic Discourse," in Yavuz and Esposito, *Turkish Islam*, 238–47 (245).

57. In general, see Peter L. Berger, "Reflections on the Sociology of Religion Today," *Sociology of Religion* 62 (2001): 443–54. For a neo-Weberian approach to the same process within Opus Dei, which has often been criticized by Catholic sociologists, however, some of them associated with the Opus Dei itself, see Joan Estruch, *Saints and Schemers: Opus Dei and Its Paradoxes* (New York: Oxford University Press, 1995).

58. See Jean-François Mayer, "The Gülen Movement: A Modern Expression of Turkish Islam—Interview with Hakan Yavuz," *Religioscope*, July 21, 2004, online at http://religion.info/english/interviews/article_74.shtml.

59. Zarcone, *La Turquie moderne*, 279,

60. See Thierry Zarcone, *Secret et sociétés secrètes en Islam: Turquie, Iran et Asie centrale XIX–XXème siècles. Franc-Maçonnerie, Carboneria et Confréries soufies* (Milan: Arché, 2002).

61. Zarcone, *La Turquie moderne*, 280.

62. See Krisztina Kehl-Bodrogi, Barbara Kellner-Heinkele, and Anke Otter-Beaujean, eds., *Syncretistic Religious Communities in the Near East: Collected Papers of the International Symposium "Alevism in Turkey and Comparable Syncretistic Religious Communities in the Near East in the Past and Present." Berlin, 14–17 April 1995* (Leiden, The Netherlands: Brill, 1997); Olsson, Özdalga, and Raudvere, *Alevi Identity*; Shankland, *The Alevis in Turkey*; Paul J. White and Joost Jongerden, *Turkey's Alevi Enigma: A Comprehensive Overview* (Leiden, The Netherlands: Brill, 2003); Elise Massicard, *L'autre Turquie: Le mouvement aléviste et ses territories* (Paris: Presses Universitaires de France, 2005).

63. See Jenny B. White, *Islamist Mobilization in Turkey: A Study in Vernacular Politics* (Seattle: University of Washington Press, 2002). For different perspectives, see Ayse Saktanber, *Living Islam: Women, Religion and the Politicization of Culture in Turkey* (London: I. B. Tauris, 2002); Çinar, *Modernity, Islam, and Secularism in Turkey*.

64. Ali Çarkoğlu and Binnaz Toprak, *Türkiye'de Din, Toplum ve Siyaset* (Istanbul: Türkiye Ekonomik ve Sosyal Etüdler Vakfı [TESEV], 2000), table 6.1.2.

65. Ronald Inglehart, Miguel Basáñez, Jaime Díez-Medrano, Loek Halman, and Ruud Luijkz, eds., *Human Beliefs and Values: A Cross-Cultural Sourcebook Based on the 1999–2002 Values Surveys* (México: Siglo XXI Editores, 2004), tables F028, F064, F065.

CHAPTER 2

The Meaning of Conservative Democratic Political Identity

■ *Yalçın Akdoğan*

The Justice and Development Party (JDP; Adalet ve Kalkınma Partisi; AK Party) views and projects itself as a conservative democratic party. It was founded under the leadership of the current prime minister, Recep Tayyip Erdoğan, on August 14, 2001, and is the thirty-ninth political party established in the history of modern Turkey. In its first general election on November 3, 2002, it captured 365 out of a total of 550 seats in parliament, making it the most powerful political party in Turkey, closely mirroring the spectacular electoral success of the Democrat Party in the early 1950s.

This chapter analyzes the conservative democratic political identity of the JDP and its role in the formation of new discourses and perspectives in Turkish politics. Furthermore, this study is an attempt to evaluate the place and importance of such a political identity and discourse in Turkish politics. As such, it will analyze the many debates arising from this novel political phenomenon in Turkish politics, as well as the important issues raised in such debates. The differences between the political identity of the JDP and the political Islamism of the National Outlook Movement (Milli Görüş), the movement from which the JDP is considered to have developed, will also be examined. The JDP's novel political identity not only affects the present political climate in Turkey, but also has the ability to influence and change Turkish political culture and institutions for years to come. These potential future effects will also be considered.

The Basic Parameters of Conservative Democratic Political Identity

The twentieth century is known as the century of ideologies, with liberalism, fascism, communism, and socialism all gaining currency and power at different times throughout the century.[1] Some thinkers regard conservatism as an important ideology that can be compared to liberalism and socialism, although its basic philosophy and constituent parameters remain subject to an ongoing debate.

According to the conservative democrats, the field of politics should be firmly grounded in the culture of reconciliation. It is possible to solve social differences and disagreements in the political arena on the basis of reconciliation. A variety of social and cultural groups should participate in politics in order to add diversity to public debate in the forum of tolerance that is generated by democratic pluralism. Participatory democracy is improved by including these diverse groups and voices in the political process.

Conservative democracy favors a limited and defined form of political power. It does not accept authoritarian or totalitarian practices that would lead to a repressive state. The greatest enemies of civil and democratic politics are authoritarian and totalitarian tendencies that, if not curtailed, lead to arbitrariness in application of laws, a downplaying of genuine representation and participation, and disregard for individual and collective freedoms.

Conservative democracy considers political legitimacy to be based on popular sovereignty and the rule of law, which, in turn, is based on constitutionality and universally accepted norms. These elements are the main bases of political power, and political leaders achieve legitimacy by accepting the will of the nation. Political legitimacy is thus based on the common acceptance of a national identity that expresses itself in commonly held norms regarding action, rules, and collective worth.

By necessity, political power and institutions must remain within a designated legal framework, thereby ensuring rule of law. The state should be functioning, small but dynamic, and effective, and excessiveness and waste in government should be prevented. The state should never insist on specific preferences for its citizens, or retreat to dogmatic and ideological stances. Instead, the state must be defined, shaped, and controlled by its citizens. Democracy becomes acceptable if it is able to mix a wide variety of social and cultural differences and demands in the political arena. A truly democratic political arena is one in which all of society's problems are referred and discussed, all social demands are given a voice, and social programs can be tested and modified. In the case of Turkey, the heterogeneity of its society will work to enrich a pluralist democracy.

Politics should be established on that basis of reconciliation, integration, and tolerance instead of conflict, the formation of cliques, and polarization. Presently, a radical rejection of the existing political structure through the establishment of a totally new order is not viewed as viable or feasible. In order to enable gradual change vis-à-vis the overall structure, it is necessary to maintain some of the values and features of the existing structure.

There must be an established balance between idealism and realism. It is natural that some people possess utopian visions, but conservative democracy does not implement these utopian ideals by forceful means and does not insist on the truth of these ideals over the truth of others. It insists on balance and on gradual, evolutionary change. Thus, conservative democracy rejects radicalism and societal engineering. The use of totalitarian means and forcible methods to change society is deemed unacceptable because of the negative socioeconomic, cultural, and political effects such methods have historically produced. Instead, conservative democracy supports a gradual and progressive transformation of its functions in order to bring about significant, even revolutionary change for the betterment of society. Such gradual improvements, by genuinely reflecting what has been acquired historically by a society and what gains can naturally evolve in the future, can produce societal transformations that are both fundamental and permanent. Changes that have not materialized gradually are not considered viable or permanent.

THE IDENTITY OF CONSERVATIVE DEMOCRATS

There is a belief in Turkish political circles that the JDP developed solely as a result of feelings of antipathy among the general public toward the ruling Kemalist elite. Before the JDP's rise to power, the political situation in Turkey was dominated by weak coalition governments and replete with repeated economic crises, corruption, poor management, and social crises precipitated by significant economic downturns, with the result that the country's international prestige was being eroded. This political situation had the effect of galvanizing diverse social classes, whose expectations for the future were being dashed, and in whose eyes Turkish political institutions were losing credibility. Negative public opinion and widespread dissatisfaction culminated in the "soft" coup of February 28, 1997.[2]

In this turbulent atmosphere decent politics and honest, hardworking politicians who sought to represent the Turkish people seemed nonexistent. It is precisely for this reason that the JDP, untested but also untainted, emerged as the only party possessing the momentum to fulfill the expectations of a discouraged electorate. The political success of the JDP was thus not based on its ability to articulate and project an identity that resonated with a large portion of the population, but rather on the electorate's dissatisfaction with the general state of politics in Turkey. This dissatisfaction was so deep and widespread that it generated millions of votes in support of this new, alternative party.

Despite the fact that its political success has been based more on public dissatisfaction with the status quo than on its own political views, the JDP has worked to carve out a separate political identity for itself. This identity is conservative democracy, announced by Tayyip Erdoğan during the founding process of the JDP. The goal of introducing this concept was to carve a separate political space for the JDP, as well as to introduce a new path of politics in Turkey.

NORMALIZATION OF THE POLITICAL LANDSCAPE

The ineffectiveness of Turkish politics and politicians in general, particularly after the February 28 "soft" coup, provided the JDP with an excellent platform from which to gain power. As has been already pointed out, this platform has been one of efficiency in providing services rather than a specific identity. The JDP's developing sense of identity is thus predicated on the normalization of the current Turkish political system. Turkish political life has been influenced and buffeted by tensions arising from several sources, including conflicts between religion and politics, tradition versus modernity, religion and the state, and the relationship of the state, society, and the individual. These acute tensions have stunted political growth in the country, and have opened a Pandora's box of questions concerning the very nature of Turkish politics and identity. The JDP has been actively working to reform the system by solving some of these problems without upsetting the status quo entirely. This reform has been accomplished, in part, by developing a modernity that accepts the traditional, a globalism that accepts the local, and a stress on smooth, rather than radical, change.

THE ATTEMPT TO HINDER UNCONTROLLED REACTION
IN FAVOR OF CONTROLLED ALTERATION

The success of the JDP in the November 2002 elections should not be read as the success of political Islam. Although the leadership of the JDP is composed largely of ex-Islamists, the people who voted to elect the JDP for the most part did not do so on the basis of its "Islamic" identity. Instead, they voted for the JDP on the basis of expectations given to them by the party's charismatic leader, Erdoğan. The JDP's electoral success in the 2002 and 2004 municipal elections thus did not rest on a rigid ideology, but rather on the party's emphasis on moderation, general continuity, and the fact that it has made "people and service" its central platform. As a result of this strategy, the individuals who voted for the JDP came from a very broad ethnic and socioeconomic background.

Before the birth of the JDP, Islamist political movements in Turkey generated negative public reactions. Erdoğan therefore wanted to create a new political party identity that fell within the parameters of Turkish politics. The JDP thus avoided espousing radical change, and it acted within the well-defined parameters of the Turkish political process. By doing so, the JDP has avoided antagonizing those sectors of society and political actors who most feared their electoral success. This particular stance will most likely affect the JDP's political future positively. The JDP's political success may have effects that go well beyond its own political future, however. The party's platform represents an opportunity to significantly change the face of Turkish political institutions through its approach of balanced and moderate policies that have popular support.

CREATING AN INDEPENDENT CONSERVATIVE PARTY

Conservatism has always been a component of Turkish politics and has manifested itself in many party platforms. Conservatism can be seen in the policies and platforms of certain center-right parties, from the Democrat Party of Adnan Menderes to the Justice Party of Demirel, and most recently in the Motherland Party of Turgut Özal. It has also been espoused by parties on the left. However, by making conservatism the engine of change, the JDP has broken new ground in the history of Turkish politics. Furthermore, before the JDP, conservatism had not manifested itself in parties that stressed tradition, religion, social values, and the spiritual.

The JDP portrays itself as the meeting point of different value systems, political styles, and individuals from across the political and socioeconomic spectrum. The JDP does not espouse "identity politics," and argues that such politics have been a hindrance and a cause of crises in Turkish politics, leading to an "us versus them" mentality that has polarized Turkish society. The JDP instead emphasizes a political style that rejects making one's religious beliefs, sect, or ethnicity the center of the party's platform. The JDP is attempting to play the role of a mass party concerned with the problems that face society in general. This type of politics further distances the JDP from other parties and movements such as the Islamist National Outlook Movement of Necmettin Erbakan and the only-Kurdish HADEP, whose emphasis on identity has led to radicalization and marginalization at the expense of perspectives that emphasized democratization and intrinsic freedoms. In his speech at the party's establishment, Erdoğan explicitly noted that "[o]ur party clearly refuses to be a party that imposes an ideology on the nation and will not denigrate religious values by exploiting them in the politics." By distancing itself from its Islamist roots and the confines of this ideology, factors that would have led to marginalization, the JDP achieved massive electoral success by creating for itself a conservative political identity. In addition, the JDP has structured itself in such a way that it is able to protect both religious sensibilities and its conservative roots, while at the same time becoming an inclusive, mass party with popular support.

DEBATE SURROUNDING THE CONCEPT OF "CONSERVATIVE DEMOCRACY"

The JDP's self-declared identity of conservative democracy has been the subject of debate and scholarly exchange, and a number of questions have been raised surrounding the concept. Conservatism as a concept has aroused much debate because it has been molded by a diverse set of events not only in Turkey, but also in the world. Because conservatism emerged in diverse cultural forums throughout the world, its articulation and implementation have been different in different contexts, thus leading to discussion of its "real" nature. For example, French conservatism defended the monarchic order against the forces of the Revolution and Enlightenment, and perhaps because this stance is difficult to comprehend in a modern political approach, this school is remembered for its fanaticism. Furthermore, the recent interventionist approach of neoconservatism has cast a long shadow on the term *conservatism* throughout the world. Western conservatism is generally considered to be a form of extreme social atavism, full of intolerance, xenophobia, and opposition to diversity.

In Turkey, conservatism is generally posited as a "political attitude" that insists on gradual change and the perpetuation of moral and family values. There is now a rich and ongoing debate in Turkey over the concept of conservative democracy itself. This interest in and discussion of the concept is taking place because of the JDP's identification with it.[3] Some journalists have compared and contrasted this concept with those of Islamic democracy, moderate Islam, and liberal democracy. The JDP is not trying to regenerate and duplicate problematic past applications of conservatism; rather it seeks to reshape the concept of conservatism within the sociocultural structure of Turkey through development of a more reasonable approach to politics, while at the same time absorbing lessons from past failures.

If the JDP is able to regenerate and localize its own brand of conservatism by learning from the negative lessons of the past, this will not only be a victory for the JDP, but also for Turkish political culture in general. The JDP faces severe problems from such a momentous gamble, but also distinct advantages and opportunities. This process is aided by the fact that even though historically Western conceptualizations of conservatism have been largely negative, conservatism today is largely viewed as acceptable and reasonable. If the JDP were to define itself along these lines, it would provide both the party and Turkey with distinct advantages. Conservatism as the JDP envisions it would play a positive role precisely because of its emphasis on "conservative" and gradual, rather than revolutionary and destructive, change.

INTELLECTUAL AND POLITICAL DEBATES

"Conservative democracy" is subject to debate precisely because it is deemed "unscientific" and has remained largely outside the purview of the political science literature. "Conservative democracy" is often critiqued as lacking both conceptual and political legitimacy." For example, Ali Bayramoğlu, a columnist of the daily *Yeni Şafak*, has argued that it is antithetical to put "conservatism" and "democracy" together to create a new political identity.[4] He also claims that there is no literature on the concept of "conservative democracy" and that this is a mistaken political identity.

Because of the novelty of this concept, however, it remains to be seen whether established schools of political thought will further the debate and conceptualization of the diverse bundle of abstract ideas contained within it. Atilla Yayla, a professor of political science at Gazi University in Ankara, disagrees with Bayramoğlu and argues that "[i]f conservative democracy becomes an accepted term in political science this will only occur in the future, maybe in 5–10 years maybe 50 years."[5] Though the term liberal democracy designates a political government style it is sometimes used to define ideological etiquette (i.e., a liberal democrat). As for social democracy, though it is mistakenly assumed to be a type of democracy, it essentially indicates an ideological location. Furthermore, social democracy, with respect to its structure, is often at odds with representative liberal democracy more than liberalism or conservatism. According to Yayla, with time "conservative democracy," like social democracy, may become a term that designates a specific sociopolitical ideological line. Mümtaz'er Türköne, a political science professor at Gazi University, provides the best nuanced argument against those who criticize the concept of conservative democracy as not existing in the political science literature, stating that theory follows in the wake of political action and

> political thought always comes after action in order to explain events that have taken place. The leader who is in the firing line makes a decision and then puts it into practice; the masses react after the fact. Intellectuals attempt to create "novelties" or new ideas to either legitimize or object to certain world conceptualizations. No leader looks at the books before acting; at most the leader will defend his actions by using extant thoughts, hoping to sustain support for that action. Thus, the essential duty of intellectuals lies not in creating utopian scenarios for politicians, but in generating theories that will help the leader explain and gain support for his/her actions.[6]

The efforts expended by the JDP, at very least, should be viewed as a modest contribution to Turkish political life. The importance of the JDP's political development should not be denigrated or verified only on the basis of its success in generating scientific inquiry. Its practical value can be judged by analysis of its new conceptualizations and its potential to generate new developments in Turkish politics.

Is Conservative Democracy Possible?

In addition to the debates revolving around the lack of literature on conservative democracy and the incompatibility of democracy and conservatism, there is also a debate regarding the actual political identity of a "conservative democrat." Ömer Çaha notes that it is not possible to make a serious distinction between liberal democrats and conservative democrats.[7] Today, in Europe and in America conservative politics are defended not only by Christian Democrats but also actively supported by right-wing parties in general. The Conservative Party in England and the American Republican Party typify this trend. These parties conceptualize politics by synthesizing both conservative and liberal values. Furthermore, the assertion that a democrat cannot be conservative and vice versa seems artificial. Yayla argues that "[f]irst, the very application of modern democracy denies this assertion through practice. Can we say that English conservatives or American conservatives are not democrats? There are powerful conservative parties existent in all the strong democracies of the world. They alternately come to power and then go away. Democracy remains in place. The very application of democracy validates the existence of conservative democrats."[8] According to Etyen Mahçupyan, if conservatism is not compatible with democracy, then it must expend the necessary effort in order to make it so. "This party's search for identity supplies it with a viable political platform, recognized universally, thereby making it possible for the party to have a lasting impact on the Turkish political stage. Conservative democrats' emphasis on the process of 're-definition' automatically opens the door of criticism, but it also opens the door to political participation. After this point, whether conservative democrats are accepted intellectually is simply a question of sociological 'digestion.'"[9]

Democracy is not an ideology, but when we talk about social, liberal, and conservative democracy it must be noted that we are making an ideological classification. Political struggle occurs because these viewpoints all possess differing political sensibilities and strategies. For example, as the social democrat works to bring about his/her ideal utopia by introducing the state into the economic and social spheres, a conservative democrat realizes this same mission by relying on volunteer groups, civil organization, and the family. While the liberal democrat places the individual at the center, that is, within the state, conservative democrats are of the opinion that the state should only be granted observer status, thereby ensuring better protection of individual freedoms.

The claimed conservative democrat identity of the JDP does not raise many questions at a practical level, and as such the debate over the concept and meaning of "conservative democracy" is confined to the literature. Nevertheless, there are some who note that the JDP limits its potential and inclusiveness by using such a confining definition of its identity. There is concern that the JDP's much-heralded reformist mission may be incompatible with classical conservatism.

If the JDP is able to establish a synthesis of classical conservative culture with Islamic values, and to remain a viable party in a functioning democracy, this will be its most lasting legacy. As Mahçupyan emphasized, the rehabilitation and reform of the old order is tied directly to the materialization of the JDP's political transformation.[10] If the JDP simply plays politics in the democratic system, its democratic sensibilities will still be questioned by the Kemalist establishment. An effort to bring about a cultural transformation that reconciles Islam with democracy will validate the maturity of Turkey's democracy, and will remove the negative assertion that the JDP is Islamist first and democratic a distant second. Presently, the JDP does not intend to exploit democracy; rather it intends to adopt a truly democratic identity that is conducive to Turkey's political needs and culture. This approach can be looked at as a stage of adaptation to the rules and institutions inherent in a democratic system. Time will show how successful the JDP is at internalizing democratic culture as it attempts to redefine itself and regenerate the discourse of inclusive politics.

THE MUSLIM DEMOCRAT DEBATE

There are some who allege that it is impossible for the JDP to project a conservative identity and modes of action and at the same time ignore concepts of piety and Islam that have previously been taboo in Turkish politics.[11] Some journalists, including Etyen Mahçupyan, argue that the JDP uses the label "conservative democrat" simply because its members cannot term themselves "Muslim Democrats." Mahçupyan writes that "[i]t is not easy to use the term 'Muslim' in a country that has transformed authoritarian secularism into an official ideology. This is especially the case if one wants to avoid any unpleasantness ... On the other hand it can be said that conservatism in Turkey encapsulates elements of Islam."[12]

The JDP's leadership declares this assertion untrue and notes that, rather than being forced to adopt this terminology and identity, they actively support it because of the overarching inclusiveness afforded by a "conservative democratic" identity. The JDP leaders argue that it would not be politically expedient to define themselves as "Muslim democrats" in a country possessing different religions, sects, and ideologies, noting that this would only lead to marginalization and exclusion of both the party and portions of the populace. Because of acute sensitivity regarding secularism and Islamization of the state in Turkey, the JDP refuses to be a representative of moderate Islam at the expense of its conservative democratic identity. The JDP leadership understands the danger of playing Islamist politics and the tension that such an approach would necessarily cause in Turkey. For these reasons, the JDP prefers to present itself as a conservative democratic party whose members and supporters consider religious values important, not Islamist politics.

According to Mahçupyan, the conservative democratic identity of the JDP has done much to normalize Turkish politics.

> It is obvious that the JDP's transformation and its desire for reform have become more powerful as it has accepted universal strategies regarding the administration of the country that include social preferences which have not caused offence because Islam has not been specifically introduced to the cultural debate. It can be said that the further normalization of Turkish politics would be helped by the formation of a "Muslim Democrat" party in terms of defining the relation between the state and society.[13]

According to Ahmet Taner Kışlalı, Turkey may be considered a Muslim democracy because of the institutionalization of secularism and the acceptance in Turkey of an identity that is both Muslim and democratic.[14] However, even in a mostly Muslim society, political partiality vis-à-vis any religion invites polarization and separatism. Yıldız interprets the JDP's rejection of a "Muslim democrat" identity for a "conservative democratic" one as positive. "It is significant that the JDP has not adopted a Muslim democratic identity. This particular approach has strengthened the connection between religion and policy in a democracy without injuring the religion and its believers by negatively distorting the religion's fundamental philosophy."[15]

THE CENTER-PERIPHERY DEBATE

Şerif Mardin's description of the center versus the periphery debate can be useful in understanding Turkish politics.[16] In Turkish politics the term "center" generally refers to an official ideology and constitutive philosophy that is espoused by the Kemalist political elite. The concerns of the "center" are generally equated with those of the "state." In other words, playing politics in the center means staying within the specific parameters that have been designated by the center. The indivisible unity of the nation and secularism constitute these parameters in Turkey. Center parties thus consider themselves "masters of the house" (*ev sahibi*). These parties are perceived as reliable and acting to ensure the continuity of the system. "Center" parties include the Motherland Party (Anavatan Partisi), the True Path Party (Doğru Yol Partisi), and the Republican People's Party (Cumhuriyet Halk Partisi).

The "periphery" refers to sectors of the population who oppose the system as it is currently constituted. Peripheral parties in Turkey have been generally short-lived and perceived as being reactionary, excessive, marginal, and even fanatical. Such parties are thought to be incompatible with the overall system and status quo, and they therefore risk being marginalized and excluded rather quickly. However, peripheral parties do possess a certain dynamism stemming from their oppositional status. The parties emanating from the National Outlook Movement, including the JDP, are generally deemed to be "peripheral parties."

Viewing the JDP as a "peripheral" party has many important political implications. Success in Turkish politics has historically been predicated on a party's implicit acceptance of "the irrevocable principles of the state" and the "indispensable values of the nation." Parties that have failed to accept these principles have been marginalized and kept out of the center. The JDP's stated opposition to ethnic, religious, and regional nationalism places them firmly within these accepted parameters. Nevertheless, in the JDP's view, it is more important to bring the demands of the periphery to the center than to be considered a "center" party. According to Ali Bulaç only "successful articulation and representation of societal demands will make the JDP a significant and successful force in Turkish politics."[17] However, there is a major difference between simply bringing social demands to the center and actually representing these demands. No party has remained in power simply by articulating societal demands in the center while failing to effectively represent these demands. The JDP is working to represent and translate the periphery's expectations and requests at the center by couching them in the language of the center. The failures of previous peripheral parties lay not so much in their exclusion from the center but rather in their inability to translate their constituents' demands into the language deemed suitable at the center.

Neither the center nor the periphery won the November 3rd elections. Corruption and scandal spelled the demise of traditional center parties long before the elections. The collapse of center parties in Turkish politics precipitated a crisis, but the fact remains that these parties had never been able to deal effectively with the demands of the periphery and, as such, other institutions and interests had already begun to involve themselves in politics, either as individual actors or as parties. However, traditional periphery politics based on ethnicity and religion had also collapsed. These peripheral parties also experienced heavy losses in the November 3rd elections, further marginalizing them. Peripheral parties such as the Democratic People's Party (DEHAP) failed to obtain more than a fraction of the Kurdish vote. The Felicity Party (Saadet partisi) failed to muster the Islamic vote and the Nationalist Action Party (Milliyetçi Hareket Partisi) and Great Unity Party (Büyük Birlik Partisi; BBP) failed to mobilize the nationalist vote. The lack of success of peripheral parties in Turkey has less to do with any inherent meaninglessness of peripheral politics and more to do with the radical and limited nature of the demands made by these particular parties.

The JDP won the election by reconciling the demands of the center with those of the periphery and vice versa. In effect, the JDP occupies a novel political space in Turkey. The center's loss of power and trust occurred simultaneously with the periphery's final acceptance of the political process in order to affect lasting change. Any future role that the JDP assumes in resolving the center/periphery problem successfully not only affects the party but the political future of Turkey. The JDP cannot afford to ignore the demands of the periphery, nor can it afford to antagonize the center. The JDP will only be considered a successful party if it can dispel the mistrust and antipathy felt by the center for the periphery and vice versa. Thus far the party appears to be succeeding. It can be said that the JDP is now a center party in terms of its political language and expression.[18] The JDP's broad and eclectic base of constituents has helped it to distance itself from what could have been a more rigid ideological identity, and as a mass party, it has a better chance than other peripheral parties of representing the demands of its constituents in the center. The JDP can be said to have successfully united the center and the periphery by employing an adept political language and adopting policies that take into account the values and expectations of the majority of Turkish society. It has successfully couched peripheral concerns in the language of the center.

THE PROBLEM OF ORIGINALITY

The political realities of Turkey dictate, in part, how the JDP has chosen to construct and portray itself as a party. The JDP has become a party of the center characterized by its lack of political enemies, moderation, and lack of originality. Consideration should be given to the methods by which the JDP has evolved into its present form, and the processes by which it has corrected its past mistakes.

The importance of identity and identity transformation in the social and cultural arena is the main source of hope and cause for worry in Turkey today. Islamists claim their cultural identity is an ideological identity. In the political arena, Islam as a way of life has unavoidably become synonymous with Islam as an ideological identity. The JDP's goal is to transform cultural values in such a way that religion as a political identity is acceptable, rather than to simply reduce religion to an ideology. Mahçupyan describes this effort as the building of a bridge between the cultural and political arenas. The search for this bridge is not antithetical to the stated mission of the JDP. Rather, because the JDP as a party is already a bridge between the center and the periphery, it may also be a bridge that connects Turkish Islam's past and future. Building this bridge is synonymous with the synthesis of the interests and demands of many diverse sectors of society. Türköne argues that

> The leaders of the JDP intend to fill any void experienced by society because of this alteration to political and cultural life with the modernity of the future, the local with the universal, logic and rationalism, and moderation as opposed to radicalism. This concept and the synthesis it projects is simply a search for political, social, and cultural reconciliation in Turkey. This is an invitation, a declaration of intention, but also a sign of JDP submission to the established political order. The search for legitimacy of the political order is also the search for legitimacy of the JDP.[19]

Acceptance of the legitimacy of the political order is a sine qua non for a party to gain legitimacy. A party that sees the political order as illegitimate cannot expect to be validated by that same system. The JDP necessarily must see the search for reconciliation in Turkish society as beginning with a basic acceptance of democracy and the norms of political behavior. To do otherwise would make reaching a consensus with the status quo regarding policies and political understanding impossible, and would handicap the ability of the JDP to seek change effectively. The Turkish political system, trapped between parties seeking legitimacy by blatant submission and those opposing any sort of compromise, has been in a state of constant crisis. For this reason, political parties that accept the political system but are able to maintain a semblance of autonomy can produce significant change.

THE RELATIONSHIP BETWEEN THE IDENTITY OF THE JDP AND THE POLITICAL ISLAM OF THE NATIONAL OUTLOOK MOVEMENT

In order to understand the JDP, its development, and its political identity, concepts such as Islamism and political Islam must be discussed. It is impossible to properly portray the Justice and Development Party's political identity or to answer critics' questions regarding its ties with tradition and religion without first evaluating its previous relationship with Erbakan's National Outlook Movement. The JDP has distanced itself from Erbakan and his policies, and this move represents a break from other parties that developed under the auspices of the National Outlook Movement. The JDP is different from the National Outlook Movement in most respects, including its organization, its political identity, its style, and its campaign slogans. According to Sedat Ergin, the JDP chose a different path to power as a result of the February 28th "soft" coup, and, this new path represents an essential break in the evolution of Turkish political Islam.[20]

Some writers have alleged that it is impossible for the JDP to cut its ties with the Islamism of the National Outlook Movement simply because of its history. These arguments focus only on the past histories of the JDP's political leaders, rather than on their current attitudes and actions. Current JDP members who began their political careers in Erbakan's National Outlook Movement have exhibited changes in their political style through their participation in the JDP government. Of course this process of evolution takes time and will likely become more definite as the party continues to govern. Through their political dialogue and projects the Justice and Development Party's leaders are attempting to demonstrate that they walk on a different political path than that of their predecessors. In the speeches given at the party's General Congress, JDP leader Erdoğan articulated the party's agenda, which demonstrated the party elite's commitment to inclusive politics based on conservative rather than religious criteria. According to Ali Yaşar Sarıbay, "If the party founders' cultural-ideological background is taken into account and its history considered by itself, then the most suitable definition of the JDP's political identity would be that of an 'Islamic Party.' However, this is an insufficient definition because if one compares the JDP's political ideology and what political strategies it employs with that of Erbakan's National Outlook Movement parties, it becomes clear that the JDP has distanced itself significantly from an 'Islamic values' platform."[21]

Analyses of similarities and differences between the JDP's style and that of the National Outlook Movement generally focus only on members of the JDP who actually began practicing politics under Erbakan's tutelage, including Recep Tayyip Erdoğan. However, the JDP also differs from the National Outlook Movement in that it is composed of members from diverse political backgrounds and persuasions. It thus has a much broader political base than its predecessor. The JDP's current emphasis on diversity and open-mindedness is reflected in the makeup of its party elite. The administration and government of the present-day JDP includes members who have come from the True Path Party, the Nationalist Action Party, and the Motherland Party. It could be said that as a conservative party the JDP, while not ignoring the importance of religious values in politics, has been able to place these religious values within its wider platform of social justice and the importance of the social structure. If the party's first year in government is studied, it becomes apparent that the JDP chose not to continue its previously active relationship with Islamism. In Ergin's opinion, the JDP has not renewed or reiterated a platform that conforms to the one drawn by the National Outlook Movement and has avoided repeating the significant mistakes made during the so-called Refahyol period. Indeed, precisely because the policy platform of the JDP differs significantly from that of the National Outlook Movement, it is incorrect to simply portray the JDP as a reflection of the Refahyol period, characterized by conflicts and crisis. John O'Sullivian points out that the JDP's actions conform to the basic paradigm and rules of the Turkish Republic. "The JDP works for moderate reform that will accept the spectrum of Muslim beliefs and expression in public life. This shows the JDP to be a conservative party and, as such, poses no threat to Turkey's secular system. Furthermore, the JDP has furthered the Kemalist goal of becoming 'European' by taking the monumental step of powerfully endorsing Turkey's membership application to the European Union, as well as passing important reform packages required by the European Union as a prerequisite for full membership."[22]

The JDP's support of development and democratization can be viewed simply as a means of gaining full European membership for Turkey or as an attempt to make the JDP's policies appear compatible with the basic paradigm of the Turkish Republic. However, the JDP argues that it did not pass these reforms simply to gain a better relationship with the state. The JDP leadership asserts that the party passed these reforms on the basis of its belief in the necessity of freedom, justice, and democracy in Turkey.

NOTES

1. Yalçın Akdoğan, *AK Parti ve Muhafazakar Demokrasi* (Istanbul: Alfa Yayınları, 2004), 16.

2. M. Hakan Yavuz, *Islamic Political Identity in Turkey* (New York: Oxford University Press, 2003), 239–74.

3. Eyup Can, "AK Parti Neyi Muhafaza Ediyor?" *Zaman*, August 27, 2003.

4. Ali Bayramoğlu, "Hem Muhafazakar, Hem Demokrat Olunur mu?" *Yeni Şafak*, January 13, 2004.

5. Atilla Yayla, "Muhafazakar Demokrasi ve Muhafazakar Demokratlar," http://www.liberal-dt.org.tr/guncel/Yayla/ay_muhafazakar%20demokrasi.htm, February 5, 2004.

6. Mümtaz'er Türköne, "Devrimci Muhafazakarlık," *Zaman*, January 15, 2004.

7. Ömer Çaha, "Muhafazakar Demokrasi, Liberal Demokrasi'nin Kardeşidir," *Zaman*, August 31, 2003.

8. Yayla, "Muhafazakar."

9. Etyen Mahçupyan, "Muhafazakar Özeleştiri," *Zaman*, August 22, 2003 [??].

10. Ibid.

11. Yalçın Akdoğan, *Siyasal Islam: Refah Partisi'nin Anatomisi* (Istanbul: Sehir Yayınları, 2000).

12. Etyen Mahçupyan, "Demokratik Muhafazakarlık ve Demokratlık," *Zaman*, August 24, 2003.

13. Etyen Mahçupyan, "Muhafazakarlık Bir Tür Merkez Mi?" *Zaman*, August 25, 2003.

14. Ahmet Taner Kışlalı, *Cumhuriyet*, December 23, 1997.

15. Ahmet Yıldız, "Muhafazakarlığın Yerlileştirilmesi ya da AKP'nin 'Yeni Muhafazakar Demokratlığı,'" *Karizma* 7 (January–March 2004): 54.

16. Şerif Mardin, "Center Periphery Relation: A Key to Turkish Politics?" *Daedalus*, Winter 1972.

17. Ali Bulaç, "Muhafazakarlığı Referansları," *Zaman*, August 23, 2003; Bulaç, "Ak Parti'nin Handikapları: Din'e Karşı Tutum," *Zaman*, April 12, 2004.

18. M. Hakan Yavuz, "Türk Muhafazakarlığı: Modern ve Müslüman," *Zaman*, January 10, 2004.

19. Mümtaz'er Türköne, "Devrimci Muhafazakarlık," *Zaman*, January 15, 2004.

20. Sedat Ergin, "AKP'nin Ikinci Yıldönümünde," *Hürriyet*, August 19, 2003.

21. Ali Yaşar Sarıbay, "AKP'nin Politik Kimliği ve Gidişatı," *Zaman*, October 11, 2003.

22. John O'Sullivan, "Türkiye Demokrasi Için Iyi Bir Model," *Zaman*, November 13, 2003.

CHAPTER 3

Christian Democracy and the JDP

Parallels and Contrasts

■ *William Hale*

Ever since its foundation in 2001, the leaders of the Justice and Development Party (JDP) have stoutly maintained that their party is not based on religion, and is strictly a "conservative democratic party." In an interview given shortly after the JDP government came into office in November 2002, Recep Tayyip Erdoğan, the party chairman, admitted that "[s]ome people may think differently. They may look towards such bodies as the Christian Democratic parties in Europe. That is their view and their reality. We do not share it."[1] Shortly before the establishment of the JDP he declared that Islam would not even be a "point of reference" (*referans*) for the party, although he had used this phrase earlier to explain his political beliefs.[2] In January 2004 he elaborated this by saying that his party supported a "conservative democracy," which incorporated pluralism and tolerance. In his words:

> While attaching importance to religion as a social value, we do not think it right to conduct politics through religion [or] to attempt to transform government ideologically by using religion... Religion is a sacred and collective value... It should not be made a subject of political partisanship causing divisiveness.[3]

Erdoğan's caution was probably motivated by the fact that if he had suggested his party was "Islamic," he could have rendered it liable to closure by the Constitutional Court, as in the cases of the Welfare and Virtue parties, and in accordance with the constitution and the Political Parties Law. His description of the party is not universally accepted. Among foreign observers, for instance, Graham E. Fuller refers to the JDP as "an overtly religious party... even though it has been prudent and careful in not advertising its religious roots."[4] More subtly, it is frequently suggested that the JDP could be considered as the Muslim equivalent of a Christian democrat party, on the grounds that it holds to liberal democratic values but is influenced and informed by Muslim beliefs. As the Turkish Islamist writer Ali Bulaç suggested soon after the JDP's victory in the general elections of November 2002, there was a gap between the proclamations of the party leadership and the attachments of its grassroots supporters. The latter had rejected an outrightly Islamist agenda, but still gave mass support to a "Muslim democrat" party, Bulaç argued.[5] The link between the JDP and Christian democracy has also been highlighted by the fact that the party has applied for attachment to the European People's Party, which links the main Christian democrat parties in the European Parliament. Paradoxically, the Christian democrats in Europe (notably in Germany) oppose Turkey's bid to join the European Union on "cultural" grounds, so the approach has so far been rebuffed, but the German Christian democrats have made efforts to build some bridges with the JDP.[6]

The position taken in this chapter is that even though the JDP leadership denies the identification, as it is quite entitled to do, there are sufficient similarities as well as contrasts between the JDP and the classic Christian democrat parties of Western Europe to make an exploration of them a worthwhile exercise. The first two sections outline the history and the identity, ideology, and policies of three such parties, in France, Germany, and Italy, and the nature of their support base. The following two sections turn the spotlight onto the JDP, assessing its ideology, policies, and social basis within this comparative framework.

EUROPEAN CHRISTIAN DEMOCRACY: A SUMMARY HISTORY

Although its origins could be traced back to the nineteenth century, Christian democracy in Western Europe was essentially a child of the period of catharsis and reconstruction that followed the Second World War. It rapidly assumed a crucial role in most countries outside Britain, Scandinavia, and the Iberian peninsula (the latter being under fascist rule until the 1970s). By 1948 Christian democrat parties had dominant or near-dominant positions in five European countries (Austria, Belgium, France, Italy, and the Netherlands),[7] to be followed shortly afterwards by the Federal Republic of Germany, established in 1949. Later, the principles of Christian democracy spread to Latin America and—after the end of communism in Eastern Europe—to Poland, Romania, Hungary, Slovakia, and Lithuania.[8] Describing and analyzing such a large number of parties, in diverse countries and periods, is obviously beyond the scope of this chapter. Instead, what follows concentrates on what can be described as three "classic" Christian democrat parties, in countries of roughly the same size as present-day Turkey—that is, the Popular Republican Movement (Mouvement républicain populaire, or MRP) in France, the Christian Democratic Union (CDU-CSU) in Germany, and the Christian Democracy party (Democrazia Cristiana, or DC) in Italy.

In the aftermath of the war, center-right and conservative political forces in all three countries faced an essentially similar challenge. The old conservative parties of prewar Europe had been fatally discredited by their role in allowing the fascists and Nazis to come to power, or, in the French case, cooperating with the Nazi occupiers. In most countries, communists had spearheaded the resistance to fascism and, in the French and Italian cases, there seemed to be a real danger of a communist takeover of the state (in Germany, the challenge was obviously different, since communism could be seen as an external rather than internal threat). Democratic socialists also appeared to be in a far stronger position than the discredited right or center-right. In the search for an effective alternative, Christianity, especially in its Roman Catholic version, played a crucial role. As Gabriel Almond remarked, "in the chaos of post-war Europe, the [Catholic] Church stood as the only ubiquitous non-communist, and non-Nazi institution."[9] This was facilitated by the fact that in 1944 the Vatican abandoned the distrust of democracy that had been the dominant attitude in Catholicism before the war, and legitimated democratic government as the "natural" political form that, according to Pope Pius XII, came closest to the church's thinking.[10] The Vatican's conversion was not entirely convincing, since it continued to support fascist and authoritarian regimes in Spain, Portugal, and parts of Latin America. However, it gave the green light to observant Catholics to play an active part in liberal-democratic political movements, where this was possible. While they reflected what could be called traditional values, Christian democrats in France, Germany, and Italy could present themselves as harbingers of a new democratic era.

Although the three parties considered here were born in similar circumstances, their subsequent trajectories diverged. In France, the MRP was founded in November 1944, under the chairmanship of Maurice Schumann. It participated in the provisional government headed by Charles de Gaulle in October 1945, and stayed on in government after the general resigned the following January. In the elections to the second Constituent Assembly in June 1946 it became the biggest party in France, with 28.2 percent of the votes. However, its relations with de

Gaulle proved to be a fatal handicap for the party. In 1946, it broke with the general when the latter opposed the proposed constitution of the Fourth Republic. Since a large proportion of the MRP's supporters had essentially been Gaullists as well as observant Catholics, much of its electoral base was lost when de Gaulle established a separate party, the Rally of the French People (Rassemblement du peuple français, or RPF) in 1947. When de Gaulle returned to power in 1958, the MRP presented itself as his loyal ally, but in 1962 it again parted ways with the general, and the party was almost wiped out in the subsequent elections. It staggered on until 1965, when it merged with like-minded politicians to form the Democratic Center (Centre démocrate). Hence, in spite of the important role played by French thinkers in the development of Christian democrat principles, it turned out to be the shortest lived and most marginal of the three parties.[11]

As the dominant party of the center-right in Germany for almost sixty years, the history of the CDU-CSU stands in sharp contrast to that of the MRP. The first national meeting of CDU leaders from the separate occupation zones of western Germany was held in December 1945. In February 1947 a "working association" was formed with the Christian Social Union (CSU), established as a separate party in Bavaria, which has lasted to this day.[12] While the CDU and CSU are formally separate organisations, they operate as a single party at the national level, forming a single group in the Bundestag and campaigning together in national elections. Under the leadership of Konrad Adenauer (until 1963) and Ludwig Erhard, CDU-CSU held continuous power between 1949 and 1966 in coalition with small centrist parties, overseeing Germany's dramatic economic revival during the 1950s and 1960s. After a short-lived "grand coalition" with the Social Democrat Party of Germany (SPD), the CDU-CSU moved to the opposition benches for the first time in 1969, returning to government under Helmut Kohl between 1982 and 1998. The CDU-CSU has been in opposition for the last six years, but has recovered its electoral support and currently shows signs that it might return to power in the next general elections, due in 2006.[13]

The history of Democrazia Cristiana falls somewhere between those of the MRP and the CDU-CSU, in that it dominated Italian government between 1945 and 1993, but eventually collapsed in the general meltdown of the Italian political system in the early 1990s.[14] DC's first leader, Alcide De Gasperi, became prime minister in June 1945. Thereafter, through support from other anticommunist parties, every Italian prime minister until 1981 was a member of DC. Even if it did not always control the premiership, DC continued to form part of every government until 1994. On the other hand, the party appeared to be in a steady state of decline after its high point in the 1950s. De Gasperi's death in 1954 removed its most effective leader, and by 1959 the party had fallen under the control of a cluster of factional oligarchs. More fatally, DC appeared to prove the adage that "permanent power corrupts permanently."[15] The vast web of corruption that engulfed Italian politics in the early 1990s was not confined to DC, since it first erupted in the Socialist Party in Milan. *Tangentopoli* ("Bribesville"), which became a nickname for Milan, was then applied to the whole of Italy. In 1993 Giulio Andreotti, seven times prime minister and regarded as the incarnation of the old Christian democrat regime, was indicted on charges of collusion with organized crime, though not convicted. In January 1994 DC split. Part regrouped as the "Christian Democrat Center." Currently the party has been revived as the "Union of Christian Democrats" but Italian Christian democracy clearly lacks the power it previously wielded.[16]

CHRISTIAN DEMOCRACY: IDENTITY, IDEOLOGY, AND SUPPORT STRUCTURES

A frequent comment about Christian democracy is that its ideology is very hard to define: in fact, the term "catch-all parties" is sometimes used.[17] The main feature that makes it distinctive is its open appeal for support from committed Christians, although in the case of the MRP this appeal was muted.[18] Both the MRP and the CDU claimed to speak for Protestant Christians as well as Catholics. In the case of the CDU this claim had some justification, as several leading members of the party (most notably Ludwig Erhard, the Federal Republic's second chancellor) were from the Protestant community. This intention was natural, given that in the former West Germany the two confessions were evenly balanced, at least nominally.[19] However, claims such as that of Anthony Trawick Bouscaren, made in 1949, that Christian democrats generally were "non-denominational" and "have avoided becoming associated with any one church," are hard to sustain.[20] In practice, support for Christian democracy in France and Italy came, almost exclusively, from Catholics, and in Germany very largely from the Catholic community.[21] Essentially, all three parties were not just Christian in their loyalties, but predominantly Catholic.

A huge debate concerns the position of Christian democracy in the contest between left and right—essentially, between capital and labor—

that dominated much of postwar European politics. In principle, a distinction is drawn between Christian democracy and classic procapitalist conservatism, by asserting that it seeks a "third way" between capitalism and state socialism, rejecting the "materialism" of both, which supposedly ignores man's moral nature. Instead of class conflict, Christian democrats advocated consultation between government, industry, and labor.[22] In the early postwar years, Christian Democrat governments in both France and Italy had partly socialist agendas, overseeing large-scale nationalizations and constructing alliances with Catholic (in effect, anticommunist) labor confederations.[23] In Germany, there was no equivalent of the Catholic labor movement,[24] but the CDU-CSU advanced the principle of a "social market economy," which would "restrain the excesses of private capitalism through the independent control of monopolies, free competitive production, and social justice for everyone."[25]

As time went on, however, the distinctiveness of Christian democracy in terms of its social and economic policies declined. Although Christian democrats in Germany and elsewhere remained relatively unaffected by the doctrines of the "new right" advanced in Britain and the United States during the 1980s,[26] it had by this stage become hard to say what distinguished them from moderate conservatives. In France, Catholic trades unionism was "essentially a middle-class movement with little appeal for industrial workers."[27] In Italy, DC became a machine for old-fashioned patronage politics rather than social justice. Similarly, in Germany the CDU-CSU drew in middle-class and rural voters regardless of their denominational affiliation.[28] As Emiel Lamberts concluded in 1995, "Christian Democracy is...gradually losing the characteristics that distinguish it from the conservative parties in Europe."[29] There is no clear evidence that this process has been reversed since then.

In one policy area, however, the Christian democrats followed a clear and unwavering line, although it had little to do with their Catholic sympathies. In the field of European integration, Adenauer, Schumann, and De Gasperi were all strong advocates of participation in NATO and the formation of what became the European Economic Community, now the European Union. All of them had suffered under totalitarian regimes and two devastating wars. Hence they had every reason for abandoning chauvinistic nationalism, embracing a new order that emphasised the rights and welfare of the individual before those of the nation state.[30] This commitment to greater European integration has continued as an important part of the philosophy of the CDU-CSU in Germany as well as the center-right in France and Italy.

Its policies on what could be called cultural or moral issues have also been a distinguishing feature of Christian democracy. The question of the role of religion in education has long been the subject of fierce dispute in many European countries, with Christian democrats predictably supporting the principle that religious instruction should be provided in state schools, and that the state should subsidize schools established by faith-based organizations (in most cases, the Catholic church).[31] In Italy the question of allowing divorce, which was opposed by the Catholic church, became a burning issue in 1970, when a new law permitted divorce in certain restricted circumstances. In 1974 DC backed a referendum campaign to repeal the law, but a majority of the voters decided otherwise. A law allowing abortion in limited circumstances was passed in Italy in 1978; this was opposed by Christian democrats, who supported a more restrictive law. However, their proposal was again defeated in another referendum in held in 1981.[32]

A characteristic claimed by Christian democrats was that their parties were "classless," reflecting their supposed opposition to classic parties of both the left and the right. It also derived from their primary appeal to observant Christians (mainly Catholics) rather than to people of any particular socioeconomic category. During its relatively brief life as an effective party, it appears that the MRP achieved this aim. Within its electorate, no social class was massively over- or underrepresented, and people of all classes were present more or less in proportion to their share of the French population.[33] In the case of DC, the position is hard to assess, since it is argued that class has never been a good indicator of voting behavior in postwar Italy. DC could justifiably claim that it was an interclass party, but this did not mean that its electorate was a mirror image of Italian society. Instead, it was disproportionately drawn from people living in rural areas and small towns (especially in the "White Belt" of northern Italy), from older voters, and from women—the last two categories being more likely to be religiously observant.[34] In Germany, the CDU-CSU has been more closely identified with farmers, the self-employed, and white-collar rather than blue-collar workers, although some industrial workers who are firm Catholics also support the party.[35]

Especially in their early days, Christian democrat parties could also be seen as part of a wider social movement, rather than as purely self-standing institutions. The role of Catholic labor organizations in the rise of the MRP and DC has already been referred to. Of the other nongovernmental organizations from which Christian democracy emerged, and with which it continued an alliance, Catholic Action was easily the most important. This has been described as a "lay apostolate" and was presumed to have purely spiritual and moral functions. In practice, with its millions of members in France and Italy, as in other countries, it acted as a meeting ground in which Catholics could develop and support political movements, and propagate policies.[36] Besides Catholic Action, both the MRP and DC drew support from Catholic youth organizations, covering workers, agriculturalists, and students, and (in the Italian case) independent cultivators. German Christian democracy appears to have a less widespread institutionalized social base, but the CDU-CSU also established a number of youth groups, women's groups, and local government organizations.[37]

While this network of organizations gave Christian democracy an important social base, in the long run it was inevitably weakened by the increasing secularization of society in all three countries. This probably strengthened the drift of the CDU-CSU toward conventional conservatism, and contributed powerfully to the extinction of the French and Italian Christian democrat parties. As the Jesuit father Bartolomeo Sorge wrote in 1976, "we are living through a change of culture and a change of civilisation."[38] As a crude yardstick, the decline in church attendance was startling. In 1956, 69 percent of adult Italians claimed to have been to mass in the previous week, but by 1972 this figure had fallen to 35.5 percent. Practicing Catholics in France were estimated to account for about 30 percent of the population up to 1956, but only about 10 percent by the 1980s. To take another indicator, Italian Catholic Action had 2.6 million members in 1966, but only half that number in 1970, and half again by 1978. In Germany, regular church attendance by Catholics fell from 61 percent in 1953 to 32 percent by 1987, with attendance by Protestants falling from 18 percent to only 4 percent between the same dates. As in other countries, the influence of organized religion steadily waned during the last decades of the twentieth century, so that by 2000 about 10 percent of the population of the former West Germany, and half that of the former East Germany, admitted to being nonreligious.[39] From this, Kees van Kersbergen has concluded that "Christian values are increasingly represented in secular terms."[40] Existing trends caused one to wonder whether, in the future politics of Western Europe, they will be seen as "Christian" values at all.

The Justice and Development Party: The Cultural, Historical, and Institutional Environment

Comparing the JDP and the European Christian democrat parties simply as institutions will give an incomplete comparative picture. In particular, the fact that Turkey is a Muslim country creates striking contrasts, since there are significant differences between traditional Islam and Christianity, both institutionally and in their attitudes toward the state. Moreover, the historical situation in which the JDP came to power in Turkey was fundamentally different from that of Europe in the immediate postwar years, the birth phase of Christian democracy.

On the first score, it seems fair to say that modern Christianity does not have a state project comparable to that of Islam in its more radical versions. This is not to suggest that Christianity gives an unqualified endorsement to democracy. For example, the Catholic church condemns the use of artificial birth-control methods, or liberal laws on abortion and divorce, even if these are legitimized by a democratically elected legislature. In this view, the idea of the sovereignty of the people is not just limited by the need to protect individual and group rights, or maintain international peace, since what is regarded as morally wrong by the church is still unacceptable even if it is the "will of the people." On the other hand, what could be called the political agenda of the church is mainly limited to debates over such topics as the role of religiously defined values in education or laws affecting sexual morality and sometimes social justice.

In contrast, radical Islamism has an explicit vision of the state, even if this is probably not supported by more than a minority of the world's Muslims. It is one that could be said to be exemplified in the cases of the Islamic Republic of Iran or the Kingdom of Saudi Arabia, and essentially consists of the proposal that the sovereignty of God takes precedence over the sovereignty of the people. Hence, all the laws of the state, in the criminal, civil, and commercial spheres, should be based on the word of God, as conveyed to the Prophet Muhammad and interpreted by those recognized as experts in Islamic law. Laws that infringe this principle can be constitutionally annulled, even if they are democratically enacted, and the state is entitled to discriminate between its citizens on the basis of religion and gender. This obliges democratic parties in Muslim societies to reject the articulated Islamist state project, and to restrict the role of religion in politics to those topics, such as education and morality, which are an accepted part of the religion-state dialogue in non-Muslim democracies. The JDP's claim to democratic credentials rests on adhering to this restriction, and in this respect it can argue that it has some affinity with Christian democrat parties.

The institutions of the two religions also differ in important respects. In particular, since the abolition of the caliphate in 1924, there has been no equivalent in Islam to the institution of the papacy in Catholic Christianity, claiming a transnational authority. Hence, Islamist political movements are relatively free to promote their own political, social, and cultural agendas without limitations or directives demanded by an external institution, and do not have to face criticisms similar to those faced by Christian democrats, that they are merely the long arm of the Vatican. There is no one in Islam to give a signal for the foundation of democratic parties, as the pope did in 1944. This gives politicians and political thinkers in Muslim societies a degree of flexibility and independence that is not always open to the leaders and theorists of Christian democracy, especially in Catholic or predominantly Catholic countries. It can be argued that the JDP has made good use of this flexibility.

The historical circumstances of the JDP's birth were also very different from those of Christian democracy. Political parties often define themselves as much in terms of what they oppose as what they support. In postwar Europe, Christian democrat parties projected themselves primarily as being anticommunist and antifascist. In 1944–49, France, Germany, and Italy all had new beginnings, as states as well as societies, with new constitutions. The war had swept away old structures as well as ideas. There was no such institutional reconstruction in Turkey at the time of the JDP's birth in 2001. Admittedly, most of the parties that had ruled Turkey during the 1990s and up to 2002 were enmeshed by a web of corruption and incompetence—a sort of *Tangentopoli alla turcha* (Bribesville Turkish style) that swept them from power in the elections of November 2002, so there were some parallels with the Italian experience of the early 1990s. However, unlike the Christian democrat parties of the 1940s, the incoming JDP government in the Turkey of 2002 had to deal with the constitutional and economic system that it inherited from its predecessors, and to work out its relationships with the existing powers and institutions in the state and the economy accordingly. While the Christian democrat parties could make an open appeal for support on the basis of Christian values, the need to stay within the secularist bounds imposed by the Turkish constitution, as well as the need to appeal to voters who would have reacted against such an appeal, meant that the JDP could not give an equal role to Islam in its public discourse.

Communism had never been more than a marginal force in Turkish politics, and was anyway fatally enfeebled after the end of the cold war, so the JDP did not have to concentrate on defeating it. Instead, it had to define its position between two contradictory forces: on the one hand, the more radical Islamist project, represented by the veteran Necmettin Erbakan's "National View" (*Milli Görüş*) tradition, to which the JDP leaders had themselves been previously attached, and on the other, the authoritarian version of secularism represented by parts of the state bureaucracy, the armed forces, and elements within the opposition Republican People's Party (RPP, Cumhuriyet Halk Partisi). To add to the list of differences, the steady contraction of religious observance that had seriously affected the Christian democrat parties by the late twentieth century does not appear to have been reproduced in Turkish Islam. A survey carried out for the Turkish Economic and Social Studies Foundation (TESEV) in 1998–99 reported that almost 63 percent of those surveyed said that they attended Muslim communal prayers every Friday, with another 19.0 percent claiming to attend nearly every week.[41] With the great majority of Turks being observant Muslims (or at least claiming to be so), it appears that the most politically important divide is not between the observant and the nonobservant, but between those who support more fundamentalist Islamic positions and those who do not. As an example, the TESEV survey reported that just over 21 percent of the respondents claimed to support the idea of a religious state dependent on the Shari'a, with around 10–14 percent expressing support for the implementation of Islamic laws on marriage, divorce, and inheritance that discriminate against women.[42] The conclusion is that although the big majority of Turks count themselves as observant Muslims, only a small minority of around 10–20 percent interpret this in ways that would conflict with the basic principles of a secular democracy. One can only speculate whether formal adherence to Islam in Turkey will decline in the future, as Christian observance has declined in Western Europe.

POLICIES AND SUPPORT BASES

Given these positions, how do the ideological principles and practical policies of the JDP compare with those of Christian democrat parties, and does its social support rest on different or similar elements? Answering these questions is not easy, partly because of the difficulties inherent in any cross-national comparisons, but more particularly because the JDP has so far had a relatively short history, and important information that would be needed for a complete comparison is lacking. Nevertheless, some tentative answers can be given, on the basis of the party's declared principles and its policies since it came into office, plus the limited conclusions that can be drawn from the election results of November 2002.

Ideologically, a striking parallel between the proposals of the JDP and those of the Christian democrats is that they both championed liberal democratic values and the rights of the individual rather than the strength of the state. For the JDP, the implementation of these principles was made easier by the fact that the European Union presented Turkey with a road map of liberal reforms and the improvement of human rights as a condition for the start of accession negotiations. Hence the JDP government continued an important program of constitutional and legal changes through a series of "Harmonization Packages," which have continued into the summer of 2004.[43]

In the field of economic and social policies, the most important difference between the JDP and Christian democracy appears to derive from the fact that the binary divide between left and right is of far lower salience in Turkey today than it was in the Europe of the 1940s and 1950s, so that the JDP does not have to concentrate on defining its position within it. It thus has no pressing need to articulate a "third way" between capitalism and socialism. More immediately, the economic crisis that rocked Turkey in 2000–2001, and the huge foreign debt that the JDP government inherited from its predecessors, virtually obliged it to adhere to the economic and financial remedies prescribed by the International Monetary Fund and other international financial institutions.[44] The "Copenhagen criteria," which it implemented in its bid for eventual membership of the European Union, required it to establish and maintain a functioning market economy.[45] In these circumstances, the JDP government had few practical options. There was almost no room for it to develop radical or original economic strategies, even if it had wanted to.

Realizing that it had to concentrate on what was practical, the JDP abandoned the ideas of the "Just Order" (*Adil Düzen*) formerly promoted by Necmettin Erbakan, which had attacked the "capitalist system based on interest" and had urged the promotion of small enterprises alongside a large state industrial sector in which interest would be abolished.[46] In its election manifesto of 2002, the party recognized that "the strength of private enterprise of our nation is the most important source of economic progress. The basic role of the state in the economy is to ensure the conditions for free competition in the market, and to remove the obstacles facing private enterprise." It supported privatization of the lumbering state industrial sector and the integration of Turkey into the global economy, while recognizing that globalization created new threats as well as opportunities for the developing economies. To secure greater social justice, it also sought to reduce the gross imbalances in income distribution as well as unemployment.[47] In its party program, it advocated the principle of a "social state" that would ensure for needy citizens a way of life "befitting human dignity."[48] However, its proposals appeared to fall well short of the more radical economic program advocated by, for instance, De Gasperi, in the early days of DC in Italy, and put far less emphasis on intervention by the state in the economy. Instead, they paralleled the relatively noninterventionist policies of the CDU-CSU in Germany, without articulating the idea of a "social market economy." They also reflected the huge changes in the global economic system over the previous half-century and the vastly increased degree of transnational integration that these entailed.

The most distinctive policy positions developed by the JDP, which distinguished it from its rivals in the electoral marketplace, were probably its policies in the fields of education and culture. In 1998 Tayyip Erdoğan had enunciated the idea that secularism could not be interpreted as hostility to religion: the state could be secular, but not individuals,[49] and the JDP has continued this interpretation of secularism.[50] In its 2002 election manifesto, the party interpreted its commitment to conservatism mainly in cultural terms, arguing that society renewed itself within the context of basic institutions such as "the family, school, property, religion, and morals," and that interference by the state in these institutions and values would lead to conflict and disorder.[51] In the field of education, the party promised that facilities of all kinds would be made available for instruction on religion "as a requirement of the principle of secularism." Apart from the regular classes on "religious culture and moral education" that are a part of the curriculum in all primary and secondary schools stipulated by article 24 of the constitution (introduced, paradoxically, by the former military regime in 1982), parents would be entitled to ask for additional instruction on religion. A further commitment by the party was that graduates of all high schools and equivalent institutions would be accorded equality in the university entrance examinations.[52] The significance of the last undertaking was that it would have allowed graduates of the special state high schools for Imams and preachers (*İmam Hatip Okulları*) to enter universities on equal terms with students from normal state or private schools. Originally, the special religious schools had been set up to train Muslim religious functionaries. However, over time their graduates have vastly outnumbered the actual need for Imams and preachers, and have been used as a means of entering nonreligious professions by families and students of conservative views.

The JDP government appeared to act on this commitment in May 2004, when Minister of Education Hüseyin Çelik tabled a new draft law on higher education that, among other things, would have allowed students from "professional" schools to compete for university entrance with those from normal high schools. Against fierce opposition from the RPP and the prosecularist establishment, including the General Staff, the JDP used its large majority in Parliament to push the bill through the house on May 13, 2004.[53] However, on May 28 President Ahmet Necdet Sezer exercised his right to return the bill to Parliament, and the government backed down. On June 1 Prime Minister Erdoğan announced that the proposal would be shelved, at least for the time being.[54] A later example of the same kind of conflict arose in August–September 2004, when the JDP conducted negotiations with the RPP designed to produce an agreed draft of changes to the Turkish Penal Code that were being required by the European Union. Most of the text was uncontroversial, since it dealt with human rights improvements that were accepted as necessary by both sides. However, the JDP also proposed that the "obstruction of freedom of religion" should be made a crime, that religious functionaries should be allowed to engage in politics in off-duty hours, and that women should be allowed to wear "Islamic" headscarves in state institutions. All these proposals reawakened suspicions that the JDP's claim that it had abandoned an Islamist agenda was false, and were strongly opposed by the RPP. As a result, after much debate, the ruling party agreed to drop them. The headscarf issue was a long-standing and contentious one: in November 2002 and April 2003 open rows had broken out between the JDP leaders and prosecularist institutions such as the presidency and the military, when it was feared that their wives might appear clad in headscarves at official functions.[55] Eventually it was agreed that offenders could be fined, but not imprisoned as had earlier been proposed.[56]

While these issues seemed to be resolved, at least for the time being, Tayyip Erdoğan and his minister of justice, Cemil Çicek, meanwhile put the cat among the pigeons by proposing that the new version of the Penal Code should also include a clause making adultery a criminal offense (as it is in traditional Islamic law).[57] After some tergiversations by its leader, Deniz Baykal, the RPP came out strongly against the proposal. In the opposite camp, Cemil Çicek claimed that there was public support for this measure, while Tayyip Erdoğan argued that "the family is a sacred institution for us," implying that the law was necessary to protect it. To critics who pointed out that adultery is not a criminal offense in any Western country, he claimed that Turkey did not have to apply "imperfect" Western morals.[58] This did not assuage his domestic critics among members of the legal profession, women's organizations, and the media, who urged that the proposed clause would be an illegitimate invasion of personal privacy by the state and emphasised that adultery is only an offense in ultraconservative Islamic countries like Saudi Arabia.[59] The most effective criticisms, however, came from Brussels, where the European commissioner with responsibility for enlargement, Günther Verheugen, strongly attacked the proposal. Accordingly, the proposed clause was dropped after Erdoğan visited Brussels for direct talks with the commissioner on September 23, 2004. Parliament duly passed the amendments to the Penal Code, without any of the controversial clauses, three days later.[60]

While not all the moral or cultural issues that have divided Christian democrat and secularist or modernist opinion in Western Europe have been reproduced in Turkey (for example, artificial birth control and divorce, which are accepted in the Turkish case), it is clear that the JDP's policies on religious education mirror those adopted by Christian democrat parties in Europe. The criminalization of adultery is not now on the agenda of European Christian democrat parties. However, the headscarf question has also become a bone of contention in several European states, even if it is not clear that Christian democrats in all countries have a distinct stand on this issue.[61] In Turkey, the evidence was that the JDP leadership was anxious to appease its more Islamist supporters on all these issues, but was eventually prepared to back down in the face of strong opposition both at home and abroad.

A final policy issue on which there is a clear correspondence between the JDP and Christian democracy is its rejection of state-centered nationalism and its commitment to international cooperation—most notably, the European Union (EU). Breaking with the anti-European, pro-Islamist views of Necmettin Erbakan, the party claims that it sees Turkish membership of the EU as a "natural result of our modernisation process," and attacks those who oppose this by adhering to ideological approaches emphasising "national sovereignty, national security, national interest [and] national and indigenous culture."[62] The party demonstrated its opposition to hard-line nationalism by its policy on the Cyprus question, giving full support for the Annan Plan for a settlement of the problem, even though this was in the event rejected by the Greek Cypriots.[63]

As a corollary of this, the party embraces the concept of multicultural-ism within Turkey. In a section on the "East and South-East" (which it admits may be referred to as the "Kurdish question"), the party program commits itself to maintaining the unitary structure of the Turkish repub-lic and keeping Turkish as the official language of the state and educa-tion. It admits, however, that the problems of the south-east are not just those of economic underdevelopment, and that policies "recognising cul-tural differences within the principle of a democratic state" are essen-tial. Accordingly, it advocates that provision be made for "cultural activ-ities, including publication and broadcasting, in languages other than Turkish."[64] This commitment (which was in any case required by the EU as one of the conditions for the start of accession negotiations) was even-tually put into practice by instituting very limited provision for Kurdish language education and broadcasting in the spring of 2004.[65] Broadcast-ing in Kurdish by private radio and television channels can be expected to follow. Not all these policies were mirrored in those of Christian democ-racy—ethnic differences within the indigenous population are not an issue, for instance, in the politics of Italy and Germany, nor were they in France during the career of the MRP. Nonetheless, they could be seen as very similar to the liberal internationalist approach embraced by Chris-tian democrat parties in the postwar period.

Like the Christian democrats, the JDP also relies on a social support base among a wide variety of nongovernmental organizations. In Turkey, there are serious legal limitations to this reliance since, under the Politi-cal Parties Law, parties are not allowed to engage in "political relations and cooperation" with societies, trades unions, foundations, cooperatives, or professional organizations "with the objective of carrying forward or strengthening their own policies."[66] Nonetheless, a number of nongov-ernmental organizations can be identified with the modernist-Islamist camp in Turkish politics, and apparently help to strengthen the JDP's social base. In the trades union field, the labor confederation Hak-İş may be seen as the Muslim equivalent of the Christian labor organizations of France and Italy, although it also has relations with other Islamist and center-right parties.[67] However, like Catholic union confederations in Europe, it only enjoys the support of a minority of industrial work-ers.[68] Among business groups, the Independent Industrialists and Busi-nessmen's Association (MÜSİAD) is also identified with the pro-Islamist camp, although its literature carefully avoids such identification. It repre-sents in particular smaller but rapidly growing firms in central and east-ern Anatolia, in contrast to the big business establishment in Istanbul and the other industrial cities of western Turkey, which are associated with the far larger Turkish Industrialists and Businessmen's Association (TÜSİAD).[69] A further significant part of the social support network that has underpinned Islamist political movements in Turkey, and that can be said to be part of the same political stream as the JDP, is made up of the large number of philanthropic foundations (*Vakıflar*) providing welfare services to the needy in the industrial suburbs of Istanbul and other cities. Their activities include traditional Islamic charity such as providing meals for the needy through public kitchens and distributing fuel and groceries to poor families, besides establishing or equipping clinics and hospitals, providing transport and dormitories for students, distributing furniture and used clothing to the poor, and providing help in finding a job or even a spouse.[70] These organizations give JDP politicians a base in the poorer sections of urban society that appears to have been lacking in Christian democracy in Western Europe.

Taking this investigation further by assessing the class or regional basis of JDP's electorate is currently extremely difficult because of the lack of survey data. It also appears that social class is in any case a poor indicator of voting behavior in Turkey, as in Italy. The limited evidence we have suggests that the party has a variegated and geographically dispersed electorate. Preliminary surveys of the 2002 election results indicate that the JDP was particularly well supported in central and eastern Anatolia, as well as in the Black Sea region, but that it also had important support in working-class districts of big cities in the west. From this, observers like Üzeyir Tekin have concluded that the JDP is a "classless party." Comparison with the Christian democrat parties of Europe is difficult, but such a picture would parallel suggestions for the support base of the MRP. It would also indicate that the JDP is a less middle-class party than, say, the CDU-CSU in Germany has traditionally been.[71] Clearly, more research on this topic is needed.

Some Preliminary Conclusions

Some of its supporters may seek to legitimize the JDP by claiming that it is the Muslim equivalent of a Christian democrat party, but the outline history of Christian democracy in the earlier part of this chapter suggests that it should not be taken as a model for Turkey. In France, the MRP had a relatively short life as an effective political movement, mainly because of the unique role of Charles de Gaulle in French postwar politics. In Italy, DC flourished for almost five decades, but then perished in the systemic collapse of the early 1990s. In Germany, the CDU-CSU continues to exist as a powerful center-right party, but the "Christian" part of its intellectual inheritance is nowadays diluted, or distorted into conventional conservatism. The JDP will clearly need to avoid these pitfalls. In particular, if it achieves long-term dominance in Turkish politics, as DC did in postwar Italy, it runs the risk of internal factional divisions and the corruptive influences of unchallenged long-run power.

At the same time, even if the leaders of the JDP reject the "Muslim democrat" label, there are intriguing similarities between their party and the Christian democrat parties of Western Europe in terms of policies, especially on moral, cultural, and educational issues; international attitudes; and support structures. The main differences appear to derive from those inherent in the Christian and Muslim religions, and in the historical circumstances of their birth and development. The most striking contrast is that while Christian democrat movements in Western Europe generally developed in a conservative, pro–status quo direction, the JDP, while culturally conservative, also projects itself as an antiestablishment force in Turkish politics, opposing the state-centered authoritarian secularists who have, it is argued, become Turkey's new conservatives.[72] Tayyip Erdoğan is taken as a fitting symbol of this resurgence—as a "man of the people" who moved up from a humble position in society, suffered imprisonment for his political principles, and then successfully challenged the old state establishment. He uses this biography as a parallel narrative of his political beliefs. As he wrote shortly before the elections of 2002,

> My story…is the story of this nation [in Turkish *millet*, implying also "the people"]. Either the people will win, they will get into power, or the monarchical rule of a minority which looks down upon the people from on high, which is a stranger to Anatolia, oppressive and obstinate, will carry on. The authority to decide rests with the people.[73]

Clearly, this radical élan had helped to sweep his party into power. What remains to be seen is whether, unlike its Christian democrat predecessors, it could survive the transition and remain an invigorating as well as dominant force in Turkish politics in the years ahead.

NOTES

1. Interview with Şeref Özgencil, *The New Europe* 1, no. 2 (December 2002): 11.

2. Ruşen Çakır and Fehmi Çalmuk, *Recep Tayyip Erdoğan: Bir Dönüşüm Öyküsü* (Istanbul: Metis Yayınları, 2001), 189. In December 1997 he had said, "As an individual

my point of reference is Islam—just as Christianity is for President Clinton" (quoted ibid., 144).

3. *Turkish Daily News*, Internet edition, www.turkishdailynews.com, January 31, 2004.

4. Graham E. Fuller, "Turkey's Strategic Model: Myths and Realities," *Washington Quarterly* 27, no. 3 (2004): 52.

5. Ali Bulaç, "'İslamcı Parti' ile 'Müslüman demokrat parti,'" *Zaman* newspaper, Internet edition, www.zaman.com.tr, November 6, 2002.

6. See the reports in the Internet editions of *Hürriyet*. www.hurriyetim.com.tr, September 26, 2003, and February 16, 2004; *Milliyet*, www.milliyet.com.tr, October 6, 2003; and *Radikal*, www.radikal.com.tr, April 21, 2004.

7. See Gabriel Almond, "The Christian Parties of Western Europe," *World Politics* 1 (1948): 31–32.

8. On the latter point, see Adrian Karatnycky, "Christian Democracy Resurgent: Raising the Banner of Faith in Eastern Europe," *Foreign Affairs* 77 (2001): 13–18.

9. Gabriel Almond, "The Political Ideas of Christian Democracy," *Journal of Politics* 10 (1948): 749.

10. Most notably, in the pope's Christmas radio address of 1944; see Paolo Pombeni, "The Ideology of Christian Democracy," *Journal of Political Ideologies* 5 (2000): 297.

11. Jean-Marie Mayeur, "La démocratie d'inspiration chrétienne en France," in *Christian Democracy in the European Union (1945/1995)*, ed. Emiel Lamberts (Leuven, Belgium: Leuven University Press, 1997), 80–85; Peter Van Kemseke, "The Societal Position of Christian Democracy in France," in Lamberts, *Christian Democracy*, 174, 181–83.

12. Geoffrey Pridham, *Christian Democracy in Western Germany: The CDU/CSU in Government and Opposition, 1945–1976* (London: Croom Helm, 1977), 36–44.

13. For a detailed account of the CDU-CSU between 1949 and 1976, see Pridham, *Christian Democracy in Western Germany*, chaps. 2–3.

14. For a fuller history of DC between 1945 and 1988, see Robert Leonardi and Douglas A. Wertman, *Italian Christian Democracy: The Politics of Dominance* (Basingstoke, UK: Macmillan, 1989), chap. 3.

15. Martin Clark, *Modern Italy, 1871–1995*, 2nd ed. (London: Longman, 1996), 334.

16. Ibid., 413–21.

17. See, for example, Kees van Kersbergen, "The Distinctiveness of Christian Democracy," in *Christian Democracy in Europe: A Comparative Perspective*, ed. David Hanley (London: Pinter, 1994), 31; however, van Kersbergen later disputes this description (ibid., 35, 37–40).

18. Thus, Jean-Marie Mayeur prefers to speak of the MRP as being attached to "democracy of a Christian inspiration" (Mayeur, "La démocratie d'inspiration chrétienne," 79). The MRP did not refer to Christianity or Catholicism in its title or articles of association, and never sought an organizational tie with the Catholic church since it feared a revival of anticlericalism. Nevertheless, it had a distinctly Catholic support base (Van Kemseke, "The Societal Position of Christian Democracy," 175, 178).

19. Pridham, *Christian Democracy in Western Germany*, 26–27, 38–39; David Broughton, "The CDU-CSU in Germany: Is There Any Alternative?" in Hanley, *Christian Democracy*, 106; Anton Rauscher, "Der Einfluss der Christlichen Demokratie

auf Gesselschaft und Kultur in der Bundesrepublik," in Lamberts, *Christian Democracy*, 377. The MRP also claimed to be nonconfessional and had some Protestant members (Mayeur, "La démocratie d'inspiration chrétienne," 80). However, the question was fairly insignificant in the French case, given that Protestants account for less than 2 percent of the population. It is even less significant in Italy.

20. Anthony Trawick Bouscaren, "The European Christian Democrats," *Western Political Quarterly* 2 (1949): 59, 61.

21. An opinion poll in 1952 found that 79 percent of the MRP electorate attended a [Catholic] church regularly. In Italy, even in the relatively secularized 1970s at least two-thirds of DC's supporters claimed to have attended church the previous Sunday. In France, all the nonattenders who voted Christian Democrat also identified themselves as Catholics (Van Kemseke, "The Societal Position of Christian Democracy," 175; Clark, *Modern Italy*, 329).

22. Van Kersbergen, "The Distinctiveness of Christian Democracy," 33: Bouscaren, "The European Christian Democrats," 60.

23. Leonardi and Wertman, *Italian Christian Democracy*, 28, 31–35; Murray Edelman, "Sources of Popular Support for the Italian Christian Democrat Party in the Postwar Decade," *Midwest Journal of Political Science* 2 (1958): 156–57; Breuno Béthouart, "L'apport socio-économique de la démocratie chrétienne en France," in Lamberts, *Christian Democracy*, 339–40; Willard Ross Yates, "Power, Principle, and the Doctrine of the Mouvement Républicain Populaire," *American Political Science Review* 52 (1958): 429; Samuel H. Barnes, "The Politics of French Christian Labour," *Journal of Politics* 21 (1959): 105–6, 119.

24. There are, however, some "Christian" labor unions outside the German Federation of Trades Unions (DGB) that, although officially neutral in party politics, have close ties with the SPD; Broughton, "The CDU-CSU in Germany," 106.

25. Pridham, *Christian Democracy in Western Germany*, 31–32.

26. Broughton, "The CDU-CSU in Germany," 112.

27. Barnes, "The Politics of French Christian Labour," 105.

28. Pridham, *Christian Democracy in Western Germany*, 334–35.

29. Emiel Lamberts, "General Conclusions: Christian Democracy in the European Union (1945–1995)," in Lamberts, *Christian Democracy*, 480.

30. R. E. M. Irving, "Italy's Christian Democrats and European Integration," *International Affairs* 52 (1976): 400, 405–6.

31. See Yves-Marie Hilaire, "L'influence de la démocratie chrétienne dans la sphère de la religion, la morale et la culture en France," in Lamberts, *Christian Democracy*, 432; and Anton Rauscher, "The Influence of Christian Democracy on Socio-Cultural Policy in Western Europe," in ibid., 42.

32. Clark, *Modern Italy*, 381–83.

33. Van Kemseke, "The Societal Position of Christian Democracy," 175.

34. Mark Donovan, "Democrazia Cristiana: Party of Government," in Hanley, *Christian Democracy*, 80; Clark, *Modern Italy*, 329.

35. Pridham, *Christian Democracy in Western Germany*, 335.

36. Almond, "Christian Parties," 51.

37. Van Kemseke, "The Societal Position of Christian Democracy," 176–78; Leonardi and Wertman, "The European Christian Democrats," 211–12, 216–21; Broughton, "The CDU-CSU in Germany," 107.

38. Quoted in Clark, *Modern Italy*, 370.

39. Ibid, 370–71; Hilaire, "L'influence de la démocratie chrétienne," 429; Leonardi and Wertman, "The European Christian Democrats," 212–13; Broughton, "The CDU-CSU in Germany," 109; Russel J. Dalton, "Politics in Germany," in *Comparative Politics Today: A World View*, 7th ed., ed. Gabriel A. Almond et al. (New York: Longman, 2000), 299.

40. Van Kersbergen, "The Distinctiveness of Christian Democracy," 43.

41. Ali Çarkoğlu and Binnaz Toprak, *Türkiye'de Din, Toplum ve Siyaset* (Istanbul: Türkiye Ekonomik ve Sosyal Etüdler Vakfı [TESEV], 2000), 42, 45.

42. Ibid., 16, 72–73.

43. See William Hale, "Human Rights, the EU and Turkish Accession," *Turkish Studies* 4 (2003): 107–26, reprinted in Ali Çarkoğlu and Barry Rubin, eds., *Turkey and the European Union: Domestic Politics, Economic Integration and International Dynamics* (London: Frank Cass, 2003), 107–26. For subsequent developments in 2003–4, see Economist Intelligence Unit, *Turkey: Country Report* (London: E.I.U., quarterly), April 2003, June 2003, September 2003, and June 2004.

44. See the special issue of *Turkish Studies*, "The Turkish Economy in Crisis," vol. 4., no. 2 (2003).

45. *Conclusions of the [EU] Presidency, Copenhagen, June 21–22, 1993*, copy kindly supplied by Foreign and Commonwealth Office, London.

46. See Ruşen Çakır, *Ne Şeriat, ne Demokrasi: Refah Partisi Anlamak* (Istanbul: Metis Yayınları, 1994), 131–39; and the manifesto issued by the Welfare Party (*Refah Partisi*) for the 1995 elections, *25 Aralık Sabahı Türkiye Yeniden Doğacak!* 13–15.

47. *Herşey Türkiye İçin: Ak Parti Seçim Beyannamesi* (2002), from JDP website, www.akparti.org.tr, 32, 35–36.

48. JDP Party Programme, *AK Parti, Aydınlığa Açik...Karanlığa Kapalı*, section 5.1, from JDP website, www.akparti.org.tr.

49. Çakır and Çalmuk, *Recep Tayyip Erdoğan: Bir Dönüşüm Öyküsü*, 115.

50. JDP Party Programme, section 2.1.

51. *Herşey Türkiye İçin*, 7.

52. JDP Party Programme, section 5.2.

53. Website of NTV television, Istanbul, www.ntvmsnbc.com, May 7, May 13, 2004.

54. Ibid., May 28, June 1, 2004.

55. Ibid., April 24, 2003; and *Briefing* (Ankara, weekly), November 25, 2002, 9, and December 2, 2002, 5–6.

56. *Turkish Daily News*, Internet edition, September 1, 2004.

57. Such a clause had been included in the Penal Code of 1926, but in 1996 and 1998 it had been struck down by the Constitutional Court on the grounds that, in its original wording, it had discriminated against women. The new clause proposed by the JDP would have overcome this objection, but this did not assuage its critics, who opposed the criminalization of adultery as a general principle.

58. *Hürriyet*, Internet edition, August 30, 2004; *The Guardian* (London, daily), September 6, 2004.

59. Ibid., and *Radikal*, Internet edition, September 1 and 2, 2004.

60. *Hürriyet*, Internet edition, September 23, 2004; NTV website, September 27, 2004.

61. For instance, France maintains the headscarf ban in schools, whereas in Britain and Germany the decision is left to individual institutions or local education authorities.

62. See *Herşey Türkiye İçin*, section 9. For a fuller discussion of the JDP's foreign policies, see Üzeyir Tekin, *AK Parti'nin Muhafazakâr Demokrat Kimliği* (Ankara: Orient Yayınları, 2004), 198–219.

63. For an earlier discussion of this, see Tekin, *AK Parti'nin Muhafazakâr Demokrat Kimliği*, 210–14.

64. JDP Party Programme, section 2.8.

65. Website of CNN Türk television, Istanbul, www.cnnturk.com.tr, April 4, 2004.

66. *Siyasi Partiler Kanunu*, no. 2820, art. 92; text in Şahver Everdi, ed., *Seçim Mevzuatı* (Istanbul: 21 Yüzyıl Yayınları, n.d.), 138.

67. Notably the Felicity Party and the True Path Party; I am indebted to Ersin Kalaycıoğlu for information on this point.

68. According to statistics issued by the Ministry of Labour and Social Security in January 2004, 2.8 million of the 4.9 million registered employees in Turkey were union members; however, of this number, the six unions affiliated to Hak-İş only had 322,000 members, or 11.4 percent of the total, the vast majority being in unions affiliated to the "supra-party" confederation Türk-İş, or the traditionally left-wing DİSK; reported in *Hürriyet*, Internet edition, January 17, 2004.

69. See Ayşe Buğra, "Class, Culture, and State: An Analysis of Interest Representation by Two Turkish Business Associations," *International Journal of Middle East Studies* 30, no. 4 (1998): 521–39; Ziya Öniş and Umut Türem, "Business, Globalization and Democracy: A Comparative Analysis of Turkish Business Associations," *Turkish Studies* 2 (2001): 94–120; Karin Vorhoff, "Businessmen and Their Organizations: Between Instrumental Solidarity, Cultural Diversity and the State," in *Civil Society in the Grip of Nationalism: Studies on Political Culture in Modern Turkey*, ed. Stefanos Yerasimos, Günter Seufert, and Karin Vorhoff (Istanbul: Orient-Institut, 2000), 143–96.

70. See Jenny B. White, *Islamist Mobilization in Turkey: A Study in Vernacular Politics* (Seattle: University of Washington Press, 2002), chap. 6.

71. Tekin, *AK Parti'nin Muhafazakâr Demokrat Kimliği*, 170–71.

72. See, for instance, İhsan D. Dağı, *Batılılaşma Korkusu* (Ankara: Liberte Yayınları, 2003), 7–19, 178–81.

73. *Yeni Şafak*, October 2, 2002, quoted in Tekin, *AK Parti'nin Muhafazakâr Demokrat Kimliği*, 32.

CHAPTER 4

The Justice and Development Party

Identity, Politics, and Human Rights Discourse
in the Search for Security and Legitimacy

■ *İhsan D. Dağı*

Since its formation in 2001 under the leadership of Recep Tayyip Erdoğan, the former mayor of Istanbul elected in 1995 from the pro-Islamic Welfare Party, the Justice and Development Party (JDP) has been seen as an outsider, an intruder, and even an anomaly by many secularists. This view is symbolically demonstrated by the exclusion of the prime minister's headscarved wife from official occasions taking place at broadly defined "public places." On National Day celebrations at the presidential palace, President A. Necdet Sezer invites Erdoğan and other JDP members of Parliament whose wives use headscarves without the company of their wives, a symbolic act of exclusion. This exclusion reflects the distrust of the JDP held by the secular state elite.

The JDP is not only excluded by the secularists; the JDP leaders themselves have also displayed an attitude of self-segregation under the psychological pressure of being regarded as outsiders and anomalies. Erdoğan's speeches in which he claims that "they are not blacks," "not aliens coming from outer space," display the degree of exclusion felt by Erdoğan himself.[1] This points to the "insecure" place the JDP occupies in Turkish politics, to a paradox of a deep sense of insecurity despite huge electoral support.

The JDP's discourse and politics of human rights can therefore be best understood in this context of permanent insecurity experienced in its encounter with the secularist establishment. The JDP emerged at a time when two previous political parties of the founding leaders of the JDP had been closed down by the Constitutional Court in the last three years; when the leader of the movement, Erdoğan, had been imprisoned and banned from active politics; and when the Kemalist/secularist cen-

ter represented by the military and the judiciary had displayed its determination to eliminate any Islamic-popular opposition as well as its social
and economic networks. Under these circumstances the JDP has developed a three-layered strategy: first, adopt a language of human rights
and democracy as a discursive shield; second, mobilize popular support
as a form of democratic legitimacy; and third, build a liberal-democratic
coalition with modern/secular sectors that recognize the JDP as a legitimate political actor.

The search for systemic legitimacy and security has thus shaped the
JDP's approach to human rights, which are expected to resolve these
problems for the JDP. This may well be regarded as the instrumentalization of human rights in daily politics rather than the internalization of
them. Yet it is argued that *instrumentalization* through the recognition of
the utility of human rights for self-preservation may also lead to *institutionalization* of human rights.

COMPOSITION OF THE JDP IDENTITY: AN ISLAMIST PARTY?

The JDP was born from the ashes of a banned political party (the Virtue
Party) by a leader who was imprisoned for "inciting hatred and enmity"
and barred from running for a parliamentary seat in the November 2002
elections. In these elections the JDP captured 34 percent of the votes and
363 seats in Parliament, a landslide victory, while its nearest contender,
the Republican People's Party, could only get 178 seats with 19 percent of
the votes, and the pro-Islamic Felicity Party received an all-time low of 2
percent.[2]

Despite its electoral victory the JDP has remained vulnerable to secularist opposition directed not only by the main opposition party, the
Republican People's Party, but also by the military and some civil sectors that see the JDP as a pro-Islamic movement with a secret agenda
to undo the Kemalist/secularist reforms. Given the closure of two pro-
Islamic political parties, from which the JDP leadership sprang, by the
Constitutional Court since 1998, the portrayal of the JDP as an Islamically oriented party has created an unsettling problem of legitimacy for
the party, generating insecurity in its relations with systemic forces. This
insecurity has in fact been the Achilles' heel of the JDP.

Questioned in the first press conference after the elections of 2002,
JDP leader Erdoğan stressed that the JDP was not "religion centric" but
"conservative and democrat."[3] This has been the JDP language spoken
constantly since its formation in an attempt to disassociate itself from the

political movement from which, to a large extent, it originated, namely the National Outlook Movement (NOM) led by Necmettin Erbakan since 1970.[4] As a mass political movement the JDP carries conservative, nationalist, Islamic, and democratic messages and credentials. Yet in its essence the JDP has emerged from the evolution of pro-Islamic NOM. It reflects the recognition by a group of politicians with pro-Islamic backgrounds of the "limits of Islamic politics" in the age of globalization and under the pressure of the Kemalist/secularist institutional and popular opposition. This owes a lot to the February 28 Process in 1997, which clearly demonstrated that not only Islam's political representation but also its social and economic networks can be violently uprooted by the Kemalist/secularist center even at a time when a pro-Islamic party was the leading political force in the country.[5]

The JDP therefore symbolizes the withdrawal of Islam from the political sphere in return for safeguarding its social network, which is the basis of the conservatism the JDP claims to represent. The JDP displays a retreat from "political" to "social" Islam out of the realization that the growth of Islam's political representation is a self-defeating success, as proved by the closure of the pro-Islamic Welfare Party in 1998, the party that won the mayorship of Istanbul and Ankara in 1994 municipal elections, came up as the leading political force in the 1995 general elections, and led a short-lived coalition government from 1996 until 1997, when it was forced to leave office under pressure from the military.[6]

There is no doubt that those who broke with the NOM formed the core of the JDP, whose leader, Erdoğan, had been elected the mayor of Istanbul from the ranks of Erbakan's Welfare Party in 1994 after years of service to the NOM at almost every level in Istanbul. Deputy chairman of the party and the current minister of foreign affairs, Abdullah Gül, was elected as a member of Parliament for the Welfare Party (WP) in 1995, and in 1999 for the Virtue Party (VP), which had replaced the WP after its closure. Bülent Arınç, the current Speaker of Parliament, was also a parliamentarian from the WP and the VP in the 1990s. In short, the trio who made up the leadership of the JDP were once disciples of the pro-Islamic Erbakan.

It should be remembered, however, that the JDP leaders who had a NOM background had come to be known as the "reformists" within the movement, as shown when Gül placed his nomination for the leadership of the Virtue Party in the party congress of May 2000 against the wishes of Necmettin Erbakan, the natural leader of the movement, who had been banned from politics by the Constitutional Court in 1998. In the race Gül was openly supported by Erdoğan and Arınç. The contest, in which Gül received nearly half of the delegate votes for the leadership of the party in the absence of Erbakan, turned out to be a catalyst for the reformists' break from the traditional leadership.[7] By placing himself in the race for the party leadership, Gül and his supporters not only acted against the traditional leadership of the NOM, but in the process they broke from the ideology symbolized by the leadership. This naturally did not take place in a vacuum; it was rather a response to a number of challenges facing Islamic politics in the late 1990s, notably the February 28 decision of the National Security Council (NSC) that displayed the determination of the military to exclude an Islamically oriented group from exercising governmental power.

As a result, when the VP was closed down by the Constitutional Court in 2001 for being a center for antisecular activities, Erdoğan tried to persuade many people with no Islamic background to join the party in an attempt to reach out to wider social and political groups.[8] The attempt to include liberal names continued during the election period, enlisting especially names from the center-right like Erkan Mumcu from the Motherland Party, and Köksal Toptan and Mehmet Dülger from the True Path Party, by which the JDP signaled that it would no longer be stuck with the NOM cadets. This reaching out was reflected in the cabinet in which moderate people with center-right backgrounds were appointed ministers of the interior, justice, industry, education, tourism, and culture.

While evaluating the change Erdoğan went through in recent years, moreover, one should remember that he served as a mayor, a local politician.[9] In local politics, even in a big metropolitan city like Istanbul, politics is about "services," not about grand ideologies, transformative projects, salvation, or reawakening of the people. Politics at the local level generally requires a different approach in which not "ideology" but "service" to people matters. It is not a field of "grand politics," but politics of possibilities within social and economic limits. Regardless of how sacred they may be considered by their followers, ideological positions and preferences would not be effective in solving the problems of roads, sewage, running water, or collection of garbage. Instead, recognizing differences in social space that encircles the city is important; mayors have to be cooperative and pragmatic, able to form alliances with broader social sectors to get various services done. Erdoğan's experience in Istanbul has certainly influenced him to a great degree to become a pragmatic, service-oriented politician. As a mayor he came to see politics as nonideological, instrumental for solving the daily problems of people—politics as problem solving, not as a means to build an ideologically oriented Islamic community.

Islamism in Turkey, as in the Middle East proper, is traditionally constructed and legitimated by a strong anti-Westernism.[10] In the face of Western political, economic, and cultural challenges the "indigenous" identity that is Islam was to be a genuine alternative to the West, to Western ideas and models. Opposition to the West thus became a defining element of Islamist identity and politics. The NOM, too, regarded the West as the "mother of all evils": corrupting, degenerating, and destroying the "national" identity and indigenous civilization that is Islam. While advocating a union of Islamic countries, the NOM strongly opposed Turkey's integration into the European Union, describing it as a "Christian club."[11]

While Islamic political identity was traditionally built in opposition to the West, to Western values and, equally important, to the history of Westernization in Turkey, pro-Islamic politicians of the late 1990s (most of whom have joined the JDP) realized that they needed the West and modern/Western values of democracy, human rights, and the rule of law in order to build a broader front against the Kemalist/secularist center, and to acquire legitimacy through this new discourse in their confrontation with the Kemalist/secularist center.[12]

Based on such a "rethinking" in recent years, the policies of the JDP in seeking integration with the EU indicate that historical animosity toward the West has come to an end.[13] Integration into the West and maintaining Islamic identity are no longer seen as mutually exclusive choices; one can remain attached to an Islamic identity yet advocate integration with the West as in the case of Turkey's EU membership bid. The JDP's position on EU membership and globalization reflects a "rethinking" that differs significantly from any conventional Islamic stand. Moreover, by seeking EU membership, the JDP leadership with its pro-Islamic background must have explicitly abandoned the idea of an Islamic government in Turkey, given that the EU membership process almost permanently eliminates such a possibility.

The JDP grass roots also reflect a pro-Western attitude. According to a public opinion poll conducted in July 2004, 79 percent of the JDP voters favor EU membership, above the national average of 73 percent. They also view NATO more positively (60 percent) compared to the national average (48 percent). The JDP voters have a positive view of "Western civilization" (50 percent; national average 54 percent) and favor aligning with the West (53 percent) instead of the East if they have to chose between these two broadly defined orientations.[14]

In accordance with this attitude, the JDP, instead of leaning toward local and nationalistic reactions, has been taking a pro-globalization stand. The party program and the election declaration have embraced globalization as a fact within which policies have to be developed. The party expresses its determination to open up Turkey to the globalized world as a competitive country. Erdoğan's speeches immediately after the November elections included specific messages for the international financial centers. He declared that the JDP government would further ease the foreign currency regulations and make the entry of foreign investments to Turkey more attractive.[15] By continuing with the previously accepted IMF program, the JDP takes a pro-globalization stand. The government has not so far confronted but cooperated with the actors, processes, and premises of globalization.

No doubt that the JDP is a peripheral force in Turkish politics, responsive to the demands coming from the periphery. Those peripheral social and economic forces the JDP represents might be expected to hold antiglobalist tendencies. On the contrary, resistance to globalization in Turkey comes from the bureaucratic elite and ideologically committed Kemalists who create obstacles to the economic and political demands of the peripheral forces. This resistance in turn has led to the formation of a strange alliance between social and economic groups supporting JDP and globalist forces. As a result the JDP has moved to cooperate with the global forces to break the resistance of the bureaucratic and ideological centers. To isolate and eliminate the bureaucratic and Kemalist-ideological center, the JDP has speeded up Turkey's integration with global structures. In sum, antiglobalist tendencies in the party have been overtaken by an analysis that places Turkey not in isolation but integrated into the external world as a precondition for further democratization that is expected to open up a broader space for the survival and the legitimacy of the party.[16]

Beyond ideological transformation of the leadership, it would be inaccurate to assume that the JDP's 34 percent vote in the general elections and 42 percent in the local elections of March 2004 represent the number of Islamists in Turkey. According to Tarhan Erdem, a public opinion analyst, in the November elections the JDP received votes from the electorates who, in the previous elections, had voted for other political parties. Compared to the 1999 general elections, 69 percent of the Virtue

Party, 38 percent of the National Action Party, 28 percent of the Motherland Party, 21 percent of the True Path Party, and 14 percent of the Democratic Left Party voters voted for the JDP in the November 2002 elections.[17] This shows that the JDP appealed to almost all sectors of society and was supported by the conservative right. In addition, the provinces where the JDP came in first were also the provinces where the Motherland Party (under the leadership of Turgut Özal) had been the front-runner in the 1983 and 1987 elections.[18] Some attributed the success of the JDP in the elections to the support of the poor and the oppressed.[19] However the JDP voters ranged from the poor of the urban periphery to conservative peasants in the depth of the Anatolia and to demanding provincial entrepreneurs. In the elections the JDP therefore enjoyed the trust of people who are ideologically, socially, and geographically diverse.

Thus the JDP, by virtue of its support base, does not represent an Islamist alternative but instead reflects demands of the periphery that is traditionally pragmatist and developmentalist, yet disenchanted with the authoritarian state tradition of Turkey. Neither the social base of the JDP nor its rhetoric and policies so far presents an Islamic posture. Given the fluctuations in the electorate's preferences, especially in the last few elections, and the shaky economic balances in the country, a search for an ideological legitimization in the name of Islamism instead of meeting social demands and expectations is unlikely. On the contrary, such a policy goes against the "basic instinct" of the JDP, which is the search for systemic legitimacy and security.

The defining point in the discussion of how close the JDP is to political Islam is that those who have an Islamist background have been questioning both the feasibility of Islam as a political project and the conformity of an Islamist project to Islam itself.[20] It seems that pro-Islamic groups, realizing that social and economic networks of Islam had been damaged most when political Islam was at its peak (1995–99), have withdrawn their support from Islamist political movements, as reflected in the results of the November 2002 general elections in which the political party representing the NOM and its leader Erbakan could get only 2 percent of the vote. Instead of political representation of Islam, voters opted for a conservative-centrist approach that is expected to create social and economic networks of Islam. It seems that this is also the route preferred by the JDP in that neither its rhetoric nor its program and policies in the government displays an Islamic orientation. The concept of a "social," not "political," Islam has gained ground,[21] as shown by the acknowledgment of the JDP, in spite of its Islamic roots, that all ideologies including Islamism have died in the age of globalization.[22] Realizing that the rise of political Islam was detrimental to Islam's social and economic influence in Turkey, the JDP defined itself as "conservative-democrat" in an attempt to escape from the self-defeating success of political Islam.

Yet while the JDP claims to be a conservative democratic party, some pro-Islamic circles, along with its secularist opponents, insist on the party's Islamic identity.[23] Based on a comparison with "Christian democrat" parties in Western Europe, they are inclined to describe the JDP as a "Muslim democrat" movement.[24] In the absence of an historical precedent for such a political movement, the attempt at describing the JDP as Muslim democrat can be best regarded as an invention that would reflect neither the social base nor the political language of the party. The JDP seems to have played a role in merging conservative/local/national sentiments with developmentalist and globalist objectives. The JDP leadership is also aware that a Muslim democrat identity does not help resolve its problems of legitimacy and security in the system; on the contrary it exacerbates them. A conservative democrat identity, on the other hand, places the JDP in a historical and social context, socializes and historicizes the party, and enables it to claim to represent a major political currency that has existed since 1946, namely the Democrat Party line in which historically peripheral forces found themselves represented vis-à-vis the Kemalist/secularist center. The JDP leaders managed to escape from the imposition on the party of an ahistorical identity inherent in the term "Muslim democrat" through an intellectual modeling of Islamic groups and a simplification of Turkish politics at the hands of Western observers.

THE LEGITIMACY PROBLEM AND INTRUMENTALIZATION OF DEMOCRACY AND HUMAN RIGHTS

Islamic groups, including the JDP leaders within the NOM, had never taken democracy and human rights seriously until the February 28 decisions of the National Security Council in 1997. Experiencing the pressures of the Kemalist/secularist center on every aspect of their lives, the Islamic groups sought protection within the language and institutions of modernity whereby they discovered the utility of human rights and democracy. After experiencing the isolation, marginalization, and even oppression of 1997 and 1998, they realized that they were seen and would always be seen as an "illegitimate" political force, an anomaly to be corrected in Turkish politics by the Kemalist/secularist center.

Responding to the pressures originating from the military's adamant opposition, which influences the attitudes of judges and high state bureaucracy as well as mainstream secular media, the JDP leadership has realized the legitimizing power of democracy. Popularity displayed by means of elections was considered to be their most valuable asset in their quest for recognition from secularist forces.[25] Thus they had to rely on democracy/democratic participation as a source of legitimacy. As they faced the state power (namely the military and judiciary) opposing them, they turned to the "people power" they knew they enjoyed. Erdoğan has constantly disavowed the religious orientation of the JDP in an attempt to disperse Kemalist/secularist criticism; instead he has insisted that the JDP is a conservative party of "average" Turkish citizens. His reference to average citizens points to the streets. He legitimates himself by claiming that he "understands" and "recognizes" the streets, and portrays himself as someone coming from the streets. He knows that he must rely on people power vis-à-vis the Kemalist/secularist opponents who are powerful in the state apparatus. For the party leadership, democracy has turned out to be a matter of survival.

However, paradoxically, the electoral successes of the JDP have not resolved its problem of legitimacy and security but instead have worsened it: the election results indicating that the JDP's popular support reached 42 percent have increased the anxiety of the Kemalist/secularist groups. Therefore the search for popular legitimacy and strength through the elections actually exacerbated the legitimacy/security problem further.

Thus the JDP adopted a discourse on democracy, human rights, and the rule of law as a means to protect itself against the power of the Kemalist/secularist center, a strategy that also enabled it to forge broad coalitions at home and abroad with liberal-democratic groups.[26] Both through the ballot box and the language of political modernity the JDP has tried to secure legitimacy.

The JDP leadership developed a similar attitude toward the value of human rights as they saw their political parties closed down, leaders banned from political activities, and associations and foundations intimidated. In response they moved to embrace the language of civil and political rights that provided both an effective leverage against the pressures of the state and a ground upon which to build international coalitions. The JDP supported the universality of human rights. JDP members make frequent references to internationally recognized human rights conventions, not those specific to Islam or Turkey. They recognize that human rights are also global, transcending national borders and traditions. They not only support the globalization of human rights, but also advocate global implementation of internationally recognized human rights.

In the election campaign of 2002 and in the party program, a heavy emphasis was placed on human rights and democracy. In fact the party program has been presented as a program on democracy and development, a sign of the importance that the party attaches to these themes. It refers to the individual and his/her happiness as the ultimate objective of the party. "The development and democracy" program of the party claims to fulfill basic rights and freedoms of the people, promising not only legal guarantees but also proper implementation of human rights provisions. Among the issues covered substantially by the 2002 election declaration are basic rights and freedoms, democracy and civil society, justice and the rule of law, and restructuring of the state. Different social, ethnic, political, and religious identities are regarded as a source of richness, not a threat. The election declaration stated that "the JDP does not only recognize their differences but encourages them to participate in politics with their identities" and promises a limited state that would respect the expanding role of the private sector and nongovernmental organizations. The party also claims to broaden the realm of politics vis-à-vis the historical domination of bureaucracy. In short, through its program and election declaration the JDP claimed to contain elements of a democratic and liberal political movement.[27]

No doubt the adoption of a modern political language based on an advocacy for democracy, human rights, and the rule of law has provided the JDP with a discursive supremacy and legitimacy over its opponents, who are not likely to risk their own legitimacy by denouncing human rights and democracy. Those who did oppose the modern political agenda put forward by the JDP have found themselves in the awkward position of being described as resisting changes toward modernity, a claim that was used to generate legitimacy for the Kemalist/secularist forces. The JDP's reference to the language of the "universal" against the "particular," that is, the exceptionalism of Turkey that would justify authoritarianism, has won the support of liberal/secular circles. The language of human rights has therefore provided the JDP with discursive legitimacy over their opponents, while democracy has enabled it to display popular legitimacy. As such, both have proved to be valuable in acquiring security in the establishment because they contribute to the standing of the JDP as a legitimate actor in Turkish politics.

The language of human rights has linked the JDP with broader social and political forces both at home and abroad as well as provided a shield against authoritarian tendencies. Around the human rights theme the JDP has therefore managed to forge a coalition with liberals and reformists both at home and abroad. The search for international coalition led the JDP leadership to look to the West, where numerous human rights nongovernmental organizations, the European Union, the European Court of Human Rights, and individual states had already been critical of the Turkish human rights record. In the end the JDP has found itself on the same side with Westerners on the need to further democratize and guarantee civil and political rights in Turkey.

UNDERSTANDING POLITICAL REFORMS

In order to achieve the reforms requested by the accession partnership document issued by the EU following the Helsinki European summit, at the beginning of 2002 the coalition government led by Bülent Ecevit of the Democratic Left Party introduced a harmonization package, a legislative technique in which amendments were made to various laws within one law passed by Parliament. The JDP government formed after the November elections has continued to use this technique with even more efficiency given its parliamentary majority, and with a clear objective of securing a date for the beginning of accession negotiations with the EU. The EU membership is regarded by the JDP leadership as a natural outcome of Turkey's modernization history. The party program reads that "meeting Copenhagen political criteria is an important step forward for the modernization of the country."[28]

Right after the November elections JDP leader Erdoğan declared that their priority was not to resolve the "headscarf" problem, as expected by many both from Islamic and secularist circles, but instead to speed up the process to get Turkey into the EU. Erdoğan toured the European capitals before the Copenhagen European summit of December 2002 to secure a specific date to start membership negotiations with the EU. The EU Council, however, postponed its decision on Turkey until its 2004 summit, at which a decision would be taken to start, without delay, the accession negotiations with Turkey provided that Turkey fulfilled fully the Copenhagen political criteria.[29] This was a challenge for the new government since Erdoğan stated that the Copenhagen political criteria were not only part of the requirement for Turkey's entry into the EU but an objective to be reached regardless of EU membership.[30] As a result, since its formation the government has introduced fundamental reforms on the Kurdish issue, human rights in general, and civil-military relations, with seven harmonization packages passed by Parliament; the government even seemed ready to compromise to resolve the long-standing Cyprus dispute.

With the first harmonization package presented by the government in January 2003, freedom of association, deterrence against torture and mistreatment, and safeguards for the rights of prisoners were enhanced. A number of changes were also introduced in the legislation on political parties. Most important of all was that closure of political parties was made more difficult. Accordingly a three-fifths majority vote is required for a decision in the Constitutional Court to close a political party. The case for the closure of a political party may be filed only for reasons specifically stipulated in the constitution, not, as formerly, in the law of political parties. Political parties are thus extended protection under the constitution. The amendment also introduced a new sanction short of closure by the Constitutional Court that can deprive political parties partially or fully of the state's financial assistance. These amendments were obviously important for the JDP given the fact that two previous parties of its leaders had been closed down by the Constitutional Court. As such these amendments were in accord with the JDP's search for security within the constitutional order and overlapped with the requirements of the EU membership bid.

In February 2003 Parliament passed another harmonization package in which provisions for improving conditions for retrial in light of the decisions of the European Court of Human Rights were enacted. Article 8 of the antiterror law was abolished in July 2003 along with the introduction of other provisions that allow political propaganda in languages other than Turkish, the lessening of sentences for so called honor-killings was ended, and the NSC representatives on the censor board and the Radio and Television Supervision Board were removed.[31] The package passed by Parliament in August 2003 introduced a significant reform with regard to civilian-military relations, limiting the jurisdiction of military courts over civilians, enabling the auditing of military expenditure and property by the court of auditors, repealing executive powers of the general secretary of the NSC, increasing the time period of regular NSC meetings from once a month to once every two months, and opening the way for appointment of a civilian secretariat general for the NSC. By turning the NSC into a merely advisory body and the Secretariat General into an administrative unit, the political weight of the military has significantly been reduced.[32]

Beside these legislative reforms, in September 2003 the government set up a Reform Monitoring Group, composed of the ministers of foreign affairs, justice, and the interior, and of high-ranking bureaucrats, in response to the EU's insistence on overseeing effective implementation of the reforms introduced.

The European Council meeting in Brussels in December 2003 welcomed the "considerable and determined efforts" of the government and recognized that the reforms undertaken "have brought Turkey closer to the Union." However the Council underlined the need for sustained efforts to strengthen the independence and functioning of the judiciary; the exercise of freedoms of association, expression, and religion; the alignment of civil-military relations with European practice; and the exercise of cultural rights.[33] Over the decision of the Council, Prime Minister Erdoğan declared that his government would complete the work necessary and "make the Copenhagen criteria as Ankara's own criteria."[34]

In April 2004 another comprehensive package of amendments to the constitution was approved by Parliament. With the amendments the State Security Courts were abolished, all references to the death penalty including in times of war were removed, international treaties were accorded precedence over Turkish law, and the military representative on the higher education board was removed.[35] Another package harmonizing the law with the constitutional amendments was passed by Parliament in July 2004. Moreover, in June 2004 four former deputies from the pro-Kurdish Democracy Party (DEP), including Leyla Zana, were released from prison while in the meantime the state-owned TRT started to broadcast in Kurdish.[36]

Furthermore a number of international conventions were signed and ratified in the post-Helsinki period. Among them are the ratifications of the International Covenant on Civil and Political Rights; the International Covenant on Economic, Social, and Cultural Rights; Protocol No. 6 to the European Convention on Human Rights; the Optional Protocol to the Convention on the Rights of the Child; and the signature of Protocol No. 13 to the European Convention on Human Rights.

These are fundamental changes in the legal system. On the outstanding issue of implementing these reforms, the government introduced a zero-tolerance policy toward the torture cases, and engaged in training of police officers, judges, and public prosecutors on human rights with the help of the EU and the Council of Europe.

All these reforms were finally recognized as meeting the Copenhagen political criteria by the European Commission in its 2004 progress report on Turkey. The Commission, noting that Turkey has "sufficiently fulfilled" the political criteria, has recommended that the Council open accession negotiations, and the European Council meeting in Brussels on December 17, 2004, decided to open accession negotiations with Turkey in October 2005.

INSTRUMENTALIZING THE EU ACCESSION

The legislative reforms introduced in less than two years have been driven by Turkey's EU membership bid. Securing a path leading to membership has been regarded as essential not only for democratizing and developing Turkey, but also for broadening legitimacy of the JDP within the modern/ secular sector. The EU membership bid turned out to be a "modern" project on which the intentions and objectives of the JDP would not be questioned, moreover one in which the JDP extracted support from modern/secular sectors, adding to its strength and legitimacy, and lessening its inherent insecurity within the system. Thus the JDP government has ceased to be seen as an outsider or an anomaly. Istanbul-based big capital represented by TÜSİAD and the liberal media have extended in a sense a conditional legitimacy to the JDP government. So long as the government has remained committed to the EU membership bid it has managed to get the support not only of TÜSİAD but also of big media and social democrat and liberal circles, including intellectuals and nongovernmental organizations, significant actors shaping public opinion. Moreover, on a more popular level, given that the idea of full membership in the EU has constantly been supported at around 70 percent, the JDP's EU orientation has been a "safe" policy choice, a choice that has further added to the JDP's popular support and legitimacy.

It is clear that the needs of the JDP have overlapped with the demands of the EU and its requirements for membership. The JDP wanted to limit the power of the military over domestic politics via the NSC or more directly to enhance civilian control over the military, strengthen civil society including pro-Islamic associations and endowments, expand freedom of expression, and make party closure more difficult. These had been the objectives of the JDP leadership since the lack of these benefits had been effectively used against them, especially after 1997. Because these objectives were defined as Turkey's "homework" on the path for EU accession, the JDP government has speeded the process of reform.

It seemed that European demands for democratization and human rights have also overlapped with the JDP's search for protection against the Kemalist/secularist center, including the military and the judiciary.[37] They came to understand that the more Turkey was distanced from the West and the EU in particular, the stronger would be the hegemony of the army that treats the JDP as an anomaly and a threat. Thus the EU emerged as a natural ally to reduce the influence of the army and to establish democratic governance within which the JDP would be regarded as a legitimate player. The expectation was that the army's interventions in politics would be significantly lessened as a result of the further democratization that was a precondition for Turkey's entry to the EU; a Kemalist state ideology guarded by the army would not be sustainable in an EU-member Turkey.[38]

Thus the JDP government has been able to introduce human rights and democracy reforms, although cautioned by many in the Kemalist/secularist center, on the basis that these were necessary for Turkey's EU membership, an objective that has always been justified as the last stage of Westernization, an unquestioned objective that has also been a legacy of the Kemalist revolution. Turkey's Westernizing elite have had to put up with the reforms required by the EU in order to reach the ultimate objective of its own project of Westernization. This necessity has reduced significantly the resistance that the JDP would otherwise have encountered. The military has had to accept the restructuring of the NSC simply because that was one of the preconditions for Turkey's accession process; because they could not disagree, at least publicly, with the greater objective of Westernization via EU membership, they had to conform to the reforms needed. The same need to accept occurred for the abolishing of the death penalty and the State Security Courts, both seen as significant leverages against the Kurdish secessionist activities. On these and other reforms the military did put up some objections.[39] But their resistance was overcome because of the legitimizing power of the Westernization project of the republican elite. Because of the role Westernization has played in the formation of modern Turkish state identity, concerns or cautions displayed by the army, the judiciary, and even diplomats have been eased by references to this greater objective.

The EU's demands for reforms have overlapped with the JDP's search for consolidating its power and acquiring wider legitimacy within the system vis-à-vis the army and other radical secularist forces through a policy of enhancing democracy, human rights, and civilian supremacy over the military. The result has been a speedy process of political reforms in Turkey. The EU membership perspective has thus enabled the government to persuade the military and wider public to accept radical reforms.

CONCLUSION

It seems that the JDP has instrumentalized both human rights and EU membership in its search for systemic legitimacy and security. Instrumentalization of human rights does highlight the need for a human rights regime. The recognized utility of human rights is the social and political base on which a sustainable regime can be built. The search in human rights for protection constitutes the practical, if not moral, ground on which a human rights regime can be established. Intrumentalization in the sense of recognizing its utility may therefore serve to institutionalize a human rights regime.[40]

Thus the fact that a political party that enjoys the support of nearly one-half of all voters in Turkey sees human rights as fundamental to its very survival is indicative both of its insecurity and the social and political strength of a human rights discourse. The JDP government has sought to secure a "legitimate" place for itself in the Turkish political arena by its discourse and mechanisms for human rights in addition to the popular legitimacy it has enjoyed through elections.

In this context some credit should be given to the constraints put up against the JDP by the Kemalist/secularist center that forced the JDP with its massive social and political power to stick to the objectives of human rights, democracy, and EU membership.[41] These constraints have had a transformative impact on Turkish political culture, particularly among the center-right voters. The JDP's popular language of human rights and democracy has contributed to the legitimization of democracy and human rights among the conservative Turkish people from the center-right political background. Yes, they traditionally valued democracy, but it was a ballot-box democracy along with a fetishistic notion of the supremacy of national will over authoritarian state elite. Yes, they have defended "their" rights against the bureaucratic center. But they have traditionally not been much interested in human rights as a general/universal category. In its search for systemic legitimacy and security within a modern/universal concept of human rights, the JDP also secures and legitimates a place for universal human rights among Turkey's conservative masses.

A similar phenomenon has developed with regard to the EU in particular and the West in general. The JDP's quest for EU membership also led its conservative voters to view the EU in a more positive way. Given the historical hesitation of the conservative periphery about the West and Westernization, the JDP's quest for EU membership has also contributed to overcoming the fear of the West and Westernization traditionally prevalent among center-right voters. As a result the JDP has led Europeanization of the center-right conservative/Islamic sectors in recent years with its pro–human rights, democracy, and the EU policies.[42] In sum, the JDP, with its pro-Islamic and anti-Western roots, has ironically played a historically important role in consolidating democracy in Turkey and in integrating Turkey into the EU.

NOTES

1. *Sabah,* "'Türkiye'de hala 'beyaz Türkler' 'zenci Türkler' ayrımı yapanlar var'," http://www.sabah.com.tr/2004/03/09siy102.html; http://www.akparti.org.tr/haber. asp?haber_id=2012&kategori=; Oya Berberoğlu, "Topal ördek misali," http://www. aksam.com.tr/arsiv/aksam/2003/04/12/yazarlar/yazarlar162.html.

2. For analyses of the election results and the JDP, see Soli Özel, "Turkey at the Polls: After the Tsunami," *Journal of Democracy* 14 (2003): 80–94; Ziya Öniş and Fuat Keyman, "Turkey at the Polls: A New Path Emerges," *Journal of Democracy* 14, no. 2 (2003): 95–107; M. Hakan Yavuz, *Islamic Political Identity in Turkey* (New York: Oxford University Press, 2003), 256–64.

3. "Erdoğan: İlk iş AB, sonra ekonomi var," *Radikal,* November 4, 2002.

4. For the ideology of the movement and its evolution, see Ahmet Yıldız, "Politico-Religious Discourse of Political Islam in Turkey: The Parties of National Outlook," *Muslim World* 93 (2003): 187–210. For an analysis of the WP's ideology and electoral performance in the 1990s, see M. Hakan Yavuz, "Political Islam and the Welfare (Refah) Party in Turkey," *Comparative Politics* 30 (1997): 63–82; Ziya Öniş, "The Political Economy of Islamic Resurgence in Turkey: The Rise of the Welfare Party in Perspective," *Third World Quarterly* 18 (1997): 743–66.

5. For February 28 decisions of the NSC, see "Recommendations of the State Council Meeting and Comment," *Briefing,* March 10, 1997, 4. For an analysis of the February 28 decisions as part of the Turkish state's exclusionary policies toward Islamic groups, see M. Hakan Yavuz, "Cleansing Islam from the Public Sphere and the February 28 Process," *Journal of International Affairs* 54 (2000): 21–42; Ümit C. Sakallıoğlu and Menderes Çınar, "Turkey 2002: Kemalism, Islamism and Politics in the Light of the February 28 Process," *South Atlantic Quarterly* 102 (2003): 309–32.

6. For "social Islam" see M. Hakan Yavuz, "Towards an Islamic Liberalism?: The Nurcu Movement of Fethullah Gülen," *Middle East Journal* 53 (1999): 584–605; M. Hakan Yavuz and John L. Esposito, *Turkish Islam and the Secular State: The Gülen Movement* (Syracuse, NY: Syracuse University Press, 2003).

7. R. Quinn Mecham, "From the Ashes of Virtue, a Promise of Light: The Transformation of Political Islam in Turkey," *Third World Quarterly* 25, no. 2 (2004): 339–58.

8. Erdoğan, before forming the party, contacted many people including businessmen like Rahmi Koç and retired general Atilla Kıyat; see *Sabah,* June 25, 2001.

9. For an overview of the ideological transformation of Tayyip Erdoğan into a moderate politician, see Metin Heper and Şule Toktaş, "Islam, Modernity and Democracy in Contemporary Turkey: The Case of Recep Tayyip Erdoğan," *Muslim World* 93 (2003): 157–85.

10. See İsmail Kara, *Türkiye'de İslamcılık Düşüncesi* (Istanbul: Risale Yayınları, 1986) for the sample writings of Turkish Islamists like Şehbenderzade Filibeli Ahmed Hilmi (pp. 3–43), Said Halim Paşa (pp. 73–174), and İskilipli Mehmed Atıf (pp. 241–72); see İsmail Kara, *Türkiye'de İslamcılık Düşüncesi*, vol. 3 (Istanbul: Pınar Yayınları, 1994) for the writings of Islamists in the republican era such as Nurettin Topçu (pp. 113–239), N. Fazıl Kısakürek (pp. 241–375), Sezai Karakoç (pp. 377–479), and İsmet Özel (pp. 595–702). See also the early writings of late Islamists such as Ali Bulaç, *Modern Kavramlar ve Düzenler* (Istanbul: Pınar Yayıncılık, 1987); and İsmet Özel, *Üç Mesele; Teknik, Medeniyet, Yabancılaşma* (Istanbul: Dergah Yayınları, 1978).

11. İhsan D. Dağı, *Kimlik, Söylem ve Siyaset: Doğu-Batı Ayrımında Refah Partisi Geleneği* (Ankara: İmge Yayınevi, 1998).

12. İhsan D. Dağı, "Transformation of Islamic Political Identity in Turkey: Rethinking the West and Westernization," *Turkish Studies* 6 (2005): 21–37; Ziya Öniş, "Political Islam at the Crossroads: From Hegemony to Co-existence," *Contemporary Politics* 7 (2001): 283–84.

13. For the changing attitude of the NOM on EU membership, see Şaban Tanıyıcı, "Transformation of Political Islam in Turkey: Islamist Welfare Party's Pro-EU Turn," *Party Politics* 9 (2003): 463–83.

14. "NATO ve Türk Dış Politikası Kamuoyu Araştırması," *Pollmark*, July 2004.

15. "Ekonomik Program Eksiksiz Uygulanır," *Radikal*, November 5, 2002; "Erdoğan: İlk İş AB Sonra Ekonomi," *Radikal*, November 4, 2002.

16. İhsan D. Dağı, "Ak Parti: müslüman demokrat mı, muhafazakar demokrat mı?" *Zaman*, January 9, 2003.

17. See "İki Parti Seçmeni AKP'ye Gitti," *Radikal*, November 6, 2002.

18. For an account of similarities between the neoliberal policies of the JDP and the Motherland Party, see Simten Coşan and Aylin Özman, "Center-right Politics in Turkey after the November 2002 General Election: Neo-liberalism with a Muslim Face," *Contemporary Politics* 10, no. 1 (2004): 57–74.

19. For this explanation, see Taha Akyol, "AKP'nin Arkasında Ne Var?" *Milliyet*, October 17–21, 2002.

20. Mehmet Metiner, *Yemyeşil Şeriat Bembeyaz Demokrasi* (Istanbul: Doğan Yayıncılık, 2004); "İslam devleti projesi çöktü," Ali Bulaç's interview with Neşe Düzel, *Radikal*, December 21, 1999.

21. Politicization of religion came to be seen as a problem by the Islamists in response to the way in which the secularists/Kemalists debated Islam in public. Also see Kadir Canatan, "Çağdaş Siyasal İslam Düşüncesinin Gelişim Seyri," *Bilgi ve Düşünce* 1 (2002): 31–38.

22. For the party program and the election declaration, see the JDP's web page at http://www.akim.akparti.org.tr/ and http://www.akparti.org.tr/beyanname.doc, respectively.

23. The party organized an international symposium on conservatism and democracy held in Istanbul on January 10–11, 2004, which began with Erdoğan's speech outlining the conservative stand of the party. For Erdoğan's speech in the symposium,

see *Uluslararası Muhafazakarlık ve Demokrasi Sempozyumu*, Ankara: 2004, 7–17. Also see Yalçın Akdoğan, *Muhafazakar Demokrasi* (Ankara: AK Parti, 2003).

24. See the special issue of *Bilgi ve Düşünce* 1 (2003), a journal published by pro-Islamic intellectuals close to the JDP leadership.

25. Even the notion of "Muslim democrat," a preferred label among pro-Islamic intellectuals close to the party, is indicative of such a search for legitimization, to be acquired through a Western experimentation in "Christian democracy."

26. This part draws on my "Rethinking Human Rights, Democracy, and the West: Post-Islamist Intellectuals in Turkey," *Critique: Critical Middle Eastern Studies* 13 (2004): 135–51.

27. See the party program and the election declaration.

28. 2002 Election Declaration.

29. Philip Robins, "Confusion at Home, Confusion Abroad: Turkey between Copenhagen and Iraq," *International Affairs* 79 (2003): 547–66.

30. "Avrupa'ya net mesajlar," *Radikal*, November 7, 2002.

31. *Briefing*, May 5, 2003, 6.

32. *Briefing*, July 28, 2003, 9.

33. *Briefing*, December 15, 2003, 4.

34. Ibid., 5.

35. *Briefing*, April 26, 2004, 8–9.

36. *Briefing*, June 14, 2004, 14.

37. Helena Smith, "New Breed of Islamic Politicians Start to Find Their Feet," *The Guardian*, March 10, 2003.

38. For an early analysis of this kind, which raises the question of whether the EU membership means "adieu to Atatürk," see "Turkey Becomes a Candidate," *The Economist*, December 16, 1999. For the justification of the Islamists for supporting the EU membership, see Ali Bulaç, "Niçin AB," *Zaman*, December 11, 1999; Ali Bulaç, "Türkiye'nin ev ödevleri," *Zaman*, February 16, 2000; Ali Bulaç, "FP, 312 ve demokrasi," *Zaman*, March 25, 2000; Ali Bulaç, "AB tartışması," *Zaman*, March 19, 2002.

39. The secretary general of the National Security Council, General Tuncer Kılınç, had warned the government many times about the reform packages, and even questioned the wisdom of the EU membership bid. See "Orgeneral Kılınç: AB bize uymaz," *Radikal*, March 8, 2002.

40. For the JDP's potential for democratizing Turkey, see Ahmet İnsel, "The AKP and Normalizing Democracy in Turkey," *South Atlantic Quarterly* 102 (2003): 293–308.

41. On the relationship between the transformation of political Islam and constraints put up by the secular framework, see Mecham, "From the Ashes of Virtue," 339–58.

42. The EU support among the JDP voters reaches 80 percent, well above the national average of 73 percent. The lead for EU support is held by DEHAP voters with 89 percent. See *Pollmark*, 2004.

CHAPTER 5

A Pro-Islamic Party?

Promises and Limits of Turkey's
Justice and Development Party

■ *Sultan Tepe*

Many observers of Islamic politics have viewed the rise of Turkey's Justice
and Development Party (JDP) as a litmus test of whether and how a
party can successfully reconcile the forces of Islam and liberal democracy.
In fact, the JDP's rise to power in the November 2002 election has been
remarkable and reveals both the resiliency of Islam as a political force and
the extremely volatile nature of Turkish politics. What has made the party's success more striking is that, despite being Turkey's youngest and
least known pro-Islamist party, and having been established only fourteen months before the election, on its first try the JDP captured 67 percent of the seats in the Turkish Parliament, more than the critical majority required to amend the constitution. The JDP formed the first majority
government in decades, without having had its first party congress or
offering a detailed political agenda, and at the same time that its charismatic and controversial leader, Recep Tayyip Erdoğan, was banned from
politics and from holding public office.

By any account, the 2002 election broke many well-entrenched patterns in Turkey's politics. Since the early 1970s, with a brief interruption
after the 1980 coup, a fragmented multiparty party system and unstable
coalition governments had defined the political competition.[1] In the
aftermath of the 2002 election, Turkish politics resumed the two-party-
dominated, multiparty structure that had been in abeyance for five
decades, when all but two major parties failed to pass the national threshold of 10 percent. The election result sparked a critical realignment
in which the support for major parties of the left (the Democratic Left
Party) and right (the Motherland Party, the True Path Party) reached its
nadir. The JDP's appearance on Turkey's political scene accompanied the

purging of conventional parties from the Turkish public sphere and a change in the political elite. Amid concerns as to how the JDP would use its power, the party launched an aggressive reform program, using the European Union's "Copenhagen criteria" as blueprint. As of March 2005, a record high number of 553 laws were proposed by the JDP government and adopted by the JDP-dominated Parliament. The JDP-sponsored reforms amounted to Turkey's first civilian-initiated reform, in Abdullah Gül's words "a silent revolution." The drastic reforms spanned a broad spectrum, from the introduction of new rights such as the Right of Access to Public Records (4982), to the devolution of Turkey's highly centralized administrative system by changing the Law on Municipalities (5215).[2] The JDP's commitment to liberalize Turkey's political and economic system despite its pro-Islamic identity led an increasing number of observers of Turkish politics to declare that under the leadership of the JDP Turkey "is moving towards resolution of its traditional issues, becoming a genuine model for the Muslim world."[3] Others have taken the argument further and have concluded that the JDP's policies proved the avoidability of the so-called "democratic gap" in the Muslim world and the conflict between Islam and democracy.

This chapter questions the evaluations that focus on the party-sponsored reforms at the expense of fully accounting for both the relationship between Islam and politics, and the political agenda and identity of the JDP. In an effort to bring to the fore some of the dimensions neglected in the existing analyses, the following study begins by illustrating how the JDP emerged from a series of political and economic impasses that culminated in the 1997 indirect military intervention and the collapse of the economic system in 2001. These events affected the JDP in contradictory ways: on the one hand they shaped the pre-2002 election context and helped the JDP to emerge and enhance its power. On the other hand, the subsequent political realignment represents the major impediment to the JDP's ability to present an innovative agenda. An inside-out look at the party's ideology, its conservative democracy, its organizational structure, and its policies pertaining to the public role of Islam shows how the party's policies are dogged by the pursuit of opposite goals.

The analysis of the discourse and praxis of the JDP presented here draws mostly on a series of interviews conducted from 1998 to 2005 with the JDP elite and on a content analysis of the party program and statute, as well as a national representative survey designed and implemented by the author.[4] The JDP-sponsored reforms emphasize the urgent need to eliminate the state's ineffective structure and authoritarian policies, while the party itself continuously limits its internal democracy and develops a hierarchical party organization. More important, the JDP promises to eliminate barriers that marginalize Islam. Meanwhile the party's own ideology either reduces Islam to a set of traditional values or treats the values as limited to the private sphere. The party's avoidance of issues derived from the public role of Islam manifests itself best in its ambivalent policies toward the İmam Hatip schools, the status of religious vocational schools, the political representation of women, and the headscarf issue. Although the JDP is perceived as a pro-Islamic party, instead of placing itself at the nexus of democracy and Islam and articulating a pro-Islamic democratic ideology, the JDP keeps Islam in the background and marginalizes the debate on the political role of Islam.

Moving beyond the cursory analysis of the JDP's role as a pro-Islamic and democratic party in Turkey and the Muslim world calls for an analytical framework that brings together the major components of its electoral success: Turkey's political power structure, the configuration of the party's internal organization and leadership cadres, and the principles and implementation of the party's ideology. When put under such scrutiny, the growing distance between the party's practice and ideals illustrates that it is not the party's capacity to introduce reforms, but the party's ability to resolve the opposing trends and paradoxical positions vis-à-vis Islam that will be decisive in defining its contribution to Turkey's democracy and democracy in the Muslim world at large.

The JDP's Rise and Centrifugal Forces of Turkish Politics?

The meteoric rise of the JDP has produced competing interpretations of the party's appeal. Some scholars view Erdoğan's charismatic appeal as the reason for the party's success, reducing the JDP to Erdoğan's party, whereas others view the JDP's as an *ad hoc* coalition and the product of contextual factors. Both of these approaches offer ahistorical, leader-centered, and context-specific analyses that disregard the JDP's position within the ongoing ideological and structural transformation of Turkish politics. A thorough analysis of the JDP, however, requires placing the party's success within its historical context, providing an analysis of the structure behind the leader's political power and assessing the constituent parts of its ideology. Accordingly, any analysis of the JDP must locate it within Turkey's historical institutional characteristics marked by the changing nature of the state's secular hegemony; the effects of economic structural adjustment reforms on the shifting of political alliances; the effect of the 10 percent threshold for national representation and the subsequent indirect disenfranchisement of voters who support parties that cannot pass it; and, finally, the volatile nature of the Turkish electorate. Given that it is uncommon for a party to receive major support in one election and fail to pass the national threshold in subsequent elections, the question of whether the JDP's success is a manifestation of deep changes or whether it reflects a temporary aberration demands an answer.[5]

The role of Islam in the party's success and the party's position vis-à-vis Islam pose further challenges to an analysis of the JDP. Since the foundation of the Turkish Republic, Islam has performed a dual and contradictory role. The state elite has often relied on Islam as a common identity marker of the peoples who constitute the Turkish nation. It has also perceived Islam as a threat, because of its inherent capacity to challenge state power by offering an alternative source of legitimacy. Many observers of Turkish politics identify the competing claims between state power and the public role of Islam as one of the defining fault lines in Turkish politics. Still today, politics in Turkey is seen by many as a power struggle between the secular elite, that is, the elite who want to exclude Islamic ideas from politics, and the traditional masses, who rely on religious symbols and ideas to form their political choices.[6] The secular elite has traditionally represented the state-created bourgeoisie, namely military and civil servants, while the counter-elite has represented petite bourgeoisie, the urban poor, and rural sectors. The political left, represented by the state's founding Republican People's Party, embodied the commitment to a state-controlled economy and secularism, while the right-wing parties represented oppositional forces against the state-centric economic policies and strict secularism. The ostensibly clear-cut distinction between the secular, state-focused center and the more traditional periphery has been refashioned to such an extent, because of the extraordinary transformation of Turkish society, that we need to question its analytical expediency.

In today's Turkey the conventional economic and political alliances have been redefined because of large-scale internal migrations, the expansion of literacy, the disengagement of the state from the economic sector through privatization, and the presence of religious revivalism. As a result, the economic and political tension between the so-called secular center and the traditional periphery has taken new forms. The traditional masses are transforming themselves into political forces and making inroads into areas controlled by secular institutions and policies. By the same token, Islam's political role is being redefined via the active participation of agents who have previously associated themselves with the Islamic periphery and were excluded from the center. The confluence of these changes manifested itself in the emergence of many new political actors and issues that traverse the boundaries of Turkey's conventional state and elite structure. Among others, these actors include the so-called *Anatolian tigers*, Turkey's local bourgoisie, MÜSİAD, the business elite who differentiate themselves from their secularist counterparts, new urban dwellers created by internal immigrations, and outwardly oriented rural populations who have started to play a defining role in Turkish politics.[7] The continuing changes to the Turkish social structure pose the question of how the agents, who were bounded by the domain of the periphery, will use their newly acquired economic and political power to redefine the role of Islam in Turkish politics and define the course of Turkish modernity.[8]

Having warned against the risks involved in narrowly focused analyses and in the neglect of underlying and less visible, yet more decisive, shifts in Turkish politics, we can turn to the background of the 2002 election.[9] The JDP's sudden appearance occurred in a political context shaped by two massive crises that shook Turkey's conventional political and economic alliances: the 1997 political crisis and the 2001 economic crisis. The first crisis marked the demise of Turkey's first generation of openly Islamic parties, named "the National Outlook" Movement. The second included one of the most severe economic crises in Turkish history, which affected the economic standing of almost all Turkish citizens, triggering a process of political realignment. These crises created two separate but converging centrifugal forces, which together reasserted the role of Turkish secularism as a hegemonic official ideology and built a political affinity among previously competing economic groups such as the finance sector, the petite bourgeoisie, and the working class. During this process the limited capacity of major parties for providing political stability became evident as well. This brief background of the JDP's meteoric rise shows that its appearance on the Turkish political scene might well not have occurred without the political alliance formed by the centrifugal forces of Turkey's political system, the polarizing effect of the Erbakan-led National Outlook Movement, and the failure of the International Monetary Fund (IMF)–sponsored economic adjustment policies.

Ironically, the decline of the JDP's predecessor, the National Outlook Movement, set in motion the ascendancy of the JDP. In the aftermath of the 1995 general election, the Welfare Party, Turkey's then only overtly pro-Islamic party, which represented the National Outlook Movement, won 158 out of 500 parliamentary seats, seizing what was up to then the highest vote share achieved by an openly religious party.[10] When the competing center-right parties failed to form a stable coalition government, the Welfare Party became the leading coalition partner. The National Outlook Movement leader, Necmettin Erbakan, was named as the first Islamist prime minister of Turkey. Many of the JDP's current leaders had active roles in this short-lived Erbakan government. There is clear evidence that the political lessons learned by the future JDP elite during this time revealed themselves later in the JDP's program. The Welfare Party's policies marked a major departure from Turkey's conventional policies and steadily alienated the secular political elite and public.[11] The increasing tension between Welfare Party supporters and the secular opposition manifested itself in relation to a public event, named "Jerusalem Night," sponsored by one of the Welfare Party mayors. Jerusalem Night, which had been intended to show solidarity with the Palestinian people, openly challenged Turkey's secular policies and came to symbolize the radicalization of the party's rhetoric.

Subsequent to Jerusalem Night, the military leadership submitted a policy proposal to Necmettin Erbakan at the next National Security Council meeting that characterized Islamists as the number one security threat in Turkey. The report's recommendations ranged from extending elementary education by three years (from five to eight years) to tightening the state's control of Qur'anic schools. Contradicting its own policies and perplexing many of its supporters, the Welfare Party did indeed adopt the policies that sought to marginalize its hard-core constituency and the political role of Islam. This interference of the armed forces and the demobilization of the Islamic forces, which came to be known as the "February 28 Process," added a new entry to the Turkish political lexicon: "a postmodern" or "soft military" coup.[12] The Welfare Party's consent to these restrictions undercut the party's own power, undermined its credibility, and triggered adverse reactions, especially among Islamic intellectuals. Still, it did not prevent the Constitutional Court from deciding to close down the Welfare Party on January 18, 1998. The court also barred Erbakan from engaging in any political activities for the next five years.

The dismantlement of Turkey's Islamists under the leadership of Turkey's first pro-Islamic government sparked a political reaction that ended in the formation of a coalition government consisting of Turkey's staunchly secular Democratic Left Party and the nationalist conservative Nationalist Action Party. In an effort to stabilize Turkey's economy, the coalition government adopted a comprehensive IMF-led structural adjustment program. Despite the parties' rhetorical commitment to the reforms, crucial postponements occurred in the implementation phase, especially in the banking sector. The lack of public knowledge about the extent and timing of the reforms, combined with the delays, raised questions about the government's willingness to implement the required changes, thereby triggering one of the most destabilizing economic crises in Turkey's history.[13] When at yet another National Security Council meeting, held on February 19, 2001, the president of the Republic questioned the government's ability to carry out the reforms, a massive economic crisis erupted that damaged the economic positions of all social groups.[14] Turkey's already very low annual per capita Gross National Product declined from $2,986 to $2,261, and the annual unemployment rate increased from 6.3 percent to 6.9 percent in just a few months.[15] Four years later, 89 percent of respondents reported on the 2005 survey that the crisis affected them in significant ways. The repeated failure of political and economic policies and their destructive consequences, the collapse of Turkey's first wave of Islamist parties, and the IMF-led structural adjustment policies may well be at least in part responsible for the exceptionally high number of nonvoters in the 2002 election. Attesting to an alarming level of apathy, 21 percent of the Turkish electorate did not vote.[16] According to the A&G 2002 election survey, educated urban residents represented a disproportionately large share of nonvoters. For instance, 49.3 percent of those who did not vote were high school and college graduates, a rate much higher than the national average of 37 percent. More than 52 percent of them were employed, and 68.9 percent lived in big metropolitan areas or in cities. The 2005 survey shows that nonvoters describe themselves politically as at the center of Turkey's ideological spectrum. The increasing number of nonvoters constitutes a significant political block in Turkish politics. Taking the high abstention rate into consideration, the JDP's support as a percent of the total number of eligible voters drops to 26 percent. More than 40 percent of Turkish voters were left unrepresented in Parliament when seventeen other political parties failed to pass the national threshold of 10 percent and did not gain parliamentary seats. Only the Republican People's Party, which had traditionally capitalized on its role as the protector of secularism, managed to return to Parliament. Nevertheless, the party's stunning failure against the JDP created intense internal divisions, leaving the JDP virtually without political opposition.

In short, the political arena into which the JDP was born was characterized by (1) a failed party system, where all other major parties were discredited because of their inability to prevent the political and economic crises; (2) a weak or absent opposition; (3) an unprecedented political alliance of otherwise conflicting social forces, such as disaffected pro-Islamic groups; economically dislocated groups, especially those typically most responsive to market forces such as the business elite, or those who lost jobs, investments, and savings; as well as fixed income groups, civil servants, and workers who were hit by rising inflation; (4) a heightened level of political apathy; (5) the search for a new pro-Islamic party; and (6) a national call for creating and maintaining economic stability at any cost. However, the combination of a political void and a grand coalition of supportive groups has been a mixed blessing for the party. The 1997 crisis gave the party the power to define the terms of Islamic politics, while the 2001 crisis created an unusual coalition of social groups that had been mired in political and economic instability. The JDP's broad political support came with somewhat contradictory political expectations: that the party would present a new identity for Turkey's Islamists without being antisystemic and enforce policies to generate economic stability and a more open public sphere.

THE JDP AS AN AGENT OF DEMOCRACY: (DE)COUPLING DEMOCRACY AND ISLAM WITHIN THE PARTY AND BEYOND?

The JDP's approach to democracy cannot be grasped without including the impact of the two interrelated processes that imprinted the party: (1) The seeds of the future JDP were sown as a reactionary movement against the structure of the National Outlook movement and Erkaban's authoritarian leadership, the antisystemic and confrontational policies of the National Outlook parties, and these parties' failure to translate their electoral power into political power. From the JDP's inception, the founders wanted to create a decentralized party, in which the leader would accommodate and be open to alternative policies. (2) The JDP leadership's opposition to the Erbakan-led National Outlook parties was also prompted by their search for more effective policies to enhance the political role of Islam and the rights of observant Muslims in the Turkish public sphere. After all, the leader of the JDP, Tayyip Erdoğan himself, was sentenced to ten months in prison in 1998 for polarizing the public and spreading hatred based on religious cleavages for reciting the lines of a poem: "the mosques are our barracks, the domes our helmets, the minarets our bayonets and the faithful our soldiers…" Although Erdoğan's imprisonment ended, he remained barred from running for office until the JDP changed the country's constitution in 2003.[17]

One can find the marks of these two processes in the JDP's party program and statute. Both documents state the party's commitment to a decentralized party structure and the protection of political rights, which are presented as venues that will ultimately ensure the restoration of the role of Islam in the public sphere. Written by about 122 founding members after extensive deliberations, the party program declares that the JDP can achieve its political agenda only through its commitment to internal democracy and transparency of the structures. "Intra-Party democracy shall be improved by ensuring that individuals and those with minority views shall enjoy legal and democratic rights to fair competition."[18] In fact, attesting to this commitment, the party program also promises to limit the party chairman's and parliamentarians' ability to dominate the party.

> Our party is determined to bring a new perception of politics to Turkey and to implement this concept firstly within its own organism, thus setting an example to other parties. In order to establish intra-party democracy and transparency: It is our priority to carry out pre-elections with the participation of all members. For the sake of politics based on principles, the term of service of Chairman of the party and that of the parliamentarians shall be as indicated in our regulations of the party to determine the candidates for the seats of deputies.

Indeed, the JDP's original party statute, which was effective only from August 14, 2001, to February 2, 2003, distinguished the JDP from other Turkish parties. It provided its delegates with extensive powers to control the Central Executive Committee. Most notably, for the first time in Turkish politics, a political party set a term limit for its leadership. Likewise, the party has become the first to establish a council of referees on internal democracy, *parti ici demokrasi hakem kurulu*.[19] Notwithstanding its initial promise and innovative institutional design, shortly after Parliament adopted a constitutional amendment that allowed its charismatic leader, Tayyip Erdoğan, to hold public office, the first party statute was altered in a top-down fashion. Along with the old rules, the new ones were incorporated into the party's fundamental documents to strengthen the role of the party chairman as the single decision-making authority. The enormous speed with which the JDP transformed itself is reflected in the revisions of the party's current statute: it includes two different methods for forming the Central Decision Making and Executive Committee (CDMEC). For instance, item 69.6 allows delegates to vote for each position on the committee, whereas item 69.9 states that, if there is a group nomination in the form of a list or lists, then delegates should vote only for those on the list.

Not only do these provisions contradict each other, but, given that the party leadership itself often puts the lists forward, the party leadership enjoys disproportionate power over the formation of the CDMEC. In addition, the party chairman is given the right to change the membership of the central executive, the group of twelve chosen by himself, with the approval of the CDMEC. Disregarding the fact that merging different decision-making powers in the hands of the party chairman presents a direct violation of the party's commitment to internal democracy, the party leadership accepted the changes without any deliberation process or solicitation of feedback from the rank and file.

Even a cursory review of the party's short institutional history reveals a clear disconnect between the party's commitment to internal democracy and its elimination of official, bottom-up feedback channels. The lack of internal debates and collective decision-making mechanisms, as well as the increasing autonomy of the party leadership, marginalizes more and more party members. One can find various expressions of growing discontent directed toward the party's authoritarian structure. According to Ertuğrul Yalçınbayır, who served as deputy prime minister under the first JDP government, the party's internal democracy diverged from its initial path and has become a "brush-off" "democracy in which dissidents are harshly swept aside."[20] In the views of other members of Parliament, such as Ersönmez Yarbay, Erdoğan's charismatic leadership has marginalized other members and has paved the way for decisions that violate not only the basic principle of democratic deliberation within the party, but also the official nomination requirements.[21]

In fact, a closer look at the party's organizational structure and policy-making process shows that Erdoğan's charismatic appeal coupled with the pace of reforms seems to have resulted in the acceptance of a diminished intraparty democracy, which makes the formation of an intraparty opposition difficult. Symbolic protests, rather than organized ones, seem politically more expedient for some members. Serpil Yıldız, one of JDP's thirteen original female MPs, ran for speaker against the party leadership's imposed appointment. Unexpectedly, her candidacy attracted enough support to delay the selection of Erdoğan's candidate until the third and final round, revealing the pervasiveness of internal opposition.

Although many ignored these oppositional moves as sporadic occurrences, no one could explain the resignation of Culture and Tourism minister Erkan Mumcu on February 15, 2005. What made this highly unusual resignation more striking is that Mumcu himself attributed his defection to the presence of an "inner cabinet" that exists within the regular cabinet, and the lack of opportunity for contributing to the policy-making process. This high-level resignation signaled that the internal fragmentation and centralization of the party has reached exceptional levels.[22] Although a highly hierarchical party structure is part and parcel of party politics in Turkey, the marginalization of a minister shows that, in a striking contradiction to its party program, the JDP is on the verge of establishing a leader-dominated and insular party organization.

One might conclude that Erdoğan's enormous popularity and the party's short history makes such centralization unavoidable. More importantly, such centralization might be a constructive step toward the party's institutionalization. Yet centralization not only contradicts the party's raison d'être, but also deprives the leadership of the positive influence of opposing viewpoints. Therefore, justifications for the party's centralization of power need to be approached cautiously, for two reasons. First, the literature on party politics shows that only parties that have open communication channels and free internal debates can survive internal crises and avoid disintegration. A few, rare examples of the devolution of intraparty power following a stringent centralization do exist, but centralization often results in party fragmentation.[23] Second, considering that the party united a broad coalition of voters with different political orientations, including a wide range of ideas is especially important in order to ensure the party's continuity. Even more important, this new institutional structure and Erdoğan's authoritarian policies raise questions regarding the extent to which the party will be able to implement policies that require intense negotiations and conflict resolution within the party and beyond, such as the headscarf issue or the status of religious vocational schools.

In short, the party's fast-paced introduction of new legislation is succeeding at the expense of intraparty democracy. The formation of an "impermeable" leadership cadre within the JDP poses critical questions vis-à-vis the party elite's willingness and ability to promote democratic competition and to protect the rights of dissenters. In its current form, the JDP leadership seems to advocate a narrow definition of democracy, one that reduces it to an electoral process and freedom from the state's control and ignores the importance of the deliberative process and the inclusion of dissidents. The JDP elite seeks to secure the *institutional* foundations of a democratic society while ignoring the importance of *agents* in the party and outside that play a crucial role in giving meaning to the institutional reforms. The increasingly vocal dissenting voices raise questions regarding the party's ability to accommodate opposition, incorporate dissenters into its decision-making process, and maintain the broad coalition of support generated by the 1997 and 2001 crises.

CONSERVATIVE DEMOCRACY: THE END OF ISLAMISM IN TURKEY?

While ideologies serve as the main tool or a shortcut for political parties to communicate their positions and attract supporters, according to the 2005 survey only 2.84 percent of those who voted for the JDP in the 2002 elections attributed their support to the party's ideology. What lies behind this finding is the puzzling fact that the JDP did not offer a clear ideological program before the 2002 elections. The JDP embraced its current ideology, conservative democracy, as a brand new ideology after its rise to power. On the face of it, its ideas can be attributed to (1) the distrust of Islam as a political force by Turkey's secular elite and (2) the political learning of the JDP leadership under the Welfare Party. Since its appearance on the Turkish political scene, perhaps because of its vague ideological stances the JDP has been assigned conflicting images. One is rooted in its short history as an Islamic opposition movement to the National Outlook, which promises an original synthesis between Islamic values and democratic ideals. The second image stems from the JDP leadership's long history under the tutelage of the Welfare Party, which suggests their predisposition to extremist ideas. Therefore, while the JDP leadership seeks to define the new terms of Islamic politics, they also need to prove that they are not an antisystemic Islamist party. Erdoğan's own statements exemplify the party's effort to strike a delicate balance:

> My political views have always been in a state of constant evolution. Naturally, I have been profoundly influenced by those that have preceded me... Our party is the product of the continuity of the Turkish national existence. In some western newspapers and publications, my party is described as "an Islamic party" or as "Muslim democrat". These characterizations are not correct. *This is not because we are not Muslim or democrat, but because we believe the two need to be considered in two different contexts*... Turkey wishes to take its "political Magna Carta", which rests on a synthesis between its Muslim identity and modern values, much further by becoming an active leader of the system of

modern values, and thus to provide the world with a new "renaissance" perspective which can be a new source of inspiration.[24]

Ironically, despite the party's claim that it is an authentic product of Turkey's values and that its programs simply mirror these values, *Muhafazakar*, or conservative, is not a conventional marker used in Turkish politics for defining political ideas.[25] In other words, the JDP's "conservative" democracy does not build on a long history of ideological and political discussions, but can be seen as strategic positioning by the leadership with the intent to carve out a new and safe place in Turkey's polarized ideological space. Although the term has now become part of the Turkish political map, its components as a political ideology are still in the making, thereby giving the party the opportunity to bring Islamic values into the political sphere in novel ways.

Perhaps because of its still ambiguous content, the party leadership describes conservative democracy in various ways. Akif Gülle, the JDP deputy chairman, offers one of the most popular explanations of the party's ideology.[26] According to Gülle, the JDP's role in Turkish politics resembles the Kızılay Circle, a key intersection in the heart of the Turkish capital, Ankara. Kızılay remains as one of Turkey's main cultural, educational, and financial districts that attracts many visitors from distinct socioeconomic communities for activities ranging from entertainment to training courses. The people of Mamak (a working-class neighborhood) and Cankaya (a community populated mostly by secular bureaucrats) come to the circle with different vehicles and for different reasons. The JDP's ideology—conservative democracy—is a political view that ensures that everyone will have a place in Kızılay, regardless of the reasons for their presence and their mode of transportation. In this regard conservative democracy serves as a pluralist and inclusive political platform just like Kızılay.

More nuanced explanations of conservative democracy put forth by the party leadership converge on the idea that conservative democracy is not an ideology but reflects an organic synthesis that gives voice to the Turkish people's values and bridges the gap between the state and the people. In the party's first congress Erdoğan introduced the party as a movement that brings the "political wisdom" and the "demands of society" to the politics of Turkey:

> The JDP represents the feelings of our cherished nation in the government of Turkey. This is our mission as a party. Values which constitute these feelings have become and shall continue to be the fundamental

values to form policies. We have achieved a great convergence by opening our door to everyone who embraced the aspirations of the nation. A
sulky and burdensome state shall be eliminated, and will be replaced by
a smiling and capable state. The concept of "a nation for the state" will
not be imposed any longer, and the concept of "a state for the nation"
shall flourish instead. The state shall be prevented from becoming fet-
ters around the legs of the nation which prevents its progress.[27]

Although very appealing, this description of conservative democracy
defines its ultimate end rather than the basic principles that inform it.
Beyond its initial promise of closing the distance between state and society, conservative democracy becomes a highly vague political project.
These popular descriptions of the party's ideology have a very appealing,
inclusive façade, but do not explain the premises of conservative democracy; instead they bring to the fore its aim to be a mass or catchall party.
Missing from these definitions is any discussion of the role the party is
expected to play in the resolution of controversial issues and in formulating new policy options. A coherent ideology requires a clear set of ideas
and the definition of an ideal political order that guides the party's policy choices. In fact, Yalçın Akdoğan, the author of the JDP's ideological
manifesto *Conservative Democracy* and a key political advisor to Erdoğan,
states that "a political movement without a political ideology, line or positioning cannot be expected to have consistent policies."[28] Thus, this con-
flation of electoral strategy and ideology requires us to inquire more
deeply into the principles that inform the JDP's policies.

Nevertheless, the way conservative democracy has been discussed
within the party shows that its role as an anchor for competing political
views is questionable. Opposing Akdoğan's conclusion, many party elite
members seem skeptical of endorsing a clear ideology. Instead, the leadership emphasizes the necessity of "realistic" policies and refrains from
taking any ideological positions. For instance, the party program states
that:

> [o]ur Party is one which aims to offer original and permanent solutions
> to our country's problems, parallel to the world's realities, with the accu-
> mulation of the past and tradition, making public service its basic pur-
> pose, conducting political activities in the platform of the contemporary
> democratic values, rather than ideological platforms. The JDP is not
> and shall not be a party forcing ideologies or distributing favors. The
> most important aspect of this program is that it does not include rheto-
> ric, which cannot be converted to action. Its correctness; realism and
> applicability are the salient characteristics of our Party's policies.

The emphasis on "real politics" creates greater maneuverability for the JDP with respect to political decisions. It consolidates the party's role in Turkish politics as an ad hoc coalition, raising the question about the party's ability to maintain its support in the face of conflict-ridden issues. In fact, Akdoğan identifies two radical approaches to politics: one creates political communities based on unquestionable allegiances, sect-like, *cemaat*, parties, and the other one creates political "companies" based solely on shared material interests. Both approaches deprive politics of ideas. Adopting conservative democracy as the fulcrum of its ideas allows the JDP to distance itself from both extremes and to present itself as a mass party with conservative roots.[29]

It is not surprising, therefore, that these ostensibly straightforward ideas become highly complicated when applied to specific policy positions. A detailed review of the premises underlying conservative democracy shows some undefined, gray areas. The core of conservative democracy is the idea that the party voices society's collective reason and informs its proposed policies with society's common values. What lies behind this perception is that the party not only assumes the presence of a set of shared social values, but it also claims full knowledge of society's needs and desires. The reification of shared values and full knowledge of values makes the party's ideology self-affirming. By treating national cultural values as the foundation of its political system, the party can present many issue positions as natural choices dictated by collective demand. This view becomes susceptible to authoritarian expansion as the party assumes that it can exercise "collective reasoning" on behalf of the public without making its rationale clear to those it is governing. Revealing potential problems with such reifications, an in-depth reading of the debate on conservative democracy indicates that the JDP's conservatism is a proactive conservatism aimed at protecting and at the same time transforming the current structure. According to Akdoğan, "what we [JDP] understand from conservatism is not the protection of [all] the existing institutions and relationship but *only some of them.* Conservation does not mean being resistant to transformation and progress, but to adjust to changes without losing your *essence.*"[30] One can hardly elicit from this and comparable statements how the party would define this essence, which values are the ones to protect, who will select them, and how the party expects to pursue the selective transformation.

The hybrid nature of conservative democracy further reveals itself in the party leadership's idea that the JDP objects to a blind rejection of tradition and modernity and emphasizes the necessity of reaching a synthesis between the two. It is the promise of this synthesis that constitutes one of the pillars of the party's ideological commitments. The question of how this fusion would be formed points to more ambivalence: "it is necessary to accept modernity in its full extent, especially its progressive pillar of advanced technology, higher education, and urbanization. Nevertheless, its philosophical foundations, individualism, secularism, rationality, and materialism should be first differentiated from their misconceived practices and descriptions, [and only then] must be mixed with local values."[31] Although such prescriptions indicate that modernity and tradition are not necessarily in conflict, they do not address whether and how modernity's philosophical foundation can be adopted selectively. When placed within the ongoing debates vis-à-vis Westernization and modernization, conservative democracy fails to provide an original answer to the perpetual question facing Turkey's Islamists: whether and how local values can be integrated with the practical results of modernity, unless modernity's foundations in individualism and rationality are accepted. If the selective adoption is *viable*, then what aspects of individualism or rationality can be accepted and how?

All in all, despite its crucial role in defining the party's worldview, conservative democracy is a rather ambivalent ideology. Its premises draw on the dichotomies, for example between individual and state, collective values and state values, and offer a questionable selective adaptation process, led by the party, in order to achieve a democratic society. Paradoxically, one can argue that, because of its ambiguities and vague structure, conservative democracy serves three significant purposes: it (1) defines the party's identity in an unthreatening way to the international community; (2) appeases the concerns of the secular public by aligning it with a political tradition that evolved into Turkey's center-right movement; and (3) assures its hard-core constituency that Islam continues to play a major role in the party's policies, as it forms the foundation of the common values that the party seeks to represent. However, because of the very same ambiguities, conservative democracy in its current form (1) is far from being a blueprint for a social transformation project; (2) reduces Islam's political role by introducing a set of innate traditional values; and (3) precludes a debate on the possible ways in which Islam can be incorporated into the Turkish public sphere without being marginalized.

Politics of Avoidance:
The JDP as Interface between Islam and Democracy

A closer look at how the JDP tackles the controversial issues derived from the public role of Islam shows that the party adopts a policy of avoidance by not addressing the issues directly. Sixteen percent of its supporters nonetheless state that the primary reason they voted for the party is its promise to solve sensitive issues. Given the institutional framework of Turkish politics and the secularist constraints, the party's approach to issues salient to its observant women supporters serves as one of the rare areas where we can question how the party positions itself between the nexus of Islam and democracy and its ability to resolve the competing policy demands. Putting the JDP's party organization under the lens of gender reveals a dual structure: (1) the level of national parliamentary representation, where female college professors and lawyers, who joined the party only during or right before the 2002 election, constitute the upper echelon of the party; (2) the party-affiliated provincial organizations, where observant women, who have been part of the movement that brought the JDP to power, play an active role. They form what can be called the lower echelon of the party. The JDP justifies its dual structure as a response to the extant restrictions on the use of Islamic symbols. This binary structure combines those women who attain higher ranks without ascending through the party's internal mechanism with the others who are forced stay in the party's women branches.

At the national level, originally only 13 of the JDP's 384 members of Parliament were women. Two of them have resigned during the party's two-year rule. If we take into account the fact that a majority of the JDP's female MPs got elected thanks to unexpectedly high levels of support in some electoral districts, in spite of their low ranking on the party's preference list, a total of thirteen seats does not reflect deliberate efforts to promote women. In light of the JDP's candidate selection process, it is fair to argue that the current representation of women happens to be a much higher number than the JDP initially targeted.[32] Questions arise not only because of the small number of women representatives, but also because of the configuration of this group. Many of these MPs were asked to join the party during or shortly after its formation; they lack experience in the political arena, and, more importantly they refrain from challenging the leadership on any issue. Corollary to that, they do not form a unified voting block in Parliament, even when issues salient to women are discussed. While the JDP's poor representation of women does not appear to be an exceptional case given the historically very weak representation of women in Turkish politics, the imbalance between the female presence in the party's ranks before and after election makes the JDP's case different. Unlike other parties, the JDP's women partisans play a pivotal role in the campaigns. It is not by coincidence that the party's program declares its commitment to promoting the political status of women in its own organization as well as in Turkish politics.

The second pillar of the JDP's women representation consists of the party's affiliated women's branches. The party requires that all of its local organizations have a separate branch for women members. The branches replicate the organizational structure of the national party and form a nationwide network. According to Selma Kavaf, the current leader of the women's branches, they strive to make their local chapters work as a political academy and prepare women to take a more active role in the near future.[33] However, the JDP's women branches seek to maintain a delicate equilibrium between removing the obstacles from women's active involvement in politics and protecting their traditional roles. The effort to reconcile the restrictions of the existing system, which prevents headscarf-wearing women from taking public office, with traditional norms keeps the JDP's women activists from using their accumulated political capital won during the party's successful election campaign. Despite regular meetings with the party center, the women's branches serve as insular organizations and rarely have a voice in the party's policies.

The dual structure of the party and the lack of organic links between them reveal themselves in the absence of a coherent women's voice within the party, especially in the discussion of controversial issues such as the headscarf issue (that is, removal of the ban on the use of headscarves in the public sphere). A 1997 decision by the Constitutional Court led to the treatment of the turban, a headscarf worn by observant Muslim women, as a religious symbol, thereby prohibiting its use in state-run institutions, including schools and universities. The ban currently prevents many observant women from fully participating in the Turkish public sphere; thus the removal of the ban clearly constitutes one of the most prominent issues for the JDP's constituency. In part because of the absence of a unified, vocal demand and the self-censorship of women's groups, the party avoids tackling the headscarf issue directly. Instead of submitting a bill to Parliament, it addresses the question through other venues.

In the view of the party leadership, the JDP is laying the groundwork for the issue's resolution by eliminating the constraints on the Turkish public sphere in general. The party's current policy is rooted in the presumption that given the lack of institutional consensus the party needs to place the issue into the sphere of civil society, where the problem can be resolved. Consequently, party leaders argue that it is women's groups who are primarily responsible for actively seeking a civil society consensus for abolishing the headscarf ban. Given the limited political sphere in the country, international institutions such as the European Court of Human Rights are also expected to facilitate a domestic solution. Various cases pertaining to the restriction of religious rights in the public sphere are before the court, and a favorable decision would set a precedent that would lead to the revocation of the ban. In policy areas where the party faces fewer constraints, it exercises its legislative power. Newly adopted laws such as the recent students' "Amnesty" bill promise to gradually restore the rights of women with headscarves. The bill allows students who were expelled from universities on academic or disciplinary grounds after June 29, 2000, to continue their studies. According to some observers, 677,000 students, of whom 270,000 are headscarf victims, will benefit from the amnesty and resume their studies.[34]

One might argue that Turkey's strict secular rule makes the headscarf issue an exceptional problem and does not allow us to gauge the party's policies. In fact, the headscarf issue lies at the heart of the conflict between the proponents of a limited role of Islam in the public sphere and those who advocate unconstrained religious expression. The JDP finds itself in a minefield and calibrates its rhetoric to represent the marginalized observant women without being considered an Islamist party. Reflecting the party's commitment not to challenge established policies and institutions directly, Erdoğan himself compares objections to the decisions of the state-affiliated institutions (for example, the constitutional courts, the Court of High Appeals, the National Security Council) to arguing with a referee at a football game in order to make the referee change one of his decisions: "Even if you are right," Erdoğan states, "there is no example that a referee reverses his decision. Likewise, it is futile to argue with the state's institutions."[35] If this is the case, however, we should be able to find policies that enhance women's representation and involvement both within the ranks of the party and in national politics in areas where the JDP's policies are not scrutinized by secular publics.

A review of JDP's policies beyond the headscarf issue reveals that the JDP's policies cannot be simply attributed to the secularist constraints. As the reforms adopted by the party have rarely been subject to public debate, it is rather difficult to pin down the party's overall vision and specifically its ideas on how to change gender roles. The party's main ideological document, *Conservative Democracy*, refers to "woman" five times, and only in the context of how their liberation is important, but without providing any framework as to what roles and positions women are to occupy in its idealized society. Perhaps because of this omission, the JDP leadership's attempt to criminalize adultery in the New Penal Code drew intense interest as a venue to understand the party's gender-related policies. According to the JDP leadership, the proposal was introduced in response to the demands of traditional women. For Erdoğan, such protection would benefit "deceived" women most, and it was a step aimed at preserving human honor.[36]

In a striking contrast to the party's expectation, however, the proposal ignited nationwide protests. A majority of women's groups, Islamist and secular alike, opposed the law, contending that criminalizing adultery could bring more harm to women, especially in eastern Turkey, where honor killings, the murder of women suspected of dishonoring their families through sexual conduct, is still not uncommon.[37] Although the party's rhetoric was put under scrutiny, Erdoğan did not hesitate to characterize the protesters as belonging to marginal groups who do not represent "the true Turkish women." Although the bill was withdrawn, the discussion raised serious question as to the party's presumed knowledge of Turkey's core values, which it has claimed to represent, and the meaning of these values. The adultery debate suggested that despite its staunch commitment to the liberalization of the political and economic spheres, the party is likely to subsume some traditional authoritarian and patriarchal values under the "traditional values" to be protected. Rather than allowing an open, public debate on these values, the party appears to have a tendency to claim a monopoly on defining them. The configuration of these values and the party's ability to define them became more controversial as the party appeared to have changed its position on the law on adultery not because of domestic negotiation and deliberation but as a result of the international community's pressure.

What makes the JDP's indirect approach to issues derived from Islam more questionable is that its ambivalent policies affect areas that do not fall into the sensitive intersection of gender and Islam. For instance, the JDP's approach to the status of religious vocational schools further illustrates the party's intricate strategy in addressing the public role of Islam. The JDP first introduced a bill in Parliament that sought to grant students of religious vocational schools better access to higher education. The current practice restricts the areas of study for graduates of the vocational schools at the college level. Vocational schools in general are mostly attended by lower-middle-class students, and the bill would grant the schools' graduates access to higher education equal to graduates of other schools. The secular public and the Council of Higher Education perceived the bill as a pretext for increasing the popularity of religious vocational schools, and President Ahmet Necdet Sezer vetoed it. According to current constitutional rules, the prime minister could have resubmitted the bill to the president for signature, and the bill would eventually have become law without the president's approval. The government decided to drop the bill, however, and thereby violated the JDP's campaign promise to ensure better access to higher education for graduates of religious vocational schools. Erdoğan himself is a graduate of this type of school, and his explanation as to why the bill was dropped captures the paradox of the JDP's policies: "the parents of those who sent their children to the vocational schools did not support the issue enough. The society did not stand up against the pressure. We could have sent the bill twice. But are you ready to pay the price? There is a price attached to it. As a government we are not ready yet to pay the price."[38] This incident and similar ones (for example, the attempts to solve the turban issue, criminalize adultery, provide student amnesty) point to a strategy whereby the party sends reminders to its core constituency that it takes their sensitivities seriously and seeks to offer solutions.[39] However, when the policies fail, then the party points to the insufficient involvement by civil society or traditional groups as reason for the failure, even though the party allows civil society only a limited role in the policy-making process. As a result the party's policies regarding the public role of Islam in general and women's representation in particular are marked by incongruous approaches. The party's gender policies constitute one of the most potent areas where the party has an opportunity to offer novel solutions and bring the public appearance of Islam into the public debate. Yet it is in this area that the party refrains from offering clear policies and discussing the issue of tradition and gender roles directly. The extent to which this approach is a function of the secularist institutions or the party's own priorities needs to be examined carefully. It is important to note that on several occasions, when the party leadership has had the opportunity to promote women's rights, its election-driven policies and its reluctance to change the traditional practices that disadvantage women seem to have taken precedence over women's rights. In the recent March 2004 local elections, the party used local popularity polls as the main candidate selection criteria, thereby failing to challenge the traditional patriarchal profile of the local political elite. Although the party's landslide success was assured before the elections, the party did not use the opportunity to increase its women's representation. The party consistently fails to challenge traditional local political structures in order to win elections.

What makes the JDP's contradictory policies toward women more puzzling is the complacency of the JDP-affiliated women's groups. Paradoxically, women's groups accept the JDP's current policies on the grounds that the party leadership is confined by the existing secular structure. This tacit consent further encourages the women's groups to treat today's politics as a transitional stage and to lower their expectations. Women remain silent even in cases where party policies have significantly impaired their chances. In fact, women's groups have rarely confronted the party center for its failure to enforce the party's policy of reserving 20 percent of local leadership positions for women. The party tolerates a sharp contrast between accepting violations of the party's own rules with respect to the advancement of women and the strict punishment of those party organizations that fail to win the election. In the aftermath of the March elections, the party center asked the leaders of eleven of its provincial organizations to resign, because of their failure in local elections, yet no sanction has been imposed on those who have consistently ignored the 20 percent female representation rule. To exacerbate the situation further, the same general lack of opposition emerges when we look at civil society's position vis-à-vis the JDP's policies. For instance, although 58.9 percent of the Turkish electorate finds the JDP's current policies on the headscarf unsuccessful, there has been no overt opposition to the party's current policies.

CONCLUSION

The JDP's success is grounded in a broad coalition of support that formed as a by-product of Turkey's failing polarized pluralist system and the political apathy induced by it. The JDP successfully translated this support into institutional reforms that promise to remove many obstacles on the way to a liberal Turkish democracy. An assessment of the JDP's contribution to Turkey's democracy and to closing the democratic gap in the Muslim world first and foremost necessitates a clear differentiation between the minimalist understanding of democracy as a system of competitive elections and a maximalist definition in which all agents of the democratic game enjoy basic individual rights and liberties. Although the first is necessary, it is not a sufficient condition of liberal democracy.

Therefore the JDP's political success yields two different results. There is no question that an institutional framework that provides all members of the polity with open and free access to political competitions and decision-making processes is the sine qua non of liberal democracy. In this regard, the JDP-initiated silent revolution has radically altered the landscape of Turkish politics. Significant gains toward liberalizing the Turkish public sphere have been made, especially in areas where restrictions on ethnic rights or persistent economic inefficiencies existed because of state-centered structures.

The quest for reform, unleashed by Turkey's pro-Islamic party, has earned the JDP a unique status in Turkish politics: it has successfully loosened the state's tight grip in many areas and has decentralized the Turkish political system. Nevertheless, liberal democracy requires more than an institutional framework. The main ingredients of democracy and the function of politics in a liberal democracy include active participants, and the opportunity for contestation and negotiation in areas where conflicts are present. What makes the JDP's reforms and its practice of politics uncertain is that the party forgoes important democratic processes. It is the crucial process of public debate, the involvement of individuals and civil society organizations that are absent from the formulation of these new institutions and rules. Furthermore, when we look beyond the JDP's effective reforms, we see a complicated picture.

As a political party and an agent of social transformation, the JDP reveals ambivalence. In its current form, the party's anchor, conservative democracy, appears to be an ideological marker chosen to define the party's ideology for others rather than to guide its policies. Its sufficiently ambiguous content serves to preserve the broad coalition of supporters brought together by the centrifugal forces of Turkish politics. Nevertheless, the second phase of JDP rule, the implementation of reforms, makes clarification of the JDP's ideas and the presence of a coherent map of its ideas more critical than ever. Addressing the concerns regarding the elusive nature of conservative democracy, Akdoğan contends that the JDP has not completed its evolution yet, and it is still an ongoing process. While this statement at first suggests that the party will clarify some of its paradoxical positions, we are immediately warned that "[the JDP] could not define the final form of this evolution by its own will. With the belief that an Islamic movement cannot be pursued in the political sphere, the party seeks to define itself to the center right."[40] Who defines the direction of the party's change, the context or the collective efforts of party elite, activists, and supporters raises an important question. The party's transformation so far has revealed the emergence of a narrow hierarchical party structure and the lack of well-defined ideological foundations and political direction. On the one hand, the European Union's progress reports often define the policy agendas of the party. On the other hand, the elusive idea of "traditional values," when coupled with the party's claim to have innate knowledge of them, justifies the party's policies. This ideological hollowness together with the party's transformation toward a leader-centered party limits the JDP's capacity to address and successfully resolve conflicts.

Behind the increasing disconnect between its initial promise and its current practices lies the party's ambivalent approach to Islam. The absence of a straightforward discussion of Islam in conservative democracy suggests that despite its clear Islamic roots, the centrality of Islam to its overall rhetoric, and the dominance of Islamic groups in its constituency, the party shies away from addressing issues pertaining to Islam. In a paradoxical way, the party's policies attempt to reinstate Islam in the public sphere without addressing the public role of religion explicitly. One might interpret the JDP's current approach to Islam as a strategy that seeks to ensure the restitution of Islam's political power in the long run by first relegating Islam to the private sphere. This approach requires that the party focus on strengthening individual rights in the expectation that this will resolve Islam-related issues. It is this teleological approach that further consolidates today's ongoing process of decoupling politics and Islam. The party seems to avoid the question of whether the public and individual aspects of Islam can be separated from each other. More important, by reducing the role of Islam in the public sphere to the question of better representation of traditional values, the party creates a crucial ideological vacuum in its political discourse that reifies Islam as an ambiguous set of values.

This politics of Islam without Islam suggests that unless the party clearly addresses the public role of Islam, its silence on Islam cannot be taken for a reconciliation of Islam and democracy. In other words, the party has established itself as a pro-Islamic party without any overt association to, or discussion of, Islam. This ironical relationship reminds us of the JDP's predecessors' relationship to Islam and the state's secularist ideology, Kemalism. Despite their overt opposition to Kemalist nationalism, the National Outlook parties went through a political secularization by limiting the role of *Nakşibendis*, a prominent religious sect in Turkey under their shelter, and acquiring an increasingly nationalist and developmentalist tone in their political ideology. Borrowing M. Hakan Yavuz's term, the Nationalist-view parties eventually became advocates of a form of "Green Kemalism."[41] Despite their efforts to revise the narrow definition of Kemalist secularism, these parties gradually transformed their agenda, mirroring the premises of Kemalism by attributing a central role to the state and its redistributive policies, not only in the economic but also in the *cultural* sphere, thereby failing to offer a novel political project that addresses the public role of Islam in a democratic polity.[42]

Despite the critical juncture at which it is located, the JDP's current policies do not seem to resolve the long-standing, intricate, and paradoxical relationship between Islam, the state, and secularism. Rather than repositioning Islam as a novel political force, the JDP seems to replicate the Kemalists' mode of politics and approach to Islam. Like Kemalist secularists before, the JDP elite has adopted a Jacobean, top-to-bottom reform project to liberalize the public at the expense of the public's contribution. Islamic values have been reified and their reflections in politics have been subsumed under a highly precarious notion of "collective values and reasoning"—resonating with the Kemalist idea of national will, *milli irade*. In the JDP's practice and rhetoric, Islam's role is reduced to a role at the individual level. The JDP elite's feeble efforts to formulate novel policies to advance the position of observant women specifically, and Turkish women in general, point out another underlying paradox. The party's rhetorical commitment to advancing the political status of women, its consent to maintaining the status quo, and, more important, its acceptance of the symbolic association between women with headscarves and one's commitment to Islamic values, contradicts the party's initial promises to resolve the conflicts that marginalize women. Perhaps more striking, the JDP's policies regarding women's representation in general show that it avoids challenging the lingering effect of the republican tradition that reduced the image of women to a political symbol instead of an important political agent of transformation. Finally, the JDP's core view, conservative democracy, assumes the role of redefining Turkey's local values against the foil of a universal conservative framework and justifies its political reform agenda by this global political stance. Nevertheless, given that conservatism is far from being a coherent political program, the party seems to be repeating the cardinal sin of the republican elite by failing to define how the public role of Islam can be incorporated into Turkish politics without relying on an externally defined model of political transformation.

To conclude, the JDP's policies have proved very successful in the short term, but the party seems to be increasingly undermining its own power and long-term contribution to Turkey's democracy as a pro-Islamic party by its politics of avoidance. The absence of open debates on the public role of Islam manifests itself in dual policies that are rather precarious. These dual policies maximize the party's immediate political appeal, while they carry the risk of dissatisfying the expectations of the party's pro-Islamic constituency as well as those of the secular public in the long run. In fact, the lack of clarity in the JDP's policies generates disproportionately high criticism undermining the party's image both as a pro-Islamist and as a democratic party. The increasingly visible detachment between the party's commitment and its practices places the party at the very crossroads that it has striven to avoid. However, only when the JDP moves from "politics of avoidance" and top-down reforms at the expense of public debate to "politics of open debate and consensus forming" by openly addressing the public role of Islam can it serve as a model of a pro-Islamic democratic party. Otherwise, it is likely to become another short-lived spark in Turkish politics, created by the political context, and it will miss out on the opportunity to forge a genuinely democratic pro-Islamic party that can serve as a model in the Muslim world.

NOTES

1. For different accounts of the 2002 elections, see Soli Özel, "Turkey at the Polls: After the Tsunami," *Journal of Democracy* 14, no. 2 (2003): 80–94; Ziya Öniş and Fuat Keyman, "Turkey at the Polls: A New Path Emerges," *Journal of Democracy* 14, no. 2 (2003): 95–107; Simten Coşan and Aylin Özman, "Center-right Politics in Turkey after the November 2002 General Election: Neo-Liberalism with a Muslim Face," *Contemporary Politics* 10, no. 1 (2004): 57–74.

2. For the details of the laws, visit www.tbmm.gov.tr.

3. Graham E. Fuller, "Turkey's Strategic Model: Myths and Realities," *Washington Quarterly* 27, no. 3 (2004); Fareed Zakaria, *Newsweek*, October 2004.

4. The fieldwork on which this analysis is based was made possible by the support provided by the United States Institute of Peace and the University of Illinois at Chicago. The survey sample includes 1,016 national representatives of the Turkish electorate. The questionnaire was designed by the author and included 120 questions pertaining to the assessment of Turkish politics in general and the policies of the Justice and Development Party in particular. The face-to-face interviews were conducted by trained interviewers, lasting about 45 minutes each. All of the findings regarding the public perceptions reported in this study are derived from this survey.

5. For instance, the Nationalist Action Party, which received 18 percent in the 1999 election and became one of the major coalition partners, failed to pass the national threshold of 10 percent in the 2002 election. For a more systematic analysis of party fragmentation in Turkey, see Cem Baslevent, Hasan Kirmanoglu, and Burhan Senatalar, "Voter Profiles and Fragmentation in the Turkish Party System," *Party Politics* 10 (2004): 307–24.

6. There is a genre of studies that explains the transformation of this tension between the center and periphery. For instance, see Şerif Mardin, *Religion and Social Change in Modern Turkey: The Case of Bediüzzaman Said Nursi* (Albany: State University of New York Press, 1989); M. Hakan Yavuz, *Islamic Political Identity in Turkey* (New York: Oxford University Press, 2003).

7. Two competing business associations, TÜSİAD and MÜSİAD, capture how the Turkish industrialists' elite has been transformed since the mid-1980s, after Turkey adopted policies to enhance the Turkish market economy. TÜSİAD (founded in 1971) represents the Western-oriented, large-firm business elite, whose members include the chief executives of Turkey's three hundred biggest corporations. MÜSİAD (founded in 1990) represents conservative religious, peripheral, or provincial businessmen, ranging from small business owners to large industrial enterprises. The first three letters of its acronym, "MÜS," are commonly perceived as the indicator of their "Muslim" rather than their "müstakil" (independent) identity. According to its 2004 reports, MÜSİAD membership is currently around five thousand. For a more detailed discussion of MÜSİAD, see Ayşe Buğra, "Class, Culture, and State: An Analysis of Interest Representation by Two Turkish Business Associations," *International Journal of Middle East Studies* 30, no. 4 (1998): 521–539; and Ziya Öniş, "The Political Economy of Turkey's Justice and Development Party," *Social Science Research Network*, 2004.

8. Fuat Keyman, "Türkiye'de Laiklik Sorunu'nu Dusunmek; Modernite, Sekulerlesme, Demokratiklesme (Thinking about the Problem of Laicism: Modernity, Secularization and Democratization)," *Doğu Bati*, no. 23, 2003.

9. For a review of how the role of Islam has been conceptualized in Turkey, see Mustafa Erdoğan, "Islam in Turkish Politics: Turkey's Quest for Democracy without Islam," *Liberal Dusunce* 4, no. 14 (1999): 103–17.

10. The Motherland Party received 19.6 percent while the True Path Party received 19.1 percent.

11. Neither being in charge of the coalition government nor the insistent critiques of the government's policies by the secular elite moderated the Welfare Party's rhetoric. On the contrary, the party's policies put it in direct conflict with the existing state structure and status-quo policies in three policy areas: (1) the Welfare Party continued to denounce Turkish secularism as a tool to suppress Islam, to deprive Turkey of its moral foundations, and to marginalize religious groups. (2) Erbakan questioned Turkey's efforts to join the European Union (EU), arguing that the EU's conflicting policies created "obstacles just for Turkey" that masked the EU's unwillingness to accept the country. (3) The party also diverged from Turkey's commitment to be part of the Western world and sought to create alternative international organizations. An economic coordination project, Developing-8, that included Bangladesh, Egypt, Indonesia, Iran, Malaysia, Nigeria, and Pakistan was introduced to form an international coalition among major Muslim countries. Erbakan introduced the Developing-8 idea during a seminar on "Cooperation in Development," held in Istanbul in October 1996. The D-8 envisioned cooperation among countries from regions stretching from Southeast Asia to Africa. The D-8 was formally established on June 15, 1997.

12. Cevik Bir, deputy chief of staff, explained the rationale of the coup and the blurred lines of the military's approach to secularism in the following way: "For almost 15 years we [the Turkish military] gave first priority to fighting the PKK [the Kurdish separatist army that is fighting a guerrilla war in southeastern Turkey]. No one said that

was politics. Now we are giving first priority to anti-secular activities, and the Erbakan government is very upset. They say it is not our responsibility to deal with these issues. But we see the Republic in danger, so we must act." Stephen Kinzer, "Turkish Generals Raise Pressure on Premier," *New York Times*, June 13, 1997.

13. Policy implementation seemed to have halted, especially with respect to the reconstruction of the banking sector. For instance, the reform package called for a new Board of Banking Regulation and Supervision as the first step toward reforming the banking system. A five-month delay in the appointment of the board suggested that the newly appointed board would be susceptible to political influences. To exacerbate the economic speculations, the full details of the adjustment program were never systematically publicized.

14. For a more detailed analysis see Ziya Öniş, "Domestic Politics Versus Global Dynamics: Towards a Political Economy of the 2000–2001 Financial Crises in Turkey," in *The Turkish Economy in Crisis*, ed. Barry Rubin and Ziya Öniş (London: Frank Cass, 2003).

15. On February 19, after the National Security Council meeting, the prime minister declared that there was a deep difference of opinion between him and the president. On this news, the overnight interest rate jumped to 2,058 percent on February 20, followed by 4,019 percent on the next day. The dollar exchange rate jumped to 958,000 lira from a level of 685,000 lira. The undersecretary of the Treasury and the governor of the Central Bank resigned, followed by the replacement of the economy minister. For more details see Fatih Ozatay, "Banking Sector Fragility and Turkey's 2000–01 Financial Crisis," *Brookings Trade Forum*, 2002, 121–60.

16. Turkish law requires eligible voters to participate in elections; therefore, those who do not vote risk financial punishment.

17. The court concluded that Erdoğan's recitation of the lines of a poem represented an invitation to conflict, drawing on religious values. For an account of the court decision and its impact on Erdoğan, see Ruşen Çakir and Fehmi Çalmuk, *1980 Sonrasi Islami Hareket, Recep Tayyip Erdoğan (Bir Dönüsüm Öyküsü* (Islamic Movement After 1980: Tayyip Erdoğan A Story of Transformation) (Istanbul: Metis Yayınları, 2001).

18. The JDP Party Program, www.akparti.org.

19. The council led by Nur Dogan Topolaglu does not divulge any information regarding the cases it covers. It has been reported, however, that it has reviewed only a limited number of cases. Given the low profile of the council among the JDP members, one can argue that it has become a symbolic intraparty institution as well. Personal interview with Nur Dogan Topolaglu, May 2004.

20. Yalcınbayır lost his position because of his outspoken opposition to the party's Iraq policies. For a more detailed discussion of the Iraqi crisis in Turkey, see Murat Yetkin, *Tezkere* (Istanbul: Remzi Kitabevi, 2004).

21. The recent election of the Speaker of Parliament stirred some debate within the party. Erdoğan declared his candidate as the incumbent. Yarbay Ersonmez officially signed a petition to have the Constitutional Court determine the constitutionality of Erdoğan's nomination to the position of Speaker of Parliament. According to Yarbay, Erdoğan violated the rules by declaring the current Speaker of Parliament as the party's only candidate.

22. NTV News, "Ex-Tourism Minister Claims AKP Excluded Him," February 16, 2005.

23. Larry Diamond and Richard Gunther, eds., *Political Parties and Democracy* (Baltimore: Johns Hopkins University Press, 2001).

24. Tayyip Erdoğan, from his speech given at the Center for Strategic International Studies on December 9, 2002.

25. Mir Dengir Mehmet Firat, *Uluslararasi Muhafazakarlık ve Demokrasi Sempozyumu* (International Symposium on Conservatism and Democracy) (Ankara: AK Parti, 2004), 20.

26. Personal interview with Akif Gülle, June 2004.

27. The text of the speech can be viewed at www.akparti.org.tr.

28. Yalçın Akdoğan, *Muhafazakar Demokrasi* (Conservative Democracy) (Ankara: AK Parti, 2003), 5.

29. Ibid.

30. Ibid., 128.

31. Ibid., 133.

32. According to the Turkish electoral rules, parties rank order their candidates in each electoral district. When the votes of the district are distributed among parties, these lists are used to assign the seats.

33. Personal interview with Selma Kavaf, the head of JDP Women Branches, July 2004.

34. The quote is cited in Ali Bulaç, "Final Solution to Headscarf Issue," *Zaman*, February 26, 2005.

35. Interview with Tayyip Erdoğan, NTV, October 2003.

36. "Erdoğan: Adultery Law Protects Deceived Women," Ankara, *Zaman*, August 9, 2004.

37. For more details see Helena Smith, "Turkey Split by Plan to Criminalize Adultery," *The Guardian*, September 6, 2004; Susan Sachs, "Adultery a Crime? The Turks Think Again and Say No," *New York Times*, September 15, 2004.

38. Recep Tayyip Erdoğan, "The Parents Who Sent Their Children to Vocational Schools Did not Pay Enough Attention" (Meslek Liselerinde Yavrularını Okutanlar Duruma Sahip Cıkamadılar), *Milliyet*, July 3, 2004.

39. What popularly came to be known as the Student Amnesty Law was approved on March 18, 2005. The law granted amnesty to students expelled from universities. According to some estimates, up to a quarter of a million students could benefit from the amnesty, including women expelled from public universities for wearing traditional headscarves during classes.

40. Yalçın Akdoğan, "Adalet ve Kalkınma Partisi" (Justice and Development Party) in *Islamcılık*, ed. Yasin Aktay (Istanbul: Iletişim, 2004), 629.

41. M. Hakan Yavuz, "Milli Görüş Hareketi; Muhalif Modernist Hareket (National Outlook Movement: An Oppositional Modernist Movement), in Aktay, *Islamcılık*, 600.

42. Ibid., 597.

CHAPTER 6

Reinterpretation of Secularism in Turkey
The Case of the Justice and Development Party

■ *Ahmet T. Kuru*

INTRODUCTION

On September 20, 2004, Turkish President A. Necdet Sezer stood before a symposium on religion and proclaimed, "Secularism is a way of life, which should be adopted by an individual. A 'secular individual' should confine religion in the sacred place of his conscience and not allow his belief to affect this world." While seemingly an ordinary statement, these words rang through the halls of the meeting for in that room sat two important figures from the Justice and Development Party (JDP)—Turkish Prime Minister Recep Tayyip Erdoğan and Speaker of Parliament Bülent Arınç. Both men, in their speeches, stressed, in contrast to the president, that secularism is a constitutional regime for the state, not a required ideology for individuals.[1] The debate on the "secular individual" between these politicians is not just a mere rhetorical debate. Rather, it is an extension of the broader ongoing conflict in Turkey's political arena, which pits the Kemalist elite against rightist parties in general and the JDP in particular.[2] The Kemalists have, generally implicitly, criticized the JDP for being antisecular and for preserving a secret agenda to replace the secular state with an Islamic one. To what extent is it a valid critique? Is the JDP an antisecular Islamist party?

In this chapter, I argue that the JDP is not antisecular, yet it defends a distinct interpretation of secularism that differs from that of the Kemalist establishment. The debate between the establishment and the JDP is not simply a conflict between secularism and Islamism, but rather a discussion over the true meaning and practice of secularism itself. Apart from marginal groups, there is an overall consensus on secularism in Turkey. The real debate occurs between the supporters of different interpretations of secularism.

I will first provide a conceptual framework based on a typology of secularism. The next section will be an historical framework to trace the roots of the current struggle on secularism. Then I will analyze the transformation of pro-Islamic groups' conceptions of secularism in Turkey. Finally, I will examine the debate between the JDP and the Kemalist elite, particularly on the issues of the headscarf, the İmam Hatip (Islamic) vocational schools, and the Qur'an courses.

Two Types of Secularism

Secularism is not one monolithic concept that has a standard meaning; rather, there are varying types of secularism with distinct normative backgrounds and policy implications. In this essay, I will develop two conceptions of secularism: passive secularism and assertive secularism. Passive secularism implies state neutrality toward various religions and allows the public visibility of religion. Assertive secularism, on the other hand, means that the state favors a secular worldview in the public sphere and aims to confine religion to the private sphere.[3] Passive secularism opposes any established doctrine that defines the "good" for its citizens, either religious or nonreligious, whereas assertive secularism regards secularism itself as an established doctrine to be promoted.[4]

I use passive and assertive modes of secularism as "ideal types" (à la Max Weber) that help analyze complex concrete cases through abstract modeling. As Jean Baubérot emphasizes, "Indeed, there is no absolute secularism. In each country and regarding each domain, secularism is relative, mixed with other elements of the social life and certain historical traditions."[5] The practices of secularism in secular states generally vary between these two ideal types.

The United States, France, and Turkey are three constitutionally secular states where the state constitution does not contain any specific reference to a particular religion.[6] Yet they have pursued different policies toward religion. State-religion relations in the United States have leaned toward passive secularism, whereas in France and Turkey the state has inclined toward assertive secularism. As an example of this distinction, there is strong official public visibility of religion in the United States that does not exist in France or Turkey.[7] In the United States, the motto that appears on all coins and printed money is "In God we trust"; the pledge of allegiance read by schoolchildren includes the statement "one nation, under God"; many official oaths, including the swearing-in of the president, customarily contain the statement "So help me God" and are made

FIGURE 6.1. The Continuum Between Two Ideal Types of Secularism

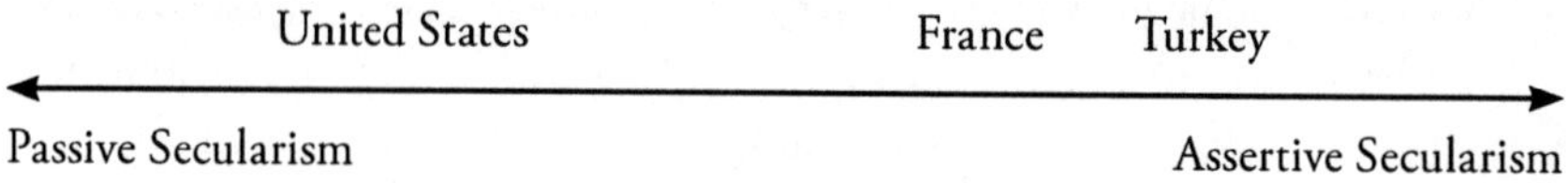

United States		France	Turkey

Passive Secularism   Assertive Secularism

by placing the left hand on a Bible; and the Supreme Court's sessions start with the invocation "God save the United States and this Honorable Court."[8]

Another example is these three states' different policies toward students' display of religious symbols, particularly the headscarf, in public schools. Figure 6.1 shows how these states' policies diverge on this issue through a continuum between the two "ideal types." The United States leans toward passive secularism, accepting the public visibility of students' religious symbols. The French state moderately resembles the ideal type of assertive secularism by prohibiting students' displays of religious symbols only in public schools. The Turkish state is closest to assertive secularism since it bans headscarves in all educational institutions, either school or university, public or private.[9]

My typology of secularism is helpful for analyzing variations not only among states, but also within states. In Turkey, despite the dominance of assertive secularist state practices, there is an ongoing debate on the true meaning and practices of secularism. I call this debate a struggle between the supporters of existing assertive secularism and those of a new shift toward passive secularism. The first group is mainly composed of the Kemalist establishment, including President Sezer, the main opposition (Republican People's Party, RPP), a majority of the Constitutional Court members, and military generals, whereas the second group involves rightist political parties such as the JDP.

Several scholars have also recognized this debate and criticized the Turkish state's rigidly secular practices as "*laikçilik*" (secularist ideology), different from the true "*laiklik*" (secularism).[10] The main problem of this categorization is its extreme normative stand that denies the legitimacy of assertive secularism. A much less normative categorization defines the first type as "laicism" and the second as "secularism."[11] Yet this categorization overemphasizes the difference between these two types as two different kinds of regimes, ignoring their substantial commonality: lack of religious control in legal and judicial processes, and official neutrality toward religions. My typology based on "passive" and assertive" types explains the distinct meanings of secularism without being extremely normative or overemphasizing the difference between these types. The following sections will employ this typology to analyze the Turkish case.

HISTORICAL FRAMEWORK

The founders of the Republic of Turkey, M. Kemal Atatürk (1881–1938) and his cadre, established secularism as the main pillar of the new state. They implemented several reforms to secularize not only the state structure, but also society. In addition to making secularism a constitutional principle and creating a totally secular legal structure, they pursued certain social reforms, particularly abolishing religious schools and monopolizing education through secular state schools and universities. During the single-party rule (1923–50) of the RPP, the party leaned toward assertive secularism by advocating the confinement of religion in individual conscience (*vicdan*) as a private issue.[12] The multiparty elections of 1950, however, started a debate on secularism. The new ruling party—Democrat Party (DP)—provided more religious freedom to society. As an example, it abolished the ban against the Arabic *ezan* (call to prayer) in the mosques. From the 1950s to the 1990s, the pro-Islamic groups defended three general views on secularism.

The liberal view. The supporters of this view were aiming to liberalize practices of the secular Turkish state. Their objective could be defined, in my terminology, as the replacement of existing assertive secularism with a more passive secularism. The central-right parties, including the DP (1946–60), the Justice Party (JP) (1961–81), the Motherland Party (MP) (1983–), and the True Path Party (TPP) (1983–), generally defended this position. One of the ideologues of this view was Ali Fuad Başgil (1893–1967), who was a senator of the JP and the dean of the Law School at Istanbul University. According to Başgil, the Muslims in Turkey should ask only one favor from the secular state (like Diogenes the Cynic asked from Alexander): "Gölge etme, başka ihsan istemem" [Stand from between me and the sun].[13]

The ascetic view. Islamic movements and communities generally tended to keep silent about secularism and preferred to focus on religious services, such as teaching the Qur'an to youth and opening dormitories for students. They avoided politics in an ascetic manner. One of the most influential of these groups was the faith-based Nur movement. Bediüzzaman Said Nursi (1876–1960), the founder of the Nur movement and the author of the *Risale-i Nur Külliyatı* (an interpretation of the Qur'an),[14] emphasized the ascetic position as the following: "Ninety-nine percent of

Islam is about ethics, worship, the hereafter, and virtue. Only one percent is about politics; leave that to the rulers."[15] He also added, "I seek refuge in God from Satan and politics."[16]

The Islamist view. The major political Islamist movement in Turkey until the late 1990s was the Milli Görüş (National Outlook) movement initiated by Necmettin Erbakan. Despite their Islamist rhetoric, Erbakan and his followers generally avoided direct criticism of secularism. They founded the National Order Party in 1970 and the National Salvation Party in 1972. Both parties were accused of being antisecular and disbanded following the military coup d'états of 1971 and 1980. In 1983, Erbakan founded the Welfare Party (WP). In the 1995 national elections, the WP received 21.4 percent of the votes and became the leading party. Erbakan became the prime minister in 1996 in the WP-TPP coalition. The WP opposed Turkey's membership in the EU[17] and led the foundation of an international organization among eight Muslim countries: Developing-Eight (D-8).[18]

Following the "soft" military coup d'état on February 28, 1997, the WP-TPP coalition collapsed, and the WP was dissolved by the Turkish Constitutional Court. The February 28 Process was destructive for Islamic education and practicing Muslims in Turkey. In that period, the headscarf was strictly banned at universities, the İmam Hatip secondary schools were closed, and teaching the Qur'an to children under age twelve became illegal. The military expelled allegedly Islamist and avowedly pious officers. In addition, pro-Islamic corporations and financial institutions faced official discrimination.[19] These oppressions ignited a transformation in pro-Islamic groups in terms of their views of Turkey's EU membership, democracy, and secularism.[20] The JDP became a leading actor in this transformation as explained in the following section.

CHANGING MUSLIM PERSPECTIVES TOWARD SECULARISM

Following the February 28 coup, pro-Islamic groups recognized that religious freedoms should be their main priority. Pro-Islamic politicians, movements, and intellectuals have tended to embrace democracy and passive secularism to be protected from the oppression of the assertive secularist state. That meant a convergence between the above-mentioned three groups: *ascetics* and political *Islamists* decided to support a *liberal* version of secularism—what I call passive secularism.

Ali Bulaç, an influential Islamist thinker, declared that "political" Islamism was dead. He called for a new "civil" Islamism, which did not contradict secularism as a political regime.[21] Along the same line, the influential Gülen movement abandoned its indifference and participated in the debate on secularism. The movement initiated by Fethullah Gülen has focused on education and opened more than four hundred schools in about fifty different countries, in addition to its international media network. This movement avoided political issues, including secularism, following Nursi's teaching.[22] Yet in the late 1990s, the Journalists and Writers' Foundation affiliated with the Gülen movement began to organize the Abant Workshops to head off sociopolitical polarization and to search for a new social consensus in Turkey. The annual workshops have included about fifty Turkish intellectuals from sharply different ideological backgrounds. The first workshop in 1998 was devoted to Islam and secularism. Its press declaration emphasized that God's ontological sovereignty is compatible with the political sovereignty of the people. The second workshop also examined the relationships among state, society, and religion.[23]

The young generation of the National Outlook Movement also transformed their ideological framework. Several of them have participated in the Abant Workshops to discuss issues such as secularism. In 2000, three leaders of the young generation—Erdoğan, Arınç, and Abdullah Gül—emphasized their prodemocratic and prosecular ideas.[24] Following the closure of their party, the WP's parliamentarians founded the Virtue Party (VP). Despite the VP's pro-EU and democratic discourse,[25] Turkey's Constitutional Court dissolved it in 2001 as well, arguing that the VP defended the freedom to wear a headscarf and therefore was antisecular. That action deepened the disagreement between the elders of the National Outlook Movement led by Erbakan, and the young generation led by Erdoğan. The former founded the Felicity Party (FP), whereas the latter established the JDP. The FP made a return to anti-EU discourse whereas the JDP took a step further to defend Turkey's membership in the EU, as well as to support democracy and secularism. In the elections of November 3, 2002, the FP was marginalized with 2.5 percent of the national votes while the JDP became the leading party with 34 percent of the votes.

The JDP has rejected affiliation with the National Outlook Movement and political Islamism.[26] It identified its normative framework as "conservative democracy" and developed it through an official publication—*Conservative Democracy*. The author of that book, Yalçın Akdoğan, defines JDP's conservatism as an ideology that stresses common sense, prudence, and gradual change, unlike its two alternatives—

socialism and liberalism—that promote ideological rationalism and radical changes. The party, therefore, rejects rationalist utopias, Jacobinism, and social engineering. At this point, the party's sources of inspiration include Michael Oakeshott and Edmund Burke.[27]

The JDP organized an international symposium to elaborate its conservative and democratic stand. At this symposium, Erdoğan emphasized that the JDP's understanding of conservatism did not mean the conservation of established institutions and relations, but implied the protection of important values and principles while pursuing progress. He stressed that using religion as a political instrument was harmful to social peace, political diversity, and religion itself. For him, the JDP aimed to synthesize local and universal values, tradition and modernity, and morality and rationality.[28]

The JDP also stresses its loyalty to the principle of secularism in its program. The program depicts secularism as "an assurance of the freedom of religion and conscience" and rejects "the interpretation and distortion of secularism as enmity against religion." It considers the discrimination against pious people because of their religious preferences as antidemocratic. The program adds that "it is also unacceptable to make use of religion for political, economic and other interests, or to put pressure on people who think and live differently by using religion."[29]

The JDP leaders have faced the trade-off between two contradictory policies. On the one hand, the state establishment has required them to show their loyalty to secularism in order to be legal and legitimate actors in Turkish politics.[30] On the other hand, their constituency has demanded that they reinterpret the established conception of secularism in Turkey.

THE JDP, PASSIVE SECULARISM, AND ASSERTIVE SECULARISM

The JDP and other rightist parties, which represent 70 percent of the votes, have by and large supported Turkey's leaning toward passive secularism. Erdoğan has frequently emphasized "state neutrality toward all religions and doctrines" to define his understanding of secularism,[31] which fits well with the ideal type of passive secularism. In January 2004, in a press conference in Washington, DC, Erdoğan stressed his desire to reinterpret Turkish secularism by analyzing the American model.[32] Another influential JDP politician, Bülent Arınç, argues that secularism should be reinterpreted in Turkey in a more liberal manner, one that emphasizes the individual's religious rights and freedoms. This new version of secularism, for him, should attach importance to the fact that Turkey is at the crossroads of civilizations. On the one hand, it is a part of the West; on the other hand, its population is overwhelmingly Muslim. For Arınç, secularism in Turkey ought to take into consideration this dual sociocultural context. A reinterpretation and true implementation of secularism in Turkey, he stresses, will greatly contribute to the worldwide debates on secularism.[33]

While explaining the JDP's view on secularism, Erdoğan's advisor Akdoğan argues that secularism needs to be empowered by democracy in order to better protect religious freedoms. For him, "A particular understanding of secularism as a monopolistic, totalitarian, and Jacobin ideology or way of life, would result in conflict, rather than social peace."[34] Akdoğan also rejects the use of religion as a political tool.[35] In my terminology, he avoids assertive secularism and argues for passive secularism.

JDP parliamentarians whom I interviewed have appreciated secularism in America, which I depict as the closest practice to the ideal type of passive secularism. Yet they stressed that they did not have a project importing the American model as a whole. They wanted to imitate the American model in terms of its content—especially the absence of an ideological state and the emphasis on religious freedoms—but not its structure.[36] The main reason why they did not have a wish to adopt the American model entirely is their statist view on state-religion relations, particularly concerning the status of the Directorate of Religious Affairs (Diyanet). These politicians have claimed that the state's coordination of religious services through the Diyanet has been necessary to maintain Islamic services efficiently and to avoid anarchy in Islamic communities.[37] An example of this statist stand is the response of Mehmet Aydın from the JDP to the criticisms on the Diyanet's hiring of fifteen thousand new Imams. Aydın, the minister of state in charge of religious affairs, said that of 75,941 mosques in Turkey 22,344 lacked an Imam from the Diyanet. In these "empty" mosques, improper people might teach religion inappropriately. He added that proper religious services were a duty of the state.[38]

Another issue in which the JDP diverges from the ideal type of passive secularism, tending instead to statism, is the debate on the obligatory religious courses in schools. In February 2005, the European Council issued a report that criticizes these courses. Several JDP politicians simply rejected that criticism, saying that those courses were not on Islam, but on "general information on religions and knowledge of ethics."[39] The JDP's divergence from passive secularism toward a more statist approach has been criticized even by its supporters in the media. Fehmi Koru, an influential columnist from *Yeni Şafak* who has strong personal connections with the JDP, has emphasized that the solution to state-religion controversies in Turkey is "more secularism." By "more secularism" Koru has implied a more liberal and less statist perspective that depends on a real mosque-state separation. He has criticized the JDP for not being bold enough to defend such a separation and for searching only for ad hoc solutions to profound problems of secularism in Turkey.[40] Because of its statist perspectives, the JDP has failed to find allies from liberal and leftist civic associations[41] and from intellectuals,[42] who have also been seeking a more liberal interpretation of secularism.

In addition to its statist view, the JDP has not had a chance to reshape secularism in Turkey because of its power limitation. Two prominent JDP politicians told me that any political party would be unable to change the structure of secularism in Turkey because of legal barriers. The Law of Political Parties, for example, forbids a political party to propose the abolishment of the Diyanet in its party program.[43] Another example of the JDP's inability to change the existing practices of secularism is the military's expulsion of its allegedly antisecular, self-professedly pious officials.[44] The number of these officers exceeded nine hundred in the last eight years.[45] Erdoğan and the JDP's minister of defense, Vecdi Gönül, could not prevent the military from this frequent discharge. They have written their dissenting opinions while signing the decisions of expulsion.

The main reason for the JDP's power limitation is the resistance of the Kemalist elite—President Sezer, the RPP, the Constitutional Court, the Council of State, and the generals—and its allies in the protection of assertive secularism: influential media groups and the Turkish Industrialists and Businessmen's Association (TÜSİAD). These individuals and institutions refer to the Constitutional Court's rigid definition of secularism as the official and unchangeable depiction of Turkish secularism.[46] According to the Court, secularism is not separation of religion and state, but "separation of religion and worldly affairs... [Secularism] means separation of social life, education, family, economics, law, manners, dress codes, etc. from religion."[47] The Court's conception of secularism is an extreme version of assertive secularism.[48] The Court's definition of *secularism* is mixed and confused with another concept—*secularization*. Secularism is a constitutional regime that determines the political boundaries between state and religion. Secularization, on the other hand, is a social process, which is claimed to result in three things: (1) the *decline* of religion, in terms of belief, affiliation, and practice; (2) *individualization* and *privatization* of religion, with the erosion of its public role; and (3) *differentiation* of religious sphere from others, such as political, economic, and legal spheres.[49] The Court combines these two separate phenomena in its definition of secularism. In short, it takes secularism as a comprehensive official doctrine, an overarching principle over and prior to all rights and freedoms, and a social engineering project to secularize society. To the Court, secularism is beyond a political regime, it is "Turkey's philosophy of life."[50]

The Constitutional Court's conception of secularism is based on two philosophical prejudgments. First, the Court adopts a *modernist* view that an evolution has occurred from backward traditional societies to the developed modern societies; one depends on religious dogmas and the other on science and reason.[51] In this regard, secularism is beyond a political system, it is "the final phase of the institutional and ideational evolution of societies."[52] Second, the Court has an *essentialist* view of religions, in the sense that it takes Islam and Christianity as frozen entities composed of unchangeable essentials. According to the Court, Turkish secularism should be more rigid than secularism in Western countries regarding the restrictions over religious freedoms because of the distinction between Islam and Christianity.[53] The tacit argument is that Islam is essentially a blueprint of society that encompasses life entirely. For controlling such a religion, a rigid secularism, which confines religion to individual spirituality and does not allow it to play any social role, is necessary, though it may not be needed in Christian societies.[54]

President Sezer, who is the former president of the Constitutional Court, agrees with and frequently refers to the Court's understanding of secularism, to which he personally contributed. Sezer stresses that the unchangeable constitutional principle of secularism in Turkey can only be interpreted by the Constitutional Court. Other institutions, including the Turkish Parliament, have no right to reinterpret it.[55] Sezer sees any attempts and even desires to reinterpret Turkish secularism as a problem. Sezer attaches importance to separating religion and "this-worldly affairs." He specifies the sphere of religion: "Religion only belongs to its sacred and special place in individuals' conscience."[56] Yet he does not specify any domain and limit to the authority of the state over individuals' religious expression.[57]

The debate between the supporters of passive and assertive secularisms in Turkey could be clearly recognized in the above-mentioned discussion on the "secular individual." Right-wing politicians, from Özal to

Erdoğan, have argued that secularism has been a constitutional regime and characteristic of the state, not a required worldview for individuals.[58] Sezer has given a clear response to this argument several times, including his speech quoted at the beginning of this chapter. He defined secularism as a way of life and ideal citizens as "secular individuals." For him, religious belief located in conscience should have no influence on this world.[59] Sezer's stand perfectly fits the ideal type of assertive secularism.

The polarization between passive and assertive secularists in Turkey does not simply reflect a state-society tension, but a fragmentation of state actors as well. The High Court of Appeals' recent decisions on freedom of expression and secularism is a good example of this division. In February 2005, the Court decided that there was no violation of law in criticizing particular secularist state policies in education, in particular, and the principle of secularism, in general. The Court emphasized that secularism no longer needed to be protected through punishing its opponents since it was overwhelmingly embraced by the Turkish people and it was impossible to eliminate an idea just by punishing it. Fourteen judges concurred with this liberal decision, whereas thirteen judges dissented and argued that antisecular ideas should be punished.[60] A month later, however, the Court made a totally opposite decision with a 24–4 vote. Several members of the Court explicitly criticized the earlier liberal decision. This time, the Court sentenced a columnist to imprisonment for twenty months for a newspaper article that included antisecular ideas. The Court members argued that they owed to secularism and if they did not protect secularism, some other forces (namely, the military) would do it. Newspapers commented on this decision as a "rövanş" (payback).[61]

The controversy between passive and assertive secularism generally focuses on the issue of education since education is seen as an arena to shape the following generations' identities and worldviews. In the following section, I analyze three controversial subjects: the ban on the headscarf, the status of the İmam Hatip schools, and the state restrictions on the Qur'an courses. These three issues are the main sources of political tensions with respect to religion in Turkey. According to TESEV's survey in 1999,[62] for example, 42.4 percent of the interviewees claim that there is oppression of religious people in Turkey: "[E]xamples of policies that are directly related to oppression in the perception of the people are primarily related to education policies such as the headscarf ban, closure of Koran courses and Imam Hatip schools. These examples cover a total of 77 per cent of all examples given by those who claim that religious people are being oppressed in Turkey."[63]

Three Controversies between Passive
and Assertive Secularists

The Headscarf Issue

The headscarf at universities became a seriously contentious issue in the
1980s.[64] Students with headscarves were expelled from universities by the
Council of Higher Education (YÖK). The Council of State confirmed
YÖK's policy of expulsion in several cases. In 1984, the Council unanimously decided that

> some of our daughters who are not sufficiently educated wear head-
> scarves under the influence of their social environments, customs, and
> traditions—without having any special thought about it. Yet, it is known
> that some of our daughters and women who are educated enough to
> resist their social environments and customs wear headscarves for just
> opposing the principles of the secular Republic and showing that they
> adopt the ideal of a religious state. For those people, headscarf is no
> longer an innocent habit, but a symbol of a world view that opposes
> women's liberty and the fundamental principles of our Republic....
> Therefore, the decision to expel the plaintiff from the university does
> not contradict the laws since she is so against the principles of the secu-
> lar state that she resists to take off her headscarf even when she comes to
> university for higher education.[65]

The Council of State's decision did not end the discussion on the
headscarf. In the late 1980s and early 1990s the leading party, the MP,
initiated several legislations to abandon the ban of the headscarf at universities. These initiations were mainly led by Turgut Özal (1927–1993),
who was the leader of the MP, prime minister (1983–89), and then president (1989–93) of Turkey. In 1988, the Parliament led by the MP majority passed legislation that provided absolute freedom to wear any dress,
including the headscarf, at universities.[66] President Kenan Evren vetoed
the law, arguing that an absolute freedom of dress is against Atatürk's
principles and reforms, modern thought, secularism, and the principle of
equality.[67] Regarding that veto, Parliament passed another bill in 1988
that made "modern dress and appearance" obligatory but allowed covering the neck and hair with a headscarf or turban for religious belief.[68]
Evren applied to the Constitutional Court, claiming the unconstitution-
ality of the legislation. The Court struck down the law as unconstitutional because of the principle of secularism and its use of religious belief
as a reason for legal exemption. According to the Court, that particular
legislation, allowing the wearing of the headscarf at universities, might

provoke religious conflicts, threaten the unity of state and nation, and destroy the public order. Moreover, the legislation "abolishes the constitutional boundaries of religious freedom by allowing religion to pass beyond the individual's spiritual life and to cause behaviors that influence social life." According to the Court, "The dress issue is limited by the Turkish Revolution and Ataturk's Principles and it is not an issue of freedom of conscience.... To attend classes with anti-modern attires [that is, headscarves] has no relevancy to freedom or autonomy." The Court referred to the above-mentioned decision of the Council of State:

> The dress code is not just an issue of physical appearance. Secularism is a transformation of mentality. It is a must for a modern healthy society. An individual is a unity composed of his/her inner and outer lives, sentiments and thoughts, and body and spirit. The dress code is a means to reflect personal character. Regardless of whether it is religious or not, anti-modern dresses that contradict the Laws of Revolution cannot be seen as appropriate. Religious dresses, in particular, constitute a deeper incongruity since they contradict the principle of secularism.[69]

Ten members of the Court concurred with this decision, while only one member, Mehmet Çınarlı, wrote a dissenting opinion. Çınarlı had four main arguments: (1) to ban wearing the headscarf is against the individual freedoms protected by the Constitution; (2) the Constitution gives the authority to Parliament to limit freedoms for the sake of public order; if Parliament decides to enrich certain freedoms, the judiciary has no authority to restrict them; (3) Atatürk's speeches and the Laws of Revolution do not include anything against the headscarf; and (4) the Court's definition of headscarves as either political symbol or backward tradition does not reflect reality; according to Diyanet's official declaration,[70] wearing the headscarf is a religious duty and many of the veiled students have tried to fulfill this duty.[71]

Regarding the decision of the Court, Parliament passed another bill, which was similar to the first legislation vetoed by Evren and lacked the issue of religious exemption: "As long as they do not violate existing laws, dress codes are free at universities."[72] The Social Democrat Populist Party, the major leftist party at that time, applied to the Constitutional Court, accusing the legislation of being unconstitutional. The Court did not declare it unconstitutional but interpreted the law as disallowing students' wearing of the headscarf.[73]

The Constitutional Court's decisions did not put an end to the problem because the assertive secularist policies toward the headscarf have had limited popular support in Turkey. According to public surveys, the supporters of the ban on the headscarf at universities constitute only 16 percent of the population while 76 percent oppose the ban.[74] A comparison with France can clarify the situation. In France, 69 percent of the population support the ban on the headscarf in public schools whereas only 29 percent are against it.[75] This public support has stabilized assertive secularist policies in France against religious symbols. The reasons for the distinction between these two countries are threefold. First, in France, the Islamic headscarf is a symbol of an immigrant religious minority and its ban is linked to rising anti-immigrant views. In Turkey, however, Islam is the religion of the overwhelming majority of society. Furthermore, about 64 percent of women wear some sort of headscarf in Turkey.[76] Second, the ban in France is confined to only public schools, whereas the ban in Turkey encompasses all educational institutions. Last but not least, the levels of religiosity of French and Turkish societies are different, as shown in table 6.1.

Exclusion of religious symbols from public schools is understandable and even desirable in less religious French society. Turkish society, on the contrary, is highly religious. It is very difficult to confine religion to the private sphere and to let a purely secular worldview dominate the public sphere in such a religious society. In sum there is a relative compatibility between less religiosity in French society and assertive secularist state policies, whereas high religiosity in Turkish society contradicts such policies that try to exclude religion from the public sphere.

Currently, although the JDP and some other rightist parties, such as the TPP, support the right to wear headscarves at universities,[77] they have almost no impact on the existing prohibition. Erdoğan has had two limited initiatives on this issue. He first suggested confining the ban to only the public schools while making it permissible at universities.[78] Since he did not receive a positive response from the Kemalist elite, he proposed to limit the ban to public universities and remove it from private universities.[79] Yet this proposition was not accepted either.

The headscarf issue is particularly a double-edged sword for the JDP. On the one hand, the JDP's constituency demands an active policy to solve this problem. Moreover, an overwhelming majority of the JDP parliamentarians (including Erdoğan, Arınç, and Gül) have wives and daughters who wear headscarves. On the other hand, the JDP could not attempt to solve the headscarf problem because the Constitutional Court took that issue as one of the reasons for the closure of the WP and the only reason to dissolve the VP. The JDP leaders have frequently emphasized

TABLE 6.1. The Levels of Religiosity of French and Turkish Societies

	BELIEF IN GOD (%)	AFFILIATION WITH A RELIGION (%)	RELIGIOUS PARTICIPATION[a] ONCE A WEEK (%)
France	60[b]	55[c]	10[d]
Turkey	97[e]	97[f]	70[g]

a. By participation, I imply going to church/mosque at least once a week.

b. The survey of *CSA/La Vie/Le Monde, Les français et leur croyances* [The French people and their beliefs], March 21, 2003, 41.

c. Dominique Vidal, "La France des 'sans-religion' [The France of those without religion]," *Le Monde Diplomatique* (September 2001): 22–23.

d. The survey of *CSA/La Vie/Le Monde*, 91; "Les Français et la prière [The French people and prayer]," *Le Pèlerin Magazine*, April 13, 2001.

e. Neither TESEV's nor Miliyet's surveys give a specific ratio of believing in God in Turkey. Therefore, I use the ratio of those who believe in God in this section: TESEV's survey in 1999, in Çarkoğlu and Toprak, *Türkiye'de Din, Toplum ve Siyaset*, 41.

f. Ibid.

g. The survey of *A&G and Milliyet 2003, Milliyet*, May 31, 2003. TESEV's survey in 1999 gives a similar ratio: 68.6, Çarkoğlu and Toprak, *Türkiye'de Din, Toplum ve Siyaset*, 45.

that they have been waiting for a consensus for a substantial solution to the problem. The party has faced similar dilemmas on the issues of the İmam Hatip schools and the Qur'an courses.

The İmam Hatip Schools

The İmam Hatip schools were opened in the late 1940s as vocational schools to train Imams and *hatips* (Muslim preachers). Their numbers particularly increased in the 1980s and the early 1990s. They became regular secondary and high schools and their graduates were oriented toward all sorts of professions beyond religious jobs. Assertive secularists—the Kemalist establishment, TÜSİAD, and influential media groups—have been concerned about these schools because they have trained an alternative pro-Islamic elite. They have argued that the transformation of the İmam Hatip schools to regular schools is against the Law on the Unification of Education of 1924, which had unified and secularized education by abolishing religious schools.

The February 28 administration pursued two policies to marginalize the İmam Hatip schools.[80] First, it implemented the policy of eight-year-education, which increased obligatory education from five to eight years.

By doing that, it closed the sixth, seventh, and eighth grades of the İmam Hatip schools, in addition to all other vocational schools and Anatolian schools that teach foreign languages. Second, through a revision in the university entrance system, it made it almost impossible for the graduates of these schools to enter universities, except the departments of theology. When the February 28 coup occurred, in the 1996–97 academic year, the İmam Hatip schools were at their peak, with 511,502 students.[81] As a result of these two particular policies, the number of students at these schools decreased to 64,534 in the 2002–3 academic year.[82]

Erdoğan has been more active on the issue of İmam Hatip schools than he has been on the headscarf problem, since the state establishment has not seemed as sensitive on the former. Many JDP politicians, including Erdoğan himself, are graduates of these schools. JDP politicians did not take the closure of İmam Hatip secondary schools as a problem and simply accepted that. What they have focused on has been to allow İmam Hatip high school graduates to enter universities again. In 2004, the JDP group passed a bill in Parliament to make relative improvements in the conditions that allowed graduates of all vocational schools, including the İmam Hatip schools, to enter universities.[83] That created a substantial reaction in the assertive secularist elite. The only support for the JDP came from other rightist parties such as the TPP.[84]

President Sezer vetoed the law by repeating his conception of (assertive) secularism.[85] He argued that, by allowing İmam Hatip graduates to enter universities, the law violated the principle of secularism, which implied "the separation of the spheres of social life, education, family, economy, and law from the rules of religion." He claimed a sharp dichotomy between "religion" and "time and the necessities of life," on the one hand, and "religious knowledge" and "reason and science," on the other.[86] Even the international media were interested in this discussion. The *New York Times*, for example, criticized Sezer's veto as "a setback to religious freedom and equal opportunity." The editorial added that "Turkey's 536 religious schools are coeducational and, with the exception of Koran study, teach the same curriculum as nonreligious schools. Their 64,500 students are as much Turkey's future as are the sons and daughters of the secular elite."[87]

The Qur'an Courses

The Turkish state has a monopoly on Islamic education; private education of Islam is prohibited. In addition to the İmam Hatip schools, there are specific public schools to teach the Qur'an, governed by the Diyanet. The February 28 administration regarded the Qur'an courses as sources of religious reaction. In 1997, in the briefings to inform the media and the high court judges, the military generals represented the Qur'anic and Imam Hatip schools as sources of votes for political Islamists. The February 28 administration substantially marginalized the Qur'an courses by using the policy of eight-year education. The Qur'an courses that had been teaching students who did not finish the eighth grade were closed. Only summer and weekend schools were allowed to teach graduates of the fifth grade. To teach the Qur'an to students under age twelve became ipso facto banned, even in summer or at the weekend. The Qur'an courses had the highest number of students—1,685,000—right before the February 28 coup.[88] As a consequence of the February 28 administration's policies, the number of students in these courses decreased to 155,285 by the end of 2004.[89]

In December 2003, the JDP attempted to improve the conditions of the Qur'an courses through a new regulation prepared by the Diyanet. The new regulation included some minor changes, such as authorization to open evening classes, reduction of the minimum student requirement from 15 to 10, removal of the time limits (which was two months) in summer, and permission to open dormitories.[90] That regulation resulted in considerable opposition by the assertive secularists. They accused the JDP of harboring a hidden Islamist agenda. President Sezer, who was against the new regulation, met with Minister Aydın and asked him to cancel the regulation; as a result, it was canceled.

The conditions of the Qur'an courses became worse in 2005 with a judgment by the Council of State. In a 16–7 vote, the Council canceled a specific regulation of these schools that had increased the education time from three days to five days a week. Moreover, the Council applied to the Constitutional Court to declare unconstitutional the law that permitted teaching the Qur'an in summer and at weekends to students who had finished fifth grade. The reasons for this decision show that the Council's understanding of secularism is a typical assertive secularism. According to the Council, it is the duty of the state to educate loyal citizens to secularism, and, therefore, it should not allow antisecular education. Secular education should be solid and continuous. Religious education, even in holidays, will negatively affect students' secular education before they finish the eighth grade.[91]

CONCLUSION

This chapter has tried to create a synergy between conceptual approach and case analysis by employing a typology of secularism to analyze the case of Turkey. On the one hand, it has used the case to develop the concepts of passive and assertive secularisms and their struggle in a Muslim context. On the other hand, it has used the typology of secularism to categorize and analyze political actors in Turkey. My typology of secularism has contributed to the analyses of the transformation of state-religion relations in Turkey. The Turkish state originally tended toward assertive secularism and still pursues policies based on that. Yet there has been a debate between the supporters of the assertive and passive secularisms. The debate will continue since it depends on the incompatibility of assertive secularist state practices with the high religiosity of Turkish society. The dispute will not end unless a shift from assertive to passive secularism occurs or unless Turkish society's religiosity declines.

My analysis has revealed the distinction between the *image* and the *practices* of the Turkish state.[92] The perceived image of the Turkish state has been of a monolithic organization isolated from the fragmentations of society. Yet the analysis has shown the fragmentations of, and struggles between, state actors in Turkey, particularly on the issue of secularism. This analysis has emphasized a sharp disagreement between the current president (Sezer) and the prime minister (Erdoğan) of Turkey on secularism. Historically, two of the three presidents that I mentioned (Evren and Sezer) were for assertive secularism, whereas the third (Özal) was for passive secularism. Similarly, political parties (JDP and RPP) have had divergent positions regardless of their being in government or opposition. Moreover, in their three recent and crucial decisions related to secularism, the members of the High Court of Appeals and the Council of State were highly polarized. These courts have made contradictory and opposing decisions as well.

Until the present, because of its own statist view and the resistance of the Kemalist establishment, the JDP has not succeeded in reforming Turkish secularism. The only exception has been the improvements in the religious rights of non-Muslim communities, such as the construction of new churches,[93] and the abolishment of state surveillance over non-Muslims.[94] The JDP could accomplish this since these reforms were a part of Turkey's adaptation to the EU and therefore supported by a fraction of the assertive secularist elite. JDP politicians were hoping that the changes in Turkish secularism expected by its constituency would occur through the EU membership process. Nevertheless, the EU's reports on religious freedoms in Turkey,[95] and the European Court of Human Rights' recent decision on the headscarf,[96] have showed that the EU would not play a direct role in the transformation of assertive secularism in Turkey. Turkey's application process for membership in the EU can play only an indirect role, through political liberalization and democratization, and therefore it is up to the JDP to demonstrate strong leadership in reshaping Turkish secularism. The JDP needs to find allies from different parts of the Turkish elite if it is to play such an active role. The more the JDP tends to passive secularism by abandoning its statist perspective, the more it may find liberal and leftist allies from the Turkish elite to reinterpret secularism in Turkey.

This chapter has argued that the JDP has not been an antisecular Islamist organization, but a defender of an alternative mode of secularism. The JDP has adopted the rightist parties' tradition of defending Turkey's leaning toward passive secularism. The old depiction of Turkish politics, particularly in the 1990s, as divided between secular forces (such as the military) and Islamist politicians is no longer valid. One needs to understand different and struggling interpretations of secularism to correctly analyze the transformation of Turkish politics.

NOTES

I thank Etyen Mahçupyan, Bekim Agai, Ziyaeddin Akbulut, Ahmet Yükleyen, Etga Uğur, the participants of Reşat Kasaba's Seminar on Turkish Studies at the University of Washington, Yüksel Sezgin, Anthony Gill, and especially Joel Migdal for their helpful comments on earlier drafts of this chapter.

1. The author's personal observation at Diyanet's Third Symposium on Religion, Hotel Dedeman, Ankara; see also "Zirvede Laiklik Atışması (Dispute on Secularism at the Summit)," *Radikal*, September 21, 2004.

2. In my terminology, Kemalism (*Kemalizm*) and Atatürkism (*Atatürkçülük*) are two different ideologies. By Kemalists, I refer to those who take M. Kemal Atatürk's six principles—secularism, nationalism, republicanism, statism, populism, and reformism—as permanent, nonnegotiable doctrines. The Atatürkists, however, are those who reinterpret and update these principles regarding changing conditions as means to achieve the end: the level of universal civilization. The former constitutes a small but still influential portion of Turkish society, whereas the latter is much larger.

3. The term "public sphere" has several definitions. In this chapter, I mean everywhere out of one's home by this term.

4. Two other scholars categorize secularism with two distinct types similar to those of my typology. Charles Taylor refers to the first type as secularism based on a "religious common ground" and the second as secularism with a "political ethic independent of religion." Wilfred McClay uses the terms "negative" and "positive" conceptions of secu-

larism. These two thinkers mainly focus on the historical roots and philosophical distinctions of the two types of secularism. This chapter makes a contribution to this discussion by analyzing a contemporary case. Charles Taylor, "Modes of Secularism," in *Secularism and Its Critics*, ed. Rajeev Bhargava (Delhi: Oxford University Press, 1988); Wilfred M. McClay, "Two Concepts of Secularism," *Wilson Quarterly* 24 (Summer 2000): 63–64.

5. Jean Baubérot, "La Laicite, une chance pour le XXIe siècle (Secularism, A Chance for the Twenty-first Century)," in *La Laicite a l'épreuve: Religions et libertés dans le monde* (Secularism under Investigation: Religions and Liberties in the World), ed. Jean Baubérot (N.p.: Universalis, 2004), 9.

6. I define constitutionally secular states as having two characteristics: (1) their legal and judicial processes are secular, in the sense of being out of religious control, and (2) they are constitutionally neutral toward religions.

7. For a comparison of the United States and France on religious symbols, see Regis Debray, *Contretemps: Eloges des ideaux perdus* (Contretemps: In Praise of Lost Ideals) (Paris: Gallimard, 1992), 22–23.

8. This short chapter neither aims nor is able to explain the debate on these monotheistic official statements in the United States. For this debate, see Mary C. Segers and Ted G. Jelen, *A Wall of Separation? Debating the Public Role of Religion* (Lanham, MD: Rowman and Littlefield, 1998).

9. For a comparison between secularism in France and in Turkey, see Jean-Paul Bury and Jean Marcou, "Laicite/*Laiklik*: Introduction," *Cahiers d'études sur la Mediterranée orientale et le monde turco-iranien* 19 (January–June 1995): 5–34; Şahin Alpay, "Mukayeseli Açıdan Türkiye'de Laiklik (Secularism in Turkey from a Comparative Perspective)," paper presented at the International Conference on Atatürk and Modern Society, Istanbul, September 25–27, 2002. For the recent ban on students' religious symbols in France, see Valentine Zuber, "La Commission Stasi et les paradoxes de la laicite française (The Commission of Stasi and the Paradoxes of French Secularism)," in Baubérot, *La Laicite a l'épreuve.*

10. Sami Selçuk, "Laiklik ve Demokrasi (Secularism and Democracy)," *Türkiye Günlüğü* 56 (Summer 1999): 45–49; Nur Vergin, "Din ve Devlet İlişkileri: Düşüncenin 'Bitmeyen Senfoni'si (Religion-State Relations: The Infinite Symphony of Thought)," *Türkiye Günlüğü* 72 (2003): 39–44; Semih Vaner, "Laiklik, Laikçilik ve Demokrasi (Secularism, Secularist Ideology, and Democracy)," in *Laiklik ve Demokrasi* (Secularism and Democracy), ed. İbrahim Ö. Kaboğlu (Istanbul: İmge Kitabevi, 2001).

11. Andrew Davison, "Turkey, a 'Secular' State? The Challenge of Description," *South Atlantic Quarterly* 102 (March 2003): 333–50.

12. Niyazi Berkes, *The Development of Secularism in Turkey* (1963; New York: Routledge, 1998); Sibel Bozdoğan and Reşat Kasaba, eds., *Rethinking Modernity and National Identity in Turkey* (Seattle: University of Washington Press, 1997).

13. Ali Fuad Başgil, *Din ve Laiklik* (Religion and Secularism) (1954; Istanbul: Yağmur Yayınları, 1977), 149.

14. See M. Ibrahim Abu-Rabi', ed., *Islam at the Crossroads: On the Life and Thought of Bediüzzaman Said Nursi* (Albany: State University of New York Press, 2003).

15. Bediüzzaman Said Nursi, *Risale-i Nur Külliyatı* (The Epistles of Light Collection) (Istanbul: Nesil, 1996), 1922.

16. Ibid., 368.

17. İhsan D. Dağı, *Kimlik, Söylem ve Siyaset: Doğu-Batı Ayrımında Refah Partisi Geleneği* (Identity, Discourse, and Politics: The Tradition of the Welfare Party at the Crossroads of the East and the West) (Ankara: İmge Kitabevi, 1998).

18. The members of D-8 are Turkey, Iran, Egypt, Pakistan, Bangladesh, Indonesia, Malaysia, and Nigeria.

19. M. Hakan Yavuz, "Cleansing Islam from the Public Sphere," *Journal of International Affairs* 54 (2000): 21–42; M. Hakan Yavuz, *Islamic Political Identity in Turkey* (New York: Oxford University Press, 2003).

20. Ahmet T. Kuru, "Globalization and Diversification of Islamic Movements: Three Turkish Cases," *Political Science Quarterly* 120 (Summer 2005); İhsan D. Dağı, "Rethinking Human Rights, Democracy, and the West: Post-Islamist Intellectuals in Turkey," *Critique: Critical Middle Eastern Studies* 13 (Summer 2004): 135–51.

21. Ali Bulaç, interview, *Aksiyon*, November 7–13, 1998; see also Ali Bulaç, "Niçin AB? (Why the EU?)," *Zaman*, December 11, 1999. For Bulaç's prosecular views, see Ali Bulaç, *Din, Devlet ve Demokrasi* (Religion, State, and Democracy) (Istanbul: Zaman Kitap, 2001), esp. 11–65.

22. See M. Hakan Yavuz and John L. Esposito, eds., *Turkish Islam and the Secular State: The Gülen Movement* (Syracuse, NY: Syracuse University Press, 2003); Ahmet T. Kuru, "Fethullah Gülen's Search for a Middle Way between Modernity and Muslim Tradition," in Yavuz and Esposito, *Turkish Islam*.

23. *İslam ve Laiklik* (Islam and Secularism) (Istanbul: Gazeteciler ve Yazarlar Vakfı, 1998); *Din, Devlet, Toplum* (Religion, State, and Society) (Istanbul: Gazeteciler ve Yazarlar Vakfı, 2000).

24. Erdoğan and Arınç's interviews, *Zaman*, February 6, 2000; Gül's interview, *Hürriyet*, February 8, 2000.

25. Ziya Öniş, "Political Islam at the Crossroads: From Hegemony to Co-existence," *Contemporary Politics* 7 (December 2001): 281–99.

26. "Erdoğan: Milli Görüş' ün Değil Demokrat Parti'nin Devamıyız (Erdoğan: We Are the Successor of the Democrat Party, not the National Outlook)," *Zaman*, May 17, 2003.

27. Yalçın Akdoğan, *Muhafazakar Demokrasi* (Conservative Democracy) (Ankara: AK Parti, 2003). Akdoğan largely used Bekir Berat Özipek's PhD dissertation on conservatism while writing this book.

28. Recep Tayyip Erdoğan, "Keynote Speech," in *International Symposium on Conservatism and Democracy* (Ankara: AK Parti, 2004).

29. AK Parti, *Parti Programı* (The Party Program), 2002.

30. See Yüksel Sezgin, "Can the Israeli *Status Quo* Model Help Post-February 28 Turkey Solve its Problems," *Turkish Studies* 4 (Autumn 2003): 47–70.

31. Erdoğan, "Keynote Speech," 7–17.

32. "Turkiye'deki Laiklik İslam Dünyasina Model Olabilir mi? (Can Secularism in Turkey Be a Model for the Islamic World?)," *Hürriyet*, April 25, 2004.

33. The author's personal observation at Diyanet's Third Symposium; see also "Zirvede Laiklik Atışması."

34. Akdoğan, *Muhafazakar Demokrasi*, 105.

35. Ibid., 132.

36. The author's personal interviews with JDP parliamentarians, April 2004, Washington, DC, and September 2004, Ankara, Turkey.

37. The author's personal interviews with JDP parliamentarians, September 2004, Ankara, Turkey.

38. "İmam Ordusunun Gerekçesi İrtica (The Reason of the Imam Army Is Religious Reactionism)," *Milliyet*, June 26, 2005.

39. "AB'ye Cevap: Din Konusu Bizim Bileceğimiz İştir (Response to the EU: Religion Is Our Own Affair)," *Yeni Şafak*, February 16, 2005.

40. Fehmi Koru, "Çözüm: Daha Fazla Laiklik... (The Solution: More Secularism...)," *Yeni Şafak*, February 9, 2005; Fehmi Koru, "Gelin Şu Adamları Şaşırtalım (Let's Shock These Guys)," *Yeni Şafak*, February 16, 2005.

41. Two examples of these associations are the Association for Liberal Thinking and Turkish Economic and Social Studies Foundation (TESEV).

42. See Etyen Mahçupyan, "Laiklik Bu Kadar Zor mu? (Is Secularism This Difficult?)," *Zaman*, February 25, 2005.

43. The author's personal interviews with JDP politicians, September 2004, Ankara, Turkey. The 89th article of the Law of Political Parties, no. 2820.

44. Adaleti Savunanlar Derneği (ASDER), *Ben Disiplinsiz Değilim* (I am not Undisciplined) (Istanbul: ASDER, 2004).

45. Ibid.

46. For example, see the speech of General Staff Deputy Chief General İlker Başbuğ, May 27, 2004, accessed at http://www.tsk.mil.tr/genelkumay/bashalk/2004basinbringleri/mayis2004/sempozyum1.htm, June 1, 2004.

47. The Turkish Constitutional Court's ruling on *The Welfare Party* case on January 16, 1997, no. 1998/1.

48. See Mustafa Erdoğan, "Religious Freedom in the Turkish Constitution," *The Muslim World* 89 (July–October 1999): 377–88.

49. Jose Casanova, *Public Religion in the Modern World* (Chicago: University of Chicago Press, 1994), 19–39.

50. The *Welfare Party* case. See also Yılmaz Aliefendioğlu, "Laiklik ve Laik Devlet (Secularism and the Secular State)," in Kaboğlu, *Laiklik ve Demokrasi*.

51. For a former Constitutional Court judge's emphasis on the dichotomy between religious dogmatic and secular scientific education, see Aliefendioğlu, "Laiklik ve Laik Devlet," 82–83.

52. The Turkish Constitutional Court's ruling on *The Headscarf* case on March 7, 1989, no. 1989/12.

53. Ibid.

54. Ibid.

55. "Sezer: Başörtüsünü Gündeme Getirmeyin (Do Not Mention the Headscarf)," *Radikal*, November 25, 2004.

56. "Laiklik Özgürlük Demek (Secularism Means Freedom)," *Radikal*, February 6, 2004.

57. Sezer does not accept any criticisms of his understanding of secularism. As an example, he disliked the U.S. State Department's *International Religious Freedom Report*, which criticized his policies that restricted religious freedoms. "Sezer'den Türban Konusunda Açıklama (Sezer's Statement about the Headscarf)," *Radikal*, March 7, 2004.

58. "Cami yerine Hastane Yapın (Build a Hospital Instead of a Mosque)," *Sabah*, June 14, 2004.

59. "Laiklik Sosyal Barış İçin Şart (Secularism Is a Must for Social Peace)," *Sabah*, February 6, 2005.

60. See "En Özgür Düşünce (The Most Free Thought)," *Radikal*, February 5, 2005.

61. "Yargıtay'da Laiklik Rövanşı (The Payback of Secularism in the High Court of Appeals)," *Hürriyet*, March 15, 2005; "Yargıtay'da Rövanş (The Payback in the High Court of Appeals)," *Sabah*, March 15, 2005.

62. TESEV's survey in 1999, published in Ali Çarkoğlu and Binnaz Toprak, *Türkiye'de Din, Toplum ve Siyaset* (Religion, Society, and Politics in Turkey) (Istanbul: TESEV, 2000), 69–70.

63. Ali Çarkoğlu, "Religiosity, Support for *Şeriat* and Evaluations of Secularist Public Policies in Turkey," *Middle Eastern Studies* 10 (2004): 129. Among these interviews, 64.8 percent mentioned the headscarf ban, 7.1 percent noticed the closure of the Qur'an courses, and 6.1 percent recognized the closure of the İmam Hatip Schools as the main examples of oppressions against religious people. Çarkoğlu and Toprak, *Türkiye'de Din*, 69; Çarkoğlu, "Religiosity," 130.

64. See Nilüfer Göle, *The Forbidden Modern: Civilization and Veiling* (Ann Arbor: University of Michigan Press, 1993).

65. The Council of State's ruling on December 13, 1984, no. 1984/1574.

66. The law passed in Parliament on November 16, 1988, no. 3503.

67. Evren's veto of law no. 3503 on November 18, 1988, no. 1662-8088.

68. The law passed in Parliament on December 10, 1988, annex 16 added to law no. 2547.

69. The *Headscarf* case.

70. The decision of Diyanet's High Council for Religious Affairs on December 30, 1980, no. 77.

71. The *Headscarf* case. For similar legal arguments on the headscarf issue, see Mustafa Erdoğan, "Başörtüsü, İnsan Hakları ve Teamüller (Headscarf, Human Rights, and Precedents)," *Türkiye Günlüğü* 56 (Summer 1999): 45–49; Ali Ulusoy, "Türban Sorunu ve Hukuk (The Headscarf Problem and the Law)," *Türkiye Günlüğü* 56 (Summer 1999): 16–35.

72. The law passed in Parliament on October 25, 1990, annex 17 added to law no. 2547.

73. According to the Court, wearing a headscarf is against the Constitution; for that reason, it violates "existing laws." The Turkish Constitutional Court's ruling on *The Second Headscarf* case on April 9, 1991, no. 1991/8.

74. TESEV's survey in 1999, in Çarkoğlu and Toprak, *Türkiye'de Din*, 59; Çarkoğlu, "Religiosity," 125. According to the survey of *A&G and Milliyet 2003*, these ratios are 24.5 and 75.5 percent, respectively: *Milliyet*, May 30, 2003.

75. The survey of *CSA* cited in "La majorité des Français favorables à une loi (The Majority of the French People Favors the Law)," *Le Monde*, December 17, 2003.

76. The survey of *A&G and Milliyet 2003*, *Milliyet*, May 27, 2003.

77. See "Siyasi Partilerden Ortak Ses: Türban Sorunu Artık Çözülmeli (A Shared Voice from Political Parties: The Headscarf Problem Must Be Solved)," *Zaman*, February 10, 2005.

78. Recep Tayyip Erdoğan, interview with Ertuğrul Özkök, "Yapma, Yıkarım (Do not Build, I Will Destroy It!)," *Hürriyet*, March 22, 2004.

79. "Türbanda Ara Formül (A Moderate Formula for the Headscarf)," *Radikal*, July 10, 2004.

80. Since the civil government was forced to share power with the military during the February 28 Process, I use the term "February 28 administration" to imply the mixture of civil and military rules.

81. "Din Öğretimi Genel Müdürlüğüne Bağlı Okullar (Schools Managed by the General Directorate of Religious Education)," accessed on the website of the Ministry of Education at http://www.meb.gov.tr/Stats/ist97/MYHTML30.htm, February 25, 2005.

82. "İmam Hatip Liseleri," CNN Turk Online, May 28, 2004, accessed at http://www.cnnturk.com.tr/OZEL_DOSYALAR/haber_detay.asp?pid=392&haberid=9269, February 23, 2005.

83. The law passed in Parliament on May 13, 2004, no. 5171.

84. "DYP'den İmam Hatip Desteği (İmam Hatip Support from the TPP), *Sabah*, May 6, 2004.

85. After that, the JDP postponed its policy instead of passing the law again.

86. Sezer's veto of law no. 5171 on higher education, May 28, 2004, accessed on the website of the Turkish Presidency at http://www.cankaya.gov.tr/tr_html/ACIKLAMALAR/28.05.2004-2729.html, June 1, 2004.

87. "Mosque and State in Turkey," *New York Times*, June 6, 2004.

88. "İşte Brifing (Here is the Briefing)," *Sabah*, June 12, 1997.

89. "İstatistiki Bilgiler," accessed on the website of the Diyanet at http://www.diyanet.gov.tr/turkish/tanitimistatistik.asp, April 18, 2005.

90. "Kuran Kursları Okullara Giriyor (The Qur'an Courses Are Entering the Regular Schools)," *Radikal*, December 5, 2003.

91. "Danıştay (The Council of State)," *Radikal*, February 10, 2005; Nazlı Ilıcak, "Laiklik Dinsizlik mi (Is Secularism Anti-Religion)?" *Dünden Bügüne Tercüman*, February 10, 2005.

92. For the duality of the state with regard to its *image* and *practices*, see Joel S. Migdal, *State in Society: Studying How State and Societies Transform and Constitute One Another* (Cambridge, UK: Cambridge University Press, 2001), 5–16.

93. In certain legal documents, the term "mosque" has been replaced by the general term "place of worship" to allow the construction of the temples of other religions. See Gareth Jenkins, "Non-Muslim Minorities in Turkey: Progress and Challenges on the Road to EU Accession," *Turkish Policy Quarterly* 3 (2004): 53–61.

94. The abolished organization was forty-two years old and named Azınlıklar Tali Komisyonu (The Subcommittee for Minorities). Şükrü Küçükşahin, "Sessiz Azınlık Devrimi (Silent Minority Revolution)," *Hürriyet*, February 23, 2004.

95. The EU's reports have only focused on the rights of the Alevis and non-Muslims. They have simply ignored violations of the majority Sunni population's religious freedoms in Turkey.

96. On June 29, 2004, in the *Leyla Şahin v. Turkey* case, the European Court of Human Rights decided that the Turkish state did not violate the Convention for the Protection of Human Rights and Fundamental Freedoms by expelling Leyla Şahin from university because of her headscarf.

CHAPTER 7

The New Generation Pro-Islamists in Turkey

Bases of the Justice and Development Party in Changing Electoral Space

■ *Ali Çarkoğlu*

The rise in support for the new generation pro-Islamists of the Justice and Development Party (JDP; Adalet ve Kalkınma Partisi) in the November 2002 general election marks a new phase in the progression of electoral collapse of centrist party politics in Turkey. The left-leaning Republican People's Party (RPP; Cumhuriyet Halk Partisi) remains the only other party that was able to pass the nationwide 10 percent electoral threshold and gain seats in Parliament. However, the RPP remained about 14 percentage points below the JDP, at around 20 percent of the vote.[1] The main question that arose in the aftermath of the November 2002 election was whether or not the center-right of the Turkish ideological spectrum is dead and will be eventually replaced by a new generation of pro-Islamists under the JDP banner. If the future of Turkish party politics will be dominated by the JDP, a healthy diagnosis of the electoral bases of its support is necessary. From where in the Turkish ideological space does the JDP support come? Who are the JDP voters? To what extent could one characterize the JDP voters on the basis of religiosity? What other attitudinal attributes best account for the supporters of the JDP? To what extent did the economic crisis of 2001 shape the electoral success of the JDP in 2002? What do we know about the impact of foreign policy options concerning the European Union (EU) and the Middle East upon decisions to vote for the JDP?

In this chapter I aim to answer these questions with the help of survey data collected before the general election of November 2002. For some of the questions I also use data collected in the aftermath of the local elections of March 2004. I first discuss the positioning of the JDP along the conventional left-right dimension and then present the results of an analysis of determinants of vote intention for the JDP. I conclude with a critical assessment of these findings.

PARTIES IN COMPETITION FOR THE NOVEMBER 2002 ELECTIONS

Despite many problems in the political and economic spheres of its development, fourteen national legislative elections have been held in Turkey since May 1950, following a questionable first experience in 1946. Among the salient features of the Turkish party system, the apparent lack of institutional continuity together with ever-increasing fractionalization and volatility of electoral support are the most significant. From the very beginning of multiparty elections, the banning of parties by military regimes or the Constitutional Court impeded the establishment of well-defined party identification among the electorate. In periods when closures ceased, incumbent party manipulations in electoral laws shaped voters' motivations and thus the outcome of elections in such a way as to render the tracing of long-term trends almost impossible. Consequently, electoral preferences have been forced to regroup behind newly founded parties as well as to switch continuously from one party to another in search mostly of a better patronage deal. As such, a long-term understanding of the ideological characteristics of Turkish party preferences remains at best blurred.[2]

In the shorter run, the characteristics of the newly founded parties remain ambiguous. Such parties typically lack organizational coherence. Charismatic leader hegemony substitutes the organizational impetus and legislative drive. Party cadres also characteristically lack an ideological consistency for targeting different electoral segments. My objective here will accordingly be to derive some ideological and electoral characteristics of the JDP and other parties that participated in the November 2002 election. I aim therefore not to give a comprehensive account of long-term questions but rather to offer a shorter-term diagnosis as to the electoral bases of support for parties in the last general election of November 2002 as a basis for a longer-term interpretation of electoral dynamics.

Admittedly, there are a number of overlapping ideological cleavages in Turkish politics. These are shaped around debates of conventional left vs. right, Islamism vs. secularism, and ethnic Turkish nationalism vs. the "Kurdish identity." Accordingly, fitting all the political parties into a multidimensional ideological space is appropriate.[3] A temporal assessment of the multidimensional developments in Turkish ideological space is another difficulty for such an analysis. A longitudinal analysis of divisions and the shifting electoral support behind them can be more easily provided for the conventional left-right scale within which I continue the following discussion.[4]

VOTERS' PERCEPTIONS

Figure 7.1 presents the profile of the Turkish party system from the perspective of the electorate. The pre-election study that forms the basis of these results is a nationwide survey of the voting-age population in October 2002 that included 1,984 face-to-face interviews in thirty-three provinces.[5]

In our pre-election study of electoral preferences, the respondents were provided with a conventional one-to-ten left-right ideology scale and asked to provide a placement for each of the major parties in the system. In a temporal assessment of these self-placements, the continual shift to the right end of the spectrum becomes quite clear. We clearly see that starting from 1990 the number of individuals at the very center of the given ideological spectrum, which comprised about 40 percent of the respondents at the time, starts to decline. In 1996, the centrist positions comprised 32.6 percent and in 2002 31.9 percent. Table 7.1 shows that since 1990 the left-of-center and centrist positions have been shrinking while the right-of-center has been growing in size. Although it is hard to time precisely the shift in ideological orientations, it seems that the

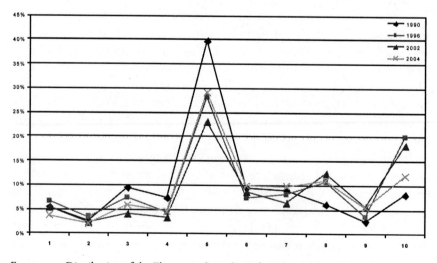

FIGURE 7.1. Distribution of the Electorate along the Left-Right Ideological Scale

TABLE 7.1. Distribution of Voters on the Left-Right Continuum

	1990[a] (%)	1996[a] (%)	2002[b] (%)	2004[c] (%)
Extreme Left (1 to 2)	7.0	9.2	7.8	5.7
Moderate Left (3 to 4)	14.8	10.7	7.2	10.3
Centre (5 to 6)	43.5	32.6	31.9	39.1
Moderate Right (7 to 8)	13.3	17.3	18.8	20.8
Extreme Right (9 to 10)	9.4	21.6	24.1	17.3
No response	11.9	8.6	10.1	6.6
	100	100	100	100

a. Kalaycıoğlu, "The Shaping of Political Preferences in Turkey," 58.

b. Ali Çarkoğlu, Üstün Ergüder and Ersin Kalaycıoğlu, "Pre-Election Study—2002" (unpublished manuscript in preparation).

c. Çarkoğlu, "Political Preferences of the Turkish Electorate."

biggest change occurred in the mid-1990s, when the country was being torn between Kurdish ethnic separatism and the rise of the pro-Islamist movement.[6] What is striking in the new data from the 2002 election is that this shift to the right is still continuing, although it appears to have slowed down. However, in 2002, while only 15 percent of the electorate is on the left-of-center, nearly 43 percent of the electorate place themselves at the right-of-center. It is noticeable that the left-of-center in the country was continuously shrinking in size in a period when the country was hit by two major economic crises, one in 1994 and another in 2001.

In April 2004, another nationwide representative sample survey was conducted.[7] While the left-of-center electorate remains constant at 15 percent, the right-of-center seems to have shrunk down to about 39 percent. Necessarily, the center seems to have grown to about 39 percent. It is interesting that as the JDP's single-party tenure completed its first year, the Turkish electorate seems to have become, once again, more centrist. One could conjecture that increasing uneasiness with fractionalized coalition governments, which cannot respond to expectations and demands of the electorate, formed the background to rising polarization in the country. As soon as the single-party government restored order and predictability in policy making and created a favorable economic environment, the polarization among the electorate seems to have reversed to centrism. Necessarily, when the center and the electoral basis of the JDP grow hand in hand, the ideological outlook for the JDP will tend to be more centrist. This tendency is primarily an outcome of the centrist relocation that took place for the whole electorate. However, I will show that even under such conditions, the overall placement of the JDP's constituency along the left-right dimension relative to other parties in the system remains predominantly unchanged.

When we look at the same picture from the perspective of party constituencies, we see that the average scores of each party as assigned by their voters correspond to most of our expectations (fig. 7.2). According to the voters, the Kurdish Democratic People's Party (DPP; Demokratik Halkın Partisi) captured the extreme left position in 2002 while the extreme right position was assigned to the JDP. While the RPP and the Democratic Left Party (DLP; Demokratik Sol Parti) are perceived to be the other two left-leaning parties of the system, Ismail Cem's New Turkey Party (NTP; Yeni Türkiye Partisi) (not shown on the figure) is placed somewhat closer to the center. Cem Uzan's Young Party (YP; Genç Parti) is given the most centrist position, reflecting a lack of ideological orientation in its populist stands. While the Motherland Party (MP; Anavatan Partisi) and the True Path Party (TPP; Doğru Yol Partisi) are seen as leaning toward right of center, the other extreme-right-wing group is placed on the distinct right-wing end of the spectrum. In other words, the constituencies of the major parties that competed in the 2002 general election place themselves on the left-right ideological spectrum almost in full agreement with our expectations about the Turkish party system.[8] NAP and TPP voters place themselves on average at the very end of the ideological spectrum while those of the JDP and MP followed them. In the eyes of their voters then, MP and TPP were within the right-of-center of the ideological spectrum. The fact that JDP voters are very close to MP and TPP voters and considerably toward the center compared to NAP voters should be emphasized here. Ideologically speaking, the differences between the NAP and the JDP voters are much larger than those found between JDP and MP as well as TPP voters. One thing is clear then: while JDP voters see themselves as similar to voters who hold the MP and TPP positions, these three parties are all in the eyes of their own voters quite far from the center of the ideological spectrum. The center (5 and 6 on our 1 to 10 scale) before the 2002 general election was left empty by all party constituencies and only YP and DLP voters see themselves as closer to the center than to either one of the extremes.

Figure 7.2 also compares the party constituency placements in the 2002 and 2004 surveys. After the municipal elections of March 2004, we

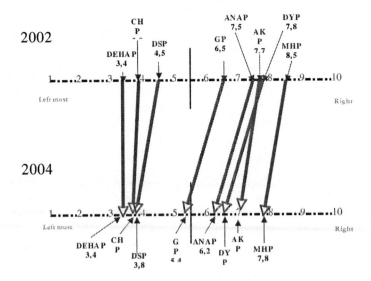

FIGURE 7.2. Party Constituencies' Positions on the Left-Right Ideological Spectrum

see that the above-mentioned move to the center of ideological orientations becomes clearer by taking the party constituencies into account. We see that with the exception of DPP voters, for whom the average position remained the same at around 3.4 on a 1 to 10 scale, all other parties' voters have changed their average positions. Typically, the center-left party constituencies, those of the RPP and DLP, have moved to the left and thus become more leftist on average during the tenure of the JDP government. The fact that on average DPP and RPP voters place themselves very similarly along the left-right ideological spectrum is also noticeable and reflects perhaps the limits of RPP appeal to a larger audience by simply maintaining a similarity to a ethnic left-wing party constituency that does not even vote for RPP.

In contrast, center-right and right-of-center party constituencies have shifted toward the center and thus mellowed their ideological stands during the course of the JDP's tenure. We also see that these shifts are not insignificant shifts. For YP, on average, the positions are 1.1 points more leftist in orientation, taking the YP voters from 6.5 points on average down to 5.4 points. Similarly, MP voters move from 7.5 to 6.2, TPP voters from 7.8 to 6.6, and JDP voters from 7.7 to 7. Even the right-most placement of the NAP moved from 8.5 on average down to 7.8, still occupying the right-most position. The only leap-frogging, to use a spatial voting jargon, occurred between TPP and JDP voters' average positions. While the

TPP voters were on average to the right of JDP voters in 2002, in 2004 they occupied on average a position to the left of JDP voters. Despite mellowing down of their ideological positions and more centrist positioning in 2004 compared to 2002, the JDP voters still occupy the second rightmost position on average. In between these two measurements, JDP constituency has grown considerably in size and thus includes a larger number of people. Nevertheless if an individual reports to have voted for JDP, he or she is on average only to the left of NAP voters and thus occupies a clear right-wing position on the ideological spectrum.

Another important point to note at this juncture is that the center position of the Turkish party system is still unoccupied by credible electoral organizations. The YP and MP command a very small group, and YP leadership has been buried under a big package of corruption charges against its leader, Cem Uzan. This picture shows that the YP constituency is still up for grabs. The constituencies mobilized by the populist rhetoric of Uzan remain to be lured by any one of the existing parties and thus form a potential threat to more responsible policy positioning in the system. However, this group is small and obviously not growing. Given the successful showing of the TPP in the 2004 municipal elections, it remains to be seen if the TPP leadership could continue its long route back to the center of Turkish politics and start appealing to the centrist constituencies.

As I emphasized elsewhere, the Turkish party system is characterized by high volatility and fragmentation, deep regional cleavages, and low nationalization of electoral forces.[9] A number of additional micro-individual-level findings complement these macro characteristics. As I demonstrated above, survey research shows a consistent shift of voters from centrist left-right ideological positions toward the extreme right end of the spectrum.[10] As a result, only a small minority seems to have remained left of center. While the centrist positions have shrunk by half, the right-of-center positions have grown continuously, and nearly 20 percent of the voters seem to be placed on the far right position; that is, at point 10 on a 1 to 10 left-right ideological scale. Multidimensional analyses show two dimensions that command the ideological competition in the Turkish party system.[11] The first and relatively more dominant dimension is the secularist vs. pro-Islamist cleavage. It is noteworthy that this cleavage largely overlaps with the center vs. periphery formations in Turkish politics and also with left-right orientations, thus being similar in many respects to Western European traditions. The second dimension is the ethnic cleavage, setting the Turkish and Kurdish identities in opposition to one another and reflecting pieces of a larger reform debate in the country around Copenhagen political criteria for EU membership.

In microindividual-level analyses, a rising disenchantment of the electorate with the existing parties becomes evident. For a long time, commercial and academic surveys have revealed that not only is a large segment of the electorate undecided as to which party to vote for, but an equally large segment simply refuses to vote for any one of the available parties.[12] The negative affect or simple anger is evident among this group of the electorate. The inability of governments to respond to emergency needs, even in the aftermath of the devastating 1999 earthquakes and the following economic crisis, obviously occupies an important place in the popular anger toward politicians and politics at large. Turkish electors seem simply unhappy with their lives and outraged with the politicians' inability to deliver satisfactory policies to counteract these tendencies.

Religiosity, more than any other variable, is found to determine Turkish voters' choice among competing parties. In only two of the most recent surveys did researchers identify varying degrees of retrospective, as well as prospective, economic evaluations on party choice.[13] Yet even when these effects are present, their magnitudes are small compared to the religiosity effect. In the 1999 elections, when the ultranationalist NAP scored high gains, Ali Çarkoğlu and Binnaz Toprak indicate that both right-of-center parties, namely FP and NAP, as well as the center-right TPP, appealed to pro-Islamist constituencies.[14] In line with the shift in ideological orientations of the voters, determinants of vote choice seem to have been molded by increasing tension between pro-Islamists and the secularists. While three of the five parties that obtained representation in the 1999 Parliament appealed to pro-Islamist sentiments, the rest of the bunch seemed to cater to secularist constituencies, thus keeping religious issues a top priority in their respective agendas.

Given the above diagnosis of the ideological characteristics of the JDP constituency from the conventional left-right ideological perspective, I turn now to the question of who were the JDP voters in November 2002.

INDIVIDUAL-LEVEL DETERMINANTS OF THE VOTE IN NOVEMBER 2002

Before I present the results of my analysis as to the determinants of party choice among voting-age respondents in a nationwide representative survey of urban and rural voters in Turkey, I present a short description of the variables used in this analysis. Table 7.2 summarizes the variables used. First of all, my dependent variable is a multinomial variable that distinguishes five groups of voters among the respondents. Those who indicated in our pre-election survey of October 2002 that they were inclined to vote for JDP, YP, RPP, NAP/FP (Saadet Partisi), and TPP/MP are included as separate categories. Those who declared that they were inclined to vote for other parties and those who were still undecided were all excluded from the vote intention function. I also joined the NAP and FP voters together and the TPP and MP voters together to form two separate categories. This was done primarily because when these parties were included as separate categories they each had too few observations to allow meaningful estimation results.

Among the independent variables I included three different dimensions of religiosity.[15] Following earlier work by R. Stark and C. Y. Glock and Riaz Hassan, the first is the ideological or faith dimension that emphasizes a set of fundamental beliefs.[16] A number of core doctrinal beliefs with which the individuals are required to comply such as belief in God, in sin, in heaven and hell, in the existence of spirit, in the afterlife, and in the existence of the devil are identified for this dimension. The second dimension is ritualistic or religious practice and comprises acts of worship through which believers are expected to show their devotion to their religion. Despite a large number of rituals in Islam, only two were used in the questionnaire, both referring to prayer. The first asked how often the respondents pray (a private act) and the second how often they go to mosque (a public act). The third dimension addresses attitudinal differences on issues related to religion. The respondents are given certain statements that they are required to evaluate by providing their degree of agreement with them on a 1 to 10 scale.[17]

As for the attitudinal dimension of religiosity, I use evaluations of a total of eleven statements to derive xenophobia, nationalism, and political inefficacy scales. Table 7.3 shows that these dimensions are clearly differentiated from one another. While increasing factor scores for the xenophobia and nationalism dimensions indicate increasing xenophobic and nationalistic attitudes, increasing factor score values for the third dimension indicates increasing political inefficacy of the respondents' feelings and attitudes.

Tables 7.4 and 7.5 show the results of my multinomial logit estimation using the above-described dependent variable with five categories of voters.[18] Table 7.4 shows that for the variables chosen in our estimation of the vote intention function, we have only 701 observations out of

TABLE 7.2. Variables Included in Party Choice Analysis

DEPENDENT VARIABLE:

Multinomial categories of party voters distinguishing JDP, YP, RPP, TPP/MP and NAP/FP voters as five different categories of respondents

INDEPENDENT VARIABLES:

Religiosity as faith, attitudes and practice (as three separate dimensions)

Religiosity as self-evaluation of respondents

Xenophobia, nationalism, and political inefficacy (as three separate dimensions)

Left-Right ideology self-placement

Sex (as dummy variable taking 1 for men as opposed to 0 for women)

Education levels (Dummy variables separating no schooling, primary and high school education from university level).

Economic condition evaluations

Kurdish speakers (as dummy variable separating Kurdish speakers from others)

Respondents' age

Respondents' income (as dummy variable separating those who are at the lowest income category from the rest)

Place of residence (as dummy variable separating rural residents from urban)

Support for EU membership (as dummy variable separating those in support =1 from non-supporters)

Support for Israel rather than other Middle Eastern countries for Turkish foreign policy (as dummy variable for Israel supporters =1 from others)

Support for Muslim countries rather than Western countries for Turkish foreign policy (as dummy variable for Muslim country supporters =1 from others)

Self-evaluated importance of the respondent's vote for the outcome of the November 2002 election

Self-reported importance of the winner of the November election for increasing the household income.

Support for the establishment of Shari'a rule in Turkey (as dummy variable separating the supporters of Shari'a from others)

TABLE 7.3. Dimensions on Xenophobia-Nationalism and Political Inefficacy

ROTATED COMPONENT MATRIX	XENOPHOBIA	NATIONALISM	POLITICAL INEFFICACY	COMMU- NALITIES
Foreigners settling in our country would harm our culture.	0.825	0.095	0.080	0.696
Foreigners settling in our country would make jobs harder to find for us.	0.745	0.167	0.097	0.593
Tourists are harming our moral values.	0.693	0.101	0.226	0.571
I would not want a foreigner to be my neighbor.	0.660	0.225	0.124	0.502
Turks do not have friends other than Turks.	0.258	0.775	0.037	0.669
Seeing Turkish flag would make me feel good.	0.041	0.729	0.055	0.536
Either one should love or should leave Turkey.	0.260	0.691	0.073	0.551
I would prefer to use a Turkish product even if it is more expensive and of lower quality.	0.152	0.674	0.158	0.503
I'm doing everything I can but I don't think I can ever reach a comfortable position.	0.144	0.144	0.723	0.564
A small and powerful group is ruling Turkey.	0.129	-0.064	0.705	0.517
Simple citizens like me are powerless to change political decisions for their benefits.	0.097	0.186	0.692	0.522
% of Variance	33.55	12.42	10.61	56.57

Extraction Method: Principal Component Analysis. Rotation Method: Varimax with Kaiser Normalization. Rotation converged in 5 iterations.

a total of 1,984, which indicates rather restrictive missing data primarily because of unanswered questions in our questionnaires for 1,283 respondents.[19] Within the subsample used, respondents intending to vote for the JDP comprised about 44 percent while those inclined to vote for the RPP comprised about 23 percent.

In order to show how JDP voters are differentiated from the rest of our comparison party constituency categories, I show on Table 7.5 summary estimation results that contrast JDP with the rest of the four categories of voters described above.[20] By so doing, we are in a position to compare the differential impact of our explanatory variables in explaining the likelihood of voting for the JDP as opposed to voting for the NAP/FP, YP, RPP, and TPP/MP. For example, looking at the comparison of those respondents who intend to vote for the JDP with those for the NAP/FP, we see that as left-right self-placement scores move to the right of the spectrum, the likelihood of voting for the JDP declines significantly. In other words, JDP voters are relatively to the left of NAP/FP voters. The likelihood of voting for the JDP significantly increases when voters with no formal education are contrasted with voters who are university graduates. In other words, relatively lower-educated respondents tend to switch from the NAP/FP to the JDP. Since the NAP was part of the incumbent coalition, it is not surprising that those who have adverse evaluations for the past year's economic performance at the time of our fieldwork would tend to vote for the JDP rather than the NAP. It is noteworthy that none of the religiosity measures included in the analysis turned out to be a significant factor in differentiating the respondents intending to vote for the JDP from those intending to vote for either the NAP or the FP. Prospective economic evaluations also turned out to be insignificant in vote intentions shifting from the NAP/FP to the JDP or vice versa. Support for EU membership also seemed unimportant in distinguishing JDP and NAP/FP vote intentions. Similarly, age, income, urban-rural divide, foreign policy preferences, and self-evaluated importance of respondent's vote for the outcome of the November 2002 elections are all found to be insignificant. In other words, apart from left-right ideology, education, and retrospective economic evaluations, NAP/FP voters and JDP voters do not seem to be different from one another.

In contrast, when we look at YP voters we see that religious practice and attitude scales both have a significant positive impact on individuals' intentions to vote for the JDP. Relatively more religious voters in our practice and attitude dimensions tend to vote for the JDP rather than the YP. Movement to the right on the left-right dimension also tends to increase

TABLE 7.4. Multinomial Logit Estimation Results of the Vote Intention Function Case Processing Summary

		N	MARGINAL PERCENTAGE
	JDP	306	43.7
	YP	90	12.8
	RPP	158	22.5
	NAP/FP	70	10.0
	TPP/MP	77	11.0
Valid		701	100
Missing		1,283	
Total		1,984	
Pseudo R-Square	Cox and Snell		0.60
	Nagelkerke		0.64
	McFadden		0.32

likelihood of voting for the JDP rather than the YP. Primary education as opposed to university education has a negative impact on people's likelihood of voting for the JDP. In other words, JDP voters tend to be more educated than YP voters. Men, rather than women, tend to vote for the JDP. Similar to contrasts with the NAP, negative retrospective economic performance evaluations tend to increase the likelihood of vote intention for the JDP compared to the YP. The JDP's credibility may thus be higher on economic issues compared to the YP. Besides retrospective evaluations, prospective ones are also working to the advantage of the JDP. If respondents' expectations about their family's finances over the next year at the time of our fieldwork gets worse, then they tend to declare intentions to vote for the JDP rather than the YP. Thus one may conjecture that the JDP has more credibility compared to the YP on the economic policy front. Another important variable that seems to shape intention to vote for the JDP, compared to the YP, is foreign policy evaluations. Those who support building closer relations with the Muslims, rather than with the Western countries, tend to declare intentions to vote for the JDP rather than the YP. In short, voters intending to vote for the JDP are distinguished from those intending to support the YP in terms of their religiosity, left-right ideological stands, education, sex, prospective economic evaluations, and foreign policy preferences. Accordingly, the JDP constituency seem to be much more different from the YP than from the NAP.

TABLE 7.5. Summary Multinomial Logit Estimation Results of the Vote Intention Function

PARAMETER ESTIMATES	JDP VS NAP/FP	JDP VS YP	JDP VS RPP	JDP VS TPP/MP
Religiosity-Faith			+	+
Religiosity-Attitudes		+	+	+
Religiosity-Practice		+	+	+
Xenophobia				
Nationalism				
Political Inefficacy				
L-R self-placement	−	+	+	
Dummy variable for no-schooling	+			
Dummy variable for primary education		−		
Dummy variable for high school				
Dummy variable for men		+		
Dummy variable for those who indicated that over the last year the economic policies followed by the incumbent government have adversely affected Turkey's economy	+	+		
Dummy variable for those who indicated that over the next year their family's economic situation will get worse				
Dummy variable for those who indicated that over the next year Turkey's economic situation will get worse		+		
Dummy variable for those who support Turkey's membership in EU			−	−
Dummy variable for those who can speak Kurdish				
Importance of the winner of November 2002 election for increasing the household income				
Self-evaluated importance of the respondent's vote for the outcome of November 2002 election				
Dummy variable for those who would want a Shari'a state to be established in Turkey				

TABLE 7.5 (CONT'D.). Summary Multinomial Logit Estimation Results of the Vote Intention
Function

PARAMETER ESTIMATES	JDP VS NAP/FP	JDP VS YP	JDP VS RPP	JDP VS TPP/MP
Dummy variable for those who prefer that Turkey builds closer relations with the Muslim rather than the Western countries		+	+	+
Dummy variable for those who prefer that Turkey builds closer relations with Israel rather than other countries of the Middle East				
Self-evaluated religiosity				
Dummy variable for those who report less than or equal to 200 million TL household income per month				
Respondent's age			-	-
Dummy variable for rural areas				

All equations were estimated with an intercept.

When we look at the results for the JDP in comparison to RPP voters, we see several patterns emerging. We see once again that religiosity
dimensions are all significant and positive, indicating that more religious
respondents tend to favor the JDP rather than the RPP. Ideological divide
along the left-right dimension is also significant in separating the JDP
voters from those of the RPP; that is, more right-wing respondents tend
toward the JDP rather than the RPP. Interestingly, RPP voters seem to be
older than those intending to vote for the JDP.

Foreign policy preferences concerning EU membership and Turkey's
building relations with Muslim rather than Western countries are both
significant in telling JDP intentions from those for the RPP. Despite the
clear pro-EU policy stand of the JDP after the election, it is clear that
respondents who are supportive of Turkey's EU membership are less likely
to vote for the JDP compared to the RPP. Similarly, respondents intending to vote for the JDP are skeptical toward Western countries rather
than supportive of the building of better relationships with the Muslim
countries. In other words, religiosity, left-right ideology, and age, together
with foreign policy preferences, distinguish respondents intending to vote
for the JDP from those who favor the RPP.

A very similar picture appears for factors that account for differences between respondents intending to vote for the JDP as opposed to the TPP/MP. The only exception is that for the case of the TPP/MP, left-right self-placement appears to be insignificant. In other words, the difference between JDP and TPP/JDP voters is insignificant along the left-right scale while religiosity, age, and foreign policy preferences between JDP and TPP/MP voters appear significantly different from one another. In fact it seems that the TPP/MP constituency is similar in these respects to the RPP rather than to the JDP, which appears as more religious, anti-EU, younger, and closer to cooperation with Muslim rather than Western countries.

It is important to note at this juncture that while the faith and practice dimensions have little policy implication, the attitudinal dimension reflects many important policy clues for the JDP government. The issue of turban and headscarves at the universities forms an integral part of this dimension and thus makes it more obvious why JDP is so insistent on changing the current policy so as to allow headscarves in the universities. The attitudinal religiosity dimension rather than the faith and practice dimensions appears to be the most influential in differentiating respondents who intend to vote for the JDP from YP, RPP and TPP/MP voters, so much so that, after controlling for the influences of other independent variables, a one standard deviation increase in religious attitudes makes voting for the JDP twice as likely compared to the YP, 3.8 times more likely compared to the RPP, and 1.9 times more likely compared to the TPP/MP. This is the highest impact among all independent variables for the case of the RPP and the second highest for the YP and the TPP/MP.

CONCLUSIONS

My aim in this chapter has been to diagnose the salient microindividual-level determinants of those voters who chose to vote for the JDP in the November 2002 general election. A number of interesting differentiating patterns arise that separate the JDP constituency from that of its major competitors. First of all, despite the ideologically mellow outlook that kept many secularists in Turkey comfortable during the tenure of the JDP, the electoral bases of the JDP in November 2002 were primarily coming from a relatively younger generation having significant religious conservative traits. This electoral base, however, had expanded considerably in the March 2004 election. Nevertheless, my analysis of the

ideological positions of party constituencies for 2002 and the postmunici-
pality election in 2004 suggests that there may be very little real mellowing of right-of-center ideological positions for JDP constituencies. While
all right-of-center party constituencies have moved to more centrist positions in 2004 compared to 2002, JDP voters still occupy the second right-
most average position on the conventional left-right dimension.

Second, the impact of the economic crisis that preceded the general
elections had a positive impact on JDP electoral support. However, this
aid from economic difficulties experienced during the tenure of the DLP-
NAP-MP coalition government has to be qualified because retrospective
or prospective economic policy performance evaluations help differentiate the JDP constituency only from the NAP/FP and the YP. My analysis excluded the DLP constituency that effectively evaporated before the
2002 election. However, the negative impact of retrospective evaluations
on the NAP vote is very much in line with our expectations. The fact that
JDP voters are distinguished from YP voters on the basis of retrospective as well as prospective evaluations is interesting. It points to the JDP's
credibility advantage over the YP, since the more negative retrospective
or prospective evaluations are, the more likely our respondents are found
to switch to the JDP rather than the YP. Since both of these parties
had a natural inclination to use economic failures of the outgoing coalition as a theme in their campaign work in much the same way, the fact
that people tended to favor the JDP over the YP is an observation wor-
thy of note. However, this credibility advantage may in the longer run
become a liability for the JDP because they stand alone in government to
take the blame for any economic failure. Like many earlier governments,
JDP's success in government is critically contingent on success in the economic sphere. For the JDP there will be no ambiguity about attributing
responsibility about the economic conditions prevailing at the time of
the next election. So, failure would be translated directly into lower levels of support. However, success may not be directly and fully translated
into higher levels of support because then the electorate will have enjoyed
the full interelection period in relative prosperity. Noneconomic factors
are then more likely to be emphasized by the opposition, which may find
ample opportunities in the Turkish foreign policy arena and EU relations
to feed their appetite.

Third, at least at the time of our pre-election survey, the JDP constituency displayed a cynical view of Turkey's bid for the EU membership. However, over its tenure in executive office, the JDP leadership has
displayed a remarkable ability to adjust to newly arising subtleties and

has manipulated all their policy tools to fulfill all requirements for the start of negotiations as soon as possible. Given this determination on the part of the leadership, my most recent analysis of EU support among voters shows a clear positive turn for the JDP constituency.[21] However, the JDP constituency was more sympathetic to building ties with the Muslim countries instead of with the EU project and the Western countries. Over the last year, the JDP leadership has criticized Israel for its policies in the occupied Palestinian territories and there was some talk in the Turkish media about a newly shaped link between the Kurdish leadership in Northern Iraq and Israel's secret service. Such speculations are destructive to any support that Turkish public opinion might have for Israeli-Turkish cooperation in the region. In short, lacking executive leadership there is very little reason to think that the JDP constituency's support for Muslim instead of Western countries has changed over the last two years. This stress between the West and the Muslim world is potentially dangerous for JDP foreign policy and needs to be dealt with in a productive way by the party leadership.[22]

Fourth, it is interesting that the main differences between the constituencies of the JDP, the RPP, and the TPP/MP turn out to be differences in religiosity of their likely supporters, their preferences concerning foreign policy, and their age. However, the JDP's difference from the NAP is more focused on left-right ideological positions, education level of their constituencies, and retrospective economic punishment effect rather than foreign policy preferences or the religiosity of their likely constituencies at the time of our fieldwork. A critical difference between the JDP and the RPP as well is reflective of a left-right ideological difference similar to the difference between the NAP and the JDP. In short, an unqualified claim that the JDP constituency is more religious than other parties is simply not tenable. The JDP constituency is differently distinguished from its major competitors. While for the NAP there seems no differentiating impact of religiosity, for the YP, the RPP, and the TPP/MP separate dimensions of religiosity become critical.

Lastly, the JDP support base does not seem to include a significant Kurdish contingent. JDP correctly diagnosed this problem and acted accordingly before municipal elections to win over significant votes for the local elections. However, it remains to be seen if the JDP will be able to hold onto this support when ethnic identity politics become more salient in the next general election. One factor that will limit the JDP's ability in this respect is the observation that the JDP constituency does not also seem to be closer to the most economically disadvantaged segments of Turkish society but rather closer to middle-income earners. Although this is comforting during economic expansion, it also could foreshadow a disaster if an economic crisis looms on the horizon because taking care of the demands of the lower income groups might be simply much easier than accommodating the losing middle-income earners. However, the JDP constituency has grown considerably over the last two years. It remains to be seen to what extent these diagnoses will remain valid as we approach the next general election.

Is the JDP well positioned to fill the vacuum in the center of the Turkish political spectrum? While some of these findings are suggestive of the prospect that the JDP can fill the empty ideological space of the traditional centrist parties of the country, other findings are in contradiction with the centrist heritage. The JDP constituency does not seem to lie in the center of the Turkish ideological space. Even after the second round of electoral expansion in the March 2004 municipal elections, the JDP constituency still is to the right of all party constituencies except that of the NAP. These results need to be evaluated with the most recent data through individual-level analyses to see if the diagnosed trends continue in their significance. The Turkish electorate is simply too volatile and still considerably fragmented when it comes to ideologically salient issues, especially concerning secularism and religiosity. The background to all these ideological stands is also the economic conditions prevailing in the country.

Perhaps most striking in the above findings is the prominent impact of primarily foreign policy issues on factors that distinguish party constituencies. Not surprisingly, membership in the EU and relations with Muslim as opposed to Western countries are among the most significant factors that explain the difference between the JDP and other party constituencies. This finding may be taken also as a reflection of a reform dimension in the making in Turkish ideological space. Membership in the EU brings with it a whole set of policy initiatives geared to adapt the Turkish politico-economic system to the European standards with a fully functioning, efficient market economy together with a libertarian democracy, creating an open, self-confident Turkish society wherein basic liberties of all citizens are equally guaranteed. The cleavage that is being built upon the European project seems to get deeper every day and is starting to dominate the political scene with clear reflections on the electoral politics of the country. Together with general attitudes toward Muslim as opposed to Western countries, this divide between pro-EU groups and resisters in the party system touches upon the very core of

Turkish republican concerns with national unity, modernization, security, economic development, minority rights, and democracy. All of these issues are direct descendents of the long-term reform movement in Turkish history predating the roots of the Republic and firmly seeded in the late Ottoman reforms. As the parties and their electoral bases start to reflect these reform efforts in their respective support camps, it becomes more and more clear that the domestic political scene will be shaped and reshaped more intensely as a result of debates and competitions around state reform as a consequence primarily of the European project and linked foreign policy issues.

NOTES

1. For an in-depth discussion of the election results and the party system before and after the November 2002 general election, see Ali Çarkoğlu, "The Rises of the New Generation Pro-Islamists in Turkey: The Justice and Development Party Phenomenon in the November 2002 Elections in Turkey," *South European Society and Politics* 7 (2002): 123–56.

2. See Ali Çarkoğlu and Gamze Avcı, "An Analysis of the Turkish Electorate from a Geographical Perspective," in *Politics, Parties, and Elections in Turkey*, ed. Yılmaz Esmer and Sabri Sayarı (Boulder, CO: Lynne Rienner, 2002), 115–35; and Ali Çarkoğlu and Ilgaz Eren, "The Rise of Right-of-Centre Parties and the Nationalisation of Electoral Forces in Turkey," *New Perspectives on Turkey* 26 (2002): 95–137, for a long-term analysis of party constituencies in Turkish elections.

3. See Ali Çarkoğlu, "The Turkish Party System in Transition: Party Performance and Agenda Transformation," *Political Studies* 46 (1998): 544–71; Ali Çarkoğlu and Melvin J. Hinich, "A Spatial Analysis of Turkish Party Preferences" (2006), forthcoming in *Electoral Studies*; William M. Hale, "Democracy and the Party System in Turkey," in *Turkish Transformation, New Century, New Challenges*, ed. Brian W. Beeley (Huntingdon, UK: Eothen Press, 2002); and see Ersin Kalaycıoğlu, "Türkiye'de Siyaset," in *Sivil Toplum için Kent, Yerel Siyaset ve Demokrasi Seminerleri* (Istanbul: World Academy for Local Government and Democracy Publications, 1998) for a multidimensional analysis of Turkish ideological space.

4. For those who are not familiar with Turkish politics, table 1 in Çarkoğlu, "The Rises of the New Generation Pro-Islamists," provides a shorthand reference point for the parties' ideological and programmatic orientations. However, this table admittedly leaves many of the subtleties concerning Turkish parties, their ideology, and their constituencies out of the picture for lack of space and simplicity. For Turkish politics specialists these categories may be too simplistic because there is also a great deal of variation of parties within each category as well.

5. The expected margin of error is +/- 2.2 at the 95 percent confidence level. Frekans Research Company conducted the field research during October 10–25. Sabancı University and the Swedish Consulate-Istanbul funded the project.

6. Ersin Kalaycıoğlu, "The Shaping of Political Preferences in Turkey: Coping with the Post-Cold-War Era," *New Perspectives on Turkey* 20 (1999): 71–72.

7. This study is again a nationwide representative sample collected as part of the Philanthropy in Turkey project sponsored by the Ford Foundation and the Third Sector Foundation (Türkiye Üçüncü Sektör Vakfı-TUSEV), conducted in February and March 2004 wherein a total of 1,536 interviews were carried out.

8. The placements here also fully agree with the depiction of Çarkoğlu, "The Rises of the New Generation Pro-Islamists," in table 1.

9. See Çarkoğlu, "The Rises of the New Generation Pro-Islamists"; and Çarkoğlu and Eren, "The Rise of Right-of-Centre Parties."

10. See also Üstün Ergüder, Yılmaz Esmer, and Ersin Kalaycıoğlu, *Türk Toplumunun Değerleri* (Istanbul: TÜSİAD, 1991); Çarkoğlu, "The Turkish Party System in Transition"; Ali Çarkoğlu and Binnaz Toprak, *Türkiye'de Din, Toplum ve Siyaset* (Istanbul: Turkish Economic and Social Studies Foundation Publications, 2000); Kalaycıoğlu, "Türkiye'de Siyaset"; Kalaycıoğlu, "The Shaping of Political Preferences."

11. See Kalaycıoğlu, "Türkiye'de Siyaset"; Hale, "Democracy and the Party System"; Ali Çarkoğlu and Melvin J. Hinich, "An Analysis of the Ideological Space underlying Turkish Party Preferences," *Turkish Policy Quarterly* 1 (2002): 87–100; Çarkoğlu and Hinich, "A Spatial Analysis of Turkish Party Preferences."

12. Ali Çarkoğlu, "The Turkish General Election of 24 December 1995," *Electoral Studies* 16 (1997): 86–95.

13. See Yılmaz Esmer "Parties and the Electorate: A Comparative Analysis of Voter Profiles of Turkish Political Parties," in *Turkey: Political, Social and Economic Challenges in the 1990s*, ed. Ç. Balım et al. (Leiden: E. J. Brill, 1995), 74–89; Yılmaz Esmer, "At the Ballot Box: Determinants of Voting Behaviour in Turkey," in *The Democratic Challenge: Elections, Parties, and Voters in Turkey*, ed. Yılmaz Esmer and Sabri Sayarı (Boulder, CO: Lynne Rienner, 2001); Ersin Kalaycıoğlu, "Elections and Party Preferences in Turkey, Changes and Continuities in the 1990s," *Comparative Political Studies* 3 (1994): 402–24; Ersin Kalaycıoğlu, "Türkiye'de Köktenci Sağ Partiler ve Seçmen Tercihleri," *Dünü ve Bugünüyle Toplum ve Ekonomi* 7 (October 1994): 65–84; Kalaycıoğlu, "The Shaping of Political Preferences in Turkey," 47–76; and Çarkoğlu and Toprak, *Türkiye'de Din*, on religiosity and voting behavior.

14. Çarkoğlu and Toprak's 2000 research on political Islam finds that the FP's, NAP's, and TPP's electorate are significantly more religious than the other parties. The voters of the other three centrist parties, namely the MP, the DLP, and the RPP, are of a significantly lower level of religiosity, thus favoring secularist stands on salient issues. See Ali Çarkoğlu, "Geography of April 1999 Turkish Elections," *Turkish Studies* 1 (2000): 149–71; and Kalaycıoğlu, "The Shaping of Political Preferences," on the claim that the NAP has effectively appealed, by using the undelivered promises of religious significance, to the alienated constituencies of the now closed Pro-Islamist RPP.

15. For a detailed description of these three dimensions, see Ali Çarkoğlu, "Political Preferences of the Turkish Electorate: Reflections of an Alevi-Sunni Cleavage," forthcoming in the special issue of *Turkish Studies* on *Religion and Politics in Turkey*.

16. C. Y. Glock and R. Stark, *Religion and Society in Tension* (Chicago: Rand McNally, 1965); and Riaz Hassan, *Faithliness, Muslim Conceptions of Islam and Society* (Oxford, UK: Oxford University Press, 2002).

17. The attitudinal evaluations are obtained on seven issues. One concerns the approval of the ban of headscarves in universities. Another asks about objection to one's daughter marrying a non-Muslim. The degree of approval of closure of restaurants and

coffeehouses during the month of Ramadan until the breaking of the fast and the degree to which one is considering sending one's child to an İmam Hatip high school are also addressed. Similar evaluations are also asked about whether a religious person is more trustworthy in commercial life than nonreligious individuals. Lastly, respondents were asked whether they approve of having boys and girls in the same class at high schools and whether or not they would favor the founding of a Shari'a-based religious state in Turkey.

18. For details of this method, see Scott J. Long, *Regression Models for Categorical and Limited Dependent Variables* (London: Sage Publications, 1997), chap. 6. Estimations are carried out with SPSS 11.5.

19. Of the 1,283 total missing observations, 142 were dropped out because of insufficient number of respondents intending to vote for the DPP/PDP (66), the DLP/NTP (38), or other parties (38); and 450 respondents were dropped out because they were undecided as to which party they would vote for at the time of our fieldwork. In other words, only 691 observations (35 percent) out of 1,984 were lost because of unanswered questions.

20. Obviously, many more such comparisons can be made. However, I only report the ones that are central to our interests here. Details of the estimation results are not reported to save space.

21. See Ali Çarkoğlu, "Who Wants Full Membership? Characteristics of Turkish Public Support for EU Membership," *Turkish Studies* 1 (2000): 171–94; Ali Çarkoğlu, "Societal Perceptions of Turkey's EU Membership: Causes and Consequences of Support for EU Membership?" in *Turkey and European Integration: Accession Prospects and Issues*, ed. Nergis Canefe and Mehmet Uğur (London: Routledge, 2004), 19–45, for details of EU support among the JDP constituency. Back in October 2002 the overall level of support for EU membership was around 65 percent, and it rose to about 72 percent in March 2004. Level of support for the EU among the JDP constituency remained below nationwide averages but significantly rose to a clear majority throughout the tenure of the JDP in government.

22. This public opinion cleavage in preferences over the Muslim world as opposed to the Western countries can be directly observed not only in Turkey-EU relations and its reflections in Greek-Turkish debate over Cyprus but also in Turkey-U.S. relations that became increasingly tense over policies in Iraq.

II.
THE JDP POLICIES

CHAPTER 8

Symbols and Shadow Play

Military-JDP Relations, 2002–2004

■ *Gareth Jenkins*

The landslide victory of the Justice and Development Party (JDP) in the November 3, 2002, general elections represented arguably the greatest challenge to the traditional concept of Turkish secularism since the foundation of the Republic in 1923.[1] For the first time a party with explicitly Islamist roots had an overwhelming majority in Parliament. Although the JDP's leadership repeatedly pledged its commitment to the principle of secularism, there appeared little doubt that it would eventually attempt to change the way in which secularism was applied. The only questions were the extent to which it would seek changes and when it would seek them.

The Turkish General Staff (TGS) sees itself as the guardian of the state ideology of Kemalism, the teachings of Mustafa Kemal Atatürk (1881–1938), the Republic's founder and first president. Kemalism's two fundamental principles are territorial integrity and secularism. As a result, for the TGS, any Islamist party, however moderate, is anathema. In the weeks following the November 2002 elections, the TGS publicly refrained from criticizing the JDP, but privately it made no secret of its concerns. Yet in practical terms, there was little it could do. Facilitating the removal of the JDP from power was not a viable option, not least because there was no effective political opposition, inside or outside Parliament, that could form an alternative government. Any explicit attempt to apply pressure to the JDP to ensure that its policies remained within what the TGS deemed to be acceptable parameters would antagonize the European Union (EU).

Civilian control of the military is a sine qua non for EU membership. Although it doubts that the EU will ever grant Turkey full membership, the TGS nevertheless supports accession because it sees it as the culmination of Atatürk's policy of Westernization and because it believes that membership will result in higher levels of welfare and education, which will in turn erode electoral support for parties such as the JDP. Equally important, the TGS is aware that the vast majority of the Turkish public supports EU membership and that being seen as being opposed to, or even preventing, accession would undermine the military's still considerable public prestige.

The JDP was also aware that the TGS was its most implacable domestic opponent. As a result, in addition to EU membership being attractive in itself, for the JDP the accession process took on a new importance as a means of restraining the political influence of the TGS. But there were limits to the military's tolerance. Any direct assault on what were seen as the foundations of Kemalism would provoke a reaction from the TGS, regardless of the consequences for Turkey's prospects for EU accession. Not only could such a reaction delay the EU accession process—and thus further reduce the restraints on the military—but the resultant political instability could derail a still fragile economic recovery. Yet the JDP was under pressure from many of its supporters, who had voted for the party in expectation that it would relax or abolish many of the curbs on expressions of Islamic piety—such as women wearing Islamic headscarves in the public arena—that were included in the Kemalist interpretation of secularism.

As a result, as it consolidated its grip on power, the JDP became engaged with the TGS in a shadow play of symbols and oblique rhetoric in which the JDP would subtly probe the boundaries of Kemalist orthodoxy only to withdraw again if it provoked a reaction from the military; and the TGS sought to preserve the orthodox Kemalist interpretation of secularism yet avoid too direct an intervention in the political sphere. Both sides kept a wary eye on the EU and the progress of the accession process.[2]

ISLAM, KEMALISM, AND THE TURKISH ARMED FORCES

In their military academies and staff colleges, Turkish officers are taught that they have a sacred duty to defend not only the territory and population of the Turkish Republic but the precepts and principles of Atatürk's ideological legacy of Kemalism. For the TGS, Kemalism is not an ideological coloring painted onto the Turkish state; it is its essence. Secularism was not only the driving force behind Atatürk's domestic reforms of the 1920s and 1930s that laid the foundations for the Kemalist state, it was also the most controversial, triggering violent protests and even rebellions.[3] The bloodshed resulted not only in a hardening of attitudes toward antisecularists in the Kemalist government of the time but in the creation of a martyrology.[4] It also reinforced a perception in the military of secularism as a security issue, with the TGS as its main protector.

Perhaps more insidiously, the violence of the opposition to Atatürk's secularizing reforms has resulted in a tendency in the Kemalist establishment to see secularism not merely as the removal of explicit references to religion in the state sphere—most critically, of course, refusing to use the Qur'an or the sayings of the Prophet Mohammed as a source for legislation—but also as state control of religion in the private sphere. The Diyanet, or Directorate of Religious Affairs, which is tied to the prime ministry, appoints and pays all Sunni Muslim clergy in Turkey[5]—who are thus civil servants—and issues standardized sermons to be read out in mosques each Friday. This is not seen as contravening the principle of secularism. Yet attempts by female students to attend schools or universities wearing headscarves is viewed by most members of the Kemalist establishment as a direct assault on secularism.[6]

The secularism that the military sees itself as having a duty to defend has thus become a specific interpretation rather than a general principle. Nor is this concept of duty merely derived from a sense of emotional responsibility; it is a legal obligation.

Kemalism is embedded in the Turkish Constitution. The preamble to the constitution states that it has been formulated "in line with the concept of nationalism outlined and the reforms and principles introduced by the founder of the Republic of Turkey, Atatürk, the immortal leader and the unrivaled hero."[7]

Article 2 of the constitution states that "[t]he Republic of Turkey is a democratic, secular and social state governed by the rule of law; bearing in mind the concepts of public peace, national solidarity and justice; respecting human rights; loyal to the nationalism of Atatürk, and based on the fundamental tenets set forth in the Preamble." Article 4 of the constitution says that "the provisions in article 2 on the characteristics of the Republic...shall not be amended, nor shall their amendment be proposed."

The most detailed statement of the legal role and obligations of the military is contained in the Turkish Armed Forces Internal Service Law of January 1961. Article 35 states, "The duty of the Turkish Armed Forces is to protect and preserve the Turkish homeland and the Turkish Republic as defined in the constitution."[8]

The Turkish Armed Forces Internal Service Directive is more explicit. Article 85/1 of the directive states, "It is the duty of the Turkish Armed Forces to protect the Turkish homeland and the Republic, by arms when necessary, against internal and external threats."

Yet the TGS has no ambitions to seize power directly, not least because—although they succeeded in their short-term aims of restoring political stability—when it staged full-blown coups in 1960 and 1980 they damaged both the military's public prestige and its internal cohesion. Its goal is rather that the civilian government pursues policies that are within acceptable parameters.

ISLAM, KEMALISM, AND THE JDP

The JDP was one of two parties to be formed from the remnants of the Virtue Party (VP), which was closed by the Turkish Constitutional Court for alleged antisecular activity on June 22, 2001.[9] Almost all of the JDP leadership—including Prime Minister Recep Tayyip Erdoğan, Foreign Minister Abdullah Gül, and Parliamentary Speaker Bülent Arınç—had also been members of the Islamist Welfare Party (WP), which had itself been outlawed in January 1998.[10]

During the early 1990s Erdoğan had often been outspoken in his criticism of Kemalism, publicly declaring, "There is no room for Kemalism or any other official ideology in Turkey's future."[11] Even after he was elected WP mayor of Istanbul in 1994, he continued to court controversy, commenting, "Praise be to God, we support *sharia* law" (1994),[12] and "Parliament should be opened with prayers" (1996).[13]

Yet despite its Islamist pedigree, ever since its foundation in August 2001, the JDP has consistently sought to portray itself as a conservative rather than a religious party. It has also striven to prove its devotion to Kemalism. When party leader Erdoğan held a press conference to launch the JDP on August 14, 2001, the hall was draped with a huge portrait of Atatürk and all present were asked to observe a minute's silence in Atatürk's memory. After the press conference was over, Erdoğan and the other founding members of the party visited Atatürk's mausoleum to pay their respects.

In December 2001 the JDP published a sixty-five-page *Development and Democratization Program*, which it said would form the basis of its policies once it took power.[14] On religion it stated, "Our party considers religion as one of the most important institutions of humanity, and secularism as a pre-requisite of democracy, and an assurance of the freedom of religion and conscience."[15]

The program defined secularism as "[a] principle which allows people of all religions, and beliefs to comfortably practice their religions, to be able to express their religious convictions and live accordingly, but which also allows people without beliefs to organize their lives along these lines. From this point of view, secularism is a principle of freedom and social peace."[16] The program committed the JDP to Kemalism, stating, "Our Party regards Atatürk's principles and reforms as the most important vehicle for raising the Turkish public above the level of contemporary civilization and sees this as an element of social peace."[17]

In a clear, if unstated, reference to the way in which secularism has been interpreted by the Kemalist establishment in Turkey, the program declared that the JDP "[r]ejects the interpretation and distortion of secularism as enmity against religion."[18] It added that "[The party] considers the attitudes and practices which disturb pious people, and which discriminate them [*sic*] due to their religious lives and preferences, as antidemocratic and in contradiction to human rights and freedoms. On the other hand, it is also unacceptable to make use of religion for political, economic and other interests, or to put pressure on people who think and live differently by using religion."[19]

The program gave no details of how the JDP would change the interpretation of secularism once it came to power. To many of the party's opponents, the distinction between different interpretations of secularism was mere sophistry and its commitment to Kemalism an example of the religiously permitted dissimulation known as *takiyye*. They feared that, once in power, the JDP would gradually erode not just the traditional Kemalist interpretation of secularism but the principle itself, eventually even removing it from the Turkish Constitution.

The fact that, by the time Parliament went into summer recess in July 2004, the JDP had not passed any laws even to change the traditional interpretation of secularism had done little to allay Kemalist fears. They still saw the JDP as an anti-Kemalist, Islamist party—if not yet in deed then in waiting.

Nor is there any doubt that, during its first twenty months in power, the JDP—sometimes as a party, at other times at the initiative of individual MPs—did take several tentative steps toward modifying both the prevailing interpretation of secularism and the personality cult surrounding Atatürk. Each time they were forced into retreat by interventions from the Kemalist establishment, primarily President Ahmet Necdet Sezer and/or the TGS.

THE DOMESTIC POLITICAL CONTEXT

Turkey has an authoritarian political culture. It does not have a tradition of change being driven from below. Political parties have tended to form around charismatic individuals rather than shared ideological conviction. Advancement within the parties has been determined by personal loyalty to the leader rather than ability, which has both institutionalized corruption and nepotism and made it very difficult to replace a leader even when s/he has lost the confidence of the electorate. Although it has grown rapidly in recent years, civil society in Turkey is still in its infancy, more visible than it is effective.

Ironically, both of the revitalizations of Turkish politics in the last thirty years have been as the indirect result of "undemocratic" interventions. The banning of all existing political parties in the wake of the 1980 military coup opened the way for the foundation of the Motherland Party (MP) in 1983. Although the MP's record in office from 1983 to 1991 was, at best, mixed, it undoubtedly heralded a new era in Turkish politics, as did the JDP's electoral triumph of November 2002. Yet it is doubtful whether the JDP would ever have been founded if its two predecessors, the Welfare Party (WP) and the Virtue Party (VP), had not been closed down by the courts, and the doyen of the Islamist movement, Necmettin Erbakan, banned from politics.[20] The 1998 prosecution of Erdoğan for allegedly inciting religious hatred by reading a poem that mixed religious and military imagery helped transform his public image from that of a competent municipal mayor to a national icon,[21] and left him perfectly placed to step into the vacuum created by the removal of Erbakan from active politics.

The foundation of the JDP also came just months after a currency collapse in February 2001 had plunged Turkey into its worst economic recession in fifty years. The crisis destroyed any vestiges of respect that the Turkish electorate had held for existing political parties. In an unprecedented demonstration of the Turkish public's holding its politicians to account for their failings, none of the political parties that had won seats in the previous general elections in April 1999 succeeded in crossing the 10 percent threshold for representation in Parliament in November 2002.

The 10 percent threshold also meant that the JDP won approximately two-thirds of the seats in Parliament with just over one-third of the national vote, while 46.3 percent of the votes cast in the November 2002 elections were not even represented in Parliament. The only parliamentary opposition to the JDP was the Republican People's Party (RPP), led by the veteran Deniz Baykal, with just under one-third of the total number of seats.

Baykal's political career had been characterized by tactical acumen in internal party disputes to the detriment of strategic vision in policy matters. In the period from November 2002 to July 2004, the RPP's record in opposition was uninspiring. Its unfailing criticism of the government was too often perfunctory, unconstructive, and unaccompanied by alternative policy proposals. Indeed, the party leadership appeared more concerned with suppressing internal dissent than with defeating the JDP at the next election. The failure to institutionalize Turkish party political culture meant that the resignation of the heads of the parties that had failed to win seats in the November 2002 elections necessitated not just a change in leadership but a complete restructuring of the party apparatus.[22]

In contrast, by the time of the March 2004 local elections the JDP was still enjoying an extended honeymoon, which had been prolonged by a combination of good fortune and cautious consistency, in deed if not always in word.[23] In fact, given the infighting in the RPP and the continuing disarray and restructuring in the political opposition outside Parliament, the JDP often appeared to be the only fully functioning political party. Not surprisingly, in the local elections on March 28, 2004, the JDP increased its nationwide vote to 41.7 percent, ahead of the RPP by 18.3 percent.

The inability of other political parties, inside or outside Parliament, to mount an effective opposition to the JDP, combined with a still developing civil society,[24] has meant that the main perceived constraint on any ambitions the government may have to change the Kemalist interpretation of secularism has remained the Kemalist state itself, primarily President Sezer, and, above all, the TGS.

Under article 89 of the Turkish Constitution, the president has the right to veto legislation within fifteen days of its being present for his/her ratification and return it to Parliament for review. If Parliament passes the same legislation in an identical form, then the president has no choice but to ratify it.[25] However, s/he does have the right to submit even ratified legislation to the Constitutional Court, where it can be annulled if it is deemed incompatible with the Turkish Constitution. However, the major constraint on the JDP is neither procedural nor judicial but the informal authority of the Turkish military.

INSTRUMENTS OF INFLUENCE

Although the Turkish military has a legal obligation under article 35 of the Turkish Armed Forces Internal Service Law to protect the constitutional principle of secularism, Turkish legislation does not define what is meant by secularism; nor does it provide the Turkish military with any instruments with which to protect it.

As a result, before the November 2002 elections, the TGS had primarily exerted political influence through informal means, setting parameters for government policy by informing governments of its "concerns" at monthly meetings of the National Security Council (NSC)[26] and in private meetings with government officials or via the media through statements at public functions and in briefings to chosen journalists. However, the election of the JDP and the enactment of legislative reforms to try to prepare Turkey for EU accession have resulted in a reduction in both institutional and informal contacts between the military and the government.

Under previous administrations, in addition to high-level meetings between, for example, the prime minister and the chief of the general staff, the military had a number of informal "contact points" that could be used as discreet conduits for the exchange of information, usually between a high-ranking member of the TGS and someone at, or close to, the top of the civilian government. Although these channels were sometimes used to exert pressure on the government and to ensure that policy remained within what the TGS saw as acceptable parameters, the two-way flow of information often served to alleviate—if never completely eradicate—mutual suspicions. Since the JDP came to power, not only has the number of high-level meetings between the TGS and the government declined, but the military no longer has multiple "back channels" through which to exchange information with the civilian government.[27]

Pressure from the EU for Turkey to comply with the Copenhagen criteria for civilian control of the military, has also reduced the potential for the TGS to apply pressure on an institutional platform at the meetings of the NSC. In July 2003 the government passed a series of reforms that included extending the period between regular NSC meetings from one to two months and lifting the requirement that the NSC Secretary General be a military officer.[28] Under article 118 of the Turkish Constitution, the president is responsible for setting the agenda for NSC meetings, "taking into account the proposals of the Prime Minister and the Chief of the General Staff."[29] However, the preparation of the briefing papers and background documents that are distributed to the members of the NSC is the responsibility of the NSC Undersecretariat under its secretary general. Traditionally, the NSC Undersecretariat has been largely, though far from exclusively, composed of former or serving members of the Turkish military working in close cooperation with other branches of the state apparatus, particularly the TGS. In December 2003 Parliament voted to dispel the secrecy surrounding the operations of the Undersecretariat by lifting the ban on the publication of NSC regulations, appointments, and personnel.

Although it remained possible for the military to apply pressure to the government at NSC meetings, the reforms made it more difficult for the TGS to do so discreetly. The disengagement of the NSC Undersecretariat from the TGS theoretically reduced the military's ability to shape discussions at the NSC in advance of the meetings.[30] It also severely restricted the military's ability to present the civilian government with detailed policy proposals at NSC meetings, something that it had done, albeit rarely, in the past.[31]

The JDP's election victory, and the reduction in the scope for exerting influence through both informal "back channels" and at the institutional level at the NSC coincided with the appointment of a relatively circumspect chief of staff. General Hilmi Özkök was officially appointed at the end of August 2002, just over two months before the November 3 elections. Unlike his predecessor, the more outspoken General Huseyin Kıvrıkoğlu, who was chief of staff from 1998 to 2002, Özkök has attempted to avoid being seen as trying to influence the political process, not least because he is aware that such attempts would be regarded in Brussels as incompatible with the Copenhagen political criteria for EU membership at a time when Turkey is edging toward being given a date for the opening of official accession negotiations.

Özkök's reluctance to engage in confrontations with the JDP has meant that he has also tended to avoid exerting leverage through giving public speeches or briefings to trusted members of the press. Yet there is no reason to believe that he is any less dedicated to protecting Kemalism than his predecessors. It seems rather that he has been trying to pursue a more subtle strategy, trying to ensure that the TGS adopts as low a political profile as possible and intervening to warn the government only if he believes that the Kemalist interpretation of secularism is in imminent danger. This strategy has led to impatience and occasional disquiet amongst hard-liners in the TGS, who believe that the JDP aims to erode Kemalism gradually in incremental steps, rather than through an abrupt demolition. In the period from November 2002 to the end of July 2004, Özkök mostly resisted pressure from these hard-liners within the military to be more assertive. But there were nevertheless times when, either publicly or behind the scenes, the TGS did intervene in the political arena. For however much Özkök may try to avoid such interventions, the ideology of Kemalism, which Turkish officers are sworn to protect, is itself in the political arena.

MILITARY-JDP RELATIONS: NOVEMBER 2000–JULY 2004

On November 4, the day after the elections that brought the JDP to power, Özkök announced that the military accepted the results of the ballot as representing the "will of the people."[32] Nevertheless, on November 10, 2002, in the first written statement issued by the TGS to mark the anniversary of Atatürk's death in 1938, Özkök vowed that the Turkish military would continue to "protect the Republic against every kind of threat, particularly fundamentalism and separatism." However, privately he told colleagues that, regardless of any other considerations, the TGS could not move against the JDP unless it actually attempted to violate secularism or indicated its intention to do so. Yet the first tensions occurred not between the JDP and the TGS but between the new government and President Sezer.

Under article 76 of the Turkish Constitution, Erdoğan's 1998 conviction meant that he was barred from holding public office. He was unable to stand as a candidate in the November 2002 elections and had to wait until the new JDP administration was able to amend the Turkish Constitution to lift his ban, finally entering Parliament through a by-election in the southeastern town of Siirt on March 9, 2003.[33]

As a result, the first JDP government was headed by the JDP's deputy chairman, Abdullah Gül. On November 18, 2002, Gül presented the list of his Cabinet members to President Sezer for official ratification. They included Besir Atalay, a former university rector who had been dismissed for alleged Islamist activism, as education minister. Sezer refused to endorse the nomination, forcing Gül to replace Atalay with Erkan Mumcu, who was widely regarded as a moderate. However, when it was suspected that the JDP was attempting to breach the headscarf ban, it was the military that responded.

On November 20, 2002, Sezer and his wife left Turkey to attend a NATO summit in Prague. Under Turkish protocol, while the president is out of the country his ceremonial responsibilities pass to the Speaker of Parliament. Sezer and his wife were seen off at the airport in Ankara by the new JDP Speaker of Parliament, Bülent Arınç, accompanied by his own wife, who, like the majority of the wives of the JDP leadership, wears a headscarf. Although Arınç denied he had been deliberately provocative,[34] to the Kemalist establishment the participation of a woman in a headscarf in what was seen as an official ceremony was an assault on secularism. On November 28, Turkey's force commanders, headed by Özkök, delivered a wordless warning to Arınç by visiting him in his office in Parliament, where they sat in complete silence for three minutes before leaving.[35]

Through the 1990s, the TGS had conducted regular purges of the officer corps, expelling hundreds of officers suspected of Islamist activism or even merely excessive piety. Under current Turkish law, officers dismissed from the military do not have the right of appeal, while military procedures mean that they are often not even allowed to present a defense to the Supreme Military Council (SMC), which hears their cases. After taking office, the JDP further antagonized the TGS by appointing as head of the Parliamentary Defence Committee Ramazan Toprak, a former soldier who had been dismissed from the military in 1997 for alleged Islamist activism. Under pressure from the TGS, Toprak resigned in January 2003. However, military suspicions of the JDP were reinforced on December 27, 2002, when both Gül and Arınç publicly declared that decisions of the SMC should be eligible for appeal, and received a sharp rebuke from Özkök, who accused them of encouraging fundamentalists to penetrate and weaken the Turkish armed forces.[36]

Yet on the one issue that overshadowed both domestic and international politics during the early months of 2003—namely the impending U.S.-led war to topple Iraqi President Saddam Hussein—rather than trying to dictate policy, both the JDP government and the TGS appeared to prefer to allow the other to assume responsibility. As early as summer 2002, the TGS had decided that war was inevitable and that Turkey would have no choice but to support the United States, even putting its troops on the ground in northern Iraq, in order both to protect its alliance with Washington and to stifle any Iraqi Kurdish aspirations of independence, which it feared might inspire Turkey's own still restive Kurdish minority. Although the Turkish military remained in regular contact with the war planners in the Pentagon through fall 2002 and into early 2003, it refrained from giving Washington an explicit commitment either to fight alongside U.S. troops or to allow them to transit Turkey on their way to opening a northern front to supplement the main thrust of the military campaign driving out of the Gulf. This was partly because the TGS was hoping that, by delaying, it could exact better terms for participation—both as regards the deployment of Turkish troops in Iraq and with a view to future military aid from the United States—and partly because any commitment would have to include not only the Turkish military but also the Turkish government.

The election of the JDP complicated the situation still further. The Turkish public was deeply—and increasingly—opposed to war against Iraq.[37] Despite the JDP's claim to be a conservative rather than a religious party, there was also no doubt that, when it came to Iraq, a large proportion of both the JDP parliamentary party and its voters were primarily motivated by feelings of anti-Americanism and Muslim solidarity. Although the JDP leadership was aware that—for reasons of international *realpolitik*—it probably could not afford to remain aloof from the coming conflict, for emotional and domestic political reasons—namely, the potential electorate fallout from supporting a deeply unpopular war—it would prefer to shift responsibility for participation onto the military. For similar reasons, the TGS was unwilling to pressure the civilian government into making a commitment to participate in the war as this could then be used by the JDP to undermine the Turkish military's domestic prestige;[38] and, given its reluctance to use armed force, the military's public prestige is now the main instrument through which the TGS can exert political leverage.[39] The severing of most of the "back channels" that the TGS had been able to utilize with previous administrations meant that there was now little communication between the government and the military.[40]

In February 2003, as Washington continued to apply pressure for a decision one way or the other as to whether Turkey would allow U.S. troops to transit the country on their way to Iraq, the JDP government decided to put the issue to a vote in Parliament on Saturday March 1. A meeting of the NSC was due to be held on February 28. The JDP appears to have calculated that the TGS would use the NSC meeting to issue a public recommendation to Parliament to pass the motion and allow the government to shift the responsibility for the U.S. troop deployment onto the military. But Özkök declined to insist on any reference to the motion in the communiqué issued at the end of the meeting.

Outmaneuvered, the JDP was left with no option but to ensure that the motion passed through Parliament. Although he was still not a member of Parliament, on the morning of March 1, 2003, Erdoğan held an informal poll of JDP MPs. Only a handful indicated that they would oppose the motion. But when it was actually put to Parliament that evening, the motion passed by only 264–250 with 19 abstentions, leaving the government three votes short of the constitutional requirement of a majority of those who participated in the vote.[41] The result was a humiliation for the government but was greeted with elation by most of the Turkish public, and with angry dismay by Washington.[42] Fearful that another defeat could split the party, the government refused to present another motion to Parliament.

The fact that the U.S.-led military campaign to oust Saddam Hussein was completed quicker, and with fewer U.S. casualties, than had been anticipated went some way toward limiting the damage to Turkish-U.S. relations. However, although ties received a boost in October 2003 with the JDP's offer to send peacekeeping troops to Iraq—a proposal that was rejected by the Iraqis—the relationship between Ankara and Washington was nevertheless irrevocably changed by the March 1 decision.[43]

The debacle of March 1 also came as a shock to the TGS, which feared that it would severely reduce Turkey's ability to prevent the emergence of a Kurdish political entity in northern Iraq, either directly through a military presence on the ground or by persuading Washington to rein in the Iraqi Kurds. There were also concerns the fallout could affect Turkish defense procurement from the United States, which remains its largest supplier of weapons and military equipment. Hard-liners inside the TGS openly complained that Özkök should have been more assertive at the February 28 NSC meeting.

However, when it came to the headscarf ban, neither Özkök nor President Sezer was willing to allow the JDP any leeway. On April 23, 2003, the TGS boycotted a reception held by Bülent Arınç to celebrate National Sovereignty and Children's Day when it learned that it would be co-hosted by his headscarved wife. At the NSC meeting on April 30, 2003, the TGS stepped up the pressure on the government, accusing it of trying to foster links with what it described as "fundamentalist organizations" amongst the Turkish diaspora in Europe. It also ensured that the subsequent statement released to the press led with the declaration that the meeting "had stressed the importance of meticulously protecting the principle of secularism which is one of the basic characteristics of the state."[44]

A few days later, on May 5, 2003, the TGS issued a press release describing itself as the "fearless guardian of Atatürk's legacy" and warning that "[i]t should not be forgotten that the united and unified Turkish Armed Forces are today, as they were in the past, the greatest guarantee of the secular, democratic and social characteristics of the Turkish Republic and shall remain at the service of our exalted nation."[45]

The tension triggered by the April 23, 2003, reception gradually dissipated, only to resurface at a reception hosted by President Sezer to mark Republic Day on October 29, 2003. Sezer refused to extend invitations to the headscarved wives of JDP MPs, with the result that most boycotted the reception. Yet the government was unwilling to confront the Kemalist establishment directly. JDP leaders, such as Erdoğan and Gül, adopted a compromise policy of taking their headscarved wives with them when they traveled abroad on official trips, but pointedly leaving them at home when they attended official functions inside Turkey. However, the issue clearly still rankled with leading members of the government. When, in mid-April 2004, Bülent Arınç was asked by a member of the press on national television why his wife's name had not been included on the invitations to the forthcoming April 23 reception, he responded with an obscenity, forcing the state-owned Turkish Radio and Television (TRT) to cut its live feed.[46]

If the confrontation over women wearing headscarves had been temporarily postponed, there were still skirmishes in other areas. In September 2003 the TGS was infuriated to read in the Turkish press that the government had signed a US$8.5 billion loan agreement with the United States, with the money being reportedly tied to a commitment by Turkey not to launch cross-border operations into northern Iraq either to deter the Iraqi Kurds or to strike at camps belonging to Turkey's own Kurdish rebels.[47] For the TGS the reported conditionality was not only unacceptable in itself but, in agreeing to it without first consulting with the military, the government had encroached on what the TGS still saw as one of its key prerogatives, namely security. The TGS communicated its unease to the government both directly in private meetings with JDP officials and indirectly through comments to the Turkish media.[48] The result was that the loan was effectively frozen.

The fall of 2003 also saw a confrontation between the government and the military in arguably the most sensitive area, that of education. Kemalists argued that government plans to reform the higher education system would encourage the growth of preacher-training high schools, known as İmam Hatip schools, and make it easier for their graduates to enter university.[49] On September 9, 2003, General Aytaç Yalman, the commander of the Turkish Land Forces, met with university rectors to discuss opposition to the draft reform bill. Yalman was generally regarded as a hard-liner, and over the previous six months there had been frequent rumors in the Turkish media that some officers had become impatient at what they saw as Özkök's passivity. Initial press reports suggested that the meeting with the university rectors had been at Yalman's initiative. On September 14, 2003, the TGS was forced to issue a written statement that the meeting had been a follow-up to one held by Özkök on September 1. The TGS statement also dismissed suggestions that education lay outside its field of responsibility, declaring that "[i]t is natural that the developments related to the national education system which is of such vital importance to Turkey should be followed closely and carefully by the Turkish Armed Forces."[50]

Over the following weeks, the TGS continued to apply pressure, both behind the scenes and through statements to the press by leading commanders. At a press conference on October 14, 2003, Deputy Chief of Staff General İlker Başbuğ bluntly questioned the motives behind the planned educational reforms, pointing out that, of the 25,000 students who currently graduated from the İmam Hatip schools each year, only 2,500 continued their studies at a faculty of theology, while the total annual recruiting requirement of the Diyanet, the only body that can legally employ Islamic clerics, was 5,500.[51]

The government subsequently postponed trying to push the educational reforms through Parliament. But rumors persisted that some commanders believed that the JDP was drawing strength from Özkök's reluctance to confront the government. On December 29, 2003, a leading JDP MP, Fehmi Hüsrev Kutlu, angrily complained that the portraits in Parliament of Atatürk in military uniform made him feel as if he was imprisoned in a barracks. On December 30, 2003, Yalman issued a furious public condemnation of Kutlu's statement. In an unprecedented break with the military hierarchy, Yalman had acted independently, publicly attacking Kutlu without first clearing what he was going to say with Özkök. Unable to punish what was virtually an act of insubordination for fear of weakening the public prestige of the TGS by implying that there were divisions in its ranks, Özkök was left with little choice but to issue his own statement on December 31, 2003, supporting Yalman and condemning Kutlu.

However, by March 2004 the tensions between Özkök and Yalman appeared to have dissipated. On March 3, 2004, Özkök delivered his most explicit warning to date to the JDP government when he dispatched Yalman at the head of a delegation of virtually all of the upper echelon of the TGS to attend a conference organized by a Kemalist nongovernmental organization, the Atatürkçü Düşünce Derneği (Association for Kemalist

Thought, or ADD), to mark the eightieth anniversary of Atatürk's abolition of the caliphate. Surrounded by television cameras, the TGS delegation occupied the entire front row in the auditorium and vigorously applauded as a succession of speakers warned of the dangers facing secularism and affirmed their determination to defend it at whatever cost.[52]

However, in early May 2004, emboldened by its victory in the March local elections, the government decided once again to reform the educational system and make it easier for İmam Hatip school graduates to enter university. The full details of the reform package were made public by Education Minister Hüseyin Çelik on May 4, 2004. On May 6, the TGS issued a statement describing the reform package as "designed to damage the principles of secular education" and delivered what was, for a government largely composed of former members of the WP, a thinly veiled warning: "The views and attitude of the Turkish Armed Forces toward the Republic's characteristics as a democratic, secular and social state ruled by law are the same today as they were yesterday and shall remain the same tomorrow. No one should have any doubt or misapprehension about the thoughts and attitudes of the Turkish Armed Forces in this regard."[53]

But the government appeared undeterred, even defiant. Prime Minister Erdoğan retorted that "[n]o one should try to put pressure on the will of the people. If they do, they will see Parliament's answer. If Parliament represents the people's will, then its decisions should be respected by all."[54]

In the early hours of May 13, after an eighteen-hour all-night debate, Parliament passed the reform package and submitted it to Sezer for presidential approval. On May 28 Sezer announced that he was vetoing the bill on the grounds that it was incompatible with the constitutional principle of secularism, which he described as "the foundation stone of all the values which comprise the Turkish Republic."[55]

In order for the law to come into effect in time for the new academic year, it would have to be passed before Parliament went into summer recess in July.[56] But, faced with the combined opposition of the TGS and the presidency, the JDP backed down. On July 3, 2004, Erdoğan admitted, "As a government we are not ready to pay the price."[57]

TOWARD COMPROMISE OR CONFLICT?

There is reason to believe that the youthful radicalism of Erdoğan and other members of the JDP has been tempered by time and the moderating impact of any experience of political power on ideological conviction. But there can also be little doubt that the JDP's concept of secularism is incompatible with the one currently being applied in Turkey by the Kemalist establishment. Perhaps more critically, the patience of hard-line elements within the party and the expectations of its grassroots support are unlikely to be unlimited. Although some Turks voted for the JDP as a reaction to the corruption and incompetence of previous administrations, many more did so because they believed that, once firmly ensconced in power, it would ease restrictions on the expression of Islamic piety in the public sphere.[58] At some point the JDP will have to deliver.

In the continuing absence of an effective political opposition to the JDP from inside or outside Parliament, many Kemalists will again look to the military for leadership and guidance. Eventually, a confrontation between the JDP and the TGS appears inevitable. The longer the confrontation can be postponed, and the closer Turkey moves toward the EU in the meantime, the more limited will be the military's room for maneuver. Yet postponing the confrontation will also require as yet unproven levels of patience, competence, and sophistication on the part of the JDP. Although Özkök has sometimes come in for criticism from hard-line secularists for his carefully calibrated attempts to avoid antagonizing the EU through a direct confrontation with the government, it would be a mistake to underestimate the level of his commitment—or that of any other leading member of the TGS—to protecting Kemalism.

NOTES

1. In the elections of November 3, 2002, the JDP won 34.3 percent of the popular vote, giving it 363 seats in the 550-member unicameral Parliament. The only other party to cross the 10 percent threshold for representation in parliament was the center-left Republican People's Party (RPP), which took 178 seats with 19.4 percent. The remaining nine seats were won by independents.

2. At the time of writing, the EU was widely expected to agree at its summit in the Netherlands in December 2004 to set a date, probably sometime in 2005, for the official opening of accession negotiations with Turkey. However, the negotiations are likely to be both long and problematic.

3. The most serious occurred in the southeast of the country in 1925. It was triggered by Atatürk's abolition of the caliphate, religious schools, and Islamic *Shari'a* law courts in 1924, which was the precursor to the redefinition of Turkey as a secular state in 1928. The revolt was led by, and subsequently named after, Sheikh Said, a Kurdish tribal chieftain; it combined elements of Islamism and incipient Kurdish nationalism. The rebellion was eventually crushed and Sheikh Said and several hundred of his supporters were tried and executed by special itinerant courts known as "independence tribunals."

4. The most famous of these martyrs is Kubilay, a young military officer who was lynched by a mob of antisecularists in the Aegean town of Menemen on December 23, 1930. The TGS holds commemorative ceremonies on the anniversary of Kubilay's death and reiterates its commitment to follow in his footsteps.

5. No reliable figures are available, but Sunni Muslims are estimated to comprise approximately 80 percent of the Turkish population of 75 million. Virtually all of the remainder are Alawites, a branch of Shia Islam. The Diyanet does not provide funding or clergy for either the Alawites or Turkey's dwindling non-Muslim minorities. The compulsory national school curriculum includes only the teaching of Sunni Islam.

6. Strictly speaking, the Qur'an does not require women to cover their heads. Sura 24, verse 31 contains the only reference to a specific part of the body and then it is the breast, not the head, which women are told to cover. The other references in the Qur'an to a dress code all instruct women merely to dress modestly: for example, sura 7, verse 26; sura 24, verse 60; sura 33, verse 55; and sura 33, verse 59.

7. Turkish Constitution, 1982, http://www.mfa.gov.tr.

8. Author's translation. Turkish Justice Ministry, http://www.adalet.gov.tr.

9. The other was the Felicity Party (FP), which consists primarily of followers of Necmettin Erbakan, the doyen of the Turkish Islamist movement.

10. The WP had in turn succeeded the National Salvation Party (NSP), which was banned following the September 12, 1980, military coup, and the National Order Party (NOP), which was closed down in the wake of the 1971 military coup. Both Erdoğan and Arınç were also members of the WP's predecessor, the National Salvation Party (NSP). In the 1970s Erdoğan and Gül were members of the National Turkish Students Union (NTSB), which combined Islamism with an assertive Turkish nationalism.

11. Interview with Tayyip Erdoğan, in Metin Sever and Cem Dizdar, eds., *2. Cumhuriyet Tartışmaları* (Ankara: Başak Yayınları, 1993).

12. *Milliyet*, November 29, 1994.

13. *Milliyet*, January 8, 1996.

14. The full text of the report is available in English and Turkish on the JDP's website, www.akparti.org.tr.

15. Section 2.1, Fundamental Rights and Freedoms, *Development and Democratization Program*, 6. This and all other quotations from the program are taken from the English language version.

16. Ibid., 6.

17. Ibid., 5.

18. Ibid., 6.

19. Ibid.

20. Erbakan founded a string of political parties, each replacing a predecessor that had been banned by the courts, namely: the National Order Party (NOP) in 1970; the National Salvation Party (NSP) in 1972; the Welfare Party (WP) in 1983; the Virtue Party (VP) in 1997; and the Felicity Party (FP) in 2001. The WP, VP, and FP were established by proxies, as Erbakan was serving a ban from politics at the time of their foundation and had to wait for his ban to finish before he could officially assume leadership.

21. In April 1998 Erdoğan was found guilty of inciting religious hatred during a December 1997 speech in the predominantly Kurdish southeastern town of Siirt. Erdoğan had recited a poem by the ultranationalist Ziya Gökalp that included the lines

"The mosques are our barracks, the minarets our bayonets, the domes our helmets and the believers our soldiers." Kemalist doctrine maintains not only that the Turkish Republic is under constant threat but that the threats have remained essentially unchanged since Atatürk's lifetime. For the Kemalist establishment, Erdoğan's decision to recite a poem mixing religious Islamic and military imagery in a Kurdish town fed fears of a revival of the Sheikh Said rebellion (see note 3 above). Erdoğan subsequently served four months of a ten-month prison sentence and was released in early 1999.

22. Of the five parties that had won seats in the April 1999 elections, one—the Virtue Party—was banned in June 2001. In the aftermath of the November 3, 2002, elections, the leaders of the other four all announced they would resign. Mesut Yılmaz and Tansu Çiller, leaders of the Motherland Party (MP) and the True Path Party (TPP), respectively, did so almost immediately. Democratic Left Party (DLP) Chairman Bülent Ecevit delayed stepping down until July 2004. While Nationalist Action Party (NAP) Chairman Devlet Bahçeli still remained in his post as of August 2004.

23. Although different ministers often publicly contradicted each other—and sometimes even themselves (for example, over Cyprus in January 2003)—in speeches, actual government policy remained relatively consistent, albeit along lines effectively set by outside institutions, namely a political reform process driven by the desire to comply with the Copenhagen criteria for EU accession and an economic stabilization program formulated in cooperation with, and supported by funding from, the International Monetary Fund (IMF).

24. Nongovernmental organizations (NGOs) played an important role in the successful campaign to oust an eleven-month-old, WP-led coalition government in 1997. However, it was the TGS that provided the catalyst and coordination for the campaign.

25. Turkish Constitution, http://www.mfa.gov.tr.

26. The members of the NSC are the prime minister; deputy prime ministers; the ministers of national defense, internal affairs, justice, and foreign affairs; the chief of the General Staff; and the commanders of the army, navy, air force, and gendarmerie, under the chairmanship of the president. Although the military has never been in a numerical majority on the NSC, decisions are taken by consensus rather than a vote, with the result that the prestige and informal authority of the chief of the TGS has often outweighed the influence of the government.

27. This has reduced both the military's leverage over and its knowledge of government policy. Instead of a reversal of the direction of authority—from military-to-civilian to civilian-to-military—the result has been a dramatic contraction in the volume of information of any kind passing between the two.

28. Although it became theoretically possible in September 2003, the first civilian secretary general was not appointed until September 2004, when Yiğit Alpogan, a career diplomat then serving as Turkish ambassador to Greece, was appointed to the post. Other reforms to curb the influence of the military included: making military spending subject to civilian scrutiny; forbidding the prosecution of civilians in military courts during peacetime; and reducing military service from eighteen to fifteen months (thus also trimming the overall size of the armed forces and the officer corps).

29. Turkish Constitution, http://www.mfa.gov.tr.

30. At the time of writing in August 2004, it was too early to assess the extent to which the theoretical disengagement would be reflected in practice. Much appeared

likely to depend on the personality and sympathies of the secretary general and the extent to which s/he would come under, or be susceptible to, pressure from the TGS or the civilian government when preparing briefing papers and background documents.

31. Most famously at the NSC meeting of February 28, 1997, when it had presented the WP-led coalition government of Prime Minister Necmettin Erbakan with a list of eighteen measures to curb what the TGS believed to be antisecularist activities. The meeting marked the beginning of what became known as the "28 February Process," a military-led campaign of pressure on the government that culminated in Erbakan's resignation on June 18, 1997.

32. *Milliyet*, November 5, 2002.

33. The new Parliament amended article 76 of the constitution on December 13, 2002. The amendment was vetoed by President Sezer and returned to Parliament on December 19, 2002. However it was passed again in its original form on December 27, 2002, leaving the president with no choice but to ratify it. Ironically, the first by-election of the new Parliament was in the very same town where Erdoğan had read the poem for which he had been imprisoned and subsequently banned from politics. As soon as Erdoğan entered Parliament, Gül resigned. Erdoğan was officially appointed prime minister on March 14, 2003.

34. He told *Milliyet* newspaper, "The president was going abroad with his wife so I saw him off with my wife. What we did was normal. Everything we did was in complete conformity with our protocol duties. There was no attempt to make anything more of it." Author's translation. *Milliyet*, November 21, 2002.

35. Arınç's father had served in the military. During a later visit to Arınç, the TGS pointedly presented him with a dossier on his father's service, including details of how he had been caught committing a misdemeanor but, instead of being expelled, had been warned as to his future conduct. He had not committed any more offenses and had been allowed to serve out the remainder of his time.

36. "AKP'ye ilk eleştiriler," *Radikal*, January 9, 2003.

37. By early 2003 opinion polls were reporting that up to 94 percent of the Turkish population was opposed to the war.

38. For example, on February 21, 2003, the TGS issued a briefing note to stress that the decision to allow U.S. troops to transit Turkey was the responsibility of the civilian government: "Without a decision from the Turkish Parliament, no foreign military elements (troops, tanks, artillery, warplanes, etc.) can be allowed onto Turkish soil." Author's translation. "TGS Briefing Note No. BN-10/03," February 21, 2003, tsk.mil.tr/genelkumay/bashalk/bilginotu/2003/bn10.htm.

39. The military has traditionally topped opinion polls of institutions most trusted by the Turkish public. However, the level of its popularity fluctuates according to perceptions of need: falling back during periods of stability and rising during times of crisis.

40. For example, in December 2002 Erdoğan met with President George W. Bush in Washington. However, the lack of communication between the TGS and the JDP meant that the military was unable to discover whether Erdoğan had committed Turkey to participating in the campaign to oust Saddam Hussein. In fact, Erdoğan gave the United States the impression that Turkey would probably participate without explicitly committing himself. Author interviews with U.S. officials, Washington, June 2003.

41. The failure of the March 1, 2003, parliamentary motion appears to have been an accident rather than a coordinated rebuff to the United States. After Erdoğan's informal poll of MPs on the morning of March 1, many MPs appear to have concluded that, as the motion was going to pass anyway, they might as well vote with their consciences in what was a secret ballot. However, it is possible that, if the TGS had applied pressure to the government, many JDP MPs would have deliberately set out to block the motion. Author interviews with JDP members, Ankara, May 2003.

42. On February 6, 2003, the Turkish Parliament had voted to allow the United States to upgrade military facilities in Turkey to be ready to handle the transit of some sixty thousand U.S. troops, a decision that made no sense unless Parliament also voted to allow the troops into the country. By March 1, U.S. personnel had already arrived in Turkey and begun work on upgrading the military facilities. At the time, the war planners in the Pentagon calculated that Turkey's refusal to allow troops to transit its territory to open a northern front would cost the United States an additional one thousand casualties. Author interviews with U.S. officials, Washington, June 2003.

43. "March 1st took the romance out of our relationship. Turkey is still our NATO ally and we are confident that we can work closely together. We want to and we need to. But the certainty, the confidence will take a very long time to return." U.S. official interviewed by the author, Washington, December 2003.

44. Author's translation, *Hürriyet*, May 1, 2003.

45. Author's translation, http://www.tsk.mil.tr/genelkurmay/bashalk/aciklama/2003/a08.htm.

46. Hakkı Devrim, "Arınç'a argo sözlüğü lazım," *Radikal*, April 16, 2004.

47. Primarily members of Kongra-Gel, the group originally known as the Partiya Karkeren Kurdistan (Kurdistan Workers' Party or PKK).

48. For example: "Askerden şartlı krediye itiraz," *Hürriyet*, October 2, 2003.

49. The İmam Hatip schools were originally established to train Muslim clergy, but they soon became popular with parents who wanted their children to have a religious opportunity but not become Imams. In 1976 they began to accept girl students, even though there are no female clergy in Islam. Kemalists suspected that the schools were producing hard-line Islamists, many of whom were then being used by antisecular groups to penetrate the civil service. According to the Turkish Ministry of National Education, by the 1997–98 academic year there were 605 İmam Hatip schools in Turkey with 192,786 students. However, reforms introduced under the "28 February Process" (see note 31 above) reduced their number to 450 with 64,534 students in 2002–3. But enrolment increased after the JDP came to power. In the 2003–4 academic year there were 452 schools and 84,898 students, of whom 49,336 were boys and 35,562 girls.

50. Author's translation, "TGS Press Statement No. BN-19/03," September 14, 2003, http://www.tsk.mil.tr/genelkumay/bashalk/aciklama/2003/a19.htm.

51. "Askerden imam hatip muhtırası," *Hürriyet*, October 14, 2003.

52. "Komutanlı hilafet paneli," *Radikal*, March 4, 2004.

53. Author's translation, "TGS Press Statement no. BN-07/04," May 6, 2004, http://www.tsk.mil.tr/genelkumay/bashalk/aciklama/2004/a07.htm.

54. *Turkish Daily News*, May 12, 2004.

55. *Radikal*, May 29, 2004.

56. In its anxiety to push the bill through Parliament, the JDP had apparently not noticed that it included an outdated description of the Supreme Electoral Board (YSK), the composition of which it had just revised. Updating the description of the Supreme Electoral Board would have necessitated changing the text of the law, which would have meant that technically it was a new draft and vulnerable to a presidential veto (see note 25 above).

57. "Erdoğan: YÖK'ü zorlamayız," *Radikal*, July 4, 2004.

58. In a survey of JDP voters after the November 3, 2002, general election, almost half (46 percent) said that it was impossible to separate religion from temporal affairs. Although only 44 percent thought that all Muslim women should cover their heads, 93 percent wanted the JDP to lift the ban on women in headscarves entering state, while 55 percent believed that the educational system should be organized according to Islamic principles. Survey conducted by Bosphorus University, Istanbul, and published in *Milliyet*, November 15–18, 2002.

CHAPTER 9

The Political Economy of Turkey's Justice and Development Party

■ *Ziya Öniş*

The extraordinary electoral success of the Justice and Development Party (JDP) in the November 2002 general elections, following a decade of political instability under successive coalition governments, represented a major turning point in Turkey's political and economic trajectory. The present study explores the economic bases of this success and advances three interrelated hypotheses for this purpose. First, the party has been extremely successful in constituting a cross-class electoral alliance, incorporating into its orbit both winners and losers from the neoliberal globalization process. Business support, notably from small- and medium-sized business units falling under the umbrella of a major nationwide business association, constitutes a crucial element of the JDP's electoral support. Second, the strong track record of the JDP'S predecessors, the Welfare and the Virtue Parties (WP and VP respectively) at the level of the municipal governments is another element of key importance. Third, the failures of the conventional or established parties of either the center-right or the center-left in achieving sustained and equitable growth, avoiding costly financial crises, and tackling the problem of pervasive corruption have also paved the way for the party's unprecedented electoral success in the recent era. In spite of its Islamist roots and a natural association in terms of its leadership and core bases of political support with the Welfare and the Virtue parties, the JDP has nevertheless managed to present itself as a new face with a claim to the very center of Turkish politics. Consequently, it has been able to construct a much broader electoral coalition judged by the standards of two major predecessors.

While explaining the rise of the JDP is an interesting issue in itself, an even more interesting question is whether the party will be able to consolidate its power and establish itself as a major hegemonic force in

Turkish politics, at least during the next decade. Clearly, an adequate answer to this question requires a systematic and critical analysis of the JDP government's performance, notably in the economic realm. A second major objective of the study, therefore, is to examine the performance of the JDP in office during a short but unique period in terms of the intensity of political and economic reforms. Our assessment in this context is quite favorable though with certain reservations. Although it might be early to provide a full-scale assessment, nevertheless, the evidence to date suggests that the JDP government's initiatives in the interrelated realms of the economy, the polity, and foreign policy have been rather successful. In the purely economic realm, the JDP government's broad commitment to the International Monetary Fund (IMF) program helped the process of economic recovery from the deep economic crisis that Turkey experienced in 2000 and 2001, with inflation rates falling to their lowest level since the early 1970s. Furthermore, the government's strong commitment to the goal of European Union (EU) membership and the associated reform agenda, on both the economic and democratization fronts, helped to inspire confidence among domestic and foreign investors.

Hence, for the first time for many years, Turkey found itself in the midst of a virtuous cycle with economic and political reforms as well as key foreign policy initiatives feeding into one another, helping to produce a favorable environment for economic growth. Given these favorable developments, my central contention is that it is unlikely that the JDP will experience a major dislocation of its power base for the foreseeable future. Only major setbacks such as another major financial crisis or a dramatically negative response by the EU to Turkish membership aspirations, such as closing the full-membership option altogether—which, in turn, may be translated to a violent negative reaction in financial markets precipitating a possible economic crisis—could seriously undermine the popularity and the electoral fortunes of the JDP. While the possibility of such an extremely negative scenario cannot be ruled out completely, at the time when this chapter is written the prospects for such an outcome appear to be rather remote.[1] What seems to be more likely is the realization of a benign scenario whereby positive signals from the EU contribute to the process of economic and political reforms that, if successful, are likely to consolidate the JDP's power base even further. There is no doubt that, as we shall discuss in some detail, the JDP will encounter a number of serious challenges to its economic, political, and foreign policy agendas over the course of the next decade. My prediction, nevertheless, is that given the achievements of the party so far, these serious challenges are unlikely to cause a dramatic loss of popularity and electoral support that would lead toward its possible marginalization on the Turkish political scene.

The Underlying Political Economy of the JDP's Electoral Success

There is no doubt that the economic crisis, the deepest crisis that Turkey has experienced in its recent history, with negative repercussions on all segments of Turkish society, rich and poor, educated and noneducated, urban and rural, had a devastating impact on the electoral fortunes of established political parties in Turkey.[2]

Clearly, the three parties that experienced major setbacks with a dramatic collapse in their electoral support were the parties that made up the coalition government that came into office following the April 1999 elections and were ironically though somewhat unintentionally responsible for some of the major economic and political reforms that Turkey experienced in recent years. The leading member of the coalition government, the Democratic Left Party (DLP) led by Bülent Ecevit, experienced a total collapse. Similarly, the Nationalist Action Party (NAP) and the Motherland Party (MP) also experienced dramatic declines in their bases of electoral support. Indeed, none of the three members of the coalition government could even pass the 10 percent threshold in the November 2002 elections, which meant that they were effectively excluded from participation in parliamentary politics after 1999. Yet another political party that was not in government in the 1999–2002 era, but was nevertheless a major political force throughout the 1990s, namely the True Path Party (TPP), also experienced a deep setback and was relegated to the sidelines. Clearly, large segments of the Turkish electorate displayed a deep dissatisfaction with established political parties on both the right and the left of the political spectrum. Center-left parties were penalized for failing to protect the interests of the poor and the underprivileged. The center-right parties suffered, in addition, from their association with widespread corruption.

Hence, the JDP as a new force in Turkish politics capitalized on the failures of conventional political parties. The JDP managed to present itself to wide segments of Turkish society as a progressive force that could come to terms with the positive aspect of economic globalization based on active participation and competition in the global market. At the same time, the JDP's approach involved a serious concern with social justice

issues involving both the distribution of material benefits and the extension of individual rights and freedoms. Compared to its rivals, the party
appeared to be forward-looking and reformist in its approach, aiming to
come to grips with the forces of globalization, meaning to capitalize on
its material benefits while aiming to correct some of its negative consequences at the same time. Indeed, in certain respects, the JDP appeared
to be more of a European-style social democratic party of the Third Way,
compared to its main rival in the November 2002 elections, the Republican People's Party (RPP). With its emphasis on the benefits of the market, the need to reform the state in the direction of a post-developmental
regulatory state, its concern with social justice issues, its commitment
to multiculturalism and extension of religious freedoms, and its transna-
tionalism as exemplified by its greater commitment to EU membership
and the associated set of reforms than any other political party in recent
Turkish society, the JDP projected the image of a Third Way political
party. In contrast, the RPP appeared much more inward-oriented and in
certain respects far more conservative judged by the standards of European-style Third Way politics.[3]

The RPP has capitalized on the benefit of the doubt of not being in
government or even in Parliament during the 1999–2002 era. In some
ways, in spite of its long history, it was also a partially new face that the
voters could turn to in the face of their deep dissatisfaction with the
principal parties in office. Nevertheless, the RPP leadership, in spite of
the recruitment of the former minister of state for the economy, Kemal
Derviş, failed to overcome its heavily nationalistic, statist, and inward-
leaning orientation. Furthermore, the party's single-minded adherence to
a rather strict and rigid version of secularism helped to alienate it from
important segments of the Turkish society that favored an extension of
religious rights and freedoms within the boundaries of a secular state.
Hence the traditionalism, the lack of adaptability, and the relative lack of
concern of the RPP with economic issues constituted some of the key factors that clearly helped to enhance the JDP's electoral fortunes, with the
gap between the parties widening even further in the municipal elections
of November 2004 (fig. 9.1). Stated somewhat differently, the JDP has
clearly benefited from the absence of a powerful and vocal opposition,
and this very absence of a genuine alternative from either the right or
the left of the political spectrum with a capacity to adapt itself to changing circumstances and the new parameters within which Turkish politics
operates may help to accentuate the dominance of the JDP even further
during the course of the next few years.[4]

% Votes

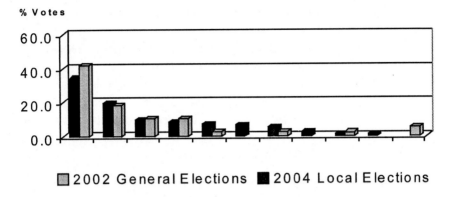

■ 2002 General Elections ■ 2004 Local Elections

FIGURE 9.1. Electoral Performance of Political Parties in 2002 and 2004.

Sources: http://www.secim2002.com; http://www.secim2004.com; and http://www.ntvmsnbc.com.

At a deeper level, any analysis of the JDP's electoral success also has to take into account the party's Islamist roots in the sense that the party, while presenting itself as a new political movement with a claim to the very center of Turkish politics, also capitalized on some of the inherent strengths as well as avoided the mistakes made by its predecessors the WP and the VP. The main lesson that the JDP learned from the record of its predecessors involved the need to construct a broad-based interclass alliance. This alliance encompassed the more dynamic and prosperous segments of society that were benefiting from the globalization process in material terms as well as the more disadvantaged and underprivileged sections of society both in rural areas and on the margins of major metropolitan areas, groups that clearly failed to participate effectively in or benefit from the operation of the global market. Indeed, the active support of small- and medium-sized business units, notably in the rising Anatolian cities, collected under the umbrella organization the MÜSİAD (Independent Industrialists and Businessmen's Association), was a key element in the rise of the Welfare Party in the mid-1990s.[5] The support of small- and medium-sized enterprises continued to be a crucial element in the rise of the JDP as well. It is ironic that center-left parties in Turkey have failed to construct the broad interclass alliances needed for electoral success, which involved mobilizing small- and medium-sized business as a key component of the broad electoral coalition.[6] From a political economy perspective, one of the crucial differences between the JDP and its rivals is that the former is able to cut across class cleavages and appeal to diverse segments of Turkish society using religion as an effective mechanism of mutual trust and bondage, whereas the latter are able to appeal only to certain segments of Turkish society that are either the winners or the losers in the globalization process. The fact that the winners of globalization are part of the broad electoral coalition also explains, in part, why Islamist politics in Turkey has been evolving in a moderate direction in recent years, because these groups, far more than the poor and underprivileged strata of society, have a lot to lose from open confrontation with the secular establishment and the state elites.

Yet another positive legacy that the JDP derived from its predecessors was the performance of local governments. The broad evidence suggests that the municipalities run by Islamist political parties were more efficient and less corrupt than their counterparts run by other political parties throughout the 1990s.[7] Islamists, and more recently the JDP with its Islamist roots, displayed a high degree of mobilization at the local level and also capitalized on the dense networks of informal relations that helped to mobilize the local community in addressing the problems of poverty and deprivation. In retrospect, the established parties lacked the kind of mobilization and supporting network of informal relations that would enable them to challenge the JDP in this regard.

In addition, Islamists in Turkey have experienced a serious learning process in recent years that effectively taught them to avoid some of the mistakes of the previous era. This learning process became particularly pronounced following the "February 28 Process," "a postmodern coup" that effectively marked the end of the coalition government led by the Welfare Party and its leader, Necmettin Erbakan, in 1997. It became increasingly clear that a party that failed to respect the principles of secularism would have no chance of sustained and effective participation in the Turkish political system given its constitutional boundaries. Hence this learning process was extremely important in pushing Islamists in Turkey toward a moderate, centrist direction. There was a learning process in the sense that hard-line Islamist politics would appeal only to a small segment of the Turkish population. Moderation was, therefore, the key toward the construction of a mass party of broad electoral support.

A parallel factor that also helped in this respect was Turkey's deepening relations with the European Union. Islamists in Turkey increasingly recognized that promoting relations with the EU would be to their advantage in the sense that it would help to protect themselves against the hypersecularism of the state elites and would create a congenial environment for the promotion of religious freedoms. At the same time, closer

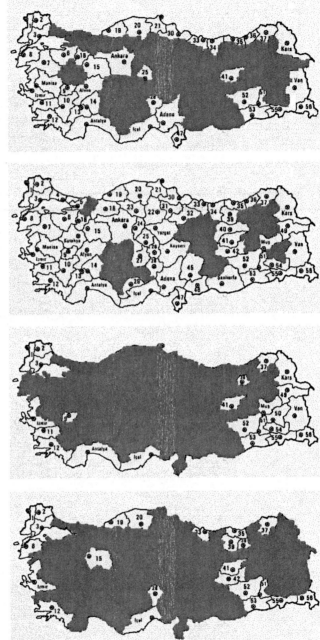

The Welfare Party
in 1995

The Virtue Party
in 1999

The JDP
in 2002

The JDP
in 2004

FIGURE 9.2. The Extent of JDP's Electoral Coalition Compared with Its Predecessors.

Sources: http://www.secimedogru.net; http://www.secimsonucu.com; and http://www.lib.utexas.edu/maps/
turkey.html.

relations with the EU placed constraints on the Islamists themselves and clearly eliminated any option of political participation without respecting the principle of secularism, broadly interpreted, in the first place. Clearly, the opportunity space or the room for maneuvering provided by the EU has been well recognized and capitalized upon by the JDP leadership in the recent era. The JDP leadership has also seen the purely economic benefits of Turkey's closer integration with the EU. Not surprisingly, therefore, the JDP has established itself as a vocal and active member of the pro-EU coalition in Turkey, a coalition in which civil society organizations led by key business associations such as the representative of big business in Turkey, TÜSİAD (Turkish Industrialists and Businessmen's Association), and MÜSİAD are also key elements. In retrospect, it is fair to say that the learning process that the Islamists have gone through during the past few decades has been far more rapid and profound than that of their counterparts in mainstream parties such as the RPP.

In the process of moving to the center, the JDP has tried to maintain its traditional Islamist core but has also tried to widen its electoral base to include broad segments of Turkish society that are conservative or religious in their orientation but have not been part of hard-line Islamist politics.[8] This broad-based character of the party is clearly projected from the electoral map that emerged after the November 2002 and March 2004 elections, a map that marks a sharp contrast with the early version of Islamist politics in Turkey that was primarily a regional, inner Anatolian phenomenon (fig. 9.2) It is fair to say that in terms of its moderate politics and its broad-based appeal, the current profile of the JDP resembles more the Menderes-style Democratic Party of the 1950s or the Özal-style Motherland Party of the 1980s than the more narrowly situated Welfare Party led by Erbakan in the mid-1990s.

THE PERFORMANCE OF THE JDP GOVERNMENT ON THE ECONOMIC FRONT: A BROAD APPRAISAL

The initial reactions to the landslide electoral victory of the JDP among key segments of the domestic business community and international financial circles were ones of serious apprehension. Arguably, the fact that Turkey for the first time for a period of over a decade had a single-party government with a comfortable parliamentary majority was identified as a factor that could contribute to economic and political stability. Yet the potential benefits of a single-party government were more than counterbalanced by the fear that, given its broad electoral base, the government was likely to deviate from the IMF program and indulge in another wave of populist spending that would bring the country once more to the verge of yet another major macroeconomic crisis. At a deeper level, there was also the fear that the political agenda of the JDP in the name of extending religious freedoms would inevitably create a head-on clash with the secular establishment and notably with the military, which, in turn, would be a major source of political and economic instability at a critical juncture of the post-crisis recovery process.

After a few months in office, however, it was quite clear that the fears and misgivings concerning the JDP government were rather exaggerated and lacked a serious basis. The government, by and large, displayed a strong commitment to the basic principles of fiscal stabilization and structural reforms embodied in the IMF program. Judged in terms of broad macroeconomic indicators, the JDP's performance could be classified as a significant success. Over the period of the past two years economic growth has been stronger than even the most optimistic forecasts and inflation lower than IMF-agreed end-of-the-year targets. The degree of commitment displayed by the government to the program helped to restore investor confidence. Indeed, during the first quarter of 2004, the Turkish economy recorded an astonishing growth of 12 percent in real GNP, which could, in part, be interpreted as a concrete sign of rising investor confidence (fig. 9.3).

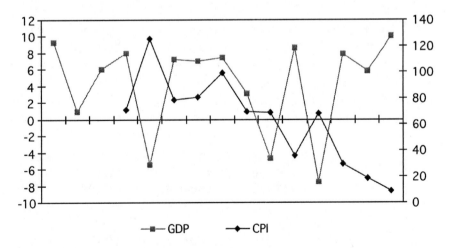

FIGURE 9.3. Turkey's Post-Crisis Inflation and Growth Performance

Note: CPI refers to the inflation rate based on the consumer price index. Sources: http://www.dpt.gov.tr and http://www.treasury.gov.tr.

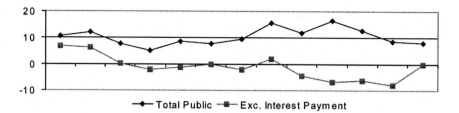

FIGURE 9.4. Public Sector Deficits: PSBR / GNP.

Note: PSBR refers to public sector borrowing requirement. Source: http://www.treasury.gov.tr.

At the heart of this process of rapid recovery was a single-minded commitment to fiscal discipline. This commitment made a sharp contrast with the experience of the Turkish economy since the late 1980s during which serious fiscal instability had been associated with a major domestic and external debt burden and successive financial crises. In spite of a serious interest burden, the government has been able to accomplish and sustain a surplus in the primary balance in line with the IMF targets (fig. 9.4). In addition, the government has been able to continue with key institutional reforms such as banking sector regulation. Consequently, most commentators would argue that by the middle of 2004 the Turkish banking and financial system is far better regulated than in the past and the Turkish economy is more resilient and robust to possible domestic and external shocks.[9] Indeed, the frequent reports published on the Turkish economy are quite unambiguous in highlighting the broad macroeconomic achievements of the government to date, while at the same time pointing toward some of the dangers and challenges that await the Turkish economy given the serious debt burden that the economy has inherited from the previous decades.[10]

In addition to its achievements on the macroeconomic front, the JDP government has been making a concerted effort for the first time to deal with the pervasive problem of corruption that has been a major negative feature of the Turkish economy during the neoliberal era. The problem has been attacked through an improvement of the legal system as well as by taking legal action against key businessmen and politicians who are accused of having been involved in corruption during the recent era. Clearly, it is too early to judge whether this concerted effort against corruption will generate widespread rather than isolated cases of success. Nevertheless, it is fair to argue that the process of dealing with the problem on a large scale has been initiated effectively by the JDP at a time when the country has been experiencing a process of rapid "European-ization" with an emphasis on democratization and the rule of law as the central elements of this process. Clearly, a successful attack on corruption will help to generate resources that could be used to finance education and other forms of social spending that are desperately needed by wide segments of the population.

In the domain of social policy, a clear gap exists between what the government has promised and what it has been able to deliver so far. Part of the explanation of this gap lies in the severe fiscal constraint that any incumbent government faces in a debt-ridden economy that is undergoing a process of massive fiscal austerity. Nevertheless, there is evidence that the government has been developing specific programs within the available budgetary limits aimed directly toward the alleviation of poverty. There is also evidence that with the recovery of the economy, the JDP government has been able to channel more resources in the form of larger volumes of lending made available to small- and medium-sized enterprises through public banks, an avenue that is crucial to addressing the basic imbalance that exists between big and small business in the Turkish context.[11]

EXPLAINING THE JDP'S SUCCESS IN THE ECONOMIC REALM: THE INTERPLAY OF ECONOMIC AND POLITICAL FACTORS AND FOREIGN POLICY INITIATIVES

Having argued that the macroeconomic performance during its early term of office has been broadly successful, it would be rather ahistorical to attribute this success exclusively to the JDP. The Turkish economy had been undergoing a series of reform initiatives during the second phase of neoliberal reforms throughout the 1990s with key turning points the signing of the Customs Union agreement with the EU (which became effective at the beginning of 1996) and the signing of an IMF program in December 1999, before the onset of an economic crisis. The decision of the EU Council in December 1999 to announce Turkey as a candidate country for full membership also exerted a dramatic impact on the incentive structure facing the economic and political actors, providing a powerful impetus for a mix of economic and democratization reforms in the process. Given the strong externally generated impetus for reform, the coalition government in office, in spite of its lukewarm approach to reform and its reservations concerning loss of national sovereignty, was nevertheless responsible for the most far-reaching set of reforms in recent Turkish history.[12]

The economic crisis of February 2001 itself, in spite of devastating consequences, had one positive unintended consequence. It helped to break down resistance to reform on the part of the Euro-skeptics and helped to accelerate the momentum of the reform process. Following the crisis, it became much easier to gather support for EU membership and its associated conditionality on the basis of the material benefits they offered. Not surprisingly some of the major reform initiatives such as the elimination of the death penalty occurred after the crisis during the critical month of August 2002. The crisis also strengthened the hand of the IMF itself, which was important in terms of breaking down resistance in domestic circles for key reform initiatives such as the regulation of the banking sector through the effective operation of the autonomous regulatory authority for the banking sector (BRSA).

The appointment by the coalition government of Kemal Derviş, from the World Bank, as the minister responsible for the economy shortly after the economic crisis also constituted an important step. Derviş and his team, through their single-minded commitment to fiscal discipline and regulatory reforms, appeared to play an important role during the crucial period between March 2001 and August 2002, during which the key ingredients of the recovery process were largely instituted. Given his links to transnational financial circles, the presence of Derviş was also important in generating confidence and securing external support for the recovery process.

It is paradoxical, therefore, that the JDP capitalized on some of the important initiatives that the coalition government introduced, notably after the crisis, while benefiting immensely from the loss of popularity of the coalition government because of its having precipitated the twin economic crises in the first place. Indeed, it was also ironic that Kemal Derviş (as a member of the DLP at the time) unintentionally helped to contribute to the subsequent success of the rival party, the JDP, first by laying the basis of the economic recovery and second by contributing to an inner party struggle resulting in the collapse of the coalition government and the calling of an early election that brought the JDP to power.

This historical background is important in placing the recent performance of the JDP into proper perspective. It is also fair to argue, however, that the JDP itself displayed a far greater degree of unity and commitment to the reform process, both on the economic and the political fronts, compared to the preceding coalition government, which was largely swimming against the tide in this process. It is striking, for example, that the JDP was far more proactive on the issue of Turkey's EU membership, meaning a commitment to undertake reform and not membership as a vague ideal in itself, than any other political party in recent history. It is striking, for example, that the party made a decisive effort to tackle the Cyprus problem through diplomatic initiatives right after the November electoral victory. This proactive stance on Cyprus, designed to eliminate one of the key obstacles on the path to EU membership, was adopted in spite of the fact that it was a risky decision for party leadership because it created the possibility of a serious clash with key segments of the military and foreign policy establishment. Nevertheless, the proactive stance paid dividends in the sense that it helped to gather further support in both external and domestic circles and to overcome the initial reservations concerning the party's alleged Islamist credentials. Indeed, the proactive stance of the JDP on the EU front was also instrumental in reshaping public opinion in Europe and in helping to mobilize support in key centers within Europe around the cause of Turkey's full membership.

In retrospect, the JDP government has been able to benefit from the synergy that has been created through its initiatives in the economy, democratization reforms, and foreign policy actions. For market actors, domestic and international, the future success of the Turkish economy was effectively tied to the prospect of EU membership. EU membership was regarded as the permanent or long-term anchor needed for the stable development of the Turkish economy given that the role that the IMF could provide was necessarily a temporary one. Given this linkage between the EU and performance of the economy, the proactive stance of the JDP on the EU issue and its ability to move beyond established nationalist rhetoric on sensitive issues such as Cyprus helped to inspire confidence and contributed to the process of economic recovery in the process.

Looking back to the economic performance of the JDP during the first two years in government, one could detect an interesting mix of commitment and pragmatism. To give an example, the government was clearly committed to the objective of fiscal austerity. Yet, in its early stages, it was much more lukewarm in its attitude toward independent regulatory bodies such as the BRSA. This lukewarm attitude perhaps reflected the pressure that came from a key component of its electoral coalition, namely small business, in the direction of a more relaxed attitude toward banking-sector regulation in order to obtain more bank credit to finance its operations. Hence there was a certain clash between the government and the IMF in the early stages on this issue, with the government putting forward the case for greater political control and accountability of

such institutions while the IMF put the primary emphasis on autonomy.[13] Yet when the government realized that this conflict would jeop-
ardize the economic program and undermine the confidence of the key
actors involved, the issue was gradually pushed aside and the conflict
over autonomous regulatory bodies faded away. One could identify similar instances of pragmatism on the part of the JDP leadership that helped
the party to come out of possible crises relatively unharmed through a
swift shift of the public debate away from the divisive issue concerned.
For example, again reflecting pressures from its more conservative, religiously inclined constituencies, the government introduced a reform bill
for higher education during the spring of 2004, key elements of which
were interpreted as providing serious concessions to the Islamists. This
initiative helped to create a crisis of considerable proportions along the
secular-Islamist axis, a crisis that had the potential to create a negative
effect on the economy. Realizing that the bill would have potentially
destabilizing consequences, the government did not contest the vetoing
of the bill by the president and the controversial piece of legislation was
effectively sidelined for the time being.

There is no doubt that the JDP government also benefited from a
certain dose of fortune. To provide a striking example, the government
was able to muddle through its relations with the United States in conjunction with the Iraq war without suffering major harm in the process.
Indeed, the fact that Turkey was able to stay out of the war completely,
by failing to allow the passage of American troops from Turkish territory
to Northern Iraq (against the wish of the JDP leadership itself) had the
unintended consequence of bringing Turkey closer to the core of Europe,
helping to break down the resistance of Euro-skeptic elements in Turkish
society even further. Hence the Iraq war was also instrumental in increasing the momentum of EU-related reforms engineered by the JDP leadership, reforms such as the closure of national security courts and broadcasting in the Kurdish language, the kind of reforms that would have
been unthinkable only a few years ago.[14]

BUSINESS PERCEPTIONS OF THE JDP GOVERNMENT'S PERFORMANCE: TÜSİAD AND MÜSİAD COMPARED

Big business in Turkey, primarily located in Istanbul and the Marmara
region and represented under the umbrella of TÜSİAD, has typically
enjoyed a tense relationship with political parties or governments with
Islamist roots or orientation. The position of TÜSİAD in protecting the

secular principles of the Republic has been rather close to the position of the established state elites. In contrast, small- and medium-sized business units represented by the other leading business organization, MÜSİAD, whose membership covers enterprises located both in Istanbul and in the dynamic inner Anatolian towns, has been closely associated with Islamist politics ever since its inception in 1990 and its strong affinity with the rise of the Welfare Party during the early and the mid-1990s. Although MÜSİAD has tried to distance itself from individual political parties following the February 28 Process, nevertheless there is no doubt that there is a considerable overlap between the agenda of this organization and that of the JDP. In recent years, MÜSİAD has followed TÜSİAD's lead, adopting a strong commitment toward Turkey's integration with the European Union and the associated democratization and reform agenda, though with a somewhat different emphasis on the need to extend religious freedoms.[15]

A systematic comparison of these two influential business associations is beyond the scope of our present inquiry. What is important in the present context is that the two organizations differ sharply in their interpretation of secularism. Consequently, whilst MÜSİAD membership is very much part and parcel of the JDP's broad electoral coalition, big business as represented by TÜSİAD has been outside this coalition and clearly was rather apprehensive about the JDP when the party established a clear parliamentary majority in November 2002. It is interesting, therefore, to compare the perceptions of government performance held by these two rather contrasting associations following a period in which the JDP has been in office for a period of nearly two years. The comparison is naturally based on the periodic reports published by the two organizations, notably on the state of the Turkish economy, as well as the public pronouncements of leading figures in these organizations.

Our comparison reveals a rather striking and paradoxical pattern. TÜSİAD, in spite of its fears concerning the possibility that the JDP could create political instability through attacks on the secular constitutional order and economic instability by engaging in populist expansionism, has been quite satisfied with the JDP government's performance to date. The periodic assessments provided by the organization highlight the overall improvement in the macroeconomic performance of the Turkish economy and praise the government's commitment to fiscal discipline as a key ingredient of stability. Similarly, the organization has been quite satisfied with the proactive stance adopted by the JDP in promoting the cause of EU membership; the initiatives taken by the government to bring the long-standing dispute on Cyprus were also welcomed.[16] What is interesting for our purposes is that the JDP in office has displayed a position, judged by the degree of commitment to IMF disciplines and the goal of EU membership, that was much closer to the position held by TÜSİAD on these critical issues.[17]

A close examination of MÜSİAD's reports during the recent era reveals a much more critical attitude toward the government's economic performance during its early term of office.[18] MÜSİAD recognizes that the government has achieved a certain degree of success in terms of fiscal stability, control of inflation, and the recovery of the real economy in the post-crisis era. Nevertheless, it strongly emphasizes the lopsided nature of the recovery process, pointing to the dangers of continued dependence on short-term capital inflows and the problems that are likely to be generated by running a large current account deficit. MÜSİAD is quite critical of what it considers to be excessively tight fiscal rules imposed by the IMF such as the primary surplus target of 6.5 percent of the Gross Domestic Product. Similarly, the organization has been critical of the tight set of regulations on bank lending imposed by the so-called autonomous regulatory agencies such as the BRSA on the grounds that such an approach puts too much emphasis on financial sector stability at the expense of the development of the real economy.[19] Indeed, MÜSİAD feels that a more appropriate strategy for Turkey would be to adopt an independent path of stabilization and reform when the current agreement with the IMF ends in February 2005. This approach sharply differs from the position of TÜSİAD as well as that of significant sections of the domestic and international community who strongly believe that a continued relationship with the IMF in some form, on top of the EU anchor, is absolutely critical for the crisis-free development of the Turkish economy over the next few years.[20] A systematic comparison of the respective positions of MÜSİAD and TÜSİAD on a number of key economic issues is presented in table 9.1.

In retrospect, the sharp difference in the perceptions of the two organizations is perhaps not that surprising in the sense that big business and small/medium-sized business find themselves in different structural locations in terms of their positioning with respect to the globalization process. A fundamental asymmetry exists between big and small capital in the sense that what matters for the former is stability at all costs whereas for the latter continued growth and competitiveness necessitates access to both bank finance and state resources. Stated somewhat differently, a large segment of TÜSİAD membership does not face the kind of financial constraints that small- and medium-sized businesses, which typically

TABLE 9.1. MÜSİAD and TÜSİAD on Government's Economic Performance and the Role of the IMF: A Stylized Comparison

	MÜSİAD	TÜSİAD
ATTITUDE TOWARD THE IMF	Rather critical of certain aspects of the IMF program. Government should bargain more effectively with the Fund over social issues and the needs of the real economy. The weight and the influence of the IMF in the policy-making process should be reduced.	Firm belief that the government should single-mindedly conform to the basic principles of the IMF program. It is also vital that an agreement with the IMF is concluded for the period after 2005. Monetary, fiscal, and structural reform components of the program are considered to be vital for long-term success.
DEGREE OF COMMITMENT TO THE PROGRAM	An alternative program of stabilization and reform is proposed, which deviates from the existing one in critical respects.	Firm commitment; deviation from program targets will generate significant costs.
GROWTH	Assessment is favorable and yet critical. Attention is drawn to the fragile and lopsided nature of the recovery process based on short-term capital inflows and rising current account deficit.	Highly favorable assessment of growth and inflation performance. Government should focus even more intensively on longer-term structural reforms.
BUDGETARY DISCIPLINE	Accepts that the government has been successful in imposing fiscal discipline but also draws attention to some of the costs of excessive budgetary discipline, notably in the sphere of public investments.	Highly supportive of the government's budgetary stance and commitment to fiscal discipline.
UNEMPLOYMENT	Highlighted as the major social and economic issue. The government is not doing enough to deal with the problem effectively. In addition to growth, direct measures are needed.	Also considers unemployment as a serious issue. Yet, the way to deal with the problem involves a commitment to the existing program rather than deviating from it.

TABLE 9.1 (CONT'D.). MÜSİAD and TÜSİAD on Government's Economic Performance and the Role of the IMF: A Stylized Comparison

	MÜSİAD	TÜSİAD
FINANCIAL SECTOR REGULATION AND THE REAL ECONOMY	Financial sector regulation should be in line with the needs of the real economy. Single-minded focus on tight banking sector regulation is costly in terms of growth and performance of the real economy.	Tight regulation of the financial sector is crucial. Weak regulations may create the basis of yet another financial crisis.
REGULATORY INSTITUTIONS IN ACTION	Critical of such institutions. These institutions should be more accountable for them to be able to adopt a balanced approach to regulation.	In line with the IMF, firm belief that for tight and effective regulation, these institutions should be highly autonomous. Not much emphasis on accountability.

fall under the umbrella of MÜSİAD, are facing. Typically they either have their own banks as part of the broader conglomerate or they have the kind of reputation needed to borrow without major problems from domestic or external sources. Moreover, big business through its close relations with the state of Turkey has enjoyed historically superior access to state resources although it is currently much less directly dependent on the state for its future performance. What is also critical here is that the typical IMF program that Turkey has been undergoing not only affects overall macroeconomic performance, but also the pattern of income distribution. One of the key distributional consequences of tight rules on budgetary discipline and financial regulation is the creation of further asymmetries between big and small business.

From a political economy perspective, another interesting lesson that could be drawn from this stylized comparison is that the existing structures of economic and political power, as well as the manner in which the economy has been integrated into the global economy and the global financial markets, severely constrain the options available to particular governments, to which the JDP government is no exception. The key to success in this environment, therefore, depends on how successfully a particular government capitalizes on the benefits offered by this structure and the extent to which it can overcome its asymmetries and negative side effects without jeopardizing its electoral prospects in the process.

IS THE TRANSITION FROM A VICIOUS TO A VIRTUOUS CYCLE
SUSTAINABLE? POSSIBLE CHALLENGES TO THE ELECTORAL
DOMINANCE OF THE JDP IN THE MEDIUM TERM

The picture presented so far suggests that Turkey in recent years has managed to overcome the instability and the impasse of the 1990s and has entered into a virtuous process whereby a series of economic, political, and foreign policy initiatives have been contributing to an unprecedented pace of democratization and a more pronounced economic recovery than many analysts had predicted in the aftermath of the 2001 crisis. Although the JDP itself did not initiate this process, it certainly helped to accelerate it by a considerable margin after November 2002. Clearly, if the recovery process continues uninterrupted and Turkey is able to obtain a date for the start of accession negotiations from the EU in December, the JDP will find itself in a much stronger position, and then it would be highly unlikely that its electoral dominance would be challenged by the time of the next general election in 2007.

Certainly, smooth developments on the EU front are likely to be translated into the economic realm and may be translated into a significant wave of long-term foreign investment in the same fashion that Poland has experienced since 1994. It is also quite likely that the government will sign a new agreement with the IMF, which will be important for an economy with a huge debt burden such as Turkey's in order to sustain investor confidence and to keep the cost of additional borrowing at acceptable levels. The alternative of trying to maintain an independent path of stabilization and reform as recommended by MÜSIAD, for example, involving experimenting with heterodox instruments such as controls over short-term capital flows and more flexible implementation of budgetary discipline and banking sector regulation, can be an exceptionally risky path to follow in the circumstances that the Turkish economy finds itself.[21] In an environment in which investor confidence is rising and foreign direct investment, which has remained at low levels by the standards of most emerging markets throughout the neoliberal era, rises by a considerable margin—and this is supported by steady improvements in productivity by domestic economic actors—then Turkish economy would be able to generate a 6–7 percent growth rate per annum on a sustained basis over time. It is this kind of sustained growth that is crucial in terms of the country's ability to raise its per capita income on a significant basis and to deal successfully with the pervasive problems of poverty and inequality. In this kind of environment, in which the JDP could capitalize on the benefits of economic growth, it would be rather difficult for opposition parties to mount a serious challenge to the JDP's electoral dominance, at least in the short run.

Yet a balanced perspective has to take into account that certain developments may occur that could upset this benign equilibrium. One such possibility that immediately comes to mind in this context is the possibility, although a remote one, that the EU provides a decisive negative response that puts an end to Turkey's membership aspirations and offers the option of a looser relationship based on a special status, an option that some German Christian Democrats recommended. Clearly, if such a bleak scenario materializes—which incidentally is rather different from another possibility: that opening up of accession negotiations is not ruled out but postponed because of a Commission recommendation that finds certain loopholes in the reform implementation process—this scenario may lead to a revival of Euro-skepticism in Turkey. It is also possible that such a bleak scenario would have an immediate negative impact on financial markets and the behavior of economic actors, both domestic and external, helping to undermine the investor confidence that has been built up over the past few years. In such an environment, the two parties that have already experienced a recovery in their electoral fortunes during the municipal elections of March 2004 (see fig. 9.2)—the center-right TPP and the ultranationalist NAP—could significantly improve their electoral fortunes and place a major challenge to the dominance of the JDP by the time of the next election.

Apart from the obvious EU factor, there are other elements that need to be taken into account in evaluating the medium-term electoral prospects of the JDP. Although the economic recovery process is under way, the process is still a fragile recovery. One has to take into account that part of the recovery process in 2003 was because of the inflow of short-term capital, which was, in part, because of low interest rates in the United States.[22] Given Turkey's huge public debt burden with a disproportionately large share of short-term debt, a widening of current account deficit, rising U.S. interest rates, and large repayments on its external debt in 2005–6 render the economy vulnerable to sudden shifts in investor sentiments (table 9.2). Hence, the possibility of yet another financial crisis with costly consequences cannot be ruled out completely although most financial analysts would argue that the risk of a debt default has diminished considerably because of a mixture of strong economic growth, large primary budget surpluses, and a flexible exchange rate policy. The risks would naturally be reduced even further if Turkey continues uninter-

TABLE 9.2. Comparative Debt Performance of the Turkish Economy, 2002

	TURKEY	ARGENTINA	POLAND	CHINA	S. KOREA	BRAZIL
External Debt / GDP[a]	72.2	53.6	38.8	12.7	28.1	49.6
Short-Term Debt[b]	15,190	20,560	9,325	18,414	42,514	26,765
Total Debt Service[b]	29,872	32,437	8,763	20,825	26,311	53,390

a. In percentage   b. Million $

Source: http://www.bradynet.com and http://www.die.gov.tr.

rupted on its EU trajectory and signs a new agreement with the IMF at the same time, strengthening the double external anchor that Turkey has enjoyed in recent years. It is important to emphasize, however, that external anchors per se are not enough and do not provide an adequate substitute for insufficient commitment to fiscal discipline and the overall reform process on the part of the policy-making elites and the key economic actors involved.

Clearly, one important issue that will affect the JDP's electoral fortunes concerns the distributional aspect of its economic policies. What is important in this context is that not only are high rates of economic growth achieved but also growth trickles down and improves the material position of large segments of the population. It will also be important for the party in government to be able to pursue an active social policy targeting those groups at the lowest end of the income scale. Although the government may face significant budgetary constraints in this respect, nevertheless a combination of high growth, the resources saved through an effective anticorruption campaign, and a downturn in defense expenditures could help to produce a significant impact in terms of poverty alleviation.[23] Unemployment is increasingly singled out as a major social and economic program in this context. The corollary of this is that if growth is not translated into a substantial improvement in employment prospects for a country with a disproportionately young population, the issue could be taken up by the rival parties and could present a major challenge to the electoral fortunes of the JDP over time.

Finally, a major challenge to the party could originate from its core supporters, who clearly expect significant progress on issues relating to Islamic identity such as the freedom to wear the headscarf in public places, the extension of opportunities for graduates of religious secondary schools (the İmam Hatip schools), and so on. Although the JDP labels itself as "Conservative Democrats," there is no doubt that it embodies a certain core of supporters who have traditionally been associated with Islamist political parties. In the early period of office, the JDP leadership could easily postpone such sensitive issues on the grounds that more immediate and pressing issues need to be tackled first, such as the economy and relations with the EU.[24] Yet such demands for cultural recognition cannot be postponed indefinitely. At the same time any attempts to respond to their demands in the current domestic and international context embodies the potential to create considerable political and economic instability, as the episode involving the controversial higher education reform bill clearly testified.[25] Hence the party faces a dilemma in the sense that in its search to capture the center and form a broad center-right coalition it may alienate some of its core group of supporters who over time could shift to other political parties such as the more radical Islamist party, the HP, or even the ultranationalistic NAP, which compete for similar segments of the electorate. The same problem exists in a different form for small- and medium-sized business that forms a significant component of the party's electoral base. Building on the earlier observation that MÜSIAD membership is quite critical of the government's unequivocal commitment to the program, the possibility that small- and medium-sized business might seek refuge in neighboring political parties should not be discarded altogether. The plight of the rural poor could constitute another cause of concern given that 35 percent of the active labor force still continues to be employed in the agricultural sector and this particular segment of society has been exposed to major cuts in subsidies as part of the IMF-induced fiscal adjustment process. Clearly, one should not discard the possibility of significant electoral swings against the JDP again in the direction of the TPP and the NAP by the disenchanted rural population.

What is crucial to highlight is that the JDP is ultimately a broad coalition that has capitalized on the failures of political parties on the left and the right of the political spectrum. This coalition is made up of a quite a different set of interests and in the Turkish setting it may be increasingly difficult to keep this broad entity together in the absence of the kind of benign scenario that we have outlined, the kind of scenario that is associated with rapid and sustained economic growth.

Concluding Observations

Economics and politics are interlinked in a peculiar way in the age of financial globalization. In this context, the JDP has been able to come to terms with globalization more than any other political party in the Turkish context. Its success so far has been based on its ability to move beyond class-based politics and to forge a broad cross-class coalition that incorporates both the winners and the losers of neoliberal globalization. Through commitment to the IMF program mixed with a certain dose of pragmatism and its proactive approach to Turkey's relations with the EU, the JDP, in office, has contributed to Turkey's economic recovery and to an intense phase of democratization reforms that was already under way before the party had actually assumed power. In spite of its Islamist roots, the party has skillfully moved toward the center of Turkish politics and has by and large successfully evaded the kinds of conflicts that could have emerged through open clashes with the state elites and the secular segments of the Turkish society. In retrospect, the JDP has capitalized on the deficiencies of both the center-right and the center-left parties in the Turkish setting. Clearly, the party itself is a hybrid formation. From a certain perspective, in line with how the party leadership tries to describe itself, with its emphasis on religion and conservative values, it constitutes a typical center-right party close to the Christian democratic tradition in Europe. Yet in certain respects the "Muslim democrats" or "conservative democrats," with their cosmopolitanism, commitment to multiculturalism, and emphasis on social justice, differ quite sharply from their Christian democratic counterparts and overlap with Third Way social democratic parties in Europe.

My basic prediction is that the party will be able to consolidate its position and maintain its electoral dominance in Turkish politics through the next general election based on the assumption that relations with Europe will develop smoothly and contribute further to the economic recovery process that is already under way. Clearly, rapid growth on the order of 6 to 7 percent per annum on a sustained basis will be critical to the ability of the party to keep its broad electoral coalition together. However, if this benign scenario fails to materialize, then the party, in spite of its success so far, may experience a significant reversal of its popularity and electoral base. With the extraordinary debt burden accumulated over time and an open capital account regime, the Turkish economy continues to be vulnerable, and one cannot rule out the possibility of a yet another costly crisis in the future even if a new IMF agreement is signed for the period after 2005. The IMF program is an important source of protection and discipline. Yet, as the experience of 2000 and 2001 has clearly illustrated, an ongoing IMF program per se cannot provide full insurance against a possible crisis. Clearly, economic success depends not only on positive signals from the EU and the IMF but also on continued commitment on the part of the government to long-term structural and regulatory reforms. Even favorable assessments of government performance during its early phase qualify their optimism by arguing that the government has not displayed sufficient commitment in key areas of reform such as privatization of state economic enterprises and the reform of the social security system. One could go even further and argue that even if crises are avoided, slow growth will not be sufficient to keep the JDP's broad electoral coalition together over a substantial period of time. The negative distributional repercussions of the IMF program under a slow growth–high unemployment scenario are likely to alienate key elements within its existing coalition, resulting in significant swings in favor of contending parties such as the TPP and the NAP.

Finally, moving beyond the purely economic realm, the debate concerning the boundaries of secularism has not been fully resolved in Turkish politics and is unlikely to be resolved through EU membership, since the EU itself does not offer a single blueprint in this context. Clearly, this observation has implications for the future of the JDP. There is a still a considerable element of mistrust concerning the JDP's centrist attitude among wide segments of the Turkish state and society. Indeed, one could argue that the degree of popularity of the JDP in international circles has been more widespread and uniform than its ambiguous position in the domestic sphere. Hence, the party is faced with a dilemma that it will ultimately have to confront. Either, it will choose to alienate its core Islamist supporters by choosing to relegate their claims for cultural recognition to the background or it will face the charge from key segments of the Turkish state and society that it is ultimately an identity-based party and its claim to being a political movement of the center is not a genuine claim. Clearly, such dilemmas or conflicts will also continue to exercise a key influence over the electoral fortunes of the party in the coming years.

NOTES

This chapter was presented as a paper at the Workshop on the Transformation of Turkish Politics: The Case of the Justice and Development Party (JDP), September 10–11, 2004, University of Utah, Salt Lake City. Valuable comments by Ahmet Faruk

Aysan, Korkut Ertürk, Fikret Şenses, and Ali Tekin as well as the able assistance of Evren Tok and Burcu Yiğiter are gratefully acknowledged.

1. The paper was written during the summer of 2004 before the critical decision of the EU on the question of opening up accession negotiations with Turkey that would lead to full membership.

2. On the nature of the twin economic crises of 2000 and 2001 that exercised such a deep impact on the Turkish economy and society, see the collection of articles in Ziya Öniş and Barry Rubin, *The Turkish Economy in Crisis* (London: Frank Cass Publishers, 2003).

3. For a further elaboration of this point involving the characterization of the JDP as a global Third Way response to Turkey's pervasive economic and political problems, see Fuat Keyman and Ziya Öniş, "Turkey's Delayed Encounter with Global Third Way Politics: The AKP and the Possibility of Democratization," *Journal of Democracy* 14, no. 2 (2003): 95–107; and Fuat Keyman and Ziya Öniş, "Globalization, Social Democracy and the Third Way: Paradoxes of the Turkish Experience," available at http://home.ku.edu.tr/~zonis/publications.htm.

4. On the nature of the Turkish party system and the principal characteristics of the political parties involved, see the articles in Metin Heper and Barry Rubin, *Political Parties in Turkey* (London: Frank Cass, 2002).

5. There is a need for qualification here that only a subset of small- and medium-sized businesses in Turkey is represented by MÜSİAD. A complete analysis has to take into account the role of the Union of Turkish Chambers and Stock Exchanges, TOBB, This is an organization in which membership is compulsory by law for all legally recognized business units. The nonconservative elements within the small- and medium-sized business community are represented under the auspices of this particular organization.

6. On the social bases of electoral support for the Welfare Party and the significance of small- and medium-sized business in this respect, see Ziya Öniş, "The Political Economy of Islamic Resurgence in Turkey: The Rise of the Welfare Party in Perspective," *Third World Quarterly* 18, no. 4 (1997); and Haldun Gülalp, "Globalization and Political Islam: The Social Bases of Turkey's Welfare Party," *International Journal of Middle Eastern Studies* 33, no. 3 (August 2001): 433–48. On the evolution of Islamist politics in Turkey since the early 1970s, see Ayşe Buğra, "Political Islam in Turkey in Historical Context: Strengths and Weaknesses," in *The Politics of Permanent Crisis: Class, Ideology and State in Turkey*, ed. Neşecan Balkan and Sungur Savran (New York: Nova Publishers, 2002), 107–45. For a recent contribution on the linkage between Islamists and the globalization process in Turkey, see Yıldız Atasoy, "Cosmopolitan Islamists in Turkey: Rethinking the Local in a Global Era," *Studies in Political Economy* 71–72 (2004): 133–63.

7. For evidence, see Uğur Akıncı, "The Welfare Party's Municipal Track Record: Evaluating Islamist Municipal Activism in Turkey," *Middle East Journal* 53, no. 1 (Winter 1999): 75–94.

8. On the forces that have been pushing political Islam in Turkey in a moderate direction, see Ziya Öniş, "Political Islam at the Crossroads: From Hegemony to Coexistence," *Contemporary Politics* 7, no. 4 (December 2001): 281–99; and R. Quinn Mecham, "From the Ashes of Virtue, a Promise of Light: The Transformation of Political Islam in Turkey," *Third World Quarterly* 25, no. 2 (2004): 339–58.

9. For further details, see various reports published by the Bank Regulation and Supervision Authority, the BRSA, available at http://www.bddk.org.tr/turkce/yayinlarveraporlar/yayinlarveraporlar.htm#1.

10. Reports by TÜSİAD, Turkish Economy 2003–4, available at http://www.tusiad.org.tr; and the Economist's Intelligence Unit, "Turkey at a Glance: 2004–05, Country Forecast," June 2004, are quite representative of the reports published in domestic and international circles concerning the broad contours of Turkey's macroeconomic performance during the recent era. For the improvement in the performance of the banking sector in the post-crisis era, see reports by the BRSA (BDDK), "Banking Sector Evaluation Report" (February 2004); "BRSA Annual Report" (2003); "Banking Sector Restructuring Program: Improvment Report VII" (October 2003). All reports were prepared by BRSA staff members and they are all available at http://www.bddk.org.tr.

11. The JDP government has been trying to follow an active social policy within the limits of fiscal austerity. Several programs have been developed to deal with the issues of poverty alleviation directly. The government has been cooperating with the Turkish Coal Mining Authorities to provide free distribution of coal to the poorest segments of society. Also, as indicated by the Ministry of Agriculture, there is an ongoing process of broadening the "Social Assistance Project" in rural areas. Similar programs have also been developed within the domain of the Ministry of Employment and Social Insurance. The details of such policies are expounded on the official JDP website, http://www.akparti.org.tr.

12. Here one needs to make the qualification that the Motherland Party, the MP, under the leadership of Mesut Yilmaz as the junior member of the coalition government, displayed a greater degree of commitment to reform on all fronts compared to the more nationalistically inclined DLP and NAP, the two dominant members of the coalition government.

13. The JDP leadership has adopted a critical attitude toward autonomous regulatory institutions. The critical attitude, however, should not be interpreted as if the government is intending to eliminate such institutions completely. The aim appears to involve a restructuring of such institutions and the style in which they operate. As Abdullah Gül mentioned, "There are some problems regarding the functioning of the Regulatory bodies, especially concerning the appointment of the members and the accountibility of these institutions." For further information please refer to http://turk.internet.com/haber/yazigoster.php3?yaziid=5858. Similar opinions are also evident in the election declarations of the JDP: "these bodies will continue their regulatory and supervisory functions, however we will make these bodies more accountable to the public and they will provide more information to the general public."

14. For a further elaboration of this point, see Ziya Öniş and Şuhnaz Yılmaz, "Turkey-EU-US Triangle in Perspective: Transformation or Continuity?" available at http://home.ku.edu.tr/~zonis/publications.htm. On the changing position of the Islamists vis-à-vis Europe, see Burhanettin Duran, "Islamist Redefinition(s) of European and Islamic Identities in Turkey," in *Turkey and European Integration: Accession Prospects and Issues*, ed. Mehmet Uğur and Nergis Canefe (London: Routledge, 2004). On the post-1999 dynamics of Turkey-EU relations and their dramatic impact on Turkish politics and the democratization process, see the collection of essays in Uğur

and Canefe, *Turkey and European Integration*, 125–47, as well as Paul Kubicek, "Turkish Accession into the EU in Comparative Perspective," *St. Anthony's College Oxford, Occasional Paper* no. 1/04, May 2004.

15. For systematic comparisons of these two key business associations, see Ayşe Buğra, "Class, Culture, and State: An Analysis of Interest Representation by Two Turkish Business Associations," *International Journal of Middle East Studies* 30, no. 4 (1998): 521–39; Ziya Öniş and Umut Türem, "Business, Globalization and Democracy: A Comparative Analysis of Turkish Business Associations," *Turkish Studies* 2, no. 2 (Autumn 2001): 94–120.

16. TÜSİAD appears to be fairly satisfied with the performance of the JDP government. Both in terms of the relations with the IMF (extension of the collaboration with the Fund) and JDP's stance and attitude toward the EU, TÜSİAD and JDP have similar opinions. As the recent report of the TÜSİAD, "Turkish Economy 2003," available at http://www.tusiad.org.tr, indicates, "the recorded growth rates in the recent period and ameliorations in some of the key macroeconomic variables establish the vital framework in order to fulfill the desired structural transformations in the economy. Together with the fall in the inflation rate, we do observe a decline in the real interest rates and, in addition to the overvaluation in the real exchange rate, we can expect continuing economic growth. Also, the success of the government in public finance will be a determining factor for the decrease of inflation and interest rates." For further information see TÜSİAD, "Public Sector Indicators in Turkey from a Comparative Perspective" (2004), available at at http://www.tusiad.org.tr; and see the positive views of the then chairman of TÜSİAD, Tuncay Özilhan, views about the contingency plan of the JDP government, available at http://www.milliyet.com.tr/2002/11/17/ekonomi/eko01.html.

17. This is not to suggest that TÜSİAD is totally receptive or uncritical of the government's actions. For example, TÜSİAD reports emphasize the need to accelerate the pace of long-term structural reforms in such areas as privatization and social security and argue that the government has not pressed ahead sufficiently to generate the kind of progress needed in these critical areas. For instance, though TÜSİAD appreciates the performce of the government, it is still suspicious about the maintainance of the high growth–low inflation trajectory. Also, from the point of the private sector, TÜSİAD's reports emphasize that the private sector should have a more competitive and productive nature. Existing levels of productivity and excess labor supply hinder new employment opportunities and limit the increase in real wages. For details, see TÜSİAD, "Turkish Economy 2003," available at http://www.tusiad.org.tr. Similarly, TÜSİAD was quite critical of the government's policy during the war on Iraq and blamed the government for the deterioration in Turkey's relations with the United States in the immediate aftermath of the war. As Tuncay Özilhan clarified, "the War in Iraq will begin outside the control of Turkey, so if we do not have the right to start and stop the war, then for the sake of protecting our interests, Turkey should not be totally outside of this war"; also, "by taking part in the War, Turkey could learn more about the prospects and objectives in that area and could take more systematic precautions." For details, see Tuncay Özilhan, "Iraq Crisis: Military Intervention and Political Outlook," opening speech, February 28, 2003, SwissHotel Istanbul, available at http://www.tusiad.org.tr/haberler/konusma/duyuruno285.pdf. In terms of the recent debates on education and universities, TÜSİAD has maintained its traditional hard-line secularist stance and its

critical attitude toward the government in this particular respect. For details, see Güntay Şimşek, "Whose TÜSİAD?" available at http://www.sabah.com.tr/2004/04/05/ simsek.html.

18. See in this context MÜSİAD report, "The Performance of the JDP Government During its First Year," December 2, 2003, Istanbul, available at http://www.musiad.org. tr. For example, the then chairman of MÜSİAD, Ali Bayramoğlu, argued that "the Government should resist some of the key demands of the IMF, notably the demands involving restrictions over wage increases and imposition of additional taxes...While the business world is expecting a decline in their costs, additional taxation would be detrimental." For details, see press release by MÜSİAD, available at http://www. musiad.org.tr/basinBultenleri.

19. For details, see http://www.musiad.org.tr/detav.asp?id=143. Also, the above-mentioned MÜSİAD report ("The Performance of the JDP Government During its First Year," December 2, 2003, 32, Istanbul, available at http://www.musiad.org.tr) is vital to having a better understanding of the approach of MÜSİAD toward the regulatory bodies

20. MÜSİAD report, "The Performance of the JDP Government During its First Year."

21. This is not to suggest that heterodox policies are inferior. Rather the argument is that such policies can be utilized much more effectively by countries that have avoided financial crises in the past and display relatively low levels of public debt.

22. See Mahfi Eğilmez, "The Background to Rapid Growth," *Radikal,* July 8, 2004; and Hurşit Güneş, "What We Have (Not) Learned from the Crisis?" *Milliyet,* July 20, 2004.

23. The downturn in defense expenditures is a new phenomenon in Turkey that clearly reflects the impact of the recent Europeanization process and democratization reforms. Clearly, the origins of this process may be traced to the end of the armed conflict with the PKK in early 1999.

24. On the characterization of the JDP as a conservative democratic party, see Yalçın Akdoğan, "AK Parti ve Muhafazakar Demokrasi," available at http://www. akparti.org.tr/muhazafakar.doc.

25. The close interaction between politics and economics, especially the finance sector, still plays a decisive role in Turkey. Negative signals from the realm of politics can easily influence the financial sector and create turmoil for a temporary period of time. As experienced a few months ago, the JDP's stance and proposals about the Imam Hatip schools created a similar kind of instability. This was an excellent example of the JDP's push for the Islamist agenda and checking out the actors' appraisal of the situation such as the military and secularists. For details, see Ömer Sabancı, "Do Not Deviate," *Radikal,* July 5, 2004; and Haluk Şahin, "The Reform Process Faces a Real Setback," *Radikal,* July 4, 2004. Also, in terms of the views of the chairman of Turkish Exporters Congress, Oğuz Satıcı, see "The Critique of YÖK from TIM," *Radikal,* July 2, 2004.

Labor Pains or Achilles' Heel

The Justice and Development Party and Labor in Turkey

■ *Engin Yıldırım*

The coming of the Justice and Development Party (JDP) to power in November 2002 initiated an interesting period in the annals of the Turkish Republic. The new government has created a momentum in the sphere of democratization. While the JDP's discourse emphasizes civil society and democratization, compared to the influence of representatives of capital, labor as an important segment of civil society seems to be, to a certain extent, marginalized by the JDP.

The question to be asked here is what factors impinge on the JDP's policies toward labor and what reasons lie behind the relative marginalization of labor. The chapter makes an attempt to understand the JDP's approach to labor in the context of the party's socioeconomic and Islamic background, membership requirements of the European Union (EU), and International Monetary Fund (IMF)–led economic policies, which create a favorable environment for a model of labor flexibility with a low level of rules. I suggest that the JDP's relations with labor are influenced by two contradictory processes: On the one hand, the JDP seems to have followed the antilabor pattern set in the early 1980s when Turkey's labor market was deregulated to achieve competitiveness through increased labor market flexibility and when its trade unions suffered from political assaults and economic setbacks. On the other hand, having received significant support from the lower classes whose interests often, if not always, clash with those of business owners, the JDP is aware that it must also please the former with its policies.

The JDP's approach to labor can be seen as an indicator of the degree to which the party has genuinely adopted democratic standards. The study of the JDP's relations with labor may stimulate the debate as to what extent the JDP has developed its political discourse along universalistic and democratic rather than Islamist lines. An analysis of the relations between the unions and the JDP will also contribute to the understanding of the problems and opportunities that some segments of Turkey's Islamist movement have been experiencing in their long march toward democracy.

The chapter begins by examining the JDP's socioeconomic background, its worldview, and its electoral base. Then it briefly outlines the main actors in the Turkish industrial relations scene. The following sections will highlight the Economic and Social Council (ESK) as an example of social dialogue, the debates on the enactment of a Job Security Act and a new Labor Act, and the use of the right to strike as specific cases illustrating the JDP's labor policies. Finally, I will deal with relations between the JDP and labor confederations representing blue-collar workers.

BETWEEN A ROCK AND A HARD PLACE: THE JDP AND CLASS

Considering that the JDP has Islamic roots, we first need to explore how Islamic political movements approach labor-related issues. Islamic movements tend to see society as functionally differentiated corporate bodies and not as classes in mutual opposition. Setting aside the rhetoric, their understanding of labor-management relationships is firmly entrenched in a traditional view of corporatism involving management based on *shura* (council), mutual respect, and a sense of responsibility shared by all workers in an enterprise. This is not surprising because Islamists, more often than not, emphasize the concept of mutual social responsibility according to which the relationship between the worker and the employer involves a mutuality of duties and rights in the spirit of brother/sisterhood, not class antagonism. Islam is viewed as "a happy marriage between labor and capital by giving the whole problem a moral bent."[1]

Given these views, it is not surprising that Islamic movements have not usually succeeded in attracting the industrial proletariat.[2] On the other hand, this does not mean that there have been no religiously motivated labor organizations in the Muslim world. An interesting example is the Confederation of Righteous Trade Unions in Turkey (known as Hak-İş). Hak-İş and similar organizations faced an important problem of legitimacy not only between secular socialist and/or nationalist labor organizations but also within the ranks of the Islamist movements, as they were usually accused of being communist when they put the problems of working children, unemployment, health and safety, job security, and so forth on the agenda.[3] The president of Hak-İş expressed rather well the way in which some Islamists consider labor-management relations: "[S]ome Muslims see the cause of all problems as the lack of moral values, but the answer should not be to present traditional Islamic morality. Muslims should understand the question of class."[4] In other words, he argues that class differences among Muslims do exist and that they cannot be alleviated by simple recourse to religious values.

Although the JDP is not a class-based party—it receives votes from various social classes including Islamic bourgeoisie, shop owners, the unemployed, peasants, and workers—commentators agree that it mostly represents a new resurgent ("Anatolian") middle class.[5] Adopting either explicitly or implicitly the center-periphery model, students of Turkish polity and society often assert that the JDP is the latest political manifestation of the social forces located in the periphery. Among these forces, the JDP is mostly identified with small- and medium-sized business owners. This "culturally conservative, politically moderate authoritarian and nationalist and economically liberal" new middle class seems to have put its weight behind the JDP.[6] Similarly, it is also pointed out that the JDP represents "the winners in the marketplace within the Islamic movements."[7] While all these arguments are certainly true, it should be borne in mind that the JDP also claims to speak for the lower classes that bore the brunt of the severe economic crises in the early 2000s, which were estimated to cost around two million jobs.[8] The main question in the November 3, 2002, election was the economy, and the issue of how to surmount the economic crisis in an efficient way, to find the solution to the devastating problems of unemployment and poverty, acquired great importance.

Summarizing several studies conducted either just before the November 3 election or in its immediate aftermath, Ergun Özbudun argues that the political fault line in Turkish politics is not class-based or related to socioeconomic problems but is pertinent to identity and cultural problems.[9] Although this argument has a certain ring of truth, we should not completely overlook the significance of socioeconomic differences among social classes in voting patterns and in influencing government policies. In addition to the backing of the new middle class, the JDP received votes from important segments of the working class. Table 10.1 shows how the JDP and its main social democrat rival, the Republican People's Party (RPP), performed in selected working-class towns in the last general election.

TABLE 10.1. Results of the November 3, 2002, General Elections in Selected Working-Class Towns

TOWN	JDP (%)	CHP (%)	VOTING RATE (%)
Aliağa	22.19	26.33	86.30
Bozüyük	24.02	18.47	89.90
Çerkezköy	26.66	21.19	76.59
Ereğli	32.05	22.97	83.86
Gebze	42.16	16.52	81.46
İskenderun	26.56	31.74	73.12
İzmit	45.68	19.58	80.89
Karabük	45.19	13.62	82.69
Kırıkkale	49.12	12.81	80.19
Körfez	40.82	18.70	76.85
Seydişehir	54.55	14.23	88.76
Zonguldak (Merkez)	28.32	21.12	76.59

Source: http://www.belgenet.net/ayrinti.php?yil_id=14, accessed on August 2, 2004.

As can be seen in table 10.1, the JDP had a strong showing in the majority of the working-class towns that are the heartlands of unionized blue-collar workers. The fact that the JDP's popular leader, Recep Tayyip Erdoğan, has risen from the bottom may make some workers associate themselves with him.[10] The support of considerable sections of the blue-collar workers for the Islamist parties has been a fact of life in the Turkish political scene since the early 1990s. The local economy in some of the towns such as Seydişehir (in Konya province), Aliağa (in İzmir province), İskenderun, and Kırıkkale is completely dependent on the state-owned enterprises, some of which are in the process of being privatized. What is interesting is that the JDP, whose program includes privatization of these enterprises, has been able to achieve the support of the workers. Before the local elections, Tayyip Erdoğan even asserted, "[P]rivatization is a must for the rationalization of the economy."[11] Interestingly, the JDP won the local election in Aliağa where a major oil refinery was being privatized and where Petrol-İş (The Oil and Chemical Industry Workers Union) explicitly urged its members not to vote for the JDP in the local elections.

While the JDP has the support of and links with the lower classes, owners of small- and medium-sized businesses, bureaucrats, and middle-class professional groups constitute its leadership and cadres. For example, this support is reflected in the composition of its deputies in Parliament. Only two trade unionists (from Hak-İş affiliates) were elected from the JDP in the November 3, 2002, elections compared to twenty-one members of the Independent Industrialists and Businessmen's Association (MÜSİAD), a conservative businesspeople's association, who were elected on the JDP ticket.[12]

Before the general elections, the JDP published a booklet entitled *The Development and Democratization Program*, which put the greatest emphasis on improving the economy, with passing references to social policies expressed in a discourse of social solidarity, which presumably means that rich people are supposed to help the needy in accordance with Islamic tenets.[13] This emphasis is reflected in the government's economic policies, which have been in line with IMF programs famous (or rather infamous) for their disregard of social and distributional issues. There were serious declines in wages and salaries in the 1980s and 1990s as a result of stabilization programs of the IMF. In its early days, the JDP government provided above-inflation wage increases for pensioners, which were sharply criticized by the IMF and financial "markets." Similarly, when the government increased the minimum wage above the inflation level, employers strongly attacked this decision.[14] While the party would like to deliver on some of its electoral promises such as increasing employment and pay levels and fighting poverty, it has to do this within the boundaries set up by the IMF. The JDP government appears to have become stuck between the demands of its constituencies, including labor, and the requirements of the IMF and financial community.

Some researchers tend to regard the JDP experience as a reflection of global Third Way policy, which "attempts to establish a linkage between state, economy and social justice."[15] On the other hand, the contention that the JDP resembles a Third Way party is open to debate given that the JDP presents itself as a center-right "conservative democratic" party. Erdoğan strongly emphasized the JDP's conservative aspects in his address to an international symposium on conservatism held by his party.[16] In addition, it is suggested the JDP culturally resembles "moderate and popular American conservatism."[17]

The JDP claims to give prominence to a democratic state, regulated market, and social justice in its policies. Erdoğan points outs that "the state should be active in social policy, whereas the private sector should take the lead in the economy."[18] On the other hand, Nühket Hotar, the JDP's deputy president responsible for social policies, suggested that the

"Turkish state is overburdened with social responsibilities."[19] Erdoğan's and Hotar's seemingly contrasting approaches to social responsibilities of the state can be seen as a manifestation of a lack of consensus among the JDP's leadership concerning social policies to be pursued.

The earlier-mentioned JDP booklet on democratization and development provided some insights into the JDP's future industrial relations policies while it was in opposition. The JDP promised, "universal standards for rights and freedoms of…labor shall be fully implemented in our country."[20] Furthermore, the JDP put a special emphasis on social dialogue and tripartite structures such as the Economic and Social Council in dealing with industrial relations issues. The booklet also mentions "the need to modernize labor law in order to decrease the cost of labor and to promote employment."[21] Finally, the JDP also promised that "unionization shall be promoted and the freedom of organizing shall be allowed." It particularly emphasized that "necessary amendments shall be made in the legislation for public employees to benefit from union rights and freedom of collective bargaining and strikes."[22]

Class-based demarcations and disagreements over economic and labor-related issues have emerged between JDP constituencies. When one considers the approach of "Islamic" capital to labor relations, one sees that it defines wage labor "not as a social stratum possessing rights pertaining to trade unions" but "as member providing services for the organist unity of the economy."[23] It is argued that one of the important contradictions the JDP has is pertinent to the possible conflict between the lower classes who carried the JDP to power and the entrepreneurs who supported it.[24]

The conflict among the social classes backing the JDP manifests itself most clearly in the field of industrial relations. The JDP's policies in this area reveal how the party deals with the conflict between capital and labor. I will now specifically examine how the JDP has approached three issues mentioned in the democratization and development booklet: social dialogue, the enactment of new labor law, and union rights. Before moving on to them, I will, nonetheless, provide a brief overview of the Turkish industrial relations scene.

The Main Actors in Turkish Industrial Relations

The state plays a dominant role in determining the basic characteristics of industrial relations in Turkey given that the public sector still employs around 40 percent of all wage earners in spite of recent privatizations.

Furthermore, around 70 percent of all unionized workers are employed in the public sector. These figures show the significance of the state in the Turkish industrial relations system.

According to the latest Ministry of Labor and Social Security (MLSS) statistics, there are 2.8 million union members out of 4.9 million workers who are under the MLSS jurisdiction. Out of 1.2 million public officials who are employed under a different jurisdiction, 788,000 are unionized.[25] The overall union density is estimated to be around 10 percent of the labor force. It should be kept in mind that the official union membership figures are inflated as a result of union competition. The percentage of the labor force covered by collective agreements, which is 5 percent, is a much better indicator of unionization in Turkey.[26] In recent years, Turkish trade unions suffered serious setbacks arising from deregulation, privatization, and the economic and financial crises. The existence of a big "informal sector" is also an important barrier to unionization. This sector contains a large number of small- and medium-sized enterprises that provide low-quality, low-wage jobs and enjoy flexible employment practices.

There are two types of labor unions in Turkey, each of which is divided into rival confederations with significant political and policy differences. The first type includes unions organizing mainly blue-collar employees under the jurisdiction of the Labor Act and operating on the basis of the Trade Unions Act and the Collective Bargaining, Strike, and Lock-Out Act. They are commonly known as *işçi sendikaları* (worker unions). Türk-İş (centrist), DİSK (leftist), and Hak-İş (Islamic) are confederations of worker unions. The second type involves unions organizing public employees who are under the jurisdiction of the Public Servants Act and operating on the basis of the Public Servants Trade Unions Act. They are called *memur sendikaları* (public servants unions). Türkiye-Kamu-Sen (nationalist), Kamu Emekçileri Sendikaları Konfederasyonu (KESK left-wing), and Memur-Sen (Islamic) are confederations of trade unions of public officials.

Established in 1952, Türk-İş is the biggest confederation of blue-collar workers' unions, with thirty-three affiliates representing 1.9 million workers. It is organized primarily in public sector establishments. It occupies, politically, a centrist position. It is mainly composed of moderate right-wing unions, but its constituent unions include some left-wing unions as well. Historically, Türk-İş has had close relations with the governments and has pursued nonpartisan "above-party" politics. While not rejecting EU membership in principle, Türk-İş has opposed reforms demanded by the EU, emphasizing the threats posed by such reforms to national sovereignty and security.[27]

DİSK was established by a breakaway group of four unions from Türk-İş in 1967. The main reason for this breakaway was a series of ideological disputes stemming from the "above-party" policy of Türk-İş. During the 1970s, DİSK followed a militant socialist trade unionism. It was closed down by the military in 1980 and resumed its activities in 1992. Today it adopts a rather less radical stance but it is still regarded as left-wing among the confederations. DİSK has a membership of 450,000 in twenty-one affiliated trade unions. Its affiliates are mostly organized in the private sector establishments in and around Istanbul.

Hak-İş was set up in 1976 with seven unions. According to the latest available Ministry of Labor statistics, Hak-İş has 330,000 members in eight affiliated unions. The basic tenet of Hak-İş was the principle of the commonality of employer and employee interests on the basis of Muslim brother/sisterhood. However, since the late 1980s Hak-İş has been transforming itself from being an Islamist labor confederation to an organization defending democracy. Hak-İş has transformed itself from adhering to Islamist principles of "labor-capital brother/sisterhood" to a present-day worldview incorporating a diversity of concepts, including democratization, European Union, and workers' rights.[28]

As far as employer organizations are concerned, they are also divided on the basis of enterprise size and organizational aims. The Confederation of Turkish Employers' Associations (TİSK) is the major employer organization specializing in labor relations and employment issues, whereas the Turkish Industrialist and Businessman's Association (TÜSİAD) and the Turkish Union of Chambers and Commodity Exchanges (TOBB) usually concern themselves with fiscal and other macroeconomic matters. While TÜSİAD represents large capital, TOBB is mainly the representative of small- and medium-sized capital. In addition, the Independent Industrialist and Businessmen's Association (MÜSİAD) has recently emerged as an important businessmen's organization representing conservative owners of small- and medium-sized businesses. In Turkey, the interests of state-owned and state-controlled undertakings are in principle represented by specific employer organizations, but these organizations in turn belong to the national confederation TİSK, which acts on behalf of Turkish employers as a whole.

The current industrial relations system was established in Turkey in 1983 during the military regime while the economic restructuring was underway. The backbone of the system was the new labor legislation, which curtailed union rights and imposed restrictions on the right to strike. Despite some recent improvements, trade union activities are still tightly controlled and restricted by the Trade Union Act. A recent particular law on the public employees' union (enacted in June 2001), allowing the establishment of trade unions for public employees, does not give the right to strike or to engage in collective bargaining.

The JDP and Social Dialogue: The Case of the Economic and Social Council

Social dialogue can be seen as a system in which the representatives of major social interests and the state establish joint bodies to achieve economic stability and maintain acceptable standards of social welfare at the same time. Social dialogue has developed for different reasons. While in Northern and Western Europe it rests on economic growth, in the transition economies of Eastern Europe it functions as a mechanism of ensuring the support of the main social groups for governments' economic policies.[29] The Turkish experience of social dialogue seems to resemble those of the Eastern European countries.

When the JDP came to power, it declared an "action plan," which included the most urgent policies to be developed and implemented in various areas. The plan's main reference to industrial relations was a promise of "redesigning the structure and working style of the Economic and Social Council (ESK) within three months."[30] Although the JDP has been in power for two years, it has not made any serious effort to redesign the ESK.

The ESK forms the institutional structure of social dialogue in Turkey. A governmental circular set up the ESK in 1995, and its composition and role were redefined in 2001 with the enactment of a special law. The ESK is designed to be a consultative body. Its goals include working toward the formation of social consensus through the expression and representation of different interests in the formulation of economic policies, to achieve and maintain enduring peace in industrial relations, and to advise the government on major economic issues such as employment, productivity, and incomes.[31] The ESK charter was later broadened to include consultation to the government in formulation of draft social legislations. The ESK charter envisages that it shall be convened every three months. The prime minister chairs the council.

The formation of the ESK was not a product of consensus formation among the social parties concerned when it was first set up. It was

TABLE 10.2. Composition of the Economic and Social Council as of 2004

Government	16
Labor (Türk-İş + Hak-İş + DİSK + Türkiye Kamu-Sen)	12
Employers (Confederation of Turkish Employers' Associations [TİSK] + Turkish Union of Chambers and Commodity Exchanges [TOBB])	6
Türkiye Esnaf ve Sanatkarlari Konfederasyonu (Turkish Confederation of Tradesmen and Craftsmen)	3
Türkiye Ziraat Odalari Birliği (Turkish Union of Chambers of Farmers)	3
Total	40

usually convened when governments needed the backing of social partners for their economic policies. The ESK lacked, until recently, a stable structure, and this lack largely impaired its work. Conflicts over representation issues were long-running. Whenever a new government comes to power, it changes the composition of the ESK without consulting social partners. Table 10.2 shows the composition of the ESK in 2004.

Among the factors of utmost importance for the success of the ESK mechanisms is confidence in the role of government. Until recently, because of political instability, weak coalition governments seemed to have misused the ESK. This has created mistrust on the part of labor and employers toward the government. Deep suspicion of tripartite cooperation particularly lurks in some labor quarters, which fear that government policy has been decided without consultations. Common causes of complaint by unions and employers have been over the selectivity exercised by the governments over when and on what to consult.

Although the JDP government has convened the ESK more frequently than its predecessors, the trade unions have felt excluded from discussions of important issues. The meetings have discussed such topics as job security, membership in the EU, minimum wage, public officials' annual pay raises, and collective bargaining in the public sector. In the last meeting, the prime minister pointed out that the ESK should also be set up at provincial levels and that the number of state officials should be reduced. The government would like to activate the ESK so that it could have the backing of social partners for its new economic and social policies. The labor side criticized the government for not discussing the enactment of a new labor code and changes in the social security system in the ESK meetings.[32] On his part, Erdoğan regards the ESK meetings as proof of how his party takes the views of social partners into account and as proof of participative democracy in action.[33]

The ESK still exhibits insufficient consultation of social partners at the national level. Its structural deficiencies, such as the dominant position of the government (sixteen of forty members), undermine the value of the council and should be reviewed together with all the social partners. Similarly, the EU, in its progress report, pointed out that reforms are necessary that will create the conditions for free and genuine bipartite and tripartite social dialogue at all levels.[34] The ESK does not legally have a bargaining function in terms of social agreements and pay policy agreements. In any case, the labor and employee participants also face limitations on their ability to deliver on their commitments that would be made in the council, since their influence over their respective constituents is far from complete.

Why does the JDP attach a special importance to the ESK? The JDP leadership, who come from an Islamist background, are likely to view tripartite structures as the most suitable solution to labor problems, as this approach resembles traditional Islamic corporatism based on "capital-labor brother/sisterhood." Social dialogue may be seen as a modern version of "capital-labor brother/sisterhood." Another factor that may explain the JDP's wish to make ESK more functional is probably related to the requirements of the EU membership. Setting up tripartite bodies is necessary to adapt Turkish industrial relations systems to the EU standards. The Joint Accession Partnership Document requires that Turkey support social partners in their efforts to achieve the EU standards. Since the development of social dialogue is one of the key elements of the European social model, the EU promotes social dialogue in industrial relations.[35] The EU has already suggested that each candidate country should have a working social dialogue that is suited to its social and industrial relations culture yet able to respond to the needs of EU membership.

BALANCING LIKE A TIGHTROPE WALKER: THE DEBATE ON THE JOB SECURITY AND NEW LABOR LAW

The debate on the job security and on the new labor law provides an interesting example of how the JDP has dealt with relations between capital and labor. While the former law drew the wrath of employers, the latter was resisted by trade unions. Although the JDP's performance related to these issues has been criticized by employers and trade unions, the latter's criticisms have been much sharper than the former. The unions accused the government of aligning itself with the employers in the debates on the laws.

The former coalition government enacted a job security law that made it difficult for employers to fire their workers without "a just cause." Employers would not be able to dismiss workers because of trade union activities, pregnancy, and legal actions against them. They would also be required to prove that the layoffs have a valid reason. The law was sharply criticized by all employer organizations including MÜSİAD, whereas all labor organizations, including Hak-İş, lobbied Parliament for the passing of the bill. Although the act was passed by Parliament, its implementation was delayed because of the earlier general election the coalition government called on November 3, 2002.

When the JDP came to power, it immediately found itself under pressure from all employers' organizations including MÜSİAD for the postponement of the implementation of the act. Although Erdoğan was initially against the postponement, when he became the prime minister his very first decree was pertinent to postpone the implementation of the act until June 2003.[36] Interestingly, while the JDP was in opposition in 2002, it strongly supported the act. For example, JDP deputies pointed out that "job security is a must for modern states" and criticized "certain pressure groups" that had previously blocked the enactment of the job security act.[37]

This decision drew heavy criticisms from labor quarters. For instance, the president of Öziplik-İş, a Hak-İş affiliate in the textile industry, expressed his concern about and deep disappointment with the decision.[38] Similarly, in a letter sent to Kürşat Bumin, a leftist columnist with *Yeni Şafak,* an JDP-sympathetic daily, the president of a Hak-İş affiliate maintained that the JDP had the mentality that views employers as a kind of benevolent group of people who provide jobs to communities and people.[39] As a matter of fact, Ali Coşkun, the minister of industry and commerce, in his address to the MESS, the powerful metal employers association, praised the industrialists and claimed, "the industrialist is a person who undergoes suffering like an ascetic."[40]

Upon losing the battle for the job security act, employers concentrated their efforts on enacting a new labor law, which would enable them to employ labor more flexibly. Employers long complained that the former labor law was a great impediment to achieving the labor flexibility deemed to be necessary for competitiveness and economic viability. According to a study by the Organization for Economic Co-operation and Development, which analyzed the former labor law and other related legislation, Turkey ranked second (following Portugal) in terms of rigidity of employment protection.[41]

As we have seen earlier, the JDP also promised to "modernize" labor law before coming to power. Murat Başeskioğlu, the minister of labor and social security, asserted that if flexible working time could not be regulated and implemented, Turkey would be an underdeveloped country.[42] In fact, all employers' organizations, including MÜSİAD, pressured the government to pass the labor law. In the course of the debate on various drafts of the new law, the JDP appeared to be caught in the cross fire. On the one hand, the TİSK president accused the JDP of "serving trade union barons rather than industry" and bowing to threats made by the unions.[43] On the other hand, all labor organizations, including Hak-İş, made efforts to prevent the passing of the bill in the parliament. Eventually it was employers who prevailed. They were generally pleased with the provisions of the new labor law. For example, TÜSİAD's president openly declared, "the law was made to our liking."[44] In contrast, the unions considered it a "slavery act in which workers become a commodity hired and fired at will by the employers."[45] They also claimed that many provisions of the labor law "emasculated the job security law." Furthermore, the unions pointed out that other right-wing parties such as the Motherland Party and the True Path Party did not dare to pass a new labor law when they were in power.[46] The labor circles tend to interpret the JDP's insistence on the act as an attempt to be seen as a respected party by capital.

The new labor law was adopted on May 22, 2003. By taking into account the relevant EU legislation, the law contains provisions regarding nonstandard employment, flexible working time, temporary employment relationship, establishment of the Severance Payment Fund, protection for workers in the event of insolvency of their employer, transfer of undertakings, employer's obligation to inform employees, job security, and effective implementation of occupational health and safety measures. Employing labor more flexibly has been the most important aspect of the new law, which has provided a legal basis for "atypical" employment relationships, namely part-time and fixed-term employment. This is the aspect of the new law most welcomed by employers. Given the emphasis on labor market flexibility, one may expect a tendency toward increasing use of fixed-term and subcontract labor.

The new labor law has also included most of the articles of the job security law but reduced the coverage of job security by excluding those establishments employing fewer than thirty workers. The job security law excluded only those employing fewer than ten workers. Therefore, the new labor law has legally provided extensive flexibility to small- and medium-sized establishments. It seems that the JDP bowed to pressures from employer organizations, particularly from MÜSİAD, to restrict the scope of the law to enterprises employing more than thirty workers rather than ten.

Many MÜSİAD members are overtly hostile to any trade union, including Hak-İş affiliates, in their workplaces. MÜSİAD advisers even previously suggested the replacement of formal industrial relations procedures by mutual trust, affection, and respect.[47] When it comes to dealing with labor, "Islamic" capital tends to adopt policies based on its own class interests. For them, unions are organizations whose existence is barely tolerated and, from an Islamic worldview, are unnecessary. As Ayşe Buğra aptly argues, despite having similar worldviews and political convictions, MÜSİAD and Hak-İş differ deeply on the questions of industrial relations and economic policies, differences that reflect, to a large extent, their class positions.[48]

"FROM OUR RECEP THE WORKER TO THEIR RECEP THE BOSS": THE JDP AND LABOR CONFEDERATIONS

Relations between labor organizations and political parties, even those sharing similar political stances, often tend to be far from harmonious. Relations between the JDP and labor are no exception to this reality. The labor organizations initially displayed guarded optimism toward the JDP government, but as time has gone by, this optimism has faded.

The main labor confederation, Türk-İş, initially approached the JDP government cautiously. Nevertheless, the enactment of the new labor law and the government's desire to continue with the privatization program forced Türk-İş to change its stance toward the government. Türk-İş-affiliated unions are largely organized in public sector enterprises, many of which are listed in the privatization program. Hence it is understandable that Türk-İş feels itself organizationally threatened by privatization. In addition, Türk-İş does not share the enthusiasm of the government regarding EU membership.[49] It also disagreed with the government's Cyprus policy and defended a nationalist line. Türk-İş, while not rejecting EU membership in principle, has opposed reforms demanded by the EU, emphasizing the threats posed by such reforms to national sovereignty and security. Türk-İş's views seem very closely associated with those of the military-security establishment on EU- and Cyprus-related issues.

Türk-İş organized five rallies against the government's privatization policy and the passing of the new labor act in 2003. In the Ankara Rally, the president of Türk-İş accused the government of supporting employers: "[T]hey said they would govern with social partners. It is now clear that by social partners they only mean TÜSİAD and TOBB."[50] In addition to Türk-İş, its major affiliates also heavily criticized the government. For instance, the president of Tek Gıda-İş (the Food Industry Workers Union) pointed out, "the indisputable fact is that the JDP government is in favour of capital in is policies."[51]

Türk-İş refrained from organizing an anti-JDP campaign in the March 2004 local elections. The Turk-İş president, Salih Kılıç, asserted that the prime minister sometimes seems to be in favor of labor but at other times he shows a tendency to support capital. "I believe he is in a dilemma."[52] However, some Türk-İş affiliates either explicitly or implicitly did not hesitate to urge their members not to vote for the JDP in the local elections. For example, Petrol-İş, which has been threatened by the massive privatization projects of the TÜPRAŞ refinery and PETKİM petrochemical complex, called for its members not to vote for the JDP in the local elections.[53] Yol-İş (the Road Construction and Maintenance Workers' Union) did not directly urge its members not to vote for JDP in the local elections. Instead, it argued that a vote for JDP would indicate a support for the Public Administration Reform Act, which the union is vehemently opposed to as the act would require the downsizing of some public agencies such as Köy Hizmetleri Genel Müdürlüğü (General Directorate of Rural Services) that have traditionally been the union's strongholds.

Hak-İş maintains that it will support "positive" policies of the JDP and will be against "negative" policies.[54] For the former position, Hak-İş gives as examples policies concerning the EU and the government's desire to make the ESK functional, whereas Hak-İş condemns the government's privatization program and strike postponements, which "have become rule rather than exceptions."[55] For Hak-İş, strike postponements dealt a serious blow to the JDP's claim of upgrading Turkish democracy to EU standards. Hak-İş also criticizes the draft trade unions and collective bargaining, strike, and lock-out acts, claiming that the new laws aim to weaken the link between the unions and the confederations. Hak-İş also required the government to proclaim May Day as an official holiday, but the government suggested that it would become an official holiday with EU membership.[56] Hak-İş president Salim Uslu also accused the government of not addressing seriously the issues of poverty and unemployment.[57]

Unlike the above unions that have left-wing leadership, some Türk-İş
affiliates with right-wing leadership concentrated on foreign policy issues
in their criticism of the government. For example, Türk Metal (the Metal
Working Industry Workers Union) criticized the JDP for its stance on
the Cyprus problem and EU membership and even implicitly accused it
of "sell-out and treason."[58]

As far as the other labor confederations are concerned, DİSK has
opted for a soft opposition against the government. It has attacked the
government for its privatization policies and amendments in labor legislation.[59] Among the public officials' confederations, left-wing KESK and
nationalist Türkiye Kamu-Sen have adopted a harsher line against the
government. They are particularly critical of the Public Administration
Reform Act, which was passed by Parliament but vetoed by the president.
While the former emphasizes the downsizing effects of the act, the latter points out that the act will pose a threat to national unity.[60] Türkiye
Kamu-Sen also heavily criticized the government for its EU and Cyprus
policies. Unlike the other confederations that organize public officials,
Islamist Memur-Sen has remained silent on the government policies and
has refrained from criticism of the JDP.

There has recently been a sudden intensification of inter-union rivalry,
particularly between Türk-İş and Hak-İş affiliates. For example, a Hak-İş
affiliate, Tarım Orman İş (the Agriculture and Forestry Workers Union),
has begun poaching workers from a rival Türk-İş-affiliated union,
Orman-İş (the Forestry Workers Union). As a result, Tarım Orman İş
has been able to increase its membership from 837 to 18,000 in just three
months. It is alleged that some bureaucrats in the relevant ministries,
several JDP deputies, and activists are behind this.[61] In addition, it is
claimed that municipal workers in Denizli and Amasya have been under
pressure to resign from their union, Genel-İş, a DİSK affiliate, and join
Hizmet-İş, a Hak-İş affiliate.[62] It can be suggested that the JDP may have
a desire to strengthen Hak-İş in order to create a friendly labor organization that will not oppose the government on every occasion. Turgut Özal
put a similar strategy into effect in the late 1980s when Türk-İş turned
against him. JDP may implicitly encourage Hak-İş as leverage against
Türk-İş.

The JDP government has also remained silent on the attacks by
employers on the right to unionize. For instance, in Eskişehir Glass
Works, the employer fired 365 workers who joined Kristal-İş (the Cement,
Glass and Earthware Workers Union).[63] Similarly, when Belediye-İş (the
Municipality Workers Union), a Türk-İş affiliate, made an attempt to

organize the workers at ISTON (a ready-made concrete producer) owned by JDP-led Istanbul Greater Municipality, in 2003, the general manager of the company actively resisted the unionization attempts.[64] As a matter of fact, the EU pressurizes Turkey to establish full trade union rights, including the elimination of restrictive thresholds for forming a trade union and the elimination of the requirement of the 10 percent threshold for a trade union to be eligible for collective bargaining at company level, as well as restrictive provisions relating to the right to strike and to collective bargaining in particular for public sector employees and public services.[65]

LIMITS OF DEMOCRATIZATION: THE JDP AND THE USE OF THE RIGHT TO STRIKE

The postponement of legal strikes has been a telling feature of Turkish industrial relations under the JDP government. When we look at recent strike statistics, one can see a downward trend, though a small upward tendency for 2004 can be observed. Turkey has not usually been a strike-prone country since the 1980s, with the major exception of the period between 1989 and 1994 (see table 10.3). Despite the insignificance of strikes, the JDP government did not hesitate to use its legal powers to postpone strikes deemed "damaging national economy".

The government twice postponed a strike in the glass sector for sixty days by 5,000 workers tied to Kristal-İş on the grounds of "threatening national security and public health." Before postponing the strike, the government asked the general secretariat of the National Security Council (NSC) whether the strike would be a threat to national security. Interestingly, (probably surprisingly for the government), the NSC advised the government that the strike would not imperil national security.[66] In previous similar cases, the NSC almost always approved government strike postponements.

The union protested to the government, accusing it of implementing policies dictated by employers.[67] The union took the case to the Council of State, which ruled that the postponement was a breach of relevant laws. The minister of justice defended the government's decision by using the same arguments put forward by the employers who successfully lobbied the government, arguing that the strikes would damage the economy, as they would risk losing their export markets. Moreover, referring to the Council of State's decision, the minister of public finance even told the employers that the government was doing its utmost to postpone the

TABLE 10.3. Strikes in 2001–2003

STRIKES	2001	2002	2003
Number of Strikes	35	27	23
Number of Workers Involved	9,991	4,618	1,535
Number of Workdays Lost	286,015	43,885	144,772

Source: Ministry of Labor and Social Security, Labor Statistics 2004.

strike but that "there are problems in the Legislative Authorities, which should be solved with your help."[68] Eventually, the government postponed the strike once again. Kristal-İş took the issue to the international arena. The International Confederation of Free Trade Unions (ICFTU) secretary general lodged a formal complaint against the government for the strike postponement. More significantly, Guentur Verheugen, the then EU commissioner responsible for enlargement, in his reply to Kristal-İş's letter regarding the issues, stressed, "the candidate countries should respect basic human, cultural and social rights as specified in the Copenhagen criteria. The right to strike is one of the fundamental social rights."[69] Notwithstanding these criticisms, the government did not hesitate to postpone another strike in the tire industry for sixty days on the grounds of "national security."

Nükhet Hotar, JDP's deputy president responsible for social polices, has made efforts to defend the government's decision to postpone two legal strikes in the tire and glass industries. The latter were postponed twice in 2003 and 2004 under the pretext of endangering national security and public health. She justified this delay by arguing, "the length and duration of strikes and workdays lost in Turkey are greater than in many countries." However, this assertion is only valid between 1988 and 1995.[70] The length and intensity of labor disputes in Turkey has rapidly declined since 1997. She also suggested that it is not suitable to go on strike in strategic industries at a time when the country has been making strenuous efforts to overcome economic crisis. As she put it, "you can not risk losing your markets." Behind this remark, it is possible to see the concerns of car manufacturers that were worried about strikes in the glass and tire industries and were fearful of losing their markets. Nonetheless, she admitted, "postponing a strike is not right in principle in a democracy."[71] She believed these postponements are "exceptions rather than rule" and hoped "no strike will ever be again postponed by the JDP government.[72]

CONCLUSION

Having come to power with great promise, the JDP has increasingly found itself cornered by the question of how economic growth will be reflected in the daily lives of the masses. Although economic indicators show improvements, the economic growth has not been particularly reflected in employment. One of the mains reasons is that the economic crises taught businesses how to be efficient even with a small number of workers. This situation creates an important challenge for the JDP government. It remains to be seen how the JDP will address the problems of unemployment and poverty. Failure to solve these problems will probably alienate the lower classes from the party.

Reconciling interests of the laboring classes and (conservative) business owners has been a real challenge for the JDP government. The JDP has oscillated between respecting labor rights and favoring policies defending the interests of employers. The JDP probably regards the ESK as the institutional mechanism for interest mediation between labor and capital. Arguably, the ESK has not so far yielded any concrete result in terms of interest mediation.

I have argued that the JDP puts a special emphasis on social dialogue among labor, employers, and the state. Originating from a political tradition with a stress on "capital-labor brother/sisterhood" discourse, the JDP found a valuable modern version of this discourse in the form of social dialogue or social partnership, which does not seem to be anachronistic in today's world and, furthermore, appears to be in line with the EU membership requirements.

My contention is that the JDP appears to have been more sensitive to the needs and interests of employers as exemplified by the changes in the labor legislation and the strike postponements. The latter case is a vivid example of how the government fell short of its own claims of democratization and of respect for democratic rights. In a country where strike levels are already low, the government's postponement (setting aside legal niceties, is, in effect, tantamount to banning) of legal strikes contradicts its own claims of democratizing the country. An awkward situation emerged in which the NSC appeared more respectful of the right to strike than the JDP government, aiming to upgrade Turkish democracy to the EU standards.

It seems that the labor question constitutes one of the outer limits of the JDP's democratization program. It is likely that beneath the surface, the JDP leadership and cadres are of the view that traditional patterns of patrimonial relations are enough to address industrial relations issues. Labor is understood from a purely moralistic viewpoint that considers it as something "to be cared for, to be done well." In this view, the employer or entrepreneur is a kind of suprahuman being creating jobs, helping the needy. The proper behavior expected from labor is to be thankful to the employers who provide them with jobs. This is the way in which small- and medium-sized business owners who are influential within the JDP tend to perceive labor relations.

The JDP's understanding of social justice probably revolves around maintaining and strengthening traditional relations of charity, solidarity, and cooperation rather than strengthening individual and social rights. How far this understanding will go in solving problems of labor remains to be seen. Although labor's political power has generally diminished worldwide in the last two decades, it can still be regarded as an important political actor that governments cannot easily brush aside. Recent Turkish political history is a witness to this reality. One of the important factors that triggered the Motherland Party's downfall was the strike wave and labor unrest in the late 1980s and early 1990s. The JDP government can only neglect the lessons of these events at its own peril.

NOTES

1. Muhammad Abdul Mannan, *Islamic Economics* (Cambridge: The Islamic Academy, 1986), 88.

2. Joel Beinin and Zachary Lockman, *Workers on the Nile: Nationalism, Communism, Islam and the Egyptian Working Class (1882–1954)* (London: I. B. Tauris, 1988), 375; Nazih N. Ayubi, *Political Islam: Religion and Politics in the Arab World* (London: Routledge, 1993), 159.

3. See "Görüşlerimiz," *Hak-İş Dergisi* 9 (March 1987): 15.

4. Salim Uslu, "A Speech," in *Mukayeseli Hukuk ve Uygulama Açısından İşçi-İşveren İlişkileri* (İstanbul: ISAV, 1992), 368.

5. Bülent Aras and Bülent Gökay, "Turkey after Copenhagen: Walking a Tightrope," *Journal of Southern Europe and the Balkans* 5 (2003): 158; Ergun Özbudun, *2002 Seçimleri Işığında Türk Siyasetinde Eğilimler* (Ankara: TÜBA, 2004), 21; Ziya Öniş and Fuat Keyman, "Turkey at the Polls: A New Path Emerges," *Journal of Democracy* 14, no. 2 (2003): 100; Üzeyir Tekin, *AK Parti'nin Muhafazakâr Demokrat Kimliği* (Ankara: Orient Yayınları, 2004).

6. Ahmet İnsel, "The AKP and Normalizing Democracy in Turkey," *South Atlantic Quarterly* 102, nos. 2–3 (Spring/Summer 2003): 297.

7. M. Hakan Yavuz, "Opportunity Spaces, Identity, and Islamic Meaning in Turkey," in *Islamic Activism: A Social Movement Approach*, ed. Quintan Wiktorowicz (Bloomington: Indiana University Press, 2003), 270–88.

8. *TİSK İşveren*, March 2003, 4.

9. Özbudun, *Seçimleri Işığında Türk Siyasetinde Eğilimler*, 13.

10. İnsel, "The AKP and Normalizing Democracy," 299.

11. Recep Tayyip Erdoğan, *Konuşmalar* (Ankara: AK Parti, 2003), 62.

12. Agah Kafkas (Çorum) and Hüseyin Tanrıverdi are JDP's only unionist deputies. Among JDP's deputies who have MÜSİAD affiliation, the following names can be given as examples: Hüseyin İrfan Rıza Yazıcıoğlu (Diyarbakır), Nimet Çubukçu (Istanbul), Ali Osman Başkurt (Malatya), Abdurrahman Müfit (Şanlıurfa), Ahmet Edip Uğur (Balıkesir), Mehmet Asım Kulak (Bartın), Hasan Arığı (Konya), Mustafa Demir (Samsun), Ahmet Uzer (Gaziantep), Niyazi Özcan (Kayseri); see http://stargazete.com/index.asp?haberid=9782, accessed on September 4, 2004.

13. Justice and Development Party, *Development and Democratization Program* (Ankara: AK Parti, 2002).

14. *TİSK İşveren Dergisi*, March 2003, 4; "Rekabet ve Türk Ekonomisi," *MESS İşveren Gazetesi*, April 2003, 10.

15. Öniş and Keyman, "Turkey at the Polls," 99.

16. Recep Tayyip Erdoğan's address to the International Symposium on Conservatism and Democracy, Ankara, AK Parti, January 10–11, 2004, 7–17.

17. İnsel, "The AKP and Normalizing Democracy," 302.

18. Adalet ve Kalkınma Partisi, *1. Olağan Büyük Kongresi, Genel Başkan Recep Tayyip Erdoğan'ın Konuşması*, Ankara, AK Parti, October 12, 2003, 83.

19. Quoted in *Türk Harb-İş Dergisi*, April 2004, 31.

20. Justice and Development Party, *Development and Democratization Program*, 14.

21. Ibid., 96.

22. Ibid., 28, 97.

23. Keyman quoted in İnsel, "The AKP and Normalizing Democracy," 298.

24. M. Hakan Yavuz, untitled paper in *International Symposium on Conservatism and Democracy* (Ankara: AK Parti, 2004), 202–8.

25. Çalışma ve Sosyal Güvenlik Bakanlığı (ÇSGB), *Çalışma Hayatı İstatistikleri* (Ankara: ÇSGB, 2004), 40.

26. Ibid., 42.

27. Erdinç Yazıcı, *Sendikal Perspektif: İşçi Liderleri Konuşuyor* (Ankara: İlke Emek Yayınları, 2004), 176.

28. For an analysis of Hak-İş, see Burhanettin Duran and Engin Yıldırım, "Islamism, Trade Unionism and Civil Society: The Case of Hak-İş Labor Confederation in Turkey," *Middle Eastern Studies* 41 (2005): 221.

29. Martin Myant, Brian Slococok, and Simon Smith, "Tripartism in the Czech and Slovak Republics," *Europe-Asia Studies* 52 (2000): 724.

30. See www.belgenet.com/eko/acileylem_161102.html, accessed on August 6, 2004.

31. See www.belgenet.com/eko/k4641.html, accessed on August 6, 2004.

32. *Türk Metal Dergisi*, August 2004, 13.

33. Erdoğan, *Konuşmalar*, 89.

34. The European Commission, *2003 Regular Report on Turkey's Progress towards Accession*, http://europa.eu.int/comm/enlargement/report_2003/pdf/rr_tk_final.pdf, accessed August 1, 2004.

35. Paul Teague, "EU Social Policy: Institutional Design Matters," *Queen's Papers on Europeanization* 1 (2000): 15.

36. *Zaman*, November 3, 2003, 5.

37. Kristal-İş, *14. Genel Kurul Çalışma Raporu 2000–2004* (Istanbul: Kristal-İş, 2004), 88.

38. "İşçi Kırgın, İşveren Mutlu," *Yeni Şafak*, March 17, 2003, 7.

39. Kürşat Bumin, "Güvence ertelemeye" okurlar ne diyor?" *Yeni Şafak*, March 18, 2003, 9.

40. *MESS İşveren Gazetesi*, May 2004, 10.

41. OECD Employment Outlook 2004, quoted in *TİSK İşveren Dergisi*, July 2004, 28.

42. *TİSK İşveren Dergisi*, March 2003, 2.

43. Refik Baydur, "'İş Güvencesi' Tartışmaları" (Istanbul: Doğan Kitap, 2004), 393.

44. See http://www.Turkishdailynews.com(old_editions/05_24_03/dom2.htm, accessed on August 3, 2004.

45. *TES-İŞ Dergisi*, May 2003, 9.

46. Kristal-İş, *Genel Kurul Çalışma Raporu*, 90.

47. Ayşe Buğra, "Labor, Capital and Religion: Harmony and Conflict among the Constituency of Political Islam in Turkey," *Middle Eastern Studies* 38 (2002): 188.

48. Ibid.

49. Türk-İş, *19. Olağan Genel Kurul Çalışma Raporu* (Ankara: Türk-İş, 2003).

50. Quoted in *TES-İŞ Dergisi*, May 2003, 6.

51. Yazıcı, *Sendikal Perspektif*, 110.

52. Kılıç, quoted in *Türk Harb-İş, Dergisi*, February 2004, 8.

53. *Petrol-İş Dergisi*, April 2004, 3.

54. Hak-İş, *10. Olağan Genel Kurul Faaliyet Raporu* (Ankara: Hak-İş, 2003), 13.

55. Ibid., 14.

56. See http://www.hakis.org.tr/arsiv/1mayis.htm, accessed on August 6, 2004.

57. Uslu quoted in http://www.hakis.org.tr/arsiv/2821-2822_panel htm, accessed on August 6, 2004.

58. *Türk Metal Dergisi*, August 2003, 3.

59. Birleşik Metal, *16. Merkez Genel Kurul Çalışma Raporu* (Istanbul: Birleşik Metal), 74.

60. See http://www.kesk.org.tr/kesk.asp?sayfa=yonet&id=41; and http://www.kamusen.org.tr/imaj/arge/akpkarne.pdf, accessed on August 3, 2004.

61. See http://www.evrensel.net/04/07/28/sendika.html, accessed on August 2, 2004.

62. See http://www.birgun.net/index.php?sayfa=61&inid=devami=2253, accessed on August 27, 2004.

63. Kristal-İş, *Genel Kurul Çalışma Raporu*, 391.

64. See http://www.evrensel.net/04/07/08/bekediye.html, accessed on August 2, 2004.

65. The European Commission, *2003 Regular Report on Turkey's Progress towards Accession*, http://europa.eu.int/comm/enlargement/report_2003/pdf/rr_tk_final.pdf, accessed on August 1, 2004.

66. Aziz Çelik, "Muhafazakar demokrasinin grevle imtihanı," *Radikal*, February 1, 2004, 10.

67. Kristal-İş, *Genel Kurul Çalışma Raporu*, 390.

68. Ibid., 144.

69. Kürşat Bumin, "Öyle bir 'grev hakkı' olsun ki, işler yine tıkırında yürüsün," *Yeni Şafak*, March 2, 2004, 5.

70. Jack Eaton, *Comparative Employment Relations* (Cambridge, UK: Polity, 2000), 140.

71. Quoted in *Türk Harb-İş Dergisi*, "Kılıç'la Söyleşi," 32–33.

72. Quoted in ibid.

CHAPTER II

Gender Politics of the JDP

■ *Edibe Sözen*

This chapter seeks to address two issues. First it examines the gender politics of the JDP by using some face-to-face interviews conducted with female members of the party. Second, it investigates the place of women in political life and their relevant political identities within the context of the party and government practices. The JDP's position on gender issues can be defined with reference to three woman typologies: the pro-JDP "Islamist women," the "conservative women" working in the party organization, and the "female members of Parliament" who represent the center-right. This chapter argues that in spite of the powerful political language produced by women in daily life, the discourse on women in political circles has more cultural codes, and thus gender policies are rooted more culturally than they are politically. Women who have entered a "resemblance (assimilation) period" with men have been found to agree with a role of "substitution thinking" when it comes to the distribution of political roles. In this framework, this chapter also examines how first lady Emine Erdoğan, who represents a conservative-democrat identity, has approached the debates on "turban/headscarf" and the public sphere. These issues are examined within the context of the relevant news published in the press. The findings here point out that as far as the JDP is concerned, the modernization process in Turkey has turned into an interactive process rather than a structural one. "Modern" has become "religious" and "religious" has become "modern," reducing the distance between various societal groups and hinting at a cross-fertilization between modernity and Islam. Simultaneously, it also becomes apparent that the same process raises a number of questions about the content and the boundary between the public and private spheres.

INTRODUCTION: THE CULTURAL GENDER POLITICS

"Liberalization," "sharing," "self-representation," and "communication" are concepts at the center of a gender politics that emancipates women from an inferior social status and myth-based understanding.[1] Within the confines of democratic culture, gender politics is about women's practices that enhance the efficacy of democracy: within the scope of gender politics are defense of women's rights and their achievement; critique of cultural and gender discriminatory policies; permanent participation in politics; articulation of violence and crimes against women, especially in wars, through women's own voices; reproduction of positive peace processes; equality of opportunity in education; and rights of abused children, among others. Gender politics also reveals the power relationships between women and men.

Gender politics as an academic interest, social activity, and political and cultural practice expands not only through the domain of necessity but also through the realm of "sensitivities." In contrast to "masculine democracy," in democracies determined by gender politics a perceptive language in conjunction with women's issues is seen to penetrate into politics: the recognition of immigrant and marginal groups, and the formation of new strategies related to constructive peace processes. Looking over the last fifty years of Turkish politics, it is hard to discover participation of women in democracy on a regular basis. In terms of women's participation in politics, the democratic rule in Turkey does not go further than an "electoral democracy." Women become visible and active only during the political campaigns before elections and on election day, rather than taking part in the entirety of the democratic process. This doesn't mean that gender politics doesn't exist; on the contrary, it shows that gender politics is determined by the cultural structure. Indeed, a definition of gender in this sense does exist.[2] Women take part in politics outside the realm of politics; however, in the political arena, they perform the social and cultural roles attributed to them. Politics in this respect is maintained by the cultural code of Turkish society.

According to a statistics report that compares the role of women in politics, Turkey ranks 110th out of 164 countries. According to the same report, the percentage of women parliamentarians is 45 percent in Sweden, 38 percent in Denmark, 37.5 percent in Finland, 36.7 percent in Holland, 36.4 percent in Norway, 36 percent in Cuba, 35.3 percent in Belgium, 30 percent in Iceland, 24.7 percent in Uganda, 22 percent in Eritrea, 21.6 percent in Pakistan, 5.7 percent in Albania, 4.4 percent in

Sri Lanka, 4.4 percent in Turkey, and 4.1 percent in Iran.³ The low percentage of women's participation in Turkish politics doesn't mean that women don't have any political ideology or are not interested in their self-representation. On the contrary, women continuously engage in politics on a daily basis. Politics is one of the dominant matters of their everyday life. Yet there are three obstacles to full participation of women in politics that highlight gender issues: First, women in the political arena enter into a process of role resemblance rather than role differentiation. In this obstacle, which can also be called gender role resemblance, women, as part of a learned cultural code, experience the success of men as their own success. In terms of gender roles in Turkey, therefore, instead of role differentiation, role substitution takes place.

The second obstacle equates self-representation with re-representation, as seen in politics on both the right and the left. As in the first obstacle, instead of representing themselves directly, women believe that they will be represented by the males. The third obstacle to women's full participation is that women do not bring forward their problems for debate, which could help create rational consensus in the society, and failure to do so leads to a lack of public discourse and poor functioning of the civil society. Democracy is construed as a concept related just to Parliament and lawmakers. In fact, gender democracy defines democracy as a daily-life reality that exists in almost all parts of society, and a process and an everyday practice without a center.

ASSIGNED ROLES AND WOMEN IN "ELECTORAL DEMOCRACY"

The JDP has come to power without questioning the secular state and has filled the social vacuum created by the February 28 Process. The overwhelming majority behind the JDP's victory had demands for freedom and transformation. How does this party define women in the political and cultural system as it relates to the continuity and transformation of democracy? In what ways do female members of the JDP want to transform the social and political system? How do JDP women define themselves and "others"?

As has been indicated in the charter of the party, problems such as gender equality, development and peace, private and public sphere give us an idea about the JDP's concept of democracy. As far as gender politics is concerned, we can talk about three types of women: First are the Welfare Party's female supporters who contributed to the success of their party in the local elections of March 27, 1994, yet remained invisible in the political arena.[4] Second are the women who have worked in Welfare Party, Virtue Party, and even National Salvation Party local bureaus in 81 provinces and approximately 934 towns. This group consists of liberal women who are well educated but have never entered the workforce; women with no political activism background; and the women who have worked for the JDP's local offices. Third are the female members of the JDP in Parliament, who are quite different from the first two types of women and who are more disposed to represent the center-right.

A woman who cannot be placed in any of the above three categories but probably can best represent the JDP is the "first lady," Emine Erdoğan. The strength of Emine Erdoğan's representation stems from the fact that she embodies the characteristics of the first two types and also communicates well with the women in the third category.

Pro-JDP Type: The Welfare Party Women

Those women who were active in the Welfare Party (WP) in the 1990s have carried the JDP to its present place. They are the ones who in the first place resist male-defined modernity and insist on the multiple modernities to which women can bring their identity. These WP women, unlike Western feminist movement women who revolted against male domination in their own interest, have carried on their activities mostly to support a "just" system that is informed by Islam.

Three main issues that determine the women's movement are "service," "unjust treatment," and "exclusion," and the method followed is sociopsychological rather than political. The sociopsychological method is followed because at the heart of the movement is the popularization of self-confidence rather than political participation or self-representation. Even though female Islamist authors are opposed, from a more sociological point of view, at the core of the women's movement is the strong desire to be the new owners (lords) of the city.

Contributing to the reversing of power relationships within women's movement terminology have been global fluidity, the new scientific paradigms, new thinking styles, the strengthening of Islamic capital, and the failure of secular groups in producing urban politics; all have pushed the Islamic groups to become "owners" in the power relationship. But I have to emphasize here the general societal tilt toward religion that took place around the early 1990s. Although the WP represented only a fraction of Islamization in Turkey, it was able to benefit from this general trend.[5]

Sibel Eraslan, one of the columnists of *Vakit* newspaper, states that during the campaign activity when Recep Tayyip Erdoğan became the mayor of Istanbul in the March 27, 1994, municipal elections, he personally mobilized the women's movement. Eraslan also underlines the important role played at this stage by Bahri Zengin, who later remained with the "traditionalists" and distanced herself from Erdoğan. Zengin was instrumental in changing the organizational structure of the thirty-two branches of the local party organization, thus enabling a women's activist network in Istanbul.[6] The purpose of these WP women was to sustain a just administrative system through a more powerful Islamic identity rather than to improve the effectiveness of democracy through gender politics. These women did not have a desire to share the power per se, but, as electoral democracy requires, they performed their roles so that males achieved the success.

The WP women, who didn't define themselves during the election stage, referred to the "other" but didn't define "other." In the women's movement during this short period, started by the WP women, housewives sided with the female students who were subject to exclusion because of the headscarf problem, but also made an effort to understand and have dialogue with the so-called "others."[7]

Cihan Aktaş describes the "others" as those who oppressed them, who neglected them. Even though the WP women described themselves as Islamists, their stance against the "other" was more social and cultural than political, and the "Islamist woman" identity was not clouded by the ambiguity of the "other."

In contrast to this thinking, Sibel Eraslan, who believes that women should have a political identity and that they are the pioneers in gaining this identity, talks about these women as having been intellectually nourished by Mawdudi and Sayyed Qutb's views until 1986, but only in the second half of the 1990s did these women gain self-confidence after starting to read the books of Ali Bulaç and Abdurrahman Aslan, and especially *The Three Problems* by İsmet Özel. And as a result, they started adopting an "antisecularist" politics.[8] Following the success of the WP in the local elections, women remained outside politics either because of the obstructive stand of Erbakan against women in the party or because of the role-substitution attitude of the women. Nonetheless, to a certain extent, Islamist women managed to come out into the public space with written cultural products.

Some of the women who were effective in this period were Necla Koytak, Seyhan Büyükcoşkun, and Fatma Bostan Ünsal; in international debates, social studies, and literature some of the leading names were Sibel Eraslan, Cihan Aktaş, Elif H. Toros, Fatma Karabıyık Barbarasoğlu, Melek Paşalı, Münire Danış, Selvigül Kandoğmuş Şahin, Yıldız Ramazanoğlu, Hülya Aktaş, Hidayet Ş. Tuksal, Nazife Şişman, Ayşe Böhürler, and Nevin Meriç.[9] As observers from outside, the studies of Nilüfer Göle, Aynur Ilyasoğlu, Deniz Kandiyoti, Binnaz Toprak, Elizabeth Özdalga, Serpil Üşür, Sevda Alankuş Kural, Abdurrahman Dilipak, Hüseyin Hatemi, and Fatmagül Berktay contributed to the formation of Islamist women's expression.

The JDP and Organization of Women

According to the figures pertaining to Turkey in general, participation of women in politics from the provincial, town, village, and district point of view is quite low. Out of 34,044 members of municipal assemblies, only 540 are women, who make up only 1.6 percent of the total. Out of 3,215 mayors, only 20 are women, representing a paltry 0.6 percent. Out of 3,122 members of the local assemblies, only 21 are women, representing 0.7 percent.[10] The percentage of women members of Parliament has risen to 4.4 percent at present from 3.8 percent in the last term.

The JDP represented the liberal wing of the Islamic movement and came to power after the closure of the WP and the VP; the JDP leadership had had the experience of municipal administration, especially after the 1994 elections. Prime Minister Erdoğan emphasizes the existence of three political platforms in Turkey, namely left, conservative, and liberal, out of which in his view the center politics is the one that is appropriate for the functioning of Turkish politics. He is not in favor of individual-centered politics, but rather favors collective politics.[11]

Nur Vergin, who analyzes the success of the JDP in terms of political sociology, maintains that "more than the ideology that they have, the success of JDP is dependent on their political party identity, which reflects the sociology of Turkey with its leader and staff."[12] Besides this apt point, M. Hakan Yavuz claims that the success of the JDP is an outcome of the opportunity spaces in politics and public space; the voters will seek a new social contract based on social justice, human rights, and global principles of democracy under the rubric of ethical principles, and the JDP will be a hope for opportunity spaces and social mobility.[13] Şerif Mardin evaluates the success of the JDP in terms of its organizational structure.

One of the most successful things is to establish a human network—which I used to claim the strategy of the weak. We only talk about his [Erdoğan's] favoritism to the people around him but this also has another side like establishing the organization and the institutions. And they are very good at it. But they are not very strong at law-making ability, which derives from an institutional background. They will only see through experience how seriously the institutional experience in the Republic of Turkey should be taken into consideration.[14]

The JDP has showed progress at the organizational level and has managed to enable women's organizations to be operational in 934 sub-provinces within 81 provinces. Selma Kavaf, the head of the JDP Women Branches, says, "Provincial Heads of the Women Branches come together every month, and in these meetings they discuss issues, especially in regards to institutionalization, topics which are in the agenda of Turkey during that month, evaluation of related projects, and work on a 'politics school' so that they can contribute to women's involvement in politics." She adds that they are following a "method" to develop a "proactive" women's movement.[15] Kavaf, who believes that women will transform the language of politics, pointed out that the conservative democrat women profile indeed represents the conservativeness of the party and that women branches of the JDP strongly represent the party, which is a centrist party itself.

One of the founders of the party, Fatma Bostan Ünsal, expresses her hesitance about gender equality and the local success of the JDP as follows: "Mr. Erdoğan became a mayor thanks to his working together with women. Although he does not speak about it openly, he knows how to work with women. But I have doubts about his team."[16] Belma Sekmen Şatır, who is a member of the Central Decision-Making Council of the JDP, says communication between the senior administrative staff of the party and the women is very respectful.[17] In such a structure where social hierarchy exists, substitution of the "political role" becomes more flexible and there is a risk of not being able to overcome male dominance because of the importance of respect within the party. Along these lines, Sema Ramazanoğlu, who studied gender politics in Sweden and who is not coming from Welfare Party tradition, is quite sensitive to developing a gender politics within the JDP. Ramazanoğlu, who wears a headscarf, is a member of Central Decision-Making Council and believes in "consultancy tradition in politics." She points out that they problematized gender politics and have done political work on establishing a political identity for the JDP women since the very beginning of the process, and that they are also seeking a role-model:

Motherland Party, TPP, WP, VP, RPP—do these parties have women branches? If they do, how do they act? PAPATYAs (Daisies) immediately come to mind when we think of Motherland Party. It is not possible to mention about women organizations. TPP has got women branches but on paper and totally virtual. In RPP there is a total oligarchic establishment. Güldal Okuducu has been the director for fifteen years continuously; they have not conducted a congress for the last eight years. After eight years there is only one meeting on "peace in the region and world." In case of the Welfare and Virtue parties, women are in active politics but there is no such thing as "institutional establishment, institutional visibility, and well-established conventions." They mostly come together at homes. And during these meetings children, mother-in-laws, mothers are there too. Teas, cookies, religious talks, reading Koran, singing hymns are the content of these meetings. There is no role model for us. We are not a religiously based party. We prefer to be transparent and clear and at the same time self-criticizing. We would like to be in politics as women and with the women's point of view. We are working on increasing the rate of female participation in municipality assemblies to 20 percent in line with Mr. Prime Minister's demand. In Erzurum, Kars, Ağrı, Iğdır, Bayburt, Artvin, Malatya, Gümüşhane provinces we worked for the women candidates to come forward. The idea that women should be in politics came to the agenda even though there were not significant numerical gains. This is an important cognitive reform.[18]

When looked at from the gender politics perspective, it can be seen that the conservative democratic expression of the JDP has not been successful in the central party organization; there is usually a more civil structure in the organization. But when local needs are considered, such a civil structuring seems appropriate for political roles and for sustainability of the democracy.

Conservative democratic structure has defined the ideology of the JDP and can be characterized as being masculine. The biggest handicap in regards to political practice is the inability to balance economic and moral values.[19] As in other conservative politics, the conservative democratic structure of the JDP has not yet been able to establish such a balance. Women can be the determinants of the moral aspect of this balance, but insufficient public discourse makes the women's position obscure. For example, although it is one of the most important issues on the agenda, corruption—which has become institutional in Turkey—looks as though it were not a woman's issue in the public sphere. Engineered public opinion has a decisive or manipulative impact over women's issues.

Gender Activism: The Women Parliamentarians of the JDP

The third type of women in the JDP is the female MPs. As a result of the February 28 Process, the JDP selected its women MPs among those who are Westernized, secular, and yet still sensitive to Islam. In addition to the case of Merve Kavakçı, whose entering Parliament wearing her headscarf created tension in Turkish politics, scarf prohibition is continuing in public places. As a result there are no MPs with a scarf, yet there are covered women in the Central Decision-Making Council, except for the Central Executive Committee and in the women's organizations of the party.

With the incorporation of the "Declaration of Preventing All Kinds of Discrimination against Women" in the JDP party program, issues have been stipulated such as the elimination of discriminative provisions against women, for example, gender discrimination in work life; measures to encourage women to become more involved in public life; and support of associations, foundations, and nongovernmental organizations promoting women's issues.

One of the issues raised by the JDP in relation to women's problems is education. According to the "Education for All 2003/2004 Global Monitoring" report, Turkey is one of twelve countries that risk not being able to realize gender equality in primary and secondary education in the society until 2015. Among the other eleven countries are Burkina Faso, Ivory Coast–Ethiopia, India, Mongolia, and Iraq.[20] In today's Turkey, where twenty-five out of one hundred women are illiterate, a campaign called "Haydi Kızlar Okula Kampanyası" (Girls to School Campaign) has been launched. This campaign, prepared by the Ministry of National Education and UNICEF, started in 2003 and will last until the end of 2005. The objective of the campaign is to foster gender equality. The campaign includes provinces such as Ağrı, Batman, Bitlis, Diyarbakır, Hakkari, Muş, Siirt, Şanlıurfa, Şırnak, and Van. In 2005, twenty more provinces will be included in the campaign.

One of the important names within the government, former minister of state Güldal Akşit, says the women parliamentarians have quite a few projects for women, such as the "1,000 jobs and food for 1,000 women" project and the "Anatolian Gardens" project, where women who are producing in their homes will be able to sell their products.[21] Akşit says they have been working to find ways to prevent violence against women.

According to Family and Social Research Department research, physical abuse exists in 34 percent of Turkish families, and verbal abuse in 53 percent. In 2006, the Office of the Status of Women will undertake a new project to be called "Violence Against Women," which will collect and form a database concerning physical and verbal abuse. This project will be funded by the EU.[22] Another achievement for JDP women MPs is the abolishing of the articles about adultery in the Turkish Criminal Law. According to the new TCK (Turkish Penal Code), sexually motivated crimes come under "crimes against individuals," while crimes in the name of "tradition" are included separately.

Another important work realized by JDP women MPs involves maternal leaves for women workers. The duration of this paid leave has been increased to sixteen weeks—eight weeks before and eight weeks after delivery. In multiple pregnancy (such as twins), this leave is eighteen weeks, and the nursing allowance is rearranged as 1.5 hours every day for one year. Unpaid birth leave is six months. Birth leave is envisaged to be twelve weeks; if desired this can be increased by six months. Zeynep Karahan Uslu, who on behalf of JDP's women MPs proposed amendments to the Labor Law and also proposed legislation about government civil servants, indicated that birth leave by civil servants, which was initially nine weeks, has been increased to sixteen weeks with this new proposal.[23]

As far as the women MPs of the JDP are concerned, the identity of women is the identity that is defined within the context of collective cultural values. Women who are pioneers of change and transformation are replaced by the ones who have accepted the central policies in the center-right party. For instance, all the women MPs in the JDP except for İzmir MP Serpil Yılmaz voted against the constitutional amendment bill that proposed the positive discrimination principle for women—in which the state would take the necessary measures for promotion of women's rights and gender equality. Minister of Justice Cemil Çicek, who explained the rejection by the majority, claims that provisions of the "Preventing All Kinds of Discrimination Against Women Protocol" (CEDAW) of the United Nations, which Turkey also signed, covers all the issues that the main opposition party, the Republican People's Party (RPP), wants to include in the constitutional amendments.[24] Despite the persistent efforts of the RPP in Parliament, the "positive discrimination" provision could not be put in the constitution. JDP MP Zeynep Ayhan Tekinbörü says they voted against the proposal because they are concerned that accepting the positive discrimination principle would probably just stay on paper given so many structural problems on the agenda of the country such as regional inequality within the country, urban problems, and lack of equal opportunity in education.[25] Canan Kalsın, the outreach coordinator in Istanbul Women Branches, says, "most of the women are inclined to accept liberal values that enable a better life" and underscores that "most of the demands from women are personal demands."[26] In the pursuit of politics concerning women, efforts to establish "better or more luxurious lives" come forth in the form of liberal values, and the "modern" aspects of life assume priority.

Islamist writer Ramazanoğlu argues that the post-1994 women's movement was different because of their struggle to exist in the public space as autonomous agents. She also argues that if there were no Muslim women, "the public sphere would not become the center of discussion" in Turkey: "We reject the concept of equality. Gender equality has gained its prominence under the second feminist wave! In a women's meeting held in Beijing in 1995 the process of 'challenge' commenced. We are putting forward the concept of 'justice.' Challenge in the name of justice. This is more humane in Africa or Asia!"[27] Those who analyze gender relations and ideologies in Muslim countries persistently focus on the role of Islam.[28] The gender policies of the JDP, which are quite sensitive to Islam, are, however, quite Western and contemporary. In terms of MPs, the women's practices are modern and secular. The political culture of the women in the party are along the lines of cultural codes, favoring consensus over disagreement and conformity over divergence. The reference point of the women MPs is the practices in the EU countries.

First Lady: Emine Erdoğan

There are three different periods in the formation of Emine Erdoğan's identity: The first formed Emine (Gülbaran) Erdoğan's political identity. She was a member of the Idealist Women Association established under the leadership of Şule Yüksel Şenler. She was very much influenced by a speech of Recep Tayyip Erdoğan,[29] whom she had dreamt about the previous night, when she went with other women members to listen to Necmettin Erbakan, then the leader of the National Salvation Party, on "National Rearing Night" in Tepebaşı in 1977. In 1978, she married Tayyip Erdoğan through an arranged marriage.

The second Emine Erdoğan is first and foremost a mother and a wife. With an attitude appropriated from cultural codes, she stands behind her husband, continues her political role by sharing it with other women, and yet is not seen in the public space or the media. Before the general elections in 2002, the media were curious about Emine Erdoğan. The second Emine Erdoğan exists in terms of her cultural gender identity. This identity was dominant until the JDP came to power in 2002.

The third Emine Erdoğan, most of the time on the agenda of the national media and from time to time on the agenda of the global media, is a first lady as well as a mother getting on well with her children. She is also a first lady who actively takes place in JDP events for women, participates in opening speeches, and openly explains her ideals to the public in parallel with the government. As a role model, she is sometimes the subject of the popular media.

Mrs. Erdoğan's articulation of the issues regarding the participation of women in political life and women's education contributes a great deal to gender democracy. She participated in the political campaigns of the March 2004 local elections to support women mayoral candidates in towns in Istanbul, in Mersin, in the Dörtyol subprovince of Hatay, and in Yeşilköy. The fact that the first lady gave the opening speech of the "Haydi Kızlar Okula Kampanyası" (Girls to School Campaign) at the national level makes the whole campaign quite effective in terms of creating public awareness and also in increasing the reliability of the campaign. However, media make their own news in their own popular language about the first lady, and from time to time this attention undermines gender democracy. This is because Turkish media have a strategy in which personal characteristics are constructed to be more meaningful than public messages. Comparing the dress styles of Emine Erdoğan with those of Semra Sezer (the president's wife), and making news out of issues such as colors, accessories, and the like, which in fact are issues of interest to the fashion designers, put the first lady's political efforts into a secondary position. Emine Erdoğan, who is sometimes harmonious and sometimes oppositional, always has to deal with the headscarf issue in the public sphere.

Mrs. Erdoğan, according to whom being covered is the symbol of Islamic life, believes that the problem can be solved through the dissemination of the ideas to be promoted by the scientific world of "freedom of thought and conscience."[30] When she, together with the other covered wives of the MPs, was not invited to the receptions given by President Ahmet Necdet Sezer, she criticized this omission by saying, "minds of the people at the top should change," which appeared in the media side by side with other ladies' vocal criticisms.[31]

In an interview by Amberin Zaman in *The Economist*, Emine Erdoğan was depicted as the woman "who managed the impossible balance." It was pointed out that she has developed her own way of dealing with diverse sectors of Turkish society:

> [W]hen E. Erdogan's husband Tayyip Erdoğan became Prime Minister 17 months ago, there were many influential Turks—both religious one like the Erdoğans, or the secular types who oppose everything they stand for—who hoped she would be a docile wife and stay at home. Secularists were unhappy about their country being represented by a woman who like more than half her female compatriots, cover her head in a sign of devotion to Islam. Pious voters had the opposite fear: they felt queasy when they saw a devout Muslim lady hobnobbing with rich and powerful Westerners.[32]

THE JDP AND WOMEN: THE TURBAN AND THE PUBLIC SPHERE(S)

During the JDP government a great deal of the intensive domestic debates have focused on the public sphere and the turban issue. Both issues have been addressed by men because of the insufficient number of spokeswomen. Some of the academics or researchers studying the JDP assert that the JDP has "normalized" this problem by putting the turban issue at the center.[33] Others believe that this issue remains unsolved even at the European level as in the case of medical faculty student Leyla Şahin, who brought the issue before the European Court of Human Rights (ECHR). In this case regarding the "prohibition of the turban in the public areas," the ECHR considered a court case against the Republic of Turkey and unanimously decided in favor of the Turkish state. According to the decision of the ECHR, the turban has "a public dimension."[34] The head of the ECHR, Luzius Wilhaber, defines secularism with reference to the "impartiality of the public area" and notably emphasizes the Islamic dogma about the legal status of women as being in contradiction with the European Human Rights Declaration.

Following the November 3, 2002, elections, the JDP faced the "protocol crisis of turban (headscarf)." The turban crisis began when the chairman of the Turkish Grand National Assembly, Bülent Arınç, went with his headscarfed wife to see the president. So the polemic about whether covered wives should take part in protocols triggered the turban-protocol crisis.

The exclusion of the covered wives of most of the JDP MPs from the receptions given at the Presidential Palace accentuated the public-sphere debate more than the turban itself. Public domain enters the agenda of the president, the prime minister, the chairman of the Turkish Grand National Assembly, and the columnists. The point reached in each and every description is whether women wearing a turban can enter the public sphere or not. In fact the turban issue has been on the agenda of Turkey since the 1980s, but its becoming a public issue is new. While turban has a singular referent, public space becomes plentiful and omnipresent. There are various public domains claimed and used as a cover for everyone separately. The Islamist female author Nazife Şişman claims that the most important factor about the perception of the veiled women who want to participate in public life is the conceptualization of the public sphere, which is thought of as a filtering mechanism to differentiate hierarchically between those who are regarded as citizens and those who are not, rather than as a framework for a common view of society and worldview. As a result of this hierarchical structure, modern women are perceived to be the real owners of this public domain and veiled women to be the ones who are infringing on this "filter."[35]

According to another Islamist writer, Yıldız Ramazanoğlu, the start of the questioning of modernization and tradition by the 1978 generation paved the way for the emergence of Islamist women, who see a scarf (turban) as a symbol of being a servant of God (Allah) rather than as being subordinate to male-dominated systems and even to one's own ego or self, and thus they get accustomed to the feeling of eternity.[36] The Islamist woman writer Cihan Aktaş, while trying to explain the veiling movement in the Islamic world in terms of a return to religious phenomena, explained headscarves as having a symbolic value to that end.[37]

In scrutinizing the headscarf problem from different angles, it should not be ignored that there is also a global dimension to this issue. In the context of post–September 11 and the increased Muslim population in Western countries such as France and Germany, Islam-phobia became a reality across the globe, and all Islamic symbols have been reinterpreted within this phobia.

The headscarf in Turkey has become a symbol to be excluded from different public spaces. During the JDP government the biggest change in the headscarf issue, which was formerly a national problem, is its becoming an "unsolved global" issue. In fact the process that has created the headscarf issue cannot be thought of apart from the issue of the modernization of tradition and is the product of a reciprocal process.

Uğur Kömeçoğlu, who conducted an empirical study on this subject, says the public appearance of covered girls has not come to life through a soft social process that originated from tradition; rather it has surfaced through the interpretation of new interactions between city dwellers and educated social groups.[38]

When compared with other parties, the highest ranking values of JDP voters are democracy and human rights, 52.8 percent; religion, 40.1 percent; and national values, 16.5 percent.[39] According to another research study that included 2,527 people (34 percent of whom voted for the JDP, 19.4 percent of whom voted for the RPP, and 9.5 percent of whom voted for the TPP in the November 3, 2002, elections), 40 percent of Turkish society considers itself as democrat, 38 percent as Ataturkist (Atatürkçü), 33.4 percent as secular, 27 percent as nationalist, and 20 percent as rightist.[40] According to both studies, no matter how much JDP voters believe in democracy and human rights with their "democratic" identity, women within the peculiar cultural gender structure of the Turkish right have not been able to transform democracy or human rights into the reality of daily life.

Before the JDP government, the turban was the issue of "girls" who could not enter universities; however, after the JDP became the ruling party it became the issue of "women" when the wives of MPs were not invited to the receptions given at the state institutions. The problem to which fathers or elders were seeking a solution has been transferred to men (husbands) who cannot solve their wives' problems. This fact is important in terms of seeing the gender hierarchy in Turkey. The problem of girls with a turban became the women's problem; the issue has become more and more intractable, and while the ideal place to look for a solution was the public sphere, the problem has been pushed to the private sphere.

The fathers or elders who had been talking on behalf of their daughters were replaced by husbands who kept quiet for their wives. This male silence about the turban issue called it to the media's attention, and the headscarf has become the most popular topic on the media agenda. Although the JDP has a gender policy in practice, the media's popularization of this policy through partial coverage with a particular emphasis on women with turbans made this issue seem ordinary. Because the language of the media is of a masculine cult (not simply men-dominated) that will undermine gender policies, this aspect of the media in Turkey is always the biggest handicap keeping gender politics from developing no matter which party comes to power. The JDP has an identity structure that can keep veiled and unveiled women together. Social distance between the two groups has narrowed and social empathy has been established. This shows that the cultural or social conservative side of the JDP precedes its political conservatism. That's because both veiled and unveiled women have the same purpose at the practical level: meeting in modernity, gaining a share from the system, and raising their life standard. The veiled women are getting modernized while the unveiled women are moving closer to Islam. From this point of view, the modernization of women is not linear or holistic as conventionally believed; on the contrary it shows cross-categorical features. It should be stressed here that the segments of the population that brought the JDP to power share this view of modernity. In addition to the bourgeoisie's lack of a class foundation in Turkey, the high level of individual mobility overlaps with this type of modernity.

Eraslan, on the other hand, especially emphasizes that the political space is not just for raising the problems of veiled women, and she asserts that this space has been narrowed by the headscarf issue. In her view, what women do for the sake of God is insufficient for women's experience and the women's movement.[41] Eraslan sees the prioritization of oral culture by the Islamist women as a hindrance against politicization and thereby touches on the importance of writing by women.

Public Sphere

Prime Minister Erdoğan defines the public sphere as one of freedom and difference, not of the state.[42] Lawyer Yüzbaşıoğlu delineates public sphere not from its physical referents but in respect to its functional referents. "You cannot say that everything is free in the public sphere. You also cannot say that everything is prohibited."[43] While European Union expert Karakaş says that the public domain is "every space outside the house," he explains that this space can be divided into "official" and "common": For the sake of maintaining the neutrality of the public sector, those who wield public power in the public sphere shouldn't wear a scarf.[44] Sociologist Ayata maintains that there is no definition of "public" and that this sphere is open to discussion: "There is no definition of the 'Public sphere' and it changes from society to society and it is a relative concept. Power wielders decide what belongs to the public sphere."[45]

Constitutional lawyer Zafer Üskül identifies the public sphere as "those spaces which are shared by the people, all but outside the private sphere, in other words, societal or public space is the realm commonly used by individuals that make up a society."[46]

The tendency in Turkey is to consider public and state as identical, and this tendency makes it difficult to define the boundaries of the public sphere. The chief columnist of *Hürriyet* newspaper, Oktay Ekşi, says, "public sphere is anywhere the presidential streamer is present." Another definition is by Erdoğan Teziç, the president of Higher Education Council: "public sphere is the area where police can ask for an identity card." Both definitions indicate that public sphere has been turned into a space where the state has subjugated the civil society and has imposed its absolute will unconditionally.[47] The speaker of the Turkish Parliament, Bülent Arınç, argues that there is no such thing as public sphere explicitly mentioned in the constitution and that nobody has the right to define a concept that does not exist in the constitution with their own way of thinking.[48]

H. Bülent Kahraman, one of the columnists of *Radikal* newspaper who has written extensively on the public sphere and headscarf, says, "if we had known the public sphere and concept of secularism in a more comprehensive way, we wouldn't have brought the debate about the headscarf to such an impasse. To this we should add that the state should believe in its citizen and should see them as matured and responsible beings."[49] By saying this he draws attention to the tension between the state and the civil society.

Public sphere in a Habermasian sense is the area to produce debates as well as ideas, and is a concept that is parallel to innovation in the historical process.[50]

In practice, the headscarf ban is being used in reference to a symbol of backwardness juxtaposed to the public sphere. Some of the incidents related to the headscarf controversy are as follows: The former head of the Supreme Court, Eraslan Özkaya, found Fadıl İnan, the head of the Fourth Penal Court, to be right in removing a suspect from the court on the grounds that she was wearing a headscarf. Özkaya defines the courts as key public spaces and says that the right to defense is a sacred one but that the right of defense of any kind should be exercised in a manner appropriate to law.[51] Another application concerns a veiled trainee in a Foreign Ministry Commission meeting of Parliament, sent by the Turkish Democracy Foundation under the "Trainee Program of the Capital." Members of Parliament from the Republican People's Party made her leave the commission hall and reminded her that Parliament is a part of the public sphere where wearing a headscarf is unacceptable.[52]

The public sphere in Turkey has been institutionalized as a medium of secularization and progress. The Turkish public sphere has been turned into an area where the state's modernist and secular ideology is exhibited. In that sense, women have been selected as the ones who constitute the most visible and conspicuous aspect of modernity, and political contestation has taken place over women's issues and bodies.

Richard Sennett investigates the historical evolution of the public sphere and its current state from a social theory perspective, describes the public sphere as a domain that is losing power in our modern society, and claims that our modern society is a "private society." According to Sennett, the last century witnessed the formation of collective personality communities, and being a community in the modern world is more about the feeling of belonging than any related action. The only action of a community is sentimental supervision to remove those who do not belong to the group because of their lack of holding the same feelings as others.[53] At the heart of the fuzzy debate on the public sphere in Turkey is the tendency for rationalization of feelings by power-feeling communities. The medium of rationalization is always "law." That is why most definitions of the public sphere are law-centered. One of the sole reasons for the continuation of the public-sphere debate in an uproar is the usage of the public sphere by stationing of secular law in it. Istanbul University, which is known for deep-rooted protests against the headscarf, opened the Beyazit Tower in the garden, which was closed for years to the public, while its acting rector, Tankut Centel, declared it to be open only for foreign visitors and banned it to the "veiled" public, claiming that the university garden was a public sphere.[54]

In terms of literary, cultural, and political public spheres that target women, approximately sixty websites and two hundred magazines in Turkey contain thousands of local and translated articles and works. Three types of discourse are prominent in these publications: secular discourse, Islamist discourse, and feminist discourse. The secular expressions are found in *Gazete (Newspaper)* and *Özgür Kadının Sesi(Voice of Free Woman)* magazines and Internet sites. The leading themes are equal opportunity in education and work, socialization, and modern participatory democracy. Some of the magazines containing Islamic discourse are *Mektup* (Letter), *Kadın ve Aile* (Women and Family), *Evrensel Kadın* (Universal Women), and *Kadın Kimliği* (Women Identity), while the dominant subjects are debates related to Islam and the tradition, maternal identity, and women's family responsibilities. In these publications it is often pointed out that women's participation in political life is not a necessity. Feminist discourse can be seen in magazines such as *Pazartesi (Monday)* and *Sosyalist Kadin (Socialist Woman)*. Most of the subjects are related to the protection of women against beating, sexual harassment, and problems of migration.[55] With regard to TV programs as the single most effective producer of public space, discourse related to women has not been produced. According to the results of a study examining how working women are represented on TV, the presentation of women in prime-time news coverage is as follows: the Fadime Şahin incident (the girl who says she had been molested by one of the religious order sheikhs), attacks against taxi drivers, pregnant woman not admitted to the hospital, interviews with women in prison, a bisexual village, problem of child singers, husband bashing, women's shelters, and religious extremism.[56]

The same research scrutinized local television series and found that women were represented mostly in housewife identities; the major issues related to women were not raised.[57] According to another study, the problems most commonly expressed by women were to study in college and to have a profession and full-time job.[58] In spite of these results, education of women and work demand are yet to assume a central position in the literary, cultural, and current political public sphere.

Conclusion

Throughout the period of change and transformation, one of the basic features of politics in Turkey is its "substitution" character. The identification of left and nationalist politics with the state, the secularism-emphasizing people with the West, the right-wing politicians with religion, and the women with the men is important from a political discourse point of view. This substitution tendency is based more on cultural codes than it is being shaped by politics. As seen in all center-right as well as left-wing parties, including the JDP, the structure that determines gender politics is not political but cultural. Ideally, gender politics should be a product of politics. Within the continuation of democracy, gender politics is reproducing and practicing democracy, and using a new language in liberal, left, and right politics. In the political language of Turkey, instead of male-female differentiation, there exists a language with characteristics of resemblance: in terms of gender roles, women are most active during elections, yet election efforts and the lion's share of success are attributed to men. In spite of the fact that most talk of daily life is politically centered, women are hesitant to participate in politics. According to research by TESEV, 65 percent of men and 74 percent of women claim that women are not given enough opportunities in politics.[59] Although the question of "equality or difference" is not found meaningful by feminists or the Islamist women in Turkey, this question makes up the foundational argument for the social and political struggle of Western women. While looking at both approaches with doubt, feminist as well as Islamist women point out that gender politics cannot be understood in terms of binary thinking.

JDP women, who don't demand either difference or equality, prefer a different approach to modernizing conservatism. There are three types of JDP women: the Islamist women, who played a role in the past of the JDP and who had been mobilized personally by Erdoğan; the women who work in the party organization and who can be found across a wide spectrum of society from Islamist to liberal groups; and the women members of Parliament representing the center-right. The common characteristic of these women is that in spite of being conservative (different from the definition of conservative in the West), they are not prejudiced against but rather have sensitivity toward Islamic values.

When all the three types of women and the practices of Emine Erdoğan are examined, one can argue that the JDP women have an identity that minimizes the social distance between women wearing scarves and the women with modern dress. In that respect, the modernization of the "conservative" and the increased Islamic sensitivity of the "modern" reveals a criss-crossing relationship between the two. The JDP can be said to be the party that has extensively dealt with women's issues more than any other political party in the last fifty years.

The triple issues of the headscarf, the public sphere, and secularism are the three obstacles to the JDP's gender policies. The tension between the JDP and other state institutions manifests itself as opposing definitions of turban–public sphere and the principles of secularism. The source of this tension, which will go down in history as the "reception crisis," is the symbolic clash between "secular" and "nonsecular." The national headscarf problem has become a global issue during the JDP government. The headscarf case in the ECHR, which has ended in favor of the secular establishment of Turkey, has especially jolted the expectations the Islamists had of European freedoms. This issue has become an indicator of the departure of the JDP from a religiously-centered party. In conclusion, the JDP, which has been a transformation party in the European Union membership period, has undertaken the transformation of the cultural gender politics of women into a political gender politics.

Notes

1. Anne Wilson Schaef, *Women's Reality An Emerging Female System in a White Male Society* (New York: Harper, 1992).

2. Barbara Hill, *Bizans Imparatorluk Kadınları, Iktidar, Himaye ve Ideoloji, Çeviren: Elif Gökteke Tut* (Istanbul: Tarih Vakfi Yurt Yayınları, 2003), 12.

3. Yıldız Temürtürkan, *Kadın ve Siyaset Paneli* (Ankara: Türk Demokrasi Vakfı and ODTÜ Mezunları Derneği, 2003).

4. The Welfare Party had won 28 percent of the seventy-five cities and had increased its votes from 9.9 percent to 19 percent. According to the result of the local elections, the RPP was seen as one of the biggest political powers of the future; for more on the Welfare Party, see M. Hakan Yavuz, *Islamic Political Identity in Turkey* (New York: Oxford University Press, 2003), 207–38.

5. Nur Vergin, "Mülakat," *Türkiye Günlüğü* 27 (March–April 1994): 5–12.

6. Interview with Sibel Eraslan (journalist), August 16, 2004.

7. Cihan Aktaş, "Cemaatten Kamusal Alana İslamcı Kadınlar," in *Modern Türkiye'de Siyasi Düşünce, İslamcılık, 6* (Istanbul: İletişim Yayınları, 2004), 835.

8. Interview with Sibel Eraslan, August 16, 2004.

9. Aktaş, "Cemaatten Kamusal Alana," 835–36.

10. Meral Tamer, "Soldaki kadın seçmen, aktif siyasete ilgisiz," www.milliyet.com, March 7, 2004.

11. Turan Yılmaz, *Tayyip, Kasımpaşa'dan Siyasetin ön Saflarına* (Ankara: Ümit Yayıncılık, 2001), 290.

12. Nur Vergin, "Siyaset ile Sosyolojinin Buluştuğu Nokta," *Türkiye Günlüğü* 76 (2004): 5–9.

13. Yavuz, *Islamic Political Identity*, 256–57.

14. Şerif Mardin's interview with Ruşen Çakır, "AKP, Neydiler ne oldular," *Vatan Gazetesi*, October 3, 2003.

15. Interview with Selma Kavaf, head of the Women Branches of the JDP, September 2, 2004.

16. Fatma Bostan Ünsal with Ruşen Çakır, "AKP, Neydiler ne oldular," *Vatan*, October 5, 2003.

17. Interview with Belma Sekmen Şatır, member of the JDP's Central Decision-Making Council, August 16, 2004.

18. Interview with Sema Ramazanoğlu, member of the JDP's Central Decision-Making Council, October 9, 2004.

19. Songül Sallan Gül and Hüseyin Gül, "The Question of Women in Islamıc Revivalism in Turkey: A Review of the Islamic Press," *Current Sociology* 48, no. 2 (April 2000): 4.

20. Herkes İçin Eğitim Küresel İzleme Raporu, April 19–25, 2004, Sabancı Üniversitesi, Istanbul.

21. Güldal Akşit, Kadın Çalışma Grubu Toplantısı Açılış Konuşması, February 21, 2004, Hilton Oteli, Istanbul.

22. "Abuse of Women Continues to Plague the Nation," *Turkish Daily News*, November 27, 2004.

23. Interview with Zeynep Karahan Uslu, a JDP woman parliamentarian, Ankara, October 20, 2004.

24. "Pozitif Ayrımcılık Yok, Reform da Yok," *Gazete: Özgür Kadının Sesi*, May–June 2004.

25. Interview with Zeynep Ayhan Tekinbörü, a JDP woman parliamentarian, Ankara, August 23, 2004.

26. Interview with Canan Kalsın, outreach coordinator in Istanbul Women Branches, August 2, 2004.

27. Interview with Yıldız Ramazanoğlu, Islamic woman writer, August 16, 2004.

28. Deniz Kandiyoti, *Cariyeler, Bacılar, Yurttaşlar, Kimlikler ve Toplumsal Dönüşümler, İng. Çev. Aksu Bora ve Diğerleri* (Istanbul: Metis Yayınları, 1997), 84.

29. Erdoğan received first place in the poetry-reading competition that was organized by the daily *Tercüman* newspaper in 1973. He demostrated his rhetorical ability as early as high school. He has a powerful voice to stir up emotions. More on Erdoğan in *Milliyet*, July 8, 2001.

30. *Milliyet*, March 23, 2004.

31. See www.nethaber.com.tr, June 28, 2004.

32. "Mrs Erdoğan's many friends," interview with Amberin Zaman, *The Economist*, August 12, 2004.

33. Nuh Yılmaz, "İslamcılık, AKP, Siyaset," in *Modern Türkiye'de Siyasi Düşünce, İslamcılık, 6* (Istanbul: İletişim Yayınları, 2004), 604–20; Üzeyir Tekin, *AK Parti'nin Muhafazakâr Demokrat Kimliği* (Ankara: Orient Yayınları, 2004), 141.

34. H. Bülent Kahraman, "Bireyselden Toplumsal Türban," *Radikal*, June 7, 2004.

35. Nazife Şişman, "Türkiye'de Çağdaş Kadınların İslamcı Kadın Algısı," in *Osmanlı'dan Cumhuriyet'e Kadının Tarihi Dönüşümü*, ed. Yıldız Ramazanoğlu (Istanbul: Pınar Yayınları, 2000), 113–38.

36. Yıldız Ramazanoğlu, "Cumhuriyet'in Dindar Kadınları," in *Modern Türkiye'de Siyasi Düşünce, İslamcılık, 6* (Istanbul: İletişim Yayınları, 2004), 804–13.

37. Cihan Aktaş, *Tesettür ve Toplum, Başörtülü Öğrencilerin Toplumsal Kökeni Üzerine Bir İnceleme* (Istanbul: Nehir Yayınları, 1992), 36.

38. Uğur Kömeçoğlu, "Örtünme Pratiği ve Toplumsal Cinsiyete İlişkin Mekansal Bir Etnografi," *Doğu Batı* 23 (2003): 49.

39. Orhan Gökçe, Birol Akgün, and Süleyman Karaçor, "3 Kasım Seçimlerinin Anatomisi: Türk Siyasetinde Süreklilik ve Değişim," *Sosyal ve Ekonomik Araştırmalar Dergisi* 4 (October 2002): 30.

40. *3 Kasım 2002'den 3 Kasım 2003'e, Türkiye'nin Bir Yılı Araştırması* (Istanbul: Genar Araştırma, 2003).

41. Sibel Eraslan, "İslamcı Kadının Siyasette Zaman Algısı Üzerine," in *Modern Türkiye'de Siyasi Düşünce, İslamcılık*, 6, ed. Yasin Aktay (Istanbul: İletişim Yayınları, 2004), 818–26; Fatmagül Berktay, *Tarihin Cinsiyeti* (Istanbul: Metis Yayınları, 2003).

42. R. Tayyip Erdoğan, www.ucansupurge.org/newhtml/, July 9–16, 2004.

43. Necmi Yüzbaşıoğlu, http://uzerlik.free.fr/modules.php?name, July 15, 2004.

44. Eser Karakaş, http://uzerlik.free.fr/modules.php?name, July 15, 2004.

45. Sencer Ayata, http://uzerlik.free.fr/modules.php?name, July 15, 2004.

46. Zafer Üskül, www.ucansupurge.org/newhtml, July 9–16, 2004.

47. Murat Belge, "Kamusal Alana Nereden Gidilir?" *Radikal*, July, 16, 2004.

48. "Bir tarif de Arınç'tan," *Radikal*, July 16, 2004.

49. H. Bülent Kahraman, "Türban ya da hepimiz suçluyuz," *Radikal*, October 27, 2003.

50. Arsev Bektaş, *Kamuoyu, İletişim ve Demokrasi* (Istanbul: Bağlam Yayıncılık, 1996).

51. "Özkaya: Mahkeme, Kamusal Alan," *Radikal*, November 7, 2003.

52. "Türbanlı öğrenci dışarı çıkarıldı," *Cumhuriyet*, June 25, 2004.

53. Richard Sennett, *Kamusal İnsanın Çöküşü, İngilizceden Çevirenler: Serpil Durak-Abdullah Yılmaz* (Istanbul: Ayrıntı Yayınları, 1996), 386.

54. Türker Alkan, "Başörtüsü ve Cinsel Ahlak," *Radikal*, December 3, 2004.

55. Afsaneh Sh.Z. Karakuş, "Türk Kadınının Siyasi Kimliğinin Oluşma Süreçleri" (PhD diss., İstanbul Universitesi, 1999).

56. Hülya Tufan-Tanrıöver ve Ayşe Eyüboğlu, *Popüler Kültür Ürünlerinde Kadın İstihdamını Etkileyebilecek Öğeler, Cinsiyetçiliğin Kültürel Pratikler Aracılığıyla Yeniden Üretilmesi:Popüler Kültürde Kadın İstihdamını Etkileyebilecek Olumlu ve Olumsuz Öğeler* (Ankara: Başbakanlık Kadının Statüsü ve Sorunları Genel Müdürlüğü, 2000), 118.

57. Tanrıöver-Eyüboğlu, *Popüler Kültür Ürünlerinde*, 109.

58. İpek İlkkaracan, *Kentli Kadınlar ve Calışma Hayatı* (Istanbul: Tarih Vakfı Yayınları, 1998).

59. Ersin Kalaycıoğlu and Binnaz Toprak, *İş Yaşamı, Üst Yönetim ve Siyasette Kadın* (Istanbul: TESEV Yayınları, 2004), 82.

CHAPTER 12

JDP and Foreign Policy as an Agent of Transformation

■ *Burhanettin Duran*

INTRODUCTION

The Justice and Development Party's (JDP) landslide victory in the November 2002 elections in Turkey has been considered a success of Kemalism by a prominent Turkish social scientist, Şerif Mardin. It is paradoxical that the new strength of Islam in Turkey has been the result of the Kemalist reforms that aimed at controlling Islam.[1] It is also paradoxical that the Kemalist ideal of becoming a part of Europe needs democratic reforms that would weaken the political influence of the military, the guardian of Kemalism.[2] Interestingly enough, this paradox has to be realized by the ex-Islamists who were ousted from power in 1997 by the military. Islamists (an internal threat to the secular Republic) have become the basic actor of transformation (deconstructing the security-based exclusive nature of the Kemalist structure) by means of a strong reliance on external factors (European Union [EU] and globalization). Turkish politics has yet to get over the paradox between the military's relative autonomy in politics on the one hand, and the consolidation of the democratic regime as an integral part of Europeanization and a fundamental condition of being a full member of the European Union on the other.[3]

The JDP has empowered itself within Turkish domestic politics first by a commitment to implement the International Monetary Fund's standby agreement and economic reforms and second by the management of serious foreign policy issues: the Iraq war and the Cyprus question. True to its commitment to membership in the EU, the JDP government has sent several packages of reforms to Parliament for approval in order to bring Turkish laws into line with EU standards. On the issue of a search for alternative options in Turkish foreign policy, Recep Tayyip

Erdoğan, the party leader and the prime minister, underlines that the EU is not a geography but a model that has no political alternative in promoting democratization.[4] In fact, the word "transformation" has become a catchword to explain the relations between Turkey and the EU. Romano Prodi, the EU Commission president, in his visit to Turkey, has noted that there has been a "profound transformation" in relations between Ankara and Brussels over the last couple of years, mostly because of the "impressive progress" that Turkey has made in meeting the Copenhagen criteria.[5]

This chapter shows that this transformation has not been limited to Turkish domestic and foreign policies.[6] A more critical process of change can be observed with respect to Islamic political identity and discourses in Turkey. What is striking about the JDP's foreign policy is that it represents a departure from the Islamism of the National Outlook Movement (NOM), which embraced an anti-Western/European stance from the 1970s to the 1990s. The JDP's foreign policy seems to balance multiple perspectives, including good relations with Middle Eastern countries and the accession to the EU. This stance creates a fertile ground for eliminating the identity crisis of Turkish domestic and foreign policies. In other words, the JDP has been transforming the parameters of both Turkish politics and Islamist politics through "Europeanization" and "internationalization" of internal issues. This task of transforming both itself and Turkey has to be based on a careful balance between Islamist and secularist expectations in domestic politics and between the United States and Europe in an international context.[7] It is certain that the JDP, more than any other Turkish political party, regards international support as a fundamental factor in attaining political legitimacy. Having learned enough from the February 28 Process, the JDP knows that electoral victory does not necessarily give legitimacy in the eyes of the state elite.

As a part of its desire for transformation, the JDP has made the issue of democratization a foreign policy objective,[8] but more interestingly, it has also resituated the domain for foreign policy as a secure way to further democratize the Turkish political system while trying to avoid a clash with conservative secularist circles. The JDP has to establish a careful balance between foreign policy and domestic politics. The JDP will face uncomfortable choices at home, especially a possible uncertainty in relations with the EU. In trying to delineate the parameters of transformation, this chapter addresses first the ideological transformation of the JDP and its "new discourse" of conservative democracy. Second, it focuses on the implications of the JDP's new civilizational discourse on foreign policy. Third, it studies the major aspects of the JDP's foreign policy: assertiveness, multilateralism, and European orientation. Last, it tries to show how domestic politics became much more subject to the processes of Europeanization and to the developments in the international arena under the JDP rule.

FROM ISLAMISM TO CONSERVATIVE DEMOCRACY: IDEOLOGICAL ROOTS AND TRANSFORMATION OF THE JDP

Since its foundation in August 2001, the JDP leaders have insisted that the JDP is a conservative democrat party seeking religious freedoms enjoyed in the West and that it will not follow an Islamic agenda.[9] Erdoğan has also stated several times that his party has no Islamist agenda by avoiding any open reference to Islam. This sensitivity reaches to the extent that he even denies being called a Muslim democrat similar to Western Europe's Christian Democrats. The JDP's political program and Erdoğan's new profile and discourse are seen by some students of Turkish politics as sincere and as a successful example of reconciliation between Islam and democracy in Turkey.[10] Indeed, the JDP's new discourse should be seen as the culmination of transformations in the various Islamic sectors in Turkey, from religious orders and communities to intellectuals. The essentialist and dogmatic aspects of Turkish Islamism have been erased and its pragmatic aspect has been strengthened by the JDP's new discourse on conservative democracy.

The concepts of "Islamic state" and "Islamic ideology" have lost their significance in the JDP's discourse. Although the ideological change in Islamists can be traced back to the public debates during the presidency of Turgut Özal (1989–93), it has been the influence of the February 28 Process that has accelerated the change. Many Islamist circles, including politicians, intellectuals, and businessmen, have come to conclude that Islamist politics are not possible and more importantly that such politics would escalate the authoritarian style of the Kemalist secularist establishment. Moreover, it is also realized that this escalation would further narrow the domestic political arena even at the expense of performing religious demands. This process has brought about some significant changes in Islamist conceptualizations of Europe, democracy, and the West in Turkey. The different circles of Turkish Islamism have abandoned their anti-European discourses and have supported Turkey's integration with the world.[11] This change of mind can be related to the conviction that the EU accession process and the integration with the world are likely to force the Turkish political system to undertake significant democratic reforms that will make the official ideology less repressive and more inclusive. In this vein, they hope that these processes will bring about a liberal democratic political environment in which their Islamic demands, related to living religious values, might be met. Certainly this transformation should not be related only to the unintended consequences of the February 28 Process. Islamist groups, as M. Hakan Yavuz underlines, have supported Turkey's integration into the EU for four reasons: (1) the rise of a new bourgeoisie within the NOM; (2) the belief that religious rights in Turkey would be better protected under the EU than they are currently under the Turkish constitution; (3) the encouragement of the NOM by Turks in Germany to support Turkey's integration into the EU; and (4) the increasing power of the new generation of NOM politicians.[12] This change of mind necessarily contributes to the transnationalization or internationalization of Islamic demands and connections.[13]

The transformation of the JDP's discourse has triggered a discussion and a confusion on how to label the party both in Turkey and the West. Though some suspicious circles have continued to call it Islamist or at least moderate Islamist, many have felt the need for renaming Erdoğan and his friends as "secular Islamist,"[14] "a European social-democratic party of the third way type,"[15] "revolutionary conservatives,"[16] "Muslim democrats,"[17] or "a Turkish version of Western Europe's Christian Democrats"[18] after declaring "the end of Islamism" in Turkey. Since the JDP opposes the idea of an Islamist party and combines traditional and liberal-democratic values, Bülent Gökay regards the rise of the party to power as "a clear evidence to the high momentum of the liberal Islam in Turkey."[19] The JDP's conservative democracy seems to be close to Anglo-Saxon conservatism, which is more liberal and moderate than the continental (French) experience.[20] Conservative democracy is depicted as "a local-oriented stance in a globalizing world." As Ömer Çaha correctly states, the JDP frames "its political understanding according to the international political and legal norms on the one hand, and to the need to protect the local institutions that serve democracy on the other." The three sources that shape the JDP's political identity are "international norms, traditional values, and the official institutions, particularly secularism, brought to life by the Republican regime."[21]

In spite of the party leaders' preference for the label of "conservative democracy," one may argue that the JDP's political identity is a two-sided phenomenon: On the one side, it is trying to forge a synthesis between liberal and conservative trends within Turkey around a new social consensus. In this sense, the JDP puts itself in the line of political tradition that comes from the Progressive Republican Party, the Democrat Party, the Justice Party, and Turgut Özal's Motherland Party. But, on the other side, there remains a discourse of (Islamic) civilization that has long been central to Turkish Islamism since the late Ottoman times. It should also be remembered that the concepts of justice and progress/development have contributed much to the evolution of Islamist discourses in Turkey, including the Welfare Party's Adil Düzen (Just Order).[22] Islamists of the Ottoman Empire were heavily influenced by the European notion of progress. Since then, with the exception of the 1980s, Islamists have accepted taking the good aspects of European civilization. Today, the JDP combines these two important themes (progress/development and justice) by naming their party as justice and development. This leads us to think that the JDP transforms the Turkish Islamist political experience by dropping the claim of establishing an Islamic state (change aspect) but still embraces some of the basic concepts of Islamism such as justice, progress, and (Islamic) civilization (continuity aspect). The JDP seems to use modernization and Europeanization as interchangeable by leaving the Islamist differentiation between these two. But at the same time, it combines modern (democratic) and conservative/local (Islamic) values to create a new synthesis. The platform for this synthesis is the idea of Islamic civilization, covered by the concept of conservative democracy. Interestingly, the idea of civilization serves two different purposes: values of Islam to be conserved and Western/European values to be emulated. The JDP's discourse on Islamic civilization is a soft version that does not essentialize the categories of Islam and the West and that considers Islam as not monolithic in political and cultural terms.

Conservative democracy represents a departure from the Islamism of the NOM. The JDP differs from the Welfare Party (WP), for example, in its understanding of politics. As Menderes Çınar states, the Welfare Party had, similar to the Kemalist outlook, an "anti-political grammar that asserts the primacy of culture in development/modernization and that sees society as a homogenous entity and as an object of government only."[23] The JDP, by recognizing the plural structure of Turkish society, advanced an inclusionary and compromising political style: "while the WP downplayed the undemocratic nature of state society relationship by concentrating on its secularist substance, the JDP primarily emphasizes the institutional setup of Turkish politics and problematizes the top-down or 'bureaucratic-statist' structures."[24] Conservative democracy, in a sense, is an answer to the ideological clash between Islamism and secularism. Although it is not declared as such, it could claim to resolve all the tensions of Turkish politics (global and local; secular and Islamic; Turkish and Kurdish). Erdoğan has often declared "politics to be an art of solving problems, but not creating them" to decrease the tensions generated by the ideological fault lines of Turkey, namely Islamism and Kurdish nationalism. But this time through foreign policy, the internal dilemmas and contradictions that Turkey has long struggled to reconcile have now become internationalized and Europeanized. At this point, the crucial question is whether the JDP can contribute to the transformation/democratization of the political culture of the Turkish elite. It is obvious that the interelite consensus (between state and political elite) is a sine qua non of a consolidated democratic rule in Turkey. One of the tasks to be accomplished is getting rid of the qualitative shrinkage of the political sphere in the February 28 Process. Apart from the EU harmonization process, it is difficult to say that the JDP has successfully triggered political debates over the sensitive issues of identity politics. Its attempts to discuss the issues of religious education and freedoms in the public sphere have been futile and have been retarded by the absence of objectives as bases for conciliation and integration—which is, after all, what politics is all about. Furthermore, the JDP's political identity, conservative democracy, is not theorized properly in order to resolve the tensions of identity politics in Turkey. The label of conservative democracy is a vague concept, and for the time being it is not possible to see a political adherence to this new political identity at the level of party members, even in the ranks of the party organization. Rather, the idea of conservative democracy seems to be an academic label, created by political advisors for the intellectual satisfaction of public opinion.

Perceptions of foreign policy and international relations have always been one of the most contested fields for Islamism, not only in Turkey in particular but also in the Muslim world in general. Perhaps the most significant aspect of transformation for Turkish Islamism has been related to the fields of foreign policy and international politics. Contrary to the Third World tendencies of the NOM's foreign policy,[25] the JDP's outlook is premised on the belief that isolation from globalization and Europeanization could lead to a deep political crisis in Turkey.

FOREIGN POLICY AND CONSERVATIVE DEMOCRACY:
A NEW DISCOURSE OF CIVILIZATION

The JDP's nonconfrontational and consensus-seeking approach in domestic politics has its equivalent in foreign policy as well. The JDP is aware that adopting anti-Western and antiglobalist discourses and policies would eradicate the possibility of transforming Turkish domestic politics. Erdoğan openly and consistently makes it clear that his party is committed to the pro-Western orientation of Turkish foreign policy. Unlike Islamism, the JDP's conception of foreign policy/international relations has not been shaped by a confrontation with the West. It is premised on the conviction of a possible harmony between Islamic civilization and the West. The JDP has distanced itself from those discourses and relations that the party thinks gave the NOM a "Third Worldist" and anti-Western perspective.[26] The WP vision of international politics was based to some extent on the conflictual and essential distinction between Islam and the West. Necmettin Erbakan's various statements on different occasions were dependent on "a perception of the West as colonial, unjust, oppressive and, ultimately, Christian."[27] As opposed to Erbakan, who visited Libya, Iran, and other Muslim countries immediately after he became prime minister, Erdoğan's first visit abroad was to Greece, and later he also toured the Western capitals. Erbakan established a D-8 (Developing Eight) group in June 1997 by bringing together the leading Muslim countries (Turkey, Iran, Egypt, Bangladesh, Indonesia, Malaysia, Nigeria, and Pakistan). In contrast to his confrontational style, Erdoğan has expressed an opposition to the idea of forming an Islamic economic bloc.[28] But this opposition does not imply that the JDP would not develop Turkey's relations with Islamic countries or would not have a desire to modify the nature of the close relations between Turkey and Israel. The JDP prefers to use existing institutions like the Organization of the Islamic Conference (OIC) to advance cooperation between the Muslim world and the West. The meetings of EU-OIC are an example of this new style of foreign policy. As a part of its strategy to interrelate the European dimension with the Islamic world, the JDP government places special importance on the second meeting that brings together the foreign ministers of the EU with those of the OIC. Although the initiator of this attempt (the first meeting was held on February 13, 2002) is the Democratic Left Party's foreign minister, İsmail Cem, it is obvious that the recent emphasis on civilizational discourse in Turkish foreign policy is parallel to the JDP's stance.[29]

The JDP's new outlook and mission in foreign policy are spoken very clearly by Abdullah Gül in this way: "We were to prove that a Muslim society is capable of changing and renovating itself, attaining contemporary standards, while preserving its values, traditions and identity." Very similar to the Islamist discourse of civilization in late Ottoman times, the JDP sees the modern values of democracy, human rights, rule of law, transparency, and accountability as the universal values shared by humanity: "These values are "universal" because no one can claim monopoly over humanistic values that are the common inheritance of civilisation. Islam has made highly significant contributions to this common civilisation."[30] The concept of Islamic civilization is employed by some Orientalists to show the irreconcilable features of Islamic and Western civilizations and to show how different (both ontologically and epistemologically) they are.[31] But the JDP's usage of the concept is directed to the creation of a platform that would integrate Turkey with Europe and that would increase Turkey's significance in the world: "With its own stable and successful model of development, its place in the Western world and its rich historical legacy and identity, Turkey will be a symbol of the harmony of cultures and civilizations in the twenty-first century."[32] In relation to the Islamic world, this conceptualization serves the task of creating self-confidence by underlining the common spiritual heritage of peace, harmony, tolerance, and affection among Muslims as they adopt Western values and institutions: democracy, good governance, transparency, and accountability. The main argument of legitimization follows in this way: "Civilizations have a lot to gain from inter-acting with each other."[33] In other words, democracy, human rights, rule of law, and good governance are "the product of the collective wisdom derived from different civilizations."[34] In this way, the JDP's instrumentalization of the concept of (Islamic) civilization seems to contribute to the transformation in the definitions of Europe in different Islamist circles. The JDP does not extend its logic in using the concept of civilizational dialogue to this level, claiming that the European civilization might more accurately be designated as "Abrahamic" than as "Judeo-Christian." Certainly this kind of argument would weaken the party's hand by disturbing secularist circles both in the Union and in Turkey.[35]

The JDP leaders believe that a compromise between Islam and democracy would bring peace to the world by reducing the tensions between Western and Muslim countries. It is clear that the party's conservative democracy, in comparison to other Islamic movements in the Muslim world, has the chance of achieving such a compromise between Islam and democracy. Abdullah Gül stressed the need for Muslim countries to democratize and pay greater attention to human and women's rights in his address to the Organization of the Islamic Conference summit in Tehran in May 2003. The party enjoys a rather supportive conjuncture of world politics in which many circles in the United States and Europe believe that if democracy is to be successfully fostered across the Muslim world, it is vital to encourage the Turkish secular democracy.[36]

The events of September 11, 2001 are seen by some as evidence of a growing polarization between Islamic civilization and Western civilization and a realization of Huntington's prophesy of "clash of civilizations." The post–September 11 era constitutes a rather suitable conjuncture for the JDP's new political identity, conservative democracy. At a time when tensions between Muslims and the West are rising and with the region full of the United States' "rogue states" like Iran and Syria, the JDP's foreign policy, which seems determined to address serious problems in a peaceful manner, could contribute much to the stability of world politics. As the discussion on the exemplary role of the Turkish model for the Muslim world shows, Turkey's relevance to the United States and Europe will depend more on its identity and less on its military capabilities.[37] Even if Turkey's secular experience has not been shared by other Muslim states, its current democratic experiment is an example from which Muslims could draw some lessons.

Foreign policy and the calculation of national interest, which are directly related to how the world and the West are seen, have been significant aspects that Islamists have challenged in the Kemalist ideology. Relations with the West had been the main domain of contestation between pro-Western Kemalists and anti-Western Islamists. However, now that the latter have modified their perception of the world, interestingly this change has created a fertile ground for developing new discourses to call for transformation in both domestic and international politics. The JDP has been redefining the notion of national interest that is the main source of legitimation in Turkish foreign policy, by depicting the Western orientation in foreign policy as complementary, not as a substitution for relations with other regions.[38] This conception of national interest seems contrary to what was perceived by either secularists or Islamists in the past. This new definition is an attempt to empower Turkey through a combination of the Western orientation of foreign policy with Turkish society's cultural and historical ties to Muslim countries. The JDP's approach, in a sense, goes beyond the identity problems of Turkish politics. This new understanding is strengthened by the recognition that in a globalized world it is no longer possible to be in isolation and that it is better to see foreign relations in terms of interdependence. After describing the direction of transformation in the JDP's approach to foreign policy, it is time to look at the implementation of foreign policy under the JDP government.

TURKISH FOREIGN POLICY UNDER JDP RULE: ASSERTIVE, MULTILATERAL, AND EUROPEAN

The JDP's new discourse of foreign policy, in general, seems to be committed to the main tenets of Turkish foreign policy: the desire to join the EU, to enhance relations with the United States, and to increase regional cooperation. The JDP also admits the basic conviction of recent Turkish foreign policy: the end of the cold war has not only enhanced Turkey's strategic importance to Europe and the United States, but has also freed it to pursue a more assertive and independent foreign policy within its region.[39] In this way, Mustafa Kemal Atatürk's famous principle of "peace at home and peace in the world" is employed by the JDP to legitimize a more assertive foreign policy. This principle had been interpreted by foreign policy makers, until recent times, to support a cautious and inward-looking policy while adhering to the international status quo. In the words of Gül, the foreign minister, the JDP's assertive policy focuses on diplomacy and multilateralism, as far as possible, to promote Turkish national interests in regions from the Middle East to Europe: "Turkey actively advocates a particular security and foreign policy approach that is based on the culture of compromise and win-win solutions to complex problems."[40] As seen during the Iraq war in 2003, the basic tool of its assertiveness is the diplomatic initiative, not the use of force. Just before the war, the JDP government organized a meeting in Istanbul of the Turkish, Iranian, Egyptian, Jordanian, Saudi, and Syrian foreign ministers, to explore ways of preventing the war in Iraq and to develop a common understanding for the future of Iraq. The JDP government continues to convene meetings of representatives from countries bordering Iraq on a periodic basis. The basic aim of these meetings is to underline the territorial integrity of Iraq as a priority in the six states' foreign policy objectives. The vision of this regional initiative is said to be based on "peaceful co-existence and the indivisible nature of regional stability." At the meeting with Kuwait, Gül gave European integration as a successful example that the regional countries need to draw lessons from to create their own "multilateral framework for cooperation and security."[41] Furthermore, the JDP's policy toward Cyprus is another example of the assertive foreign policy. Turkey under Erdoğan rule backed a UN referendum on the reunification of Cyprus, held in the spring of 2004 against the wishes of hard-line nationalists. The consequences of Turkish Cypriots' vote of "yes" and Greek Cypriots' vote of "no" have contributed much to the prestige of the JDP's activist and nontraditional foreign policy in the eyes of the EU and the United States. However, this activist policy has not produced enough responses from the United States and Europe to end the isolation of northern Cyprus from international society.

The Turkish foreign policy in the post-Helsinki period is colored by the belief that the only way in which Turkey can face the challenges of the twenty-first century is by establishing a balance of relations between the United States and Europe. Similarly, the JDP's foreign policy has to find a delicate balance between the United States and Europe. In fact, because of post–cold war realities, "Washington must recognize that Turkey will play an increasingly strong role in the Middle East but along lines designed to serve Turkish national interests...Turkey's national interests are changing to strengthen Turkey's regional and EU ties and to lessen the centrality of the US role."[42] However, this is not an easy task to deal with. For instance, in the Iraq war, the JDP oscillated between keeping strategic relations with the United States and Europeanizing its foreign policy. Indeed, in the Iraq war the JDP government has taken a rather vague stance that was accused of not being able to develop its own approach to foreign policy and of adaptation to the traditional "securitization-oriented policy."[43] The JDP's way of managing in the Iraq war was criticized as being "based on saving the day, rather than being grounded on carefully-crafted, and well-formulated conceptualization of Turkish foreign policy."[44] Saban Kardaş also points out how the JDP government reproduced "the dominant authoritarian-hegemonic discourse" by placing it at the core of their foreign and domestic policies. The JDP's vague stance is explained by Ahmet Davutoğlu as a conscious and determined attempt at multidimensional diplomacy to keep all different alternatives alive. The JDP discussed the United States' demands while consulting with the EU and keeping contact with the groups in Iraq. If Turkey had let U.S. soldiers pass through Turkish territory, relations between Turkey and the EU would have had to be repaired. The JDP knew that it was not possible to prevent the war, but still there were many things to do: a search for a peaceful solution to the Iraq crisis, including the regional meetings of Iraq's neighbors, an effort to decrease war damages in Turkey and the region.[45] These meetings are indicative of the JDP's willingness to act as a mediator in regional or global disputes. Fortunately, the consequences of this vague policy have strengthened the JDP's international prestige without undermining its support bases in domestic politics. The failure in the passage of the resolution has been praised in the majority of European capitals and in the Arab world. However, the JDP's Iraq policy has not been able to satisfy the traditional tensions of Turkish foreign policy (red lines) toward Kurdish political autonomy in Northern Iraq and the existence of the PKK (the Kurdistan Workers' Party) in this area, especially after the Second Gulf War.

The election of a Turkish candidate, Ekmeleddin İhsanoğlu, as secretary general of the OIC could be read as a sign of the growing prestige of the JDP and its activist foreign policy toward Middle Eastern and Muslim countries. The party's leadership wants to make the Turkish elite aware of Turkey's historical, cultural, and strategic potential in shaping foreign policy. Its historical and cultural background assigns it an importance incomparable to that of any other regional powers. The correct evaluation of Turkey's potential is of crucial importance.[46] The party's activism is also directed toward imbuing Turkish foreign policy with a sense of genuine self-confidence and empowerment in relations with other countries. The JDP aims to turn the uncertain security environment around Turkey's borders into a field of peace, stability, and prosperity. The attainment of compromise among the different interests of its neighbors is of key value. This new policy brought about a significant improvement in Turkish-Syrian relations, as reflected in Syrian president Bashar Al-Assad's visit to Turkey in January 2004. The JDP also tries to review Turkey's relations with neighbors and regional alliances in the Middle East; for example the changing nature of relations with Israel. The JDP is sure that this new style of foreign policy will strengthen Turkey's regional and global importance.[47]

The JDP's multidimensional foreign policy aims to move Turkey beyond being a bridge between East and West and to turn it into a point of convergence. The JDP's foreign policy, as Davutoğlu, chief advisor to the prime minister and foreign minister, explains, is premised on the basic conviction that Turkey is not a bridge but a central country (*merkez ülke*). Turkish foreign policy should be based on five interdependent principles: (1) democratization without risking security and stability (broadening the sphere of freedoms and strengthening domestic political legitimacy); (2) good relations (zero problem) with neighbors; (3) proactive, multidimensional, and complementary policies; (4) a new diplomatic style (self-confidence); and (5) transition from static diplomacy to rhythmic one (to increase the influence of Turkey in international organizations to become a global power).[48] At this point, one may argue that the party's foreign policy makers appear to exaggerate Turkey's geopolitical position and its cultural and historical connections, that the JDP's aim of turning Turkey from a regional power into a global power seems to be too ambitious. However, up until now, the JDP's multidimensional foreign policy has not contradicted the basic contours of Turkish foreign relations (pro-Western orientation). Still, we have to wait for the possible outcomes of the JDP's new foreign policy perspective.

One of the fundamental features of Turkish modernization and foreign policy has been its Western orientation.[49] Turkey's European orientation is a cornerstone of the JDP's foreign policy. For the JDP, Turkey's EU membership and its strategic partnership with the United States are complementary. But the nature of this relationship is Europeanized. Gül redefines the basis of the strategic partnership by creating a synthesis between the United States and the EU in a European way: "Our bonds with the United States are based on certain values: *democracy, rule of law and market economy.*"[50] As a sign of Europeanization, the JDP "managed to stay out of Iraq and shied away from using 'Hobbesian' or confrontational means of foreign policy, in contrast to the Turkish policy of a few years back. A good example of Turkish foreign policy evolving towards a more 'Kantian' or 'Europeanized' approach to foreign policy is the manner in which the crisis of Turkey's veto over the use of NATO capabilities for European security force operations was finally resolved in November 2001."[51]

While in the past Turkish foreign policy had focused on the importance of military security and balance of power politics, "it now increasingly appreciates the value of civilian instruments of law, economics and diplomacy, as well as of multilateral settings in which to pursue its aims. Related to this, the Turkish example demonstrates the value of European integration as a key external anchor to domestic processes of modernisation."[52]

Europeanization can decisively affect many core areas of national policies and national identities, such as those related to foreign and security policy. Europeanization can act in a dynamic way that shows that "agent and context can be co-determining."[53] Spain constitutes an important example of the fact that Europeanization is a two-way street: "once Europeanization pressures enter the domestic realm, if they resonate with the identities of national actors, they can lead to the institutionalization of national interests at the European level and a strengthening of European foreign policy capacity which may be difficult to reverse if domestic conditions change and different actors with different identities come to power."[54] The JDP's will to be a part of the EU also has an ambitious agenda. Through Europeanization it expects not only a process of convergence on foreign policy but also a remarkable degree of policy transfer from Turkey to the EU. Europeanization of foreign policy has been apparent, at least at the level of legitimizing its critical preferences such as the changing relations with Israel. After Israeli security forces assassinated the Hamas leader Sheikh Yassin, Turkey withdrew its ambassador from Tel Aviv for consultations, and Erdoğan accused Israel of "state terrorism": "Israel is not contributing to the peace process, is killing women and children indiscriminately and destroying Palestinian houses, and there is no way to describe such actions except as state terrorism."[55] Upon reactions to his harsh language, Erdoğan said, "Our attitude is in line with the E.U.'s."[56]

True to their commitment to the multidimensional approach, the policy makers of the JDP aim to export parts of Turkey's own foreign policy agenda to the EU on areas such as the Middle East, Central Asia, and the Muslim world in which the EU has some important interests of its own.[57] For example, in the case of the Islamic world, the JDP is inclined to use the EU to increase the international status of Turkey as spokesman for the Muslim world both within and outside the Union. Turkish membership in the EU would substantially strengthen the Middle Eastern profile of European foreign policy. Europeanization will have a qualitative influence on Turkish foreign policies vis-à-vis the Middle East, the Muslim world, human rights, and promotion of democracy. Turkey's membership would send a strong message about the compatibility of liberal democracy with Islam, and of the multireligious inclusiveness of the Union, thus denouncing the idea of the "clash of civilizations."[58]

The JDP has also taken the lead in consolidating European norms and values in Turkey through the EU's legal system. Europeanization has come to mean a promoter of transformation in the domestic political structure: domestic is European.

DOMESTIC IS EUROPEAN: EU AS A PROMOTER OF TRANSFORMATION

Europeanization has been a significant source of transformation in Turkey since the times of the Tanzimat. At various times, European politics have forced Ottoman statesmen or the Republican elite to take reformist steps. Similar to the proclamation of constitutional rule in 1876, the EU membership process has been strengthening human rights, rule of law, and civil society, especially in the post-Helsinki period.[59] This time, the transformational effects of Europe should be seen not just in the reforms of the Westernist elite but also in the level of desires (integration with the EU) of societal groups, including Islamists (once strong Euro-skeptics). Ironically, the hard-liner Kemalists have become pro–status quo and Euro-skeptic while the ex-Islamists have become reformist and Euro-philia to Europeanize the country. What is more ironical is that like the Islamists of the Second Constitutional period, today's Islamist circles demand what Europe urges Turkey to do by means of the requirements of the Copenhagen criteria. The implication of the EU accession process is that transformation is a multifaceted phenomenon whose time has come for Turkey. But at the same time, the idea of transformation has generated a significant amount of discomfort among the state elite: "the instinctive reactions and fears of the laicist elite in the face of the JDP and the political stance that it represents have their source mainly in the anx-iety of losing a hegemonic position; they reflect a certain kind of class position"[60]

Yavuz argues that Turgut Özal's economic liberalism "created an assortment of new 'opportunity spaces'—social sites and vehicles for activism and the dissemination of meaning, identity, and cultural codes."[61] Following this line of thinking, one may further claim that the JDP's pro-European foreign policy would broaden the framework of these opportunity spaces, which has been narrowed through the Febru-ary 28 Process. In fact, many Islamists see the EU as an open political arena where different religious groups can assert their identities with-out any oppression.[62] On the issue of an alternative option to the EU, Islamist writer Fehmi Koru insists that the Westernization process has eradicated any possibility of "an Eastern option" for Turkey and that today the West is closer to being "the contemporary civilization" than yesterday when the Kemalists attributed universality to Europe and it is not reasonable to oppose the European freedoms and rule of law on the grounds of "national interest."[63] The Copenhagen criteria, which call for the broadening of individual and liberal freedoms and for the lessening of state intervention into cultural identities and beliefs, were in conflict with the criteria of the February 28 Process. Furthermore, transformation of Islamist discourses toward Europe epitomizes the dilemma that the achievement of "reaching at the level of contemporary civilization" would particularize the Kemalist discourse on modernization. What is more problematic here about Kemalism is that its hegemonic position over the definition of modernity, which is equated with Europeanization, could be challenged by a reference to its source of aspiration: Europe. Similar to Kemalist "orientalization"[64] of Islam in the 1920s, Islamists point to the gap between the standards of the European secularism/democracy and the Kemalist conception of secularism. Kemalism is seen in terms of a lack: the absence of European secularism and the absence of European human rights. Hence, the process of Turkey's integration, like globalization, "forces Kemalism to confront the possibility that it is but one particularistic group amongst many in contemporary Turkey."[65]

The EU accession process necessitates the consolidation of Turkish democracy in accordance with the Copenhagen criteria, while empowering the JDP's legitimacy in transforming the political system: "Europe's insistence on not starting negotiations without significant progress towards these criteria allows the JDP to tackle some of the more controversial aspects of state-society relations in Turkey, including the role of religion, the military's intrusive nature, and the Kurdish minority question."[66] The repercussions of the ongoing transformation are far-reaching; as Ahmet İnsel expresses it, the JDP "has undertaken the mission of ending the September 12 regime whether it likes it or not."[67] The JDP confronts the domestic resistance coming from nationalist circles by calling the EU membership process the fulfillment of Turkish modernization. It is also certain that in the process of Turkey's integration with the EU, the domestic issues of identity politics, such as the headscarf, religious education, and the Kurdish language, will move beyond the Turkish national agenda. The EU harmonization process involves a number of issues on which the military, in particular, is highly sensitive. It is obvious that to achieve entry into the EU, significant changes have to be made in the way in which Turkey is ruled and in how it conducts its domestic, regional, and international affairs. Through this opportunity space, the JDP has been trying to transform Turkish domestic and foreign policy.

Turkey's accession process represents a fruitful example for the transformational effects of Europeanization on the domestic actors of new members as well. The JDP's strategy of turning the EU accession process into an amplifier of its political program enables it to transform both the Kemalist state structure and Islamist circles and demands. Islamic identities have to be redefined in relation to the European social, cultural, and political environments. In particular, a commitment to the idea of secularism in the EU would oblige us to discuss the similarities and differences between Western and Islamic cultural/religious practices. Islamists will have to bring their religious views to the democratic dialogue in order to be effective in persuading European public opinion and they will have to develop democratic discourses to integrate their religious demands in ways that resonate with people who do not share Islam. Turkey's integration in the EU could deconstruct the Islamist imagination of the West as a monolithic entity opposed to Islam. Turkey's membership will provide a fertile ground for the elimination of the stereotypes about Islam and European civilization: Islam as a violent and fatalist religion; the imperialism of Christian Europe and its moral decay.[68]

The JDP leadership has realized that having a democratic and European agenda would open a new path for transforming Turkish domestic politics. Turkish politics is involved in a struggle to implement the reforms made in the process of the JDP candidacy, with significant implications for the future restructuring of the political system. It is obvious that the supranational nature of the EU generates "new opportunities to exit from domestic constraints, either to promote certain policies or to veto others, or to secure informational advantage."[69] The notion of an internal threat is losing its significance in defining domestic politics, and many reforms are introduced regarding the sensitive issues of Turkish politics. These issues are no longer regarded as internal problems emanating from Turkey's unique position in the region or its domestic problems. The JDP promises to consolidate the Turkish democracy in an effort not just for the sake of meeting the Copenhagen criteria, but to make the country a liberal democracy with all of its basic principles and institutions in place. That is to say that the Copenhagen criteria will be internalized and implemented as the Ankara criteria. The adoption of European norms and institutions is an incentive especially for Turkey, which continues the process of democratic consolidation.[70] In other words, the EU influence on Turkey is "an important factor in the dual processes of political harmonization and domestic democratization."[71] Not only domestic policies need to be changed to conform to European-wide norms, but also the institutional structure needs restructuring.

Since the times of Tanzimat, Europeanization has weakened the capability of the Turkish elite to withstand pressures from European powers on the conduct of its domestic political life. The JDP leadership acknowledges the idea that in the context of the EU accession process, democratization and human rights issues cannot be regarded as domestic affairs. This position contradicts the Kemalist stance that oscillates between the liberal position and the nationalist position that denounces external interference in domestic issues.[72] Clearing up any nationalistic concern on outside interference, the JDP has a strong political will to embrace EU norms on democracy and human rights. "We are fully aware that it is in Turkey's own interest to proceed with the reforms. This will work to the will and benefit of our people. The reform process in Turkey is not complete; however it is already irreversible."[73] The JDP denounces the perception that these reforms are taken as a concession to the EU and does not mind that these reforms are externally imposed, because the leaders think that the desire of reform is the reflection of Turkish society's expectations. This is the rationale behind their declaration that the Copenhagen criteria are the Ankara criteria. Cemil Çicek, the minister of justice, refers to the EU harmonization process as "a quiet law revolution" and "a second revolution in the field of law and justice following the foundation of the Republic."[74]

Now it is time to discuss the domestic implications of the JDP's agenda of transformation and of its EU-dominated foreign policy.

CONCLUSION: FAILURES AND SUCCESSES OF NEW POLITICS

It is clear that international conjuncture strengthens the JDP's position regarding the reforms of domestic politics. The JDP, as a single-party government, also has the advantage of working in harmony to implement the economic stability program and the political reforms necessary for meeting the Copenhagen criteria. It is true that the JDP has taken the lead in consolidating European norms and values in Turkey through the EU legal system. The harmonization packages reduced the military's autonomy by limiting its role in the National Security Council and by putting military expenditures under parliamentary scrutiny.[75] These packages have also allowed broadcasting in Kurdish dialects. Moreover, the JDP government has passed laws on public administration and local governments to restructure public services in accordance with the new public administration techniques. These laws relegate some of the powers of the central government to local administrative entities.

In spite of the remarkable reforms in the EU harmonization process, the JDP's performance in managing the opportunity spaces to enlarge freedoms about identity issues should be questioned. One of the most critical challenges for the JDP leadership is how to handle the domestic tensions over the sensitive and symbolic issues of Turkish secularism (headscarf issue, İmam Hatip schools) while shaping foreign policy according to its own outlook. The JDP has so far avoided antagonizing the secularists on these sensitive issues. However, the JDP's consensual style (waiting until a "broad social consensus" is reached) is not successful in managing the issues of Islamic demands (headscarf and İmam Hatips). Its new political style has not produced a compromise on the sensitive issues of the Republic either, although the JDP has emphasized that they will seek consensus with the opposition parties and civil society institutions before introducing any major policy. In a very short time, it became obvious that achieving consensus is easier said than done. In spite of the wide consensus of the public on the need for restructuring the system, the government, which is entitled to reform, is under constant suspicion. The burden of this suspicion necessitates smooth management of tensions while pushing reforms in the political system. On the one hand, on several occasions, the military, President Ahmet Necdet Sezer, the RPP (Republican People's Party), and some elements of civil bureucracy have underlined their determination to protect the secular nature of the Republic against any Islamist change. Again, the president has often vetoed laws enacted by the JDP-dominated Parliament on the grounds that they violated the secular foundations of the Republic. On the other hand, the JDP is far from meeting the expectations of Islamic conservative circles. The party's hesitant style about the reforms of education and the Council of Higher Education (YÖK), and its inertia in solving the problem of headscarves, are interpreted by some Islamist circles as a psychology of being restricted (*kısıtlılık psikolojisi*). According to Ahmet Taşgetiren, a columnist in the Islamist daily *Yeni Şafak*, the JDP government acts as if it is under supervision while being so vulnerable to the accusations of *takiyye* (hidden intentions). The EU harmonization reforms are exceptions to this but still the negative psychology of JDP power creates a public conviction that it is only possible to reform the system with the help of external dynamics and that the value of the national will is limited in this respect.[76] For the time being, the party is not able to meet Islamic expectations on the issues of religious education and headscarves but at the same time it could bring new definitions to "conservative values" (religiosity and unity of family). The JDP's intention in presenting the bills on YÖK and religious education and later their withdrawal seems to be twofold: first to show its Islamist constituency that it is not possible to achieve their demands at this time, and second to reduce resistance to policies that accord legitimacy to religious considerations in public life by putting forth proposals one after another.[77]

In conclusion, the JDP's new politics still have to confront the political tensions regarding headscarves, religious education, and Kurdish cultural rights while transforming the domestic political structure through the EU legal system. Its success in this respect is highly dependent on its ability to facilitate agreement and to prevent excessive conflict and fragmentation over sensitive issues. One may argue that the need for transformation (integration with the EU) forces the JDP to take a post-Kemalist stand. As a reflection of the JDP's both reformist and conservative political agenda, it tries to reach a post-Kemalist stage at which the basic ideals of Kemalism such as Europeanization and secularism would be fulfilled through integration with the EU while the Kemalist fears about the divisive effects of identity politics are being calmed down. In the context of the EU accession process and globalization, the primary challenge of the JDP's foreign policy is to redefine the Turkish national identity. In this respect, the JDP has to enrich its political discourse of conservative democracy to integrate the demands of identity politics (Kurdish and Islamic identities) into the Turkish national identity. Conservative democracy is still a vague concept and it is not theorized yet to meet the demands of identity politics in Turkey.

NOTES

1. Şerif Mardin, "AKP'nin İktidarda Olması Kemalizmin bir Başarısı Sayılmalıdır," *Vatan*, September 30, 2003.

2. See Hasan Kösebalaban, "Turkey's EU membership: A Clash of Security Cultures," *Middle East Policy* 9 (2002): 131–42.

3. Ali L. Karaosmanoğlu, "The Evolution of the National Security Culture and the Military in Turkey," *Journal of International Affairs* 54 (Fall 2000): 215.

4. Recep Tayyip Erdoğan, "European Union Should Be About Values, Not Borders," *NPQ* 20 (Spring 2003): 58–59.

5. *Turkish Daily News*, January 16, 2004. Prodi said the reform performance under Erdoğan's government was remarkable, calling him one of the three greatest leaders of Turkey. These leaders are Kemal Atatürk, Turgut Özal, and Tayyip Erdoğan.

6. For the transformation of Turkish foreign policy, see Kemal Kirişçi, "Between Europe and the Middle East: The Transformation of Turkish Policy," *MERIA* 8 (March 2004): 39–51.

7. Nilüfer Göle, "AKP hem Kendi Dönüşüyor Hem Türkiye'yi Dönüştürüyor," *Vatan*, October 1, 2003.

8. Kirişçi, "Between Europe and the Middle East," 48.

9. "To make religion an instrument of politics and to adopt exclusive approaches to politics in the name of religion harms not only political pluralism, but also religion itself. Religion is a sacred and collective value. It should not be made the subject of political partisanship causing divisiveness." Yalçın Akdoğan, *Muhafazakar Demokrasi* (Ankara: AK Parti, 2003).

10. Metin Heper and Şule Toktaş, "Islam, Modernity, and Democracy in Contemporary Turkey: The Case of Recep Tayyip Erdoğan," *Muslim World* 93 (April 2003): 157–85; Ruşen Çakır and Fehmi Çalmuk, *Recep Tayyip Erdoğan: Bir Dönüşüm Öyküsü* (Istanbul: Metis, 2001).

11. See Burhanettin Duran, "Islamist Redefinition(s) of European and Islamic Identities in Turkey," in *Turkey and European Integration: Accession Prospects and Issues*, ed. Mehmet Uğur and Nergis Canefe (London: Routledge, 2004), 125–46; İhsan D. Dağı, "Rethinking Human Rights, Democracy, and the West: Post-Islamist Intellectuals in Turkey," *Critique: Critical Middle Eastern Studies* 13 (Summer 2004): 135–51.

12. M. Hakan Yavuz, "Cleansing Islam from the Public Sphere and the February 28 Process," *Journal of International Affairs* 54 (Fall 2000): 21–42.

13. Duran, "Islamist Redefinition(s)," 125–46; Heiko Henkel, "Rethinking the dar al-harb: Social Change and Changing Perceptions of the West in Turkish Islam," *Journal of Ethnic and Migration Studies* 30 (2004): 961–77.

14. Owen Matthews and Carla Power, "Europe Stumbles; By Rights, the EU Should Celebrating. Instead, It's Ensnarled in Debate Over Turkey and Its Own Identity," *Newsweek*, December 2, 2002, 19.

15. Ziya Öniş and E. Fuat Keyman, "Turkey at the Polls: A New Path Emerges," *Journal of Democracy* 14 (April 2003): 102.

16. Murat Belge, "Devrimci Muhafazakarlar," *Radikal*, January 23, 2004.

17. Gareth Jenkins, "Muslim Democrats in Turkey?" *Survival* 45 (Spring 2003): 45–66.

18. Olivier Roy, "AKP Hristiyan Demokratlarla Aynı Saflarda Yer Alıyor," *Vatan*, October 5, 2003; John Esposito, "Beyond the Headlines: Changing Perceptions of Islamic Movements," *Harvard International Review* 25 (Summer 2003): 18.

19. Liberal Islamist interpretation denies that the idea of an Islamic leviathan is supported by the Qur'an and the Sunnah. It argues that only a small part of Islamic teaching deals with state affairs while the overwhelming majority of the ethical codes directly address people's experience of religion and personal conduct of faith. Bülent Gökay, "Turkey in Europe or Europe in Turkey?" December 10, 2002, http://www.ejil. org/forum/messages/655.html.

20. Yalçın Akdoğan, interview, "Merkezde Din Yok," *Tercüman*, August 18, 2003.

21. Ömer Çaha, "Turkish Election of November 2002 and the Rise of 'Moderate' Political Islam," *Alternatives: Turkish Journal of International Relations* 2 (Spring 2003): 108.

22. While capitalism and socialism put the emphasis on the principles of freedom and equality respectively, Islamic political literature underlines the principle of justice. İbrahim Erol Kozak, *İnsan Toplum İktisat*, 2nd ed. (Istanbul: Değişim, 1999), 243.

23. Menderes Çınar, "The Justice and Development Party in Turkey," http://www. networkideas.org/themes/world/jan2003/print/prnt290103_Turkey.htm.

24. Çınar, "The Justice and Development Party."

25. Necmettin Erbakan accused the JDP of being part of the foreign plot designed for dividing the Welfare Party. In his opinion, the JDP government has taken the country away to the Second Sevres. "Erbakan'dan AKP Tarifi," *Vatan*, September 25, 2003.

26. For the division of the NOM into two political parties and the ideological transformation of Yenilikçiler (Reformists) within the Virtue Party, see R. Quinn Mecham, "From the Ashes of Virtue, A Promise of Light: The Transformation of Political Islam in Turkey," *Third World Quarterly* 25 (2004): 339–58.

27. Yavuz, "Cleansing Islam from the Public Sphere," 21–42.

28. *Turkish Daily News*, January 20, 2004.

29. The idea that Turkey stands at the meeting point of civilizations has become common in the mouths of Turkish politicians in the post-Helsinki era.

30. Abdullah Gül, *OIC Business Forum During the 10th OIC Summit Meeting in Malaysia*, October 15, 2003, http://www.abdullahgul.gen.tr/EN/Main.asp.

31. Bernard Lewis, *Islam and the West* (Oxford, UK: Oxford University Press, 1993).

32. Recep Tayyip Erdoğan, "Conservative Democracy and the Globalisation of Freedom," at the American Enterprise Institute, January 29, 2004, www.akparti.org.tr.

33. Abdullah Gül, *30th Session of the Islamic Conference of Foreign Ministers Tehran*, May 28, 2003; *The Islamic Conference Of Foreign Ministers at The Thirty-First Session Istanbul*, June 14, 2004, http://www.abdullahgul.gen.tr/EN/Main.asp.

34. Erdoğan, "Conservative Democracy and the Globalisation of Freedom," 2004.

35. The latter term excludes Islam from the values that Jews and Christians are presumed to share. It can be easily argued that Islam shares with Judaism and Christianity a long common history and many of the same religious beliefs and cultural orientations; see Antony T. Sullivan, "The West, Mediterranean Islam and the Search for a New Beginning," *Middle East Policy* 7(October 1999): 38–49. Sullivan argues that the West does not stop at the Bosporus, but in Indus.

36. For example, according to Graham E. Fuller, Turkey's newer model under the JDP rule is much better for Turkey and the world. This new model is "based on serious utilization of democratic process; a willingness to act not just as a Western power but as an Eastern power as well; a greater exercise of national sovereignty supported by the people; a greater independence of action that no longer clings insecurely to the United States or any other power in implementing its foreign policies; considerable progress toward the solution of a burning internal ethnic minority (the Kurdish) issue; and a demonstrated capability to resolve the leading challenge to the Muslim world today: the management and political integration of Islam." "Turkey's Strategic Model: Myths and Realities," *Washington Quarterly* 27, no. 3(Summer 2004): 51.

37. H. Tarık Oğuzlu, "Changing Dynamics of Turkey's U.S. and EU Relations," *Middle East Policy* 11(Spring 2004): 98–105.

38. Adalet ve Kalkınma Partisi, 1. *Olağan Büyük Kongresi, Genel Başkan Recep Tayyip Erdoğan' in Konuşması*, Ankara, AK Parti, October 12, 2003, 77.

39. See Malik Mufti, "Daring and Caution in Turkish Foreign Policy," *Middle East Journal* 52 (Winter 1998): 32–50.

40. Abdullah Gül, "Turkey's Foreign Policy and the NATO Istanbul Summit," *Turkey Bulletin* (Summer 2004): 13.

41. Abdullah Gül, *At the Regional Countries' Meeting on Iraq, Kuwait*, February 14, 2004, http://www.abdullahgul.gen.tr/EN/Main.asp.

42. Fuller, "Turkey's Strategic Model," 63.

43. Saban Kardaş, "On AKP, Turkey, and Iraq: Critical Investigations into the Debate on Turkish Contribution to Stability Force in Iraq," *Turkish Daily News*, October 2–4, 2003.

44. Kardaş, "On AKP, Turkey, and Iraq."

45. Ahmet Davutoğlu, "Türkiye Merkez Ülke Olmalı," *Radikal*, February 26, 2004.

46. For a new paradigm for the Turkish foreign policy, see Ahmet Davutoğlu, *Stratejik Derinlik* (Istanbul: Küre Yayınları, 2001).

47. See Recep Tayyip Erdoğan, *Konuşmalar: Yeni Siyasetimiz* (Ankara: Ak Parti, 2004), 47–48.

48. Davutoğlu, 2004. The multiregional activism of Turkish foreign policy in the post–cold war era, especially in the Özal era, is sometimes called Neo-Ottomanism. Although the JDP envisions a major role for Turkey in the regions of the Middle East, the Caucasus and Central Asia, the Balkans, and Europe, its international outlook goes beyond the Neo-Ottomanist model. For different depictions of Neo-Ottomanism in Turkish foreign policy, see M. Hakan Yavuz, "Turkish Identity and Foreign Policy in Flux: The Rise of Neo-Ottomanism," *Critique* (Spring 1998): 19–41; Stephanos Constantinides, "Turkey: The Emergence of a New Foreign Policy, the Neo-Ottoman Imperial Model," *Journal of Political and Military Sociology* 24 (Winter 1996): 323–34.

49. Mustafa Aydın, "Determinants of Turkish Foreign Policy: Historical Framework and Traditional Inputs," *Middle Eastern Studies* 35 (October 1999): 152–86.

50. Italics are mine; see Abdullah Gül, Luncheon given by the American-Turkish Society, New York, September 22, 2003, http://www.abdullahgul.gen.tr/EN/Main.asp.

51. Kirişçi, "Between Europe and the Middle East," 48.

52. Michael Emerson and Nathalie Tocci, "Integrating EU and Turkish Foreign Policy," *Turkey in Europe Monitor* 7 (July 2004): 7, http://www.ceps.be/files/TurkeyM/TMonitor7.pdf.

53. José I. Torreblanca, "Ideas, Preferences and Institutions: Explaining the Europeanization of Spanish Foreign Policy," *ARENA*, UNED University and Juan March Institute, May 29, 2001, http://www.arena.uio.no/publications/wp01_26.htm

54. Ibid.

55. *Radikal*, May 21, 2004.

56. Christopher Caldwell, "The Turkey Paradox," *Weekly Standard* 9 (July 26, 2004).

57. Gül in his speech argued that the EU membership is not the only perspective in Turkish foreign policy. Turkey should try to develop an effective policy in other regions as well. He gave Spain as an exemplary country that transferred its national interests in Latin America to the EU; "Geçmişten günümüze Türkiye—AB ilişkileri," November–December 2000, http://www.abdullahgul.gen.tr/EN/Main.asp.

58. There is a widely shared argument in Turkish public opinion that rejection of Turkey by the EU would provoke domestic conflicts in Turkey and a backlash in the wider Muslim world and would increase the risk of a "clash of civilizations." See the several statements of Prime Minister Erdoğan and articles of columnists from daily newspapers; Hasan Cemal "Şimdi Sıra AB'de!" *Milliyet*, June 16, 2004.

59. EU membership has been a central goal of Turkish foreign and domestic policy since 1963. Since 1987, this goal took the form of aspiring to become a full member of the EC/EU. It is also in many ways now closer than ever to fulfillment, since the EU decided at the Helsinki summit of 1999 to place Turkey on the list of countries that were up for candidacy and since the Copenhagen summit of December 2003 concluded that if the European Council in December 2004, on the basis of a report and a recom-

mendation from the Commission, decides that Turkey fulfils the Copenhagen political criteria, the EU will open negotiations without delay.

60. Ahmet İnsel, "The AKP and Normalizing Democracy in Turkey," *South Atlantic Quarterly* 102, nos. 2–3 (Spring/Summer 2003): 299.

61. A major product of these new opportunity spaces is the empowerment of society-centered Islamic movements, rather than state-centered groups; M. Hakan Yavuz, "Opportunity Spaces, Identity, and Islamic Meaning in Turkey," in *Islamic Activism: A Social Movement Approach*, ed. Quintan Wiktorowicz (Bloomington: Indiana University Press, 2003), 385.

62. Yavuz, "Cleansing Islam from the Public Sphere."

63. Fehmi Koru, "Biraz Daha Açıklık Lûtfen," *Yeni Şafak*, March 9, 2002.

64. Boby S. Sayyid, *A Fundamental Fear: Eurocentrism and the Emergence of Islamism* (London: Zed Books, 1997), 270–71.

65. Chris Rumford, "Placing Democratization within the Global Frame: Sociological Approaches to Universalism, and Democratic Contestation in Contemporary Turkey," *Sociological Review* 50 (2002): 259.

66. Henri Barkey, "Cyprus between Ankara and a Hard Place," *Brown Journal of World Affairs* 10 (Summer/Fall 2003): 233.

67. İnsel, "The AKP and Normalizing Democracy," 301.

68. For a critique of the supposed centrality of Islam in European identity formation, see Paul Rich, "European Identity and the Myth of Islam: A Reassessment," *Review of International Studies* 25 (1999): 435–51.

69. Klaus Goetz and Simon Hix cited in Jeffrey J. Anderson, "Europeanization and the Transformation of the Democratic Polity, 1945–2000," *Journal of Common Market Studies* 40 (2002): 796.

70. However, the EU is criticized for its "democratic deficit" (executive dominance and disempowerment of parliaments) in the member states on the basis that the Europeanization of national decision-making undermines the horizontal and vertical balance of powers in favor of the executive for ensuring the democratic legitimacy of domestic politics; see Tanja A. Börzel and Carina Sprungk, "Undermining Democratic Governance in the Member States? The Europeanization of National Decision-Making," http://www.boerzel.uni-hd.de/forschung/docs/boerzel_sprungk_2003.pdf; for the need on democratization of the EU, see Philippe C. Schmitter, "Democracy in Europe and Europe's Democratization," *Journal of Democracy* 14 (October 2003): 71–85.

71. Chris Rumford, "Human Rights and Democratization in Turkey in the Context of EU Candidature," *Journal of European Area Studies* 9 (2001): 97.

72. Rumford, "Human Rights and Democratization," 100. He further argues that it is possible "to have Kurdish cultural autonomy and territorial integrity, or pluralist political representation and secularism breaks with the rigid form of binary thinking that characterizes Kemalism and curtails the democratic potential of contemporary Turkey," 103.

73. Abdullah Gül, *At the Symposium "Turkey and The EU-Looking Beyond Prejudice" Maastricht*, April 4–5, 2004, http://www.abdullahgul.gen.tr/EN/Main.asp.

74. Cemil Çicek, "Legal Reforms in the EU Process," *Turkey Bulletin* (Summer 2004): 24.

75. The decrease in the military's political role is not sufficient to establish civilian control over the military. In order to attain this control, "the military's autonomous intelligence and surveillance functions, and jurisdiction over crimes against internal security and terrorism," should be abolished; Ümit Cizre Sakallıoğlu, "The Military and Politics: A Turkish Dilemma," in *Armed Forces in the Middle East*, ed. Barry Rubin and Thomas A. Keaney (London: Frank Cass, 2002), 190.

76. Ahmet Taşgetiren, "Kısıtlılık Psikolojisi," *Yeni Şafak*, August 23, 2004.

77. İlter Turan, "The Justice and Development Party: The First Year In Power," TÜSİAD-US website, www.tusiad.us.

CHAPTER 13

Turkey and the Iraqi Crisis

JDP Between Identity and Interest

■ *Saban Kardas*

INTRODUCTION

Turkey's inability to successfully conclude the negotiations with the United States on the eve of the Iraq war, highlighted by Parliament's refusal of a governmental motion on March 1, 2003, was one of the hallmarks of Turkish foreign policy during this period. The resulting limited Turkish cooperation with the United States fell short of fully living up to American expectations for opening a northern front through the territory of a long-standing partner. This situation increasingly pitted the two close allies against each other, throwing serious doubts on the viability and future of the so-called strategic partnership, supposedly reinvigorated in the post-9/11 era. This situation even led many to question Turkey's place in the Western camp.[1] For one, Turkey has found itself in a situation whereby the rapid pace of events has eroded many of the priorities underpinning its policy toward Iraq and the region. Turkey's growing disappointment with this state of affairs was further exacerbated when it realized that it was in no position to take decisive action to affect developments, a position directly connected to its lukewarm relations with the United States—hence its gradual exclusion from the political processes shaping the future of Iraq and the region in the aftermath of the war. As a result, a great deal of Turkey's subsequent efforts has been spent on repairing the damage caused by this foreign policy failure.

It is hard to reach a definite judgment on why and how Turkey got to this point and what actor(s) was responsible for this state of affairs. There is still a great deal of controversy over the making of Turkish foreign policy during that period. Beyond understanding the peculiar conditions of Turkish foreign policy during the period under consideration, a critical examination of this particular case will help us comprehend the possible transformation of Turkish foreign policy under the JDP, which in turn is essential for adequately understanding the JDP's role in Turkish politics. Perhaps nowhere is this need more visible than in the question about the main foreign policy orientation of the JDP government(s).

The JDP's managing of the relations with the United States in the context of the war and its interaction with the establishment created a critical case for putting the government's foreign policy orientation to the test. The major questions addressed in this chapter are the following: What drives the JDP's foreign policy understanding: identity or interest? Is there a JDP security vision on foreign policy, as distinct from that of the secular establishment? Is there a unified JDP approach to foreign policy, or could one identify contending views within the party?

To this end, I first investigate the JDP's formulation of Turkey's policy during the crisis, its framing of cooperation or discord with the United States, and the language its leadership used to that effect. In this analysis, I treat JDP leadership as a monolithic entity, comparing it with the foreign policy establishment represented by the military-civilian bureaucracy. By comparing its leadership's strategic language with that of Turkey's security and foreign policy elite, we could better account for the dynamic interaction between continuities and changes and between identity and interest in Turkish foreign policy. Then, I intend to make inroads into the black box of the JDP, by highlighting competing tendencies within the party regarding foreign policy.

I argue that, on a *rhetorical* level, JDP leadership employed a discourse that dismissed an ideological-ideational approach to foreign policy and prioritized the country's national interests, paying due attention to material and practical considerations. Moreover, they operated from a mindset similar to that of the establishment with regard to the definition of the crisis, specification of the country's national interests, and formulation of the policy. The differences between the JDP leadership and the establishment, to the extent that they existed, were more in the details than in the substance of the policy. As a result, the official policy was based on two pillars: cooperation out of necessity and unilateral intervention. Yet, the JDP's failure to materialize this policy highlighted *actual* dynamics that existed within the party. On that count, I argue that the JDP is far from having a unified foreign policy vision. Two layers of divisions interact in the party: within the leadership itself, and within the party group. I argue that these divisions are largely managed by the strong leadership of Recep Tayyip Erdoğan, and by the prospects for European Union membership. The eclectic identity of the JDP is suppressed by these two strong influences, and the making of Turkish foreign policy toward the region, as in many other domestic and foreign issues, has been harmonized with the contingencies arising from the country's integration process with the EU.

JDP's Foreign Policy: Escape from Identity?

Despite the party's claims to the contrary, the leadership's Islamist credentials have stimulated interest in the possible course they might adopt in foreign policy. However, to the dismay of skeptics, the JDP leadership seemed determined to follow a policy that is heavily pro-Western. What is more, the leadership even went so far as to denounce vocally any resemblance of Islamism.[2] Their concern to convince the skeptics of the ideological transformation that they had gone through led to an overtly pro-Western outlook on the part of the leadership.[3] In more practical terms, in an attempt to bolster its position vis-à-vis other power centers within the country and to strengthen internal legitimacy, besides accelerating the integration process into the EU, the leadership laid a particular stress on maintaining, and when possible deepening, friendly relations with the United States, for a more receptive attitude toward the United States might have been seen as a proof of the JDP's overcoming of its Islamist past. Because gaining "American endorsement" had been viewed as one of the unwritten rules of governing Turkey, the JDP leadership took pains to establish close contacts with the Bush administration. At the same time, the leadership endeavored to deepen Turkey's economic and political connections with the countries in its own Muslim neighborhood. This policy was rationalized more on the basis of such material and practical concerns as enhancing regional cooperation and following a multidimensional foreign policy than on immediate ideational motivations. Even in this case, there was a visible attempt to deemphasize identity as a reference point in Turkey's foreign relations. Nonetheless, the ongoing tensions in the region inevitably affected almost all facets of Turkey's external relations and domestic politics, causing great worry for the new JDP leadership and confronting it with an enormous challenge.

Turkey and the Iraqi Crisis

The crisis had been at Turkey's door long before the JDP came to power. Turkey's encounter with it can be traced back to late 2001, if not to the immediate aftermath of the 9/11 incident. Because of the crisis of government and opposition of the then government to a possible war, the Turkish political elite avoided facing the reality head on, failing to make bold decisions and to implement a comprehensive policy on Iraq. This situation, however, did not prevent contacts between Turkish and American politicians or between civilian and military delegations to discuss Turkey's possible contribution to American war plans. Turkish military and foreign ministry officials evaluated likely scenarios about the future of Iraq in the event of a war, laid down Turkey's "red lines," and proposed several policy options about Turkey's cooperation with the United States.[4] In the meantime, the Ecevit government bowed to American pressures and accepted some of the American demands. In close coordination with the bureaucracy, the government authorized the initiation of a process for working out the actual details of Turkey's role in the war. Because of the upcoming elections, the government did not take resolute action, which would have provided the bureaucracy with a clear mandate to put into practice the proposals they had brought before the government. The period between the establishment of the new JDP government and its taking full control over Turkish politics partly contributed to Turkey's delay in taking a clear stance on Iraq.

Shortly after the JDP's election victory, the Bush administration started pressuring the new government to offer Turkey's full support. Because the JDP leadership had taken an overtly pro-American stance in the meantime, optimism was prevalent among American politicians about Turkey's collaboration. Delighted with the election results, specific American demands from Turkey were conveyed by the Bush administration to Turkish politicians even before the new government was fully formed. As a result, the new government had to sit at the negotiation table and bargain over the conditions of Turkey's participation in the warring coalition.

TURKEY'S IRAQ POLICY: AVERT THE WAR

The same set of concerns that had shaped Turkish policy toward Iraq since the first Gulf War continued to determine the calculations of Turkish actors in this case as well. In that sense one could discern a strong continuity in the main principles of Turkish policy. This continuity at the same time suggested that the lessons learned from the experience of almost unconditional support for the United States in 1991, and the subsequent negative consequences on Turkey of the war, had continuously hovered in the background. To a large extent, the JDP leadership adopted these same basic parameters and operated from a mindset similar to that of the establishment. There was almost no questioning of the country's so-called "red lines" on Iraq, formulated earlier during the Ecevit government in collaboration with the bureaucracy. The JDP leadership continued to approach the problem from the same perspective, focusing exclusively on the security challenges and economic hardships to be caused by the war on Iraq.

CAUTION OVER DARING

Faced with the American determination to go to war, Turkish policy makers evaluated whether the war was in Turkey's interest, or whether Turkey's policies coincided with American plans. Although there were some hawkish views that the opportunity of the war could be seized to boost Turkey's role in the region, such as reclaiming Turkish rights over Mosul and Kirkuk, overall the policy actors reacted to this development negatively. Those arguing that the crisis presented opportunities to be reaped "if Turkey could think and act strategically" remained a minority view, and Turkish policy makers were extremely cautious not to give the appearance of pursuing a selfish agenda in Iraq even when they were simultaneously engaged in negotiations with the United States.[5]

Turkish policy makers perceived the upcoming crisis as creating more troubles than opening up opportunities; therefore they maintained Turkey's traditional status quo–oriented foreign policy and avoided revisionism. Domestic, regional, and international conditions, which were unfavorable to actively assisting the American agenda in Iraq, further augmented Turkey's placing caution over daring. The dominant mood in Turkey was to make every attempt to find a peaceful solution to the crisis in order to evade war because the war would affect the country's national interests negatively. In more specific terms, the major concerns that shaped the thinking of Turkish policy makers could be briefly discussed as follows.

The first cluster of factors is mainly security related, stemming from Turkey's greatest headache, the Kurdish problem. The indeterminate status of Northern Iraq posed several challenges to Turkey's national security. The authority vacuum there had led the separatist Kurdistan Workers' Party, using the region as a rear base, to conduct terrorist activities inside Turkish territory. Countering this threat was one of the priorities of Turkey throughout the 1990s. Another by-product of the situation in Northern Iraq had been the embryonic Kurdish state that gradually took shape within the de facto autonomous region. The eventual emergence of an independent Kurdistan had been one of the nightmare scenarios for Turkey.[6] One could also note a newfound issue, the Turkish concern to protect the rights of Turkomans in Northern Iraq. Turkey was worried that the Kurds might dominate the politics of Northern Iraq in the post-Saddam era and that they could establish full control over this oil-rich region. In this sense, strengthening the role of Turkomans was seen to be in the interest of Turkey, as a stronger role would counterbalance the power of the Kurds in the region. However, needless to say, the Turks would have preferred the continuation of the status quo—if not the restoration of Baghdad's full control in the region—over setting sail to an uncertain war, likely to shake the political and geographical map of the region.[7] That by default put Turkey and the United States at odds with each other.

The second set of factors concern the economy. The first Gulf War and the subsequent sanctions dealt a great loss to Turkey. In many instances Turkish governments had been lobbying for the phasing out of UN sanctions and trying to enhance relations with Iraq to compensate for Turkey's economic losses. Most of these attempts were met with American criticism. As in the security-related concerns, whereas Turkey's stakes lay in the normalization of economic relations with the Baghdad regime and the reinstating of its authority over the country, the United States insisted on its policy. Because it was assumed that war in the region would severely affect the Turkish economy and undermine Turkey's attempts to boost trade with the Middle East, economic considerations heightened Turkey's desire to prevent the war.

COMING TO TERMS WITH REALITY

Although Turkish policy makers had these concerns, the U.S. determination to carry war plans through, however, made it difficult for Turkey to escape the war. Moreover, because of its critical position in American war plans, there was no way that Turkey could isolate itself from the discussions on war. Last but not least, its long-standing alliance with and dependence on the United States perforce made total disengagement extremely difficult. Consequently, the American diplomatic blitz to get Turkey on board made the no-war option practically obsolete. Thus it became necessary for Turkish decision makers to come to terms with the reality that they needed to cooperate with the United States in one way or another, and to develop a justification for this policy.

Pillar I: Cooperation Out of Necessity

From this perspective, cooperation with the United States emerged as the inevitable option available to Turkey. The argument was constructed as follows: Turkey's economic and security-related concerns necessitated that it do its utmost to avoid a war. If the war was going to happen irrespective of its objections, Turkey then would need solid economic and political guarantees to minimize damage. Turkish policy makers were confronted with the unwanted situation of reluctant cooperation with the United States. They calculated that in the worst-case scenario of an unavoidable war, they could preserve the country's national interests and compensate for economic losses best only through cooperating with the United States in order "to sit at the negotiation table" in the aftermath of the war.[8]

Because the Turks had learned the lessons of cooperating with the United States the hard way, this time they did not want to commit the same mistakes that they had in 1991. Therefore they avoided offering support to the coalition without receiving complementary concessions and written guarantees on issues of importance to Turkey. Moreover, it is also the case that Turkish decision makers interpreted this instance as a unique opportunity to settle the score from the first Gulf War, especially in economic terms, which partly explains excessive Turkish demands—hence the tough Turkish bargaining strategy, which was interpreted as horse-trading by many outside observers and President Bush.

Pillar II: Unilateral Intervention

The second pillar of this strategy was to guarantee Turkey's right and ability to act unilaterally and, when necessary, independently of the warring coalition to protect its interests in Iraq. In more concrete terms, this policy first meant that Turkey would be in a position to take military action to prevent the Northern Iraqi Kurds from controlling Mosul and Kirkuk and driving toward independence. Second, the policy was understood as Turkey's maintaining of its own military presence in Northern Iraq and deploying additional military forces to fight against the Kurdistan Workers' Party formations there.[9]

This twin-pillar policy was reflected in the content of the governmental motion put before Parliament on March 1, 2003: stationing and transfer of American forces in Turkey en route to Iraq, and deployment of Turkish forces abroad. The two pillars of the policy also constituted much of the basic line of thinking in the Turkish debate on the war. Although some actors had different opinions on the first pillar, there was a broad consensus on, if not obsession with, the idea of Turkey's right to unilateral intervention.[10] Ensuring American acquiescence to Turkey's right to intervene in Northern Iraq constituted the iron rule of Turkish national interests, as almost all major actors agreed on the necessity and rightfulness of this action. However to the extent that it was essential for Turkey, these demands led to delays in diplomatic negotiations as Turkey's concerns were not compatible with American calculations. American resistance to the Turkish presence in Northern Iraq angered Turkish policy makers, including Prime Minister Abdullah Gül, because they perceived it as the only policy instrument to protect Turkey's interests. On many occasions they expressed their discomfort with what they called "reducing Turkey to a Gulf sheikhdom," or Qatar, meaning that Turkey's role could not be limited to providing bases, and Turkey could not be treated as a minor player. On both scores the government adopted the official line of thinking. Therefore, as the war became inevitable, cooperation with the United States and securing Turkey's right to unilateral intervention became the basis of the country's policy.

Double-edged Diplomacy

Implementing this policy, however, confronted the government with the difficult task of selling the idea to domestic and international constituents. When the no-war option was not viable, and Turkey had to come to terms with taking part in the coalition's war plans, the government was confronted with the challenge of striking the right balance between the demands of domestic and international constituencies on the one hand, and protecting the country's national interests while paying due attention to the contingencies of the relationship with the United States on the other. Given the extremely dismissive conditions, Turkey's collaboration with the United States was seen as choosing the lesser evil. Not only the negotiations with the United States, but also selling the deal to constituencies at home became challenging issues.

Both domestically and internationally, the government then embarked on a campaign based on a dual language. On the domestic front, publicly, it underlined its commitment to international legitimacy, and expressed its political and moral discomfort with the possible conflict in a neighboring country. On the other hand, it had to resort to *realpolitik* arguments, justifying Turkey's support as a last-resort measure in the face of an inevitable war even if the war was lacking in international legitimacy and was troubling from a moral perspective. On the international front, the government initiated the bargaining negotiations with the United States to acquire sufficient guarantees to compensate for Turkey's strategic, political, and economic losses from a possible war. At the same time, it embarked on several diplomatic initiatives to clarify its position on Iraq to the international community, especially the countries in its region. In particular, it took pains to convince them of the nonaggressive, precautionary nature of the demands it put forward in its negotiations with the United States.

Part of this policy was to harmonize Turkey's position with the requirements of the EU process. Given the troubled course of transatlantic relations, it was a delicate balancing act. The JDP government also engaged in regional diplomacy, which basically served two purposes: to find a peaceful solution to the crisis, and to present Turkey's activities in the event of an unavoidable war as defensive in nature. For a long time Gül sincerely believed that Turkey could play a constructive role in preventing the war. Thus initially the former aspect of this policy was more prevalent than the latter. This was at least the case until his last attempts to convince Saddam to comply with American demands failed in early February 2003. Then the latter concern became more pronounced in Turkey's regional diplomacy.

MARCH I

Gül's failure to avert the war through a peaceful solution at the regional level removed much of the rationale behind resisting American demands. In the meantime, the chances for preventing the war through global pressures on the United States and Iraq had been weakened, further constraining Turkey's options. These developments undermined whatever opposition the government had to the two-pillar policy developed by the civilian-military bureaucracy. The negotiations with the United States, a joint project between the government and the civilian-military bureaucracy, on economic and political/strategic issues were conducted simultaneously. These attempts eventually paid off and Turkey received most of the concessions it demanded from the United States to secure its interests.[11]

The government, however, could not repeat the same success in seeking domestic ratification for its international deal. Its inability to materialize the two-pillar policy despite the seeming consensus between the JDP leadership and the country's foreign policy establishment raises questions about intra-JDP divisions. Indeed, the case of the March 1 vote was where the frictions between the JDP leadership and its constituency and organization, as well as within JDP leadership, came into play. I discuss these issues in the next section.

OPENING THE BLACK BOX OF THE JDP

The JDP's track record during the Iraqi crisis is of valuable help in understanding how the tension between identity and interest was resolved by the new leadership, for it was a case in which the country's relationship with both Islamic and Western worlds was at stake. The JDP leadership avoided using a language reminiscent of an ideological or ideational approach to foreign policy in its dealings with both the United States and regional countries during this period. On the contrary, the arguments used to justify Turkey's policy were the reflection of a strategic understanding that heavily prioritized practical concerns and the country's national interests.

This period in Turkish foreign policy implies a substantial shift away from the policies of the JDP's predecessors, who under Necmettin Erbakan's leadership did not refrain from toying with the traditional foreign policy orientation of the republican Turkey, confronting the international power centers, and pursuing a more identity-oriented approach in their relationship with the countries in the Middle East. During the period under consideration here, it is striking to observe the high degree of similarity in the language used between the JDP leadership and the military-civilian bureaucracy and other political parties, including the previous government. There was no viable attempt stemming from the leadership's identity to advocate different definitions of Turkey's national interests and to suggest different ways of perceiving the substance and limits of Turkey's collaboration with the American agenda in Iraq. The JDP leadership adapted to the established strategic culture and to foreign policy habits and perceptions of the country. As a result, the "government policy" formulated by JDP governments reflected "state policy," represented by the bureaucracy.

This conclusion, however, needs to be qualified. The JDP's delicate balancing act was eased by the nature of the crisis and by the way the secular establishment viewed Turkey's collaboration with the United States. The overlap in the end results, namely avoiding full support of the American-led coalition, brought together diverse political actors. Because the internal and external environments confronted Turkish policy actors with extremely unfavorable conditions for Turkey's support for the United States, there was a broad resistance against the government's declared policy. Even if one assumes that they in fact acted out of ideological concerns, operating under those conditions, the JDP leadership did not need any overt ideological reasoning to justify their initial opposition to American demands because there was a wide range of practical reasons available to make a case for opposing the war, and the JDP was not alone in advocating this course of action. Therefore, the JDP's approach resonated well with that of the secular establishment, which removed any need for employing an ideological language.

The difference between the JDP leadership and the establishment, to the extent that it existed, was more in the details than in the substance of the policy. If there was a unique JDP stamp on Turkey's policy during this period, it could be said that it was the regional diplomacy formulated by the main figure on Gül's own foreign policy team, Ahmet Davutoğlu. Gül advocated this idea initially at a mini-summit at the president's residence on December 18, 2002. To convince the foreign ministry about the plan, he utilized the president's sympathy with the idea of international legitimacy and consensus.[12] This was indeed a good example of how the JDP utilized the available practical justifications shared by—and the cleavages within—the establishment to garner support for its antiwar position without resorting to an identity-based justification. Once the government agreed to cooperate with the coalition, a similar difference between Gül and the civilian-military bureaucracy emerged about the concrete steps to be taken in materializing the plan for lending support to the United States. Whereas the bureaucracy argued for a package deal to finalize all aspects of Turkey's collaboration with the coalition in one single governmental motion, Gül preferred a gradual, step-by-step approach to negotiate each specific Turkish contribution separately, hence maximize compensation.[13]

Gül's "salami tactic," taken together with the government's insistence on regional diplomacy, hardened Turkey's position. Gül used this opportunity to buy more time for his efforts for a peaceful solution, while at the same time continuing to bargain. Because it came at a time when quick and decisive action was necessary, Gül's policy contributed to delays in making resolute decisions. This lingering, coupled with the government's slow pace in lobbying for the motion within the JDP party group, made the civilian-military bureaucracy more anxious. Therefore the foreign policy establishment had to push the government to bring the matter before Parliament, though the prime minister himself was not confident about the likely support from the MPs of his own party for the motion.[14] Indeed, these "state institutions" acted as the major promoters of the two-pillar policy. The bureaucracy had made their position clear, and when they realized that the government was slow in responding to developments, they prompted the government to initiate legal processes and make necessary political decisions.[15] The pushes from the military were an important signal to end Gül's insistence on peaceful solution and forced him to turn to military options. Only after that did the negotiations between Turkey and the United States really start.

INTRA-JDP DIVISIONS

With his reluctant attitude Gül was in conflict not only with the military-civilian bureaucracy, but also to a certain extent with party leader Erdoğan. Such disagreements highlighted the underlying divisions and the patchy nature of the party and its leadership structure and their effect on foreign policy making. The problematic nature of Turkey's collaboration with the United States was aggravated by the JDP's inner troubles and controversial identity. In this section I will look at two layers of divisions that have haunted the JDP. First, I will examine top party leadership and the diverging perspectives of Erdoğan and Gül. Then I will move on to discuss the broad lines of friction within the party.

Top Leadership

Because Erdoğan had been banned from politics, he was not able to run in the November 2002 elections. Before his political rights were fully restored, the party had undergone a process of double leadership: the party leader vs. prime minister, which hindered effective control over party members. Gül and Erdoğan were two of the three leading founders of the JDP, and there were speculations about a rivalry between the two. Although they avoided confronting each other openly, and these speculations never materialized, there definitely appeared "a difference of style," if not difference of policy, between the two figures. Their different approaches were also related to their foreign policy advisors.

Erdoğan has been surrounded by more pragmatically oriented people, acting out of *realpolitik* concerns. These people included Cüneyt Zapsu, Egemen Bağış, and Ömer Çelik. For them, assuring American support was essential in order for the JDP to attain control over the establishment and competing sources of power within the country. Moreover, they felt that in foreign policy, the best course of action for Turkey was to ally with, if not bandwagon, the single global hegemon. Furthermore, they appeared to support American discourse about the war on terror and the promotion of democracy in the Middle East. They advocated a position that was based on Turkey's providing support to American war plans. Their personal connections added to the critical role played by these people. They had established close contacts with key figures within the Bush administration, such as Paul Wolfowitz, who promoted the idea of a northern front in Washington's war plans. Therefore, Erdoğan's advisory team acted like a transmission belt between Turkey and the United States, and most of the American efforts to garner Turkish cooperation were carried out through these people. Their lobbying came to be interpreted as strong signs of Turkish support for the war. Domestically, however, Erdoğan's advisers' commitment to American plans was interpreted as "American advice and threats through Erdoğan's advisers."[16] Coupled with their unpopularity within the party, their attitude turned many swing MPs to the antiwar coalition.

Gül has been aided and counseled by people who are more academically and ideologically oriented. His chief advisor was Professor Ahmet Davutoğlu, known for his extensive work on international relations, Turkish foreign policy, Islamic thought, and clash of civilization.[17] Davutoğlu has a clear civilizational approach to international relations. He is concerned with the economic, technologic, military, and political backwardness of the Islamic world. He attempts to help revitalize Islamic civilization in the age of globalization, and to spread Islam's message through a change in mentality. Although Davutoğlu does not reject the Western orientation of the country, in his notion of multidimensionality he reintroduces Turkey's Middle Eastern, Asian, and most importantly Islamic identity. He complements this notion with his emphasis on Turkey's geographical depth, historical background, and cultural heritage.

In Davutoğlu's understanding, there is little difference between Istanbul, Sarajevo, Grozny, or Baghdad for they belong to the same geopolitical and civilizational map, that is, the Islamic world in general and the Ottoman cultural zone in particular. He harbors no sense of ethnic nationalism but adheres to a form of Islamic internationalism. In his writings, Turkey's fate and story are very much integrated into the trajectory of the Islamic world. Turkey has to overcome the dilemmas resulting from the incompatibility between its political boundaries—being confined to a nation state—and its geocultural and historical breadth—its imperial legacy. To overcome the contradictions in its identity and reformulate it under the pressure of globalization, Turkey needs to participate in the globalization process as an active agent, drawing on its own geographical, historical, and cultural depth, and fertilizing Western modernity with the Ottoman-Islamic civilizational heritage.

Translating these ideas into the foreign policy realm, he argues for abandoning the traditional status quo–oriented approaches and pursuing a more proactive and dynamic foreign policy agenda. Thus, in his reading, Turkey emerges as a central country destined to lead in its cultural and geographical reach. Because of this depth, Turkey cannot be seen as an ordinary nation-state that is a product of conjectural conditions, such as other countries in its region. Therefore, Turkey has the potential to affect and be affected by what is happening in its surrounding regions. Through his rebuff of static foreign policy and emphases on Turkey's geostrategic importance and historical legacy, he rejects an isolated peripheral role for Turkey and aims at restoring its central state status on the East-West, North-South axes. As such, he also criticizes the unidimensionality of traditional Turkish foreign policy and calls for a multidimensional approach that can eventually transform Turkish political culture and fit it to the country's cultural and historical realities.

After the formation of the first JDP government, Davutoğlu was appointed as the top foreign policy advisor to the prime minister. He has been considered as the person behind Gül's Iraq and Cyprus policies. As he made clear in his several statements and interviews, Davutoğlu viewed the Iraq crisis from his grand scheme of international politics and Turkey's international position.[18] In his understanding, the reason why Turkey found itself at the center of the discussions about Iraq was the very same geographical and historical depth that it was not able to escape. Because of its unique role and historical responsibilities in the region, Turkey could not remain aloof to the developments in its proximate land basin of the Middle East. In his view, when Turkey did act in the crisis, it had to avoid acting in a way that would undermine its central position and relegate itself to a peripheral role. Turkey had to develop its own vision as an active agent. Moreover, Turkey had to refrain from prioritizing one axis of its foreign relations over others. Rather, Turkey had to calculate the implications of its Iraq policy on other dimensions of its foreign policy, and maintain its relations with other regions and powers in line with its own vision about Iraq. Most important, this implied that Turkey need not isolate itself from its own civilizational context. Moreover, for him Turkey's support for the coalition was also a stark choice between endangering relations with the United States versus undermining the relations with the European Union. Since the latter appeared to be more important than the former on the JDP's foreign policy agenda, he was inclined to tilt the balance toward the European Union at the expense of the United States. As a result, not surprisingly, he was opposed to Turkey's support for the American-led coalition and has defended Parliament's rejection of the March 1 motion on several occasions.[19]

Fed with these opposing intellectual streams of pragmatism and moralism, Erdoğan and Gül developed different reflexes throughout the crisis. These differences were further strengthened by their own personal approaches to politics. Cengiz Çandar's remarks capture the differences between the two leaders cogently: "Erdoğan is much more of a pragmatic person than Abdullah Gül...The elite think Gül is a soft-spoken man and Erdoğan is a wild man. But they are mistaken in that Gül is more doctrinaire and Erdoğan is much more concerned with the dictates of realpolitik."[20] As a result, whereas Erdoğan seemed more eager to incorporate Turkey in American war plans, Gül favored a more cautious approach.

Throughout the crisis, the making of Turkish foreign policy was dominated by Erdoğan or Gül at different periods. The courtship between Erdoğan's team and the Bush administration put its stamp on the first phase of the contacts, as was reflected in Wolfowitz and Marc Grossmann's visit to Ankara and Erdoğan's visit to Washington. This close relationship heightened the expectations from Turkey of the Bush administration. American "miscalculations" by overutilizing this channel to get quick results, however, backfired, as it caused irritation on the part of not only the government but also the military-civilian bureaucracy. Erdoğan afterwards maintained a lower profile, leaving the scene to Gül. Despite earlier offers of a cooperative attitude, the Gül government slowed down the process, by delaying the work of the American advance engineering teams and launching Gül's Middle East initiative. This lingering was the reason behind Bush's letter dated December 20, 2002, which Gül likened to Johnson's letter. The Americans had a hard time figuring out why, after a prelude of clear signs of cooperation, the Turkish side had adopted a reserved approach. The Turks started to raise new demands, avoided clear pledges, and postponed making decisions.[21] As the delay in war plans made the Bush administration impatient, its diplomatic pressure on Turkey accelerated and turned aggressive and threatening.

As "the American bullying" on Turkey through several public ultimatums mounted, and as Gül could not extract any results from his attempts, many started to grow worried about the course of Turkish foreign policy and about how to protect Turkey's strategic priorities in Iraq.

After the failure of Gül's last-ditch effort on February 3, 2003, Erdoğan moved in to put the train back on the track. On February 4, he addressed the JDP party group and warned against the dangers of being left out of the equation. This strong intervention prompted Gül to announce that Turkey would act along with the United States to protect the country's national interests.[22] Then the Gül government "hit the button" and finally initiated the legal process for receiving authorization from the Turkish Grand National Assembly.

In the run-up to the vote, Erdoğan and Gül started a campaign to convince JDP lawmakers of the necessity of cooperation with the United States. Although both Erdoğan and Gül utilized the arguments that constituted the basis of the twin-pillar policy, differences between the two leaders' style persisted. In his addresses to JDP lawmakers, Erdoğan did not refrain from underlining the country's economic weakness and dependence on external support, and from resorting to a pro-American discourse. For instance, before the parliamentary vote on the modernization motion, after telling JDP MPs that no one could defy the United States, he added, "Think rationally. Don't let yourself be deceived by the RPP-opposition party. Look at Iran, Libya, and Sudan. They have oil, but challenged the United States. What happened? Some countries and some circles are talking about Turkey as 'the leader of the Islamic world.' Don't make a fool of yourself."[23] Oftentimes he appeared to be telling the deputies what to do. Such statements, coupled with his advisers' highly war-prone attitude and speeches, generated resentment among the JDP constituency and led to a backlash.

Gül, on the other hand, never took such a clear stance. When he forwarded different motions to the parliament, he never pressured the members of his cabinet and the MPs. Rather, he preferred persuasion, which became part of his delaying strategy. He kept underlining that the prospects for a peaceful solution still existed and that the motions were never meant to declare a war. In implementing his delaying tactic, he argued that with these steps the government was buying time for a peaceful solution. Gül always postponed facing the reality head on and never confronted the gradually mounting inner-party opposition until the parliamentary vote on March 1, 2003. Because Erdoğan was going to replace Gül anyway, it could also be the case that this inner-party division played a further role. Gül did not exert pressure on the MPs before the vote in order to leave the final decision to the incoming Erdoğan government as the sole entity responsible for Turkey's involvement in war. As a result, some Turkish commentators interpreted the March motion as a reflection of the lack of unifying leadership and the underlying clash between pro-Gül and pro-Erdoğan groupings within the party.[24]

Frictions within the JDP

The broad divisions within the JDP leadership were paralleled by the eclectic nature of the party. The JDP was a newly established party, with no experience in governing the country. Nonetheless most of the founding figures had been involved in active politics in different forms. The party was founded by a group of politicians coming from the reformist wing of the National Outlook Movement (NOM), who were able to form a broad coalition out of a diverse body of politicians. The latter group ranged from liberal voices to conservative, nationalist, and Kurdish constituencies. Many people within this group had been influential political figures, particularly in center-right political parties. Because of the core party leadership's past in Islamic-oriented political parties, however, they were by definition not part of the establishment. Perhaps the realm of foreign policy presents the best example of this fact. Whereas many founders of the JDP and its predecessors had served in several governmental positions, foreign policy bureaucracy had preserved its elitist nature over decades.

It was this lack of experienced figures that led to the appointment as the foreign minister of an "outsider," Yaşar Yakış, a retired career diplomat, who had happened to join the party right before the elections. He favored the official policy and advocated a balanced cooperation with the United States. Yet he held little leverage to mobilize support for this position among the JDP constituency. What is more interesting, in addition to his lack of significant support within the party, he was not fully embraced by the foreign ministry either. He was thus occasionally at odds not only with the prime minister, but also with the bureaucracy at the ministry.

Yakış, however, was only the tip of the iceberg. One could identify four distinct groups: NOM; center right—those coming from the Motherland Party; nationalists; and those coming from Kurdish-populated regions. The strongest support for a proactive policy came from those members of the JDP coming from other center-right parties, such as Abdülkadir Aksu, Cemil Çicek, Vecdi Gönül, Ali Coşkun, and Erkan Mumcu. This group had little ideological baggage and pursued a foreign policy agenda that was based on pragmatic considerations. They were cognizant of Turkey's inability to prevent the war from happening, and they did not share the view that Turkey was indispensable to American war plans. For them, the protection and advancement of the country's national interests under those circumstances necessitated that Turkey side with the American-led coalition. They further argued that foreign policy should not be dictated by the emotions prevalent in the streets. In other words, they underlined the need to avoid intermingling domestic concerns with foreign policy. What is interesting about this group is that some of them had served in Özal's cabinet during the first Gulf War and had observed the negative implications of failing to materialize Özal's proactive policy. During cabinet meetings, this group first rejected Gül's gradual approach and in January 2003 argued that the government should hand a single motion to Parliament. Later, when the cabinet had a debate on forwarding the controversial March motion to Parliament, the same group constituted the major supporting block behind the motion. Ministers with close ties to Erdoğan, such as Kemal Unakıtan, Hilmi Güler, and Binali Yıldırım, put their weight behind this pro-cooperation group.[25]

The counterweight to this group came from diverse voices within the JDP. The factors that guided this group's behavior ranged from humanist motivations to legal considerations and to Islamic sensitivities or parochial ethnic interests. For instance, then deputy prime minister Yalçınbayır, another "outsider" to the JDP, acted in close coordination with the president and underlined the lack of constitutional basis for the governmental motion. Moreover, his main agenda was democratization, and he opposed Turkey's involvement in the war because of its likely repercussions for the EU membership process.[26] Bülent Arınç was also a key figure in the JDP before he was elected as the Parliament's speaker. Although his post requires him to disengage himself from partisan politics, he is believed to have a support base within the JDP. By voicing his discomfort with the governmental decree on public grounds similar to those of the president and Yalçınbayır, that is, lack of legitimacy behind the government's policy, he had exerted a certain influence on several MPs.

The anticooperation coalition was partly strengthened by the reflexes of JDP deputies who were elected from provinces where Kurdish-speaking people were in the majority.[27] They were worried about the repercussions of the crisis for the region. To the extent that the Turkish establishment was concerned about the revival of Kurdish separatism and terrorism in Turkey, these MPs were wary of the revival of a military approach to the Kurdish problem inside Turkey. They were worried that Turkey's active contribution to the coalition in exchange for deploying its own forces in Northern Iraq would complicate the resolution of Turkey's own Kurdish problem. Not least, Turkey's involvement in the war would lead to reinstitution of the state of emergency in the region, giving the Turkish military an upper hand in the Kurdish issue and hindering the process toward democratization and civilian control in politics.[28]

The strongest antiwar reactions came in the form of cultural-religious sentiments and the feeling of affinity with the Iraqi people, which were most vividly observed in the case of some JDP deputies coming from the NOM tradition.[29] These arguments found supporters during the discussions on Iraq among some members of the JDP cabinet, such as Abdüllatif Şener, Besir Atalay, Zeki Ergezen, and Hüseyin Çelik, as well as inspired a large body within the JDP party group. Because this group stood against the former group, some commentators argued that the JDP cabinet in fact consisted of two opposing blocks: those originating in the NOM versus those coming from the Motherland Party.[30] This group viewed the government's proposal to help a war against a Muslim country unacceptable on cultural grounds. Moreover, this group had a strategic outlook different from the official rhetoric employed by the establishment and the leadership; or at least they had different interpretation of some concepts. For them, given the centrality of the northern front for American war plans, the United States depended on Turkey; hence, Turkey held the power to avert the war by refusing to cooperate. Because Turkey was part of the same cultural map, they understood Turkey's special geopolitical positioning as dictating for it a historical responsibility to prevent the killing of a Muslim population. Furthermore, for them, the long-term cultural and psychological costs of collaboration with the United States far outweighed the tangible benefits to be gained from supporting the coalition. Hence the motto "our acts will be truly appreciated ten years later." Last but not least, this group shared a deep skepticism toward the United States. They were not convinced of the genuineness of American commitments to alleviate Turkey's economic and strategic concerns. Throughout the negotiations, American reluctance to provide Turkey with written guarantees and insistence that the agreement would need eventual congressional authorization did nothing but magnify the worries of this group.

Besides overall public pressure, an active role in infusing these myriad ideas into the JDP was played by several institutions within the Islamic media. Through their coverage of events they kept the religious-cultural dimension of the crisis intact. In this way, not only did these institutions help form opinion among JDP deputies, but they also exerted strong pressure on them. For instance, the *Yeni Şafak* daily has been an important channel through which such ideas have been transmitted to the JDP.

The newspaper's commentators interpreted the coalition's determination to invade Iraq as a step, part of a project for the establishment of American hegemony. They further linked this project to the advancement of the interests of Israel in the region. Several newspaper commentators took a stance against the government's declared policy to cooperate with the United States. One, Fehmi Koru, a close associate of Gül, likened the American demands from Turkey to an "indecent proposal."[31] Through his several TV appearances and opinion pieces, he promoted the idea that without Turkey's involvement the U.S. war plans would likely collapse. By saying no to war, in his view, Turkey could have undone the plots of the global war coalition. Another columnist argued that "if Turkey could become an active Agent and act in a way to materialize its authentic projects by leaving Western orbit, it could develop strategies that will play a key role in the writing and making of not only the regional history but also world history."[32] Along the same lines, Mustafa Özel criticized the campaign to convince the Turkish people of the obligation to join a war against the Muslim world on the side of the neo-cons. He rejected pragmatism because following such policies was not the kind of attitude that could be expected from a nation with centuries of state tradition. According to him, the benchmark for Turkey was "an idealism rooted in religion and history, which would cover all regions," rather than "a pragmatism serving a vague Turkness, undefined for a hundred years." In other words, the proper course of action for Turkey was to follow the example of the Ottomans and "refrain from becoming proxies in infidels' policies."[33] At a time when the world was counting down to war in Iraq, there was strategic fantasizing if not romantic-idealistic illusion on the part of some people who had the idea that Turkey was under a historic, civilizational responsibility to prevent the war. As the title of one editorial of *Yeni Şafak* implies, these views definitely found supporters among JDP politicians: "*Yeni Şafak* readers know the impact of their newspaper."[34]

This patchy nature of the JDP and the contrasting streams influencing the party in terms of the formulation of Turkey's policy led some to argue that the "JDP is not a unitary party, but a coalition." Although this observation may have some element of truth, the conclusion of this specific analysis begged qualification: "From now on, let's be prepared to hear the gossips that JDP is splitting up."[35] As a matter of fact, these political influences did not possess the capacity to generate a centrifugal force by forming themselves into organized oppositional blocks within the party. They remained as sporadic frictions stimulated by the crisis. Nonetheless the motion crisis was important as it highlighted the underlying divisions within the party, which in the longer term may constitute the nucleus of political groupings stemming from the JDP.

These divisions were also clear reflections of a lack of unified JDP foreign policy vision and the role played by identity in Turkey's Iraq policy. Contrary to the party leadership's seeming adoption of the interest-driven policy of the establishment and attempts to escape from identity, identity politics persisted below the surface. Identity-based concerns, be it in the form of Kurdish votes or Islamic sentiments, made their way into final Turkish policy.

CONCLUSION: MANAGING JDP's INNER DIVISIONS

The JDP avoided coming to terms with the reality of its internal divisions and the lack of a coherent identity by suppressing them through two strong influences: Erdoğan's leadership and the EU membership process. The strongest glue that bound those opposing points of view together was the leadership and personal charisma of Erdoğan.[36] The power of the leader is further strengthened by his central and almost exclusive competences in the allocation of resources and benefits accrued from the government. The brief but crucial period of double leadership, however, hindered effective control over party group at a critical juncture in the making of Turkish foreign policy. This problem manifested itself in the specific case of the motion crisis as the lack of a strategic leadership over the party's parliamentary group. Given Erdoğan's subsequent management of the differences of opinion within the party under his premiership, it would be safe to think that a more coherent and resolute leadership could have easily gathered support for the government's policy. Indeed, two critical decisions of the second JDP government attest to this fact: the decision to open the Turkish airspace to coalition operations, and the October 2003 decision of the Turkish Parliament to authorize the government to contribute to a stability force in Iraq. Despite the existence of similar degrees of opposition, Erdoğan as prime minister could exert his influence over the party members and orchestrate the divisions.

The need to harmonize Turkey's foreign policy with the requirements of the EU process has been the second force that directed attention away from the JDP's inner troubles. Turkey's European vocation provided the JDP with much needed raison d'état for the coexistence of diverse views. The rapid deterioration of Turkish-American relations and the diminishing importance of Turkey's geostrategic standing following the war eventually led to the collapse of the strategic approach as a viable option for guiding Turkey's relations with the world. In return, pro-reform and democratization circles dominated both intellectual and actual political debates and shaped the course of recent Turkish politics. In an *ex post* manner, the JDP leadership capitalized on this new phase in Turkish-European relations to rationalize its incoherent policy—or lack of perspective—toward Iraq and relations with the United States. For instance, in the aftermath of the motion crisis, Gül was arguing that "although it was not our intention, we got closer to Europe" owing to Turkey's policy on Iraq.[37] A natural outcome of this new phase was to shift the focus onto the domestic reforms demanded by the EU and accelerate Turkey's European vocation, a process that already had started during the previous coalition government. The corollary of this new situation for the foreign policy realm came in the form of further prioritizing caution over daring and avoiding any external adventure that might hinder reforms and divert Turkey from its path to the EU membership.

This new policy was most visible in the case of Turkey's so-called "red lines." As discussed, those who argued for Turkey's collaboration with the coalition justified it primarily on the basis of a concern to minimize possible risks to Turkey's national interests. If the war was going to happen anyway, Turkey had to be at the negotiation table after the war so that it could have a say in the reshaping of the region and protect its interests vocally. Many of those concerns were about the future of Iraq and the role of the Kurds in the north. However the lack of a coherent strategic vision in the end led to *ad hocary*: declared positions and highly assertive statements increasingly could not be matched by deeds. The developments so far indicate that the priorities Turkey set for its regional policy already have been undermined. Under the pressure of not only Americans but also Europeans, Turkey has been increasingly excluded from the region only to find itself watching its red lines being crossed one after another. The only policy option left at Turkey's disposal seems to be issuing declarations. Turkey appears to be nothing more than an observer in the region. So far, Turkey's calls for decisive U.S. action to allay Turkey's fears about the activities of Iraqi Kurds, or the elimination of Kurdistan Workers' Party formation in Northern Iraq, fell on deaf ears.

Ironically, this seems to be the price paid by Turkey under the JDP's "multidimensional" foreign policy. As in other vital foreign policy issues such as Cyprus, Turkey's traditional claims have been curtailed in the hope that doing so will facilitate the country's integration with Europe and provide it with new openings in a multidimensional setting. However, this new policy has increasingly marginalized Turkey's capability for unilateral action to protect its interests—second pillar. The calls for multidimensional policy reproduced unidimensionality in a new form.

NOTES

1. Cengiz Çandar, "Turkish Foreign Policy and the War on Iraq," in *The Future of Turkish Foreign Policy*, ed. Lenore G. Martin and Dimitris Keridis (Cambridge, MA: MIT Press, 2004), 47–60.

2. This conforms to the transformation of Islamist thinking in Turkey. See İhsan D. Dağı, "Rethinking Human Rights, Democracy, and the West: Post-Islamist Intellectuals in Turkey," *Critique: Critical Middle Eastern Studies* 13, no. 2 (2004); 135–51.

3. For an early note of caution that the JDP's search for legitimacy through external leverages might create a dependence on external sources of power and undermine its popular legitimacy, hence render it hostage to American pressures to utilize Turkey in its military campaigns in the region, see M. Hakan Yavuz, *Islamic Political Identity in Turkey* (New York: Oxford University Press, 2003), 262.

4. Fikret Bila, *Sivil Darbe Girişimi ve Ankara'da Irak Savaşları* (Ankara: Ümit Yayıncılık, 2004), 165–66, talks about a series of meetings in July 2002; for the content of these meetings, see appendix 3. Moreover, in response to specific American demands, the foreign ministry proposed a series of options on September 26, 2002; see Bila, *Sivil Darbe Girişimi*, 179–81 and appendix 4; similarly, Ergin also notes that after the JDP government came to power, Abdullah Gül was briefed by the military wherein he was proposed a range of policy options about the modalities of Turkey's support to the United States, which seem to be a derivative of earlier reports. Sedat Ergin, "Bizden Saklananlar—IV," *Hürriyet*, September 20, 2003.

5. Nonetheless, one should not overlook some of the Turkish demands of the United States throughout the negotiations, which go beyond mere compensation of Turkey's specific war-related costs. The policy of asking for linkages took shape during the previous government's first encounter with the crisis in July 2002, and the JDP government borrowed the same policy; Murat Yetkin, "Irak Krizinin Perde Arkası—II," *Radikal*, January 19, 2004; Bila, *Sivil Darbe Girişimi*, 172.

6. Nihat Ali Özcan, "Could a Kurdish State be Set Up in Iraq," *Middle East Policy* 11, no. 1 (2004): 119–22.

7. Therefore, Turkey declared respect for the sovereignty and maintenance of the territorial integrity of Iraq as the guiding principle of its Iraq policy. M. Hakan Yavuz, "Provincial Not Ethnic Federalism in Iraq," *Middle East Policy* 11, no. 1 (2004): 126–31.

8. The basic lines of this policy were formulated by the foreign ministry bureaucracy, supported by the military, under the previous coalition government, as a response to Wolfowitz's visit to Ankara in July 2002. Similarly, after the formation of the JDP government, during the meetings between the cabinet and the civilian-military bureaucracy, the same reasoning underpinned the basis of Turkey's policy; Sedat Ergin, "Bizden Saklananlar—I," *Hürriyet*, September 17, 2003.

9. This policy was laid down during the last days in power of Ecevit government, following Foreign Minister Şükrü Sina Gürel's visit to Washington. The emphasis on independent action from the United States appeared to be the single most important

concern driving the military elite throughout the crisis; Bila, *Sivil Darbe Girişimi*, 179–83.

10. It was mainly some liberal analysts that argued for total disengagement from the American agenda in Iraq, mainly because of its likely consequences for Turkey's European vocation and democratization. Smaller political parties on the left and, as will be discussed below, the religious right also argued along similar lines.

11. An unofficial text of the memorandum of understanding is provided in Bila, *Sivil Darbe Girişimi*, appendix 7.

12. Murat Yetkin, "Irak Krizinin Perde Arkası-V," *Radikal*, January 22, 2004.

13. Sedat Ergin, "Bizden Saklananlar-VI," *Hürriyet*, September 22, 2003.

14. Murat Yetkin, "Genelkurmay İstedi," *Radikal*, March 12, 2003.

15. "Askerden Meclis'e: Saddam Vurabilir," *Milliyet*, January 7, 2003; "Asker, Savaş Yetkisi İstedi," *Milliyet*, February 1, 2003.

16. Ali Bayramoğlu, "Demokrasinin Zaferi," *Yeni Şafak*, March 2, 2003.

17. See his work: *Sratejik Derinlik: Türkiye'nin Uluslararası Konumu* (Istanbul: Küre Yayınları, 2001); *Küresel Bunalım* (Istanbul: Küre Yayınları, 2002); Hasan T. Kösebalaban, "Review of Strategic Depth: Turkey's International Position," *Middle East Journal* 55, no. 4 (2001): 693–94. I am indebted to Erman Topçu for letting me read his unpublished manuscript: "Turkish Foreign Policy under JDP" (Ankara: Unpublished paper, 2004).

18. See Derya Sazak's interview with Davutoğlu, "Sohbet Odası," *Milliyet*, January 13, 2003.

19. Ahmet Davutoğlu, "Türkiye Merkez Ülke Olmalı," *Radikal*, February 26, 2004.

20. Ilene R. Prusher, "New Turkish Leader Lifts US Hopes," *Christian Science Monitor*, March 10, 2003.

21. Mehmet Ali Birand, "ABD Ankara'nın ne Yaptığını Anlamıyor," *Hürriyet*, January 7, 2003. Foreign Minister Yakış defended the Turkish position by maintaining that Turkey slowed down the process in response to the American side that made its proposals concrete gradually (Mehmet Ali Birand, "Yakış'ın Sözlerini Tercüme Edersek," *Hürriyet*, January 8, 2003). However, as discussed before, the role expected from Turkey was already conveyed in early December.

22. Bülent Alirıza and Seda Çiftçi, *Turkey Update* (Washington, DC: CSIS, February 14, 2003).

23. "Irak Tezkeresi AKP'yi Çatlattı," *Milliyet*, February 7, 2003.

24. "Erdoğan Şokta: Bu Nasıl Oldu?" *Milliyet*, March 2, 2003; this interpretation was partly shared by the Bush administration. Yasemin Çongar, "AKP'ye Bakış Nasıl?" *Milliyet*, March 3, 2003.

25. Sedat Ergin, "Bizden Saklananlar—VIII," *Hürriyet*, September 24, 2003.

26. He made the point after Parliament rejected the motion that this would boost Turkey's EU bid. *Turkish Daily News*, March 3, 2003.

27. "AKP Grubu Böyle Dağıldı," *Milliyet*, March 2, 2003; for the comments of the chair of TGNA's Foreign Affairs Committee to that effect, see "Dülger: Turkey Needs Government with Strong Voice," *Turkish Probe*, March 9, 2003.

28. Nonetheless, this interpretation was met with caution by some observers, because according to other sources, the majority of the rejecting camp came from western provinces. Deniz Gökçe, "Tayyip Partisi Mi?" *Akşam*, March 17, 2003.

29. See Dülger's comments, note 26 above.

30. Şükrü Küçükşahin, "Kabinede Milli Görüş ile ANAP Çatıştı," *Hürriyet*, March 24, 2003.

31. Fehmi Koru, "Ahlaksız Teklif," *Yeni Şafak*, March 3, 2003.

32. Yusuf Kaplan, "Türkiye Özne Olabilirse Dünya Tarihini Yeniden Yazabilir," *Yeni Şafak*, March 3, 2003.

33. Mustafa Özel, "Özerklik Krizinden Liderlik Krizine," *Yeni Şafak*, March 2, 2003.

34. "Yeni Şafak Okuru, Gazetesinin Etkisini Biliyor," *Yeni Şafak*, March 3, 2003.

35. Cüneyt Ülsever, "Redd-i Tezkiye," *Hürriyet*, March 3, 2003.

36. Hakan Yavuz, "Ideology and Organization of JDP," paper delivered at The Transformation of Islamic Movements in Turkey, Salt Lake City, September 10–11, 2004.

37. Sedat Ergin, "Gül: AB ile Yakınlaştık," *Hürriyet*, March 23, 2003. He paid attention to emphasize that enhanced relations were not meant as an alternative against the United States.

APPENDICES

APPENDIX I

Conservative Democracy and the Globalization of Freedom

■ *Recep Tayyip Erdoğan*[1]

JANUARY 29, 2004

One of the qualities of globalization is its ability to bring international dynamics to the local level and to give global visibility to what is local. The process of interaction that is now present at the international level places on us the responsibility to better understand other societies and to think with empathy. The global significance of this responsibility has gained prominence in political and social, as well as economic, terms.

Living in a world where violence and conflict are still with us, we need to understand against the negative consequences of globalization not only for the good of our own societies but also for others. Similarly, we have to make the positive consequences of globalization available to all societies. Otherwise, the sense of deprivation and injustice, poverty, and political suppression that prevail in various parts of the world will continue to be weaknesses which can be abused by groups wanting to disrupt international peace and stability. The most effective source to make societies more prosperous, open, and democratic, and thus render regimes stronger and more peaceful, can be found within those societies themselves. On the other hand, other countries can also wholeheartedly support, encourage, and facilitate this process and can act as examples.

Mr. Chairman, distinguished guests, one of the greatest common denominators of mankind's existence on earth is the development of humanistic values over centuries. Universal values that are embodied in the concept of democracy and supported by principles such as human rights, rule of law, good governance are the product of the collected wisdom derived from different civilizations. Historically, Judaism, Christianity, and Islam have all played a central role in forming this collective wisdom. However, the present instability and the conflict in the very region which gave birth to these three great religions prevent the realization of the vast potential which exists there, and stall collective wisdom.

As a society consisting predominantly of Muslims, Turkey will continue to make contributions toward disseminating and developing universal values in this region. Turkey feels this responsibility as a result of its democratic structure, rich historical legacy and identity, economic potential, and its membership in Western institutions. Moreover, these givens also shape Turkey's national interests. To be successful in this endeavor, we are first establishing these values firmly at home, and we will continue to do that.

I would like to share with you today the path we take and the political approach we employ in our efforts to make this vision a reality. I call this "conservative democracy." This approach rests upon Turkey's experience as a meeting point of civilizations, its values, and its people's wish and desire to adapt to contemporary values. I believe you will also find elements in this approach which you will be able to associate with.

The political party of which I am the leader, AK Party, represents a new political style and understanding in Turkish political life. I believe that this new approach, based on a political identity I call "conservative democrats," has a significance that goes beyond the borders of Turkey. One observes that, like in the case of socialism, liberalism, and conservatism, all political movements are going through a substantive process of interaction with each other. We now witness not a differentiation and polarization of ideologies with sharp and bold lines of division between them, but the formation of new political courses accompanying the pervasiveness of different ideologies. We have before us, therefore, a more colored and multidimensional picture rather than a sharp black-and-white image. We in Turkey believe that, based on this reality, it is important to renew and strengthen politics and governance through the understanding of conservative democracy.

We have seen that political approaches—we can say that there may not have been any concepts of conservative democracy, but it is not necessary to always act on the previously established ideas and approaches. We are bringing about a new concept not in an abstract manner, but also in a concrete manner, and this is something that needs to be discussed, debated. These are our ideas. And for that reason, very recently we convened in Istanbul an international conference on international conservatism and democracy. And so we have opened a platform of discussion for the concept of conservative democracy.

Our objective here is to look at all sorts of different approaches and attitudes to find out what we can accumulate from them. In other words, we go from each idea, each perspective to another one and we look at the developments around the world so that we can learn and understand what we can add to our approach.

We have seen that political approaches which run on narrow ideological frameworks, or which see politics merely as a way of distributing unequitable income, cannot respond to the people's needs. Nor can these properly allocate the country's resources or grasp the dynamics of market economy. This sort of mentality either radicalizes or intellectually impoverishes politics when it manages to come to power. Although democratic mechanisms remove such mentality from office in the end, societies do lose time in this process. In countries where democracy doesn't function, however, such political approaches harm not only their own societies, but also their periphery.

As a mass political party based on conservatism, AK Party takes its strength from the center of the social spectrum and has consequently become the largest party in the center right. With our strong position in the parliament, we have launched a comprehensive and participatory process of reform in order to develop our society in all fields. The success we achieve in Turkey may serve as an example for many countries. I believe in this strongly. The last 50 years have shown us that our party is the only party that the people have strongly supported, as the result of which we have 65 percent of the seats in the parliament.

A significant part of the Turkish society desires to adopt a concept of modernity that does not reject tradition, a belief of universalism that accepts localism, an understanding of rationalism that does not disregard the spiritual meaning of life, and a choice for change that is not fundamentalist. The concept of conservative democracy is, in fact, and answers to this desire of the Turkish people.

This new understanding of conservative democracy is developed on the basis of general principles of conservatism which have stood the test of time. It also rests upon the social and cultural traditions of our people. Our aim is to reproduce our system of local and deep-rooted values in harmony with the universal standards of political conservatism. We are for a conservatism that is modern and open to change, not one which rests on keeping the status quo.

Supporting a process of change that is evolutionary, gradual, and based on transformation in its natural course, we emphasize the importance of preserving values and achievements, rather than the preservation of present institutions and relations. Preservation should not prevent making changes and advances. It should allow for adapting to developments without losing the self. In other words, we believe in the need to reach a new synthesis without following a sort of traditionalism that rejects modern achievements.

Much distance has been covered in Turkey toward establishing and institutionalizing democracy in its fullest sense, a democracy which incorporates pluralism and tolerance, not a self-styled democracy. The ideal is not to have a mechanical democracy that is reduced to elections and certain institutions, but an organic democracy that pervades into the administrative, social, and political fields. We refer to this—we coined a new term for it, and I'd like to underline it—we refer to this as "deliberative democracy."

We are against the employment of discourses and organizational approaches that create divisions of Us and Them and make one specific fact—ideology, political identity, ethnic element, or religious thought—the center of the polity, thereby antagonizing all other choices. We don't accept that kind of an approach. This supposition is also the most effective measure against those who try to abuse people's spiritual and moral feelings, including religion as for secularism. We define this as an institutional attitude and method which ensures the state to remain impartial and equidistant to all religions and thoughts, a principle which aims to ensure peaceful social coexistence between different creeds, sects, and schools of thought.

We also believe that secularism needs to be crowned with democracy in order for fundamental rights and freedoms to be accorded constitutional guarantees. This allows secularism to function like an arbiter institution and provides an environment of compromise. While attaching importance to religion as a social value, we do not think it right to conduct politics through religion, to attempt to transform government ideologically by using religion, or to resort to organizational activities based on religious symbols. To make religion an instrument of politics and to adopt exclusive approaches to politics in the name of religion harms not only political pluralism but also religion itself. Religion is a sacred and collective value. This is how we should interpret it, how we should understand it. It should not be made the subject of political partisanship causing divisiveness. Therefore, it is important that conservatism—as a political approach which accords importance to history, social culture, and, in this context, religion as well—reestablishes itself on a democratic format. This is our opinion.

Mr. Chairman, distinguished guests, we also consider conservative democracy as an effective approach in upgrading Turkey's present economic, political, and social achievements to the level of high standards we would like to attain in the twenty-first century. The concept of conservative democracy that we are developing is being shaped by the Turkish people's experiences in history and their multidimensional cultural accumulation. And yet, this concept incorporates universal values that allow it to serve as a source of inspiration for other countries. In this context, conservative democracy foresees an attitude based on compromise, not only in domestic politics but also in external relations. Social and cultural diversity provided by democratic pluralism at home will help to develop tolerance and mutual understanding at the international level.

The future of the world lies not in a clash of civilizations but in the cooperation, harmony, and meeting of civilizations. And if the future of the world is reshaped along these lines, we will also witness the globalization of peace. But for this to gain acceptance, there needs to be a change in the prejudices that affect societies and how they view others. The secular and democratic structure of Turkey, a country which acts as a bridge between the East and the West, Islam and Christianity, as well as Europe and Asia, lives in harmony with traditions rooted in Islamic culture. The existence of such a model demonstrates that, when channels between different civilizations are kept open, cooperation does produce concrete results. Now, there might be those who do not find this mission to suit their interests and who wish to fuel a clash of civilizations. Yet, it is possible to summarize the common goal of the people of the world today as the development of dialogue, cooperation, which will ensure peace, stability, and prosperity. And to reach this common goal, we will have to strengthen democracy and respect for human rights. We need to attain sustainable and balanced economic and social development, increase measures against poverty, and improve mutual understanding between cultures.

Communication and dialogue is the path to peace and compromise. It will not be possible for societies which turn their backs on dialogue and compromise to have an effective place in the world in the future. Countries which fail to integrate with today's world, which cannot internalize universal values and develop concepts such as democracy, human rights, and the rule of law, and which cannot establish gender equality are being driven into isolation. We have to help them find the right path, and we have to be ready to do this all together.

A dialogue to be established between civilizations will also serve this end. For our part, we need to take the necessary confidence-building steps so as to build a platform of dialogue and a common language of peace. With its own stable and successful model of development, its place in the Western world, and its rich historical legacy and identity, Turkey will be a symbol of the harmony of cultures and civilizations in the twenty-first century. Turkey will achieve this not merely through its economic and military power, but its ability to make contributions to the universally accepted values and facilitate their dissemination and interaction among various parts of the world. In this sense, Turkey in its region and especially in the Middle East will be a guide in overcoming instability, a driving force for economic development, and a reliable partner in ensuring security.

Turkey's democratization is a self-imposed process. In other words, it is the result of the free choice of the predominantly Muslim Turkish society. I do not claim, of course, that Turkey's experience is a model that can be implemented identically in all other Muslim societies. However, the Turkish experience does have a substance which can serve as a source of inspiration for other Muslim societies, other Muslim peoples. Muslim societies have to find their own solutions to their problems, and each country should determine for itself what is to be done as well as its method and speed. But the time to make that decision has come.

We speak about this with all political leaders we meet, and we express this in all of the meetings we attend. Muslim societies cannot solve their problems by blaming outside forces because, first of all, we all have to accept our own responsibilities, and we also have to take upon ourselves that responsibility. On the other hand, Western countries need to be more sensitive toward societies they consider to be non-Western, and have to rid themselves of unfair generalizations and historical prejudice. It is important in this context to note that developed nations have an obligation to act in recognition of the fact that possibilities and freedoms they see as right for their people are also basic human needs for other societies. As a global power, the United States has before it an important opportunity in this sense. Carrying the responsibility of being a global power, the U.S. should use this opportunity well to ensure that the developing world understands the developed world better. Turkey is ready to assist the U.S. in this endeavor. We are always ready to do that. For this we can benefit from the solidarity of the Transatlantic Alliance and from the possibilities provided by the Turkish-American relations. Indeed, the opportunities and possibilities provided by the Turkish-American relations may have had certain disruptions for different reasons, but what happened in the past should be put behind us. We have to look toward the future and we have to talk about how we will build the future, because this would be what would be required of us if we wanted to look at the future with a vision. Our relations in the future should be developed with more substance and common understanding to facilitate the realization of the regional and global vision that we share. The complex dynamics that are in action around the world make it necessary for us to more carefully analyze the political and social development of societies as well as the role played by identity in domestic politics and foreign policy. In this vein, to better understand Muslim societies, a more objective view of Islam should be employed. It should clearly be seen that those who resort to violence in the name of Islam do not represent Islam, because Islam never supports terrorism. In fact, none of the monotheistic religions of the Abrahamic tradition support terrorism, neither Christianity, nor Judaism, nor Islam. None of them support terrorism. And when a person of one of these faiths is involved in a terrorist act, it should not be generalized to characterize the religion of that person because it will hurt the other believers of that religion. We have to refrain from this kind of an approach because religions are there to bring people together. Religions are there to bring people together with love, with peace. This is the main objective of religion.

I would like to underline one more point here. Our religion, Islam, considers the killing of a person as destroying the house of God. In other words, killing one person is seen as though killing the whole of humanity. This is the approach of our religion. Therefore it's very wrong to equate our religion with terrorism. This will hurt us, this will hurt all of the Muslim people. I think the same for Christianity; I think the same for Judaism. Therefore, it is very important to employ this objective perspective to better understand the Muslim people.

The view that there is an antagonism between the Islamic world and the West is derived from a misleading parochialism. There are people on both sides, unfortunately, who are deceived by this fallacy. Intellectuals, politicians, and shapers of public opinion are well placed to prevent such misunderstandings. In this sense, we all have to work together. The American academic institutions and think tanks have an important role to play here. As one of the historical cradles of cross-cultural interaction, Turkey remains ready to do its share today to help establish a harmony of civilizations. That the Turkish society is predominantly Muslim, has not prevented Turkey from engaging in a comprehensive interaction with the West and from becoming an important member of Western institutions and organizations. Turkey's successful conclusion of its accession process to the European Union will effectively demonstrate the harmony of a Muslim society with predominantly Christian societies on the basis of common universal and democratic values. This will constitute the first big step of the twenty-first century to be taken in the name of harmony of civilizations. Let me very clear state the following; in every summit, in every meeting we go to, we specifically stress the following: Our world today should not be a world where there is a clash of civilizations. Humanity needs to put this behind. We need to create a world where there is the meeting and harmony of civilizations, where different organizations work toward this end. We need to get together in various meetings, conferences, et cetera, so that it will be peace that will win, love that will win, and not war that will win. This is what we need to do. This is what we believe in.

NOTES

1. Prime Minister Recep Tayyip Erdoğan's speech at the American Enterprise Institute, January 29, 2004.

APPENDIX 2

The Need for Reform in the Islamic World and the Role of Civil Society

- *Abdullah Gül, Deputy Prime Minister and Minister of Foreign Affairs of Turkey*[1]

The most valuable asset we have today in resolving the problems created by the phenomenon called globalization, and in benefiting from the opportunities it presents, is our human resources. Therefore, states must establish and further strengthen free, open and participatory structures in order to make the most out of this human potential. In this regard, civil society organizations are of great assistance to us. As Turkey, we have expressed on many occasions the need to benefit from the contributions of civil society organizations in overcoming the problems infecting the countries in the Islamic world.

The Islamic world has the capacity to catch up with our times on the basis of its rich culture and the universal values which Islam has also contributed to. We now need to mobilize this potential at the level of both governments and societies. We see that the urgency of achieving the desired development in political, economic and social fields is increasingly reflected in our public opinion. Muslim countries have to assume their responsibilities and be more active to find their own solutions for their problems and to pave the way for positive change. The need for reform is being openly expressed in our societies. We have to recognize this demand and assume the ownership of the necessary process of change.

On the other hand, in order to be practicable and sustainable, the process of change should be responsive to the expectations of our societies and must be owned by them. Civil society will play an indispensable role in successfully pursuing this endeavour. Adaptation of societies to the realities of our age while preserving their own identity will be possible only with the active involvement of civil society. Acting as a bridge between governments and the people, civil society organizations carry great potential to facilitate the reform processes.

We recognize that the problems of the Islamic world which are yet to be resolved date back before the geopolitical changes that we have witnessed in recent years throughout the whole world and particularly in the Middle East. However, it is also a fact that the developments affecting international order, and in particular the increasing power of globalization to influence all walks of life have rendered the need to find solutions to our problems even more urgent.

In today's world, technological and scientific advances affect our lives in all fields. Through television and the Internet, events in far away corners of the world can be watched. Access to information has become ever easier. As information becomes globalized, everyone can follow everyone else. Consequently, with the phenomenon of globalization, the classical notion of sovereignty has also changed. States are now responsible for their actions not only to their people, but to the whole international community. Therefore, we need to have a wider and more realistic perspective in order to accurately diagnose the problems. The important thing is not to be led by a simplistic approach that contents itself with presenting our problems solely as others' faults. Clearly, societies are adversely affected by certain problematic elements of international politics. External factors should, of course, not be ignored. However, putting the blame on others for every issue will not solve our problems. To see the causes of our problems we have to look at ourselves as well. Representatives of civil society have an important responsibility in this regard. Obviously, the growing role of civil society organizations in political life is a relatively new phenomenon. Accordingly, the "state" which is increasingly confronted by these new actors in its traditional domains of sovereignty shows certain reflexes against them. At times, civil society organizations, in their capacity as the advocate of individual and societal rights, criticize the state. This is an important function, and, in the final analysis, contributes to improving the administration of societies.

In our era, the demands of the so-called "third sector," the power of the community which ensures that decisions affecting daily life are shaped by the input coming from the people, are articulated through civil society organizations. As such, the public itself is given a say in the equitable and rational allocation of resources. Civil society organizations enjoying a strong position in the West also perform the function of controlling Governments and, as such, play a guiding role without seeking merely their narrow self-interest. They function as opinion formers, highlighting the priorities of the people. The strengthening of civil society in Muslim countries too will improve the quality of public services and their efficiency. In international meetings, declarations by government representatives make an impact up to a certain point, whereas, initiatives and/or statements coming from the civil society can sometimes be more credible and direct. Volunteerism, sacrifice, and serving the public interest are important features of Islamic tradition and faith. It is therefore a significant shortcoming that, despite this fact, civil society organizations in Muslim countries are not adequately strong in our modern age.

Governments have to function in line with what the responsibility of governing requires, but they should also attend the advice and criticism coming from civil society. On the other hand, it is also important that civil society organizations express their criticisms in a constructive manner. In terms of the problems of the Islamic world, two main categories come to mind. The first category relates to the problems or misperceptions that arise in the relations between the countries with Muslim populations and others, in particular the West. For sure, in our world today terrorism cannot be condoned in any way. It has unfortunately had a negative impact on the image of the Islamic world. This important issue which needs to be well-addressed, puts responsibility on both sides. I sincerely believe that the platform you intend to develop today in this meeting can be of great help in this regard. Recently, the international interest in the Islamic world has increased throughout the entire world. However, in many cases, we observe with great dissatisfaction that the point of departure for this interest derives rather from the negative considerations or perceptions regarding the Islamic world. I believe that we have to turn this international interest into an opportunity so as to better present Islam and the Islamic community to the world at large.

Today, particularly in the West, the Islamic world is being studied from various perspectives and certain projections are being made. In order to benefit from this interest and to paint a more accurate picture of Islam and Muslim, we should not turn our backs to these efforts, but on the contrary, contribute to them as equal intellectual partners. The higher the scientific and philosophical level and the representative quality of contributions emanating from within Islam, the more their chances will be to influence the debate around the world. It is, therefore, of great importance that, based on the fundamental principles of the Islamic tradition, such as tolerance and moderation, we take an open-minded, realistic but equally visionary approach. Another important issue which I would like to draw your attention to is the risk of generalizations and reductionism that certain parts of the West demonstrate towards the Islamic world, to creep into our view of the West as well. Our relationship with the West should not develop on an adversarial basis.

Turkey's Islamic identity has not prevented it from having a close interaction with the West and from being an important member of the Western institutions and organizations. We pursue and further develop our integration with the West on the basis of mutual interest. The successful completion of Turkey's EU membership process will signify yet again the harmony of a Muslim society with the European peoples by coalescing around common, universal and democratic values. In relation to problems, the second, and I believe the more important, category points to a more essential and comprehensive issue: The problems that the Islamic world faces within itself. We see that these relate primarily to matters of human development that have political, economic and social dimensions.

Civil society organizations are among the main driving forces that contribute to forming an environment of freedom where human creativity can be mobilized so as to find rational solutions to problems. In seeking solutions to their problems, it may be possible for Muslim societies to form rules and concepts appropriate to their own circumstances. However, the universal values and principles that aim to promote human well-being are well known and are inseparable parts of Islamic belief. Therefore, universal values, which have been fed by mankind's collective wisdom and conscience as developed though the interaction among different civilizations throughout history, serve as guiding principles for Muslim societies as well. There is indeed a rich and useful common core shared by Muslim societies. This core is in full harmony with universal values. Principles such as justice, sense of helping and sharing, compassion, moderation, equality, struggle with injustice and corruption and respect for diversity that are at the root of Islam have contributed to universal values throughout centuries. In this respect, what needs to be done is to approach the issue with self-confidence and an open mind and without any complexes. Surely, there is no one single formula in attaining the aspired goal of development of our peoples. The different historical experiences and the qualities of different societies need to be taken into consideration. What is important is to remain in the right direction and follow the path of reason that the Islamic tradition also indicates.

Turkey has been drawing attention to the need for reform within the Islamic world for a long time. I, too, since the beginning of my term in office, have emphasized on various occasions, including in OIC meetings, that time has long come for addressing the political, economic and social shortcomings of our societies. In this connection, underlining the importance of universal values, I pointed to requisites such as democracy, rule of law, human rights, good governance, transparency, accountability, gender equality, the rejection of violence, and economic structures that function more effectively and freely. I made the point that, it is primarily our responsibility to put our house in order, and that no one else can accomplish this better than us. If we cannot do this ourselves, others will do it for us. And the way to put our house in order is to engage in a healthy process of change, that is, to put in place a realistic reform agenda. Clearly, the reform that is needed here pertains to the governance of Muslim societies, not to Islam itself. Islam does not, of course, need to be reformed. The need is for governments to respond to the demands of change. In this sense, one should not fear the phenomenon of reform.

In conclusion, we have to diagnose our problems freely, and engage in a responsive and constructive exchange of views. Problems that social reality presents us in the form of multivariable equations need to be addressed with a multidisciplinary approach. To the degree that we are successful in this, we will be able to defend the interests of our nations in a stronger way.

Notes

1. This article is compiled from Minister Gül's speech to the "International Conference of Islamic Civil Society Organizations: In Search of a New Vision in a Changing World," held on May 1, 2005, in Istanbul.

Contributors

■ YALÇIN AKDOĞAN is an advisor to Prime Minister Erdoğan. He has published *Siyasal Islam* (2000); *Ak Parti ve Muhafazakar Demokrasi* (2004); *Kırk Yıllık Düş: Avrupa Birligi'nin Siyasal Geleceği ve Türkiye* (2004).

■ ALI ÇARKOĞLU is currently an associate professor in the Faculty of Arts and Social Sciences at Sabancı University, Istanbul. His publications have appeared in the *European Journal of Political Research, Electoral Studies, Turkish Studies, New Perspectives on Turkey, Middle Eastern Studies,* and *Political Studies* and in edited books. He coauthored *The Political Economy of Cooperation in the Middle East* (1998) and *Turkey and the European Union, Domestic Politics, Economic Integration and International Dynamics* (2003). He currently works on the relations between mass public opinion and Turkey's bid for EU membership and on voting behavior in the last general elections of November 2002.

■ İHSAN D. DAĞI is a professor of international relations at the Middle East Technical University in Ankara. His studies mainly focus on the issues of human rights and Islamic identity in Turkish politics.

■ BURHANETTIN DURAN is an assistant professor of political science in the International Relations Department of Sakarya University. His research interests include the ideological transformation of Islamism, Islamist intellectual tradition, Turkish political thought, and Turkish foreign policy. He has published in the *Journal of Muslim Minority Affairs* and *Middle Eastern Studies.*

■ WILLIAM HALE is Professor of Turkish Politics and formerly Head of the Department of Political and International Studies in the School of Oriental and African Studies of the University of London. He is a specialist on the politics of the Middle East, especially Turkey. His publications include *The Political and Economic Development of Modern Turkey* (1981, 1984); *Turkish Politics and the Military* (1994); *Turkish Foreign Policy 1774–2000* (2000, 2002); and a number of papers and edited books on modern Turkish politics and history. He is currently working on a study of Islamism, conservatism, and democracy in modern Turkey.

■ SABAN KARDAŞ is a research assistant at the Department of International Relations at both Middle East Technical University and Sakarya University, Turkey. He is also currently a PhD student in political science, attending the University of Utah.

■ AHMET T. KURU is a PhD candidate in the Department of Political Science at the University of Washington, working on state-religion relations in three secular states: the United States, France, and Turkey. He has publications on nation-building in Central Asia, Islam and modernity, and Islamic movements and globalization in *Journal of Muslim Minority Affairs*, *Political Science Quarterly*, and *Central Asian Survey*.

■ MASSIMO INTROVIGNE is a lecturer at Holy Cross University in Rome and the managing director of CESNUR (Center for Studies on New Religions) in Torino, Italy. He is the author of forty books including the forthcoming *La Turchia e l'Europa: Religione e politica nell'Islam turco* (*Turkey and Europe: Religion and Politics within Turkish Islam*) (2006).

■ GARETH JENKINS is an independent scholar. He has published a number of articles on the Turkish military.

■ ZIYA ÖNIŞ is a professor of International Political Economy at Koç University in Istanbul, Turkey. His articles have appeared in *Government and Opposition*, *Development and Change*, *Journal of International Affairs*, *Mediterranean Quarterly*, *Mediterranean Politics*, *Comparative Politics*, *Journal of Democracy*, and *Third World Quarterly*. He is the author of *State and Market: The Political Economy of Turkey in Comparative* Perspective (1998) and coeditor of *The Turkish Economy in Crisis* (2003).

■ EDIBE SÖZEN is a professor at Istanbul University. She has published five books, including *Medyatik Hafiza* (1997); *Söylem* (1999); and *Haklari: Bir Gündelik Pratiği* (2006), and over twenty articles on communication and gender.

■ SULTAN TEPE is an assistant professor at the University of Illinois, Chicago. She is the author of several publications focusing on the relationship between religion and democracy.

■ M. HAKAN YAVUZ is an associate professor of political science at the University of Utah. He specializes in transnational Islamic networks in Central Asia and Turkey; the role of Islam in state-building and nationalism; and ethno-religious conflict management, especially Turkish and

Kurdish nationalism. His publications include *Islamic Political Identity in Turkey* (2003, 2005) and, with John Esposito, *Turkish Islam and the Secular State* (2003). He is currently writing a book, The Transformation of the Islamic Movement in Turkey: the Case of the AK Party, and another book on the social origins of Kurdish Nationalism in Turkey.

■ ENGIN YILDIRIM is a professor in the Department of Labor Economics and Industrial Relations at Sakarya University, Adapazarı. His publications include "The Metal Workers of Gebze" (1996, edited collection). His research interests lie in the sociology of work and organizations and social theory.

Index